Examining AI Innovations in Gaming and Entertainment

Jeff Saltz
Syracuse University, USA

Jasmina Tacheva
Syracuse University, USA

Shamik Tiwari
IILM University, Gurugram, India

Anurag Jain
IILM University, Gurugram, India

IGI Global
Scientific Publishing
Publishing Tomorrow's Research Today

Vice President of Editorial	Melissa Wagner
Director of Acquisitions	Mikaela Felty
Director of Book Development	Jocelynn Hessler
Production Manager	Mike Brehm
Cover Design	Jose Rosado

Published in the United States of America by
IGI Global Scientific Publishing
701 East Chocolate Avenue
Hershey, PA, 17033, USA
Tel: 717-533-8845 | Fax: 717-533-7115
Website: https://www.igi-global.com E-mail: cust@igi-global.com

Library of Congress Cataloging-in-Publication Data

Names: Saltz, Jeffrey S. editor | Tacheva, Jasmina, 1991- editor | Tiwari, Shamik, 1981- editor | Jain, Anurag, 1981- editor
Title: Examining AI innovations in gaming and entertainment / Edited By Jeff Saltz, Jasmina Tacheva, Shamik Tiwari, and Anurag Jain.
Other titles: Examining artificial intelligence innovations in gaming and entertainment
Description: Hershey, PA : IGI Global Scientific Publishing, [2026] | Includes bibliographical references and index. | Summary: "This book features the blending of cutting-edge research, case studies, and expert opinions regarding the impact of AI in the future of interactive media, gaming, and entertainment production"-- Provided by publisher.
Identifiers: LCCN 2025027513 (print) | LCCN 2025027514 (ebook) | ISBN 9798337336909 h/c | ISBN 9798337336916 s/c | ISBN 9798337336923 ebook
Subjects: LCSH: Artificial intelligence--Technological innovations | Interactive multimedia | Video games industry | Amusements--Technological innovations
Classification: LCC Q335 .E93 2026 (print) | LCC Q335 (ebook) | DDC 006.3--dc23/eng/20250902
LC record available at https://lccn.loc.gov/2025027513
LC ebook record available at https://lccn.loc.gov/2025027514

British Cataloguing in Publication Data
A Cataloguing in Publication record for this book is available from the British Library.

Table of Contents

Detailed Table of Contents

This chapter explores the revolutionary intersection of artificial intelligence (AI) and virtual reality (VR) in the emergent paradigm of the Metaverse and emphasizes the degree to which both of these technologies are redefining the future of gaming and immersive entertainment. The chapter takes an introspective look at the eradication of AI needed for dynamic world building, the use of non-player character autonomy, emotionally attuned spaces, and an adaptive narrative system which respond to a real-time user interaction. As such it shows AI's a priori position in the transformation of ever-adapting self-adaptive digital environments where boundaries between human agency and machine autonomy gradually disappear. Critical issues are systematically addressed. Finally, the chapter traces out some ways that futuristic pathways involving decentralized AI governance, cognitive augmentation and inhuman virtual civilizations.

The combination of Artificial Intelligence (AI) and Virtual Reality (VR) in the Metaverse represents a paradigm shift in the online interaction, and it changes the sphere of education, healthcare, business, and government. AI enhances VR space by facilitating flexible, customized, and intelligent interactions, but VR gives humans rich, and immersive human interaction. This cooperation facilitates the active virtual worlds with real-life-like avatars, real time generation of content, and context responsive engagement. Nevertheless, the problem of data privacy, algorithm bias, digital identity protection, and psychological outcomes should be brought up to ensure ethical and fair development. This chapter also explores the technological backgrounds, industry-related usage, and social impacts of AI-VR integration .Through the emphasized transparency, justice, and autonomy to the users, stakeholders can be able to maximise the potential of the Metaverse and reduce the dangers associated with the technology.

This chapter examines how context-aware artificial intelligence (AI) enhances virtual reality (VR) by increasing immersion, user engagement, and adaptive interactivity. Drawing on foundational theories of presence and immersion (e.g., Slater, 2009; Csikszentmihalyi, 1990), this investigation examines how AI systems interpret environmental, behavioural, and verbal cues to personalise and enrich immersive experiences. Reviewing recent innovations in generative AI, reinforcement learning, and intelligent agent design, the chapter analyses the capacity of these technologies to support dynamic content generation, adaptive gameplay, and naturalistic interaction. Complementing the literature review, a user-centred survey captures VR user perceptions and priorities regarding intelligent, adaptive systems. The chapter concludes with a discussion of ethical considerations, user modelling challenges, and future research directions, offering a timely contribution to ongoing debates in AI-driven entertainment design.

Named Giants in the Making, Mr Drain's company is the proud focus of a song sung by China's pop princess.Creating dynamic open worlds and providing endless replay value, Generative AI revolutionizes both what content is produced and how it is consumed. Rather than being a mere tool for people to use, the technology uses advanced algorithms to generate interactive virtual worlds, artificial intelligence-driven storylines that can learn from players and adaptable characters whose actions are determined by the decisions made by players as they play.By examining user behaviors and preferences in real time, generative AI guarantees customized interaction rather than watered down content re-selling to the masses. This leads onto a win-win situation where the audience is happy when they're subjected to it. Here's some examples of what it does. In effect, automated witticisms and half-baked content come from the hands of generative AI.

This chapter explores the application of Artificial Intelligence (AI) to analyze and customize the behavior of individual players in contemporary digital games. It explains the application of AI tools such as machine learning, deep learning, and reinforcement learning to personalize interactions, upgrade systems, dynamic story generation, and gamification to reduce player churn. The chapter also examines sociological and computational theories of player profiling, ethical issues regarding the use of data, and the personalization of immersive gaming experiences through AI technologies. The chapter places particular emphasis on inclusive and adaptive design, and responsible innovation.

This chapter explores for the integration of AI -operated games to enhance quality education in engineering and technology. By providing adaptive education, real-time feedback and gaming problems, AI-powered educational games promote fictional understanding, complex thinking and engagement of students. These tools personalize learning experiences based on personal performance and preferences, making complex engineering and technical concepts more accessible and interactive. This chapter also features case studies and best efforts that show the improved results and skills acquisition of education. Emphasizing innovation and incorporation, the chapter presents AI-powered gaming as a transformative approach to modern educational patterns and industry readiness.

Developments in video content across various learning platforms require new advanced techniques to efficiently manage and streamline vast video data access. Using Recurrent Neural Networks (RNNs) and Bidirectional Long Short-Term Memory (BiLSTMs) together with attention mechanisms the paper addresses real-time video summarization for learning long duration videos and courses. The developed system demonstrates functionality to detect essential keyframes while maintaining control over time-based sequence relations in video content. Video summaries created by humans serve together with raw video content to enable the model to discover vital visual data and contextual associations. Standards measuring effectiveness include BLEU and ROUGE which help assure both clear and coherent results from generated summaries. The proposed method demonstrates real-time summary generation accuracy for different video types in learning courses based on user preferences which makes it a strong practical automatic video summarization technique for the learning platform.

This chapter examines the evolving landscape of gamification, shaped by the convergence of artificial intelligence, immersive environments, blockchain, and social technologies. Once reliant on simple point-and-reward mechanisms, gamification has matured into a dynamic, intelligent, and decentralized ecosystem. AI and machine learning now drive hyper-personalized experiences; augmented and virtual reality enable embodied engagement; and blockchain technologies introduce verifiable rewards, digital ownership, and decentralized governance. These innovations expand gamification's purpose, from individual motivation to community building, equity, and sustainable behavior change. Emerging frontiers such as emotional AI and multimodal interfaces promise even deeper responsiveness by integrating gesture, voice, and biometric data. As gamification systems increasingly permeate education, healthcare, the workplace, and civic life, ethical design becomes imperative, prioritizing inclusion, autonomy, and well-being.

Preface

INTRODUCTION

The rapid advancement of artificial intelligence has fundamentally reshaped the gaming and entertainment industries, transforming not only how content is created but also how it is experienced, consumed, and understood. From intelligent non-player characters and procedural content generation to adaptive gameplay and real-time player analytics, AI has become deeply embedded in the core architecture of modern games. These innovations have elevated interactivity, realism, and immersion, while also enabling more efficient game testing, enhanced security against hacking, and personalized player experiences through adaptive difficulty and behavior-aware systems.

Beyond gaming, AI's influence across the broader entertainment landscape is equally profound. In film, music, and digital media, AI-driven tools now support advanced computer-generated imagery, deepfake technologies, automated scriptwriting, music composition, and sophisticated content recommendation systems. The emergence of digitally realistic human avatars and hyper-personalized streaming experiences on platforms such as Netflix and Spotify illustrates how AI is redefining creativity, production workflows, and audience engagement.

It is within this dynamic and evolving context that we present *Examining AI Innovations in Gaming and Entertainment*. This edited reference work brings together cutting-edge research, industry case studies, and expert perspectives to critically examine the applications, challenges, and future potential of AI across these interconnected sectors. The chapters in this volume explore how AI is shaping interactive media, redefining storytelling, and influencing the production and consumption of entertainment content, while also addressing the ethical, technical, and business implications that accompany these advances.

This book aims to provide a comprehensive examination of AI-driven innovations in gaming and entertainment. It addresses pressing ethical concerns, including issues of bias, fairness, player addiction, and the misuse of technologies such as deepfakes. It highlights emerging trends such as AI-generated games, virtual influencers, emotion-driven gameplay, and hyper-personalized entertainment experiences. Additionally, the volume seeks to bridge the gap between academic research and industry practice by presenting real-world examples of AI applications in game development, interactive storytelling, and media production.

A key objective of this work is to encourage interdisciplinary collaboration among AI researchers, game developers, media professionals, educators, and policymakers. By offering a platform for scholarly contributions, industry insights, and experimental case studies, this book fosters dialogue on responsible AI development and its sustainable integration into gaming and entertainment ecosystems.

This reference book is designed for a diverse readership, including academics and researchers in artificial intelligence, machine learning, game design, and interactive media; game developers and designers seeking practical insights into AI-powered mechanics and storytelling; media and entertainment professionals involved in film, animation, music, and streaming services; students and educators in computer science, digital arts, and media studies; as well as industry leaders and policymakers concerned with AI ethics, regulation, and governance.

By compiling state-of-the-art research and practical applications, *Examining AI Innovations in Gaming and Entertainment* contributes to the growing body of literature on AI-driven interactive media. We hope this volume will serve as a valuable and enduring resource for understanding how artificial intelligence is shaping—and will continue to shape—the future of gaming and entertainment.

ORGANIZATION OF THE BOOK

Chapter 1 examines the powerful convergence of artificial intelligence and virtual reality within the emerging Metaverse, positioning these technologies as foundational to the future of immersive gaming and entertainment. The chapter highlights AI's role in dynamic world-building, autonomous non-player characters, emotionally responsive environments, and adaptive narrative systems that evolve through real-time user interaction. By addressing critical challenges alongside visionary concepts such as decentralized AI governance, cognitive augmentation, and non-human virtual civilizations, this chapter sets a forward-looking tone for understanding self-adaptive digital ecosystems where the boundaries between human agency and machine autonomy continue to blur.

Chapter 2 builds upon this foundation by offering a comprehensive exploration of AI-enabled virtual reality in the Metaverse, focusing on its underlying technologies, real-world use cases, and ethical challenges. The chapter demonstrates how AI enhances VR environments through intelligent, personalized, and context-aware interactions across sectors such as education, healthcare, business, and governance. At the same time, it critically addresses concerns related to data privacy, algorithmic bias, digital identity, and psychological well-being, underscoring the importance of transparency, fairness, and user autonomy in responsible Metaverse development.

Chapter 3 delves into multimodal context-awareness in AI-driven virtual reality, emphasizing how intelligent systems interpret environmental, behavioral, and verbal cues to deepen immersion and engagement. Grounded in established theories of presence and flow, the chapter reviews recent advances in generative AI, reinforcement learning, and intelligent agents that enable adaptive gameplay and naturalistic interaction. Through both literature analysis and user-centered survey findings, this chapter contributes valuable insights into ethical considerations, user modeling challenges, and future research directions in immersive entertainment design.

Chapter 4 explores the transformative role of generative AI in entertainment, focusing on its capacity to create dynamic worlds and deliver infinite gameplay experiences. Moving beyond AI as a supporting tool, the chapter positions generative systems as active creative agents capable of producing adaptive storylines, responsive characters, and personalized content in real time. By analyzing how player behavior and preferences shape AI-generated experiences, this chapter highlights the shift toward highly customized, continuously evolving entertainment ecosystems.

Chapter 5 focuses on the integration of virtual reality and artificial intelligence for immersive storytelling, particularly within educational contexts. Recognizing storytelling as a fundamental human and pedagogical practice, the chapter argues that VR and AI can reinvigorate narrative-based learning that has been sidelined in content-heavy curricula. By demonstrating how these technologies support experiential and inclusive education, the chapter underscores their potential to improve learning outcomes and address the diverse needs of learners across disciplines.

Chapter 6 introduces G-GenAI, an innovative AI-driven framework designed to support co-creative game development. By leveraging generative AI models for storytelling, visual asset creation, and procedural level design, the framework enables developers—particularly indie creators—to rapidly prototype and scale game content using natural language prompts. The chapter demonstrates how human–AI collaboration can significantly reduce development time while preserving creative quality, offering a compelling vision for the future of AI-assisted game design pipelines.

Chapter 7 focuses on AI-driven player behavior analysis and personalization in contemporary digital games. It explores how machine learning, deep learning, and reinforcement learning techniques enable adaptive gameplay, dynamic storytelling, and personalized reward systems aimed at enhancing engagement and reducing player churn. The chapter also addresses sociological theories, data ethics, and inclusive design principles, emphasizing responsible innovation in the personalization of immersive gaming experiences.

Chapter 8 explores the use of AI-powered games to enhance quality education in engineering and technology. By integrating adaptive learning, real-time feedback, and game-based problem solving, the chapter shows how AI-driven educational games make complex technical concepts more accessible and engaging. Supported by case studies and best practices, this chapter positions AI-powered gaming as a transformative approach to modern pedagogy and industry readiness.

Chapter 9 addresses the challenge of managing extensive video-based learning content through an AI-driven real-time video summarization system for learning management platforms. Employing deep learning techniques such as RNNs, BiLSTMs, and attention mechanisms, the chapter presents a practical solution for generating coherent and accurate video summaries. This contribution underscores the role of AI in improving accessibility, efficiency, and personalization within digital learning environments.

Chapter 10 concludes the volume by exploring emerging trends in gamification and its evolution into an intelligent, immersive, and decentralized ecosystem. The chapter discusses how AI, immersive technologies, blockchain, and emotional computing are reshaping gamification beyond simple reward systems toward community building, equity, and sustainable behavior change. Emphasizing ethical design, inclusion, and well-being, this chapter offers a forward-looking perspective on the expanding role of gamification across education, healthcare, work, and civic life.

CONCLUSION

As the chapters in *Examining AI Innovations in Gaming and Entertainment* collectively demonstrate, artificial intelligence is no longer a peripheral technology but a central force reshaping how games and entertainment experiences are designed, delivered, and experienced. From immersive virtual worlds in the Metaverse and AI-driven storytelling to personalized gameplay, emotional computing, educational applications, and ethical governance, this volume captures the breadth and depth of AI's transformative impact across interactive media. Together, the contributions illustrate how AI enables richer immersion, adaptive narratives, intelligent personalization, and new forms of creativity that redefine the relationship between users and digital environments.

At the same time, this book underscores that innovation must be accompanied by responsibility. The ethical, social, and regulatory challenges discussed throughout the volume—ranging from data privacy and algorithmic bias to behavioral manipulation and deepfake misuse—highlight the need for transparent, inclusive, and accountable AI systems. Addressing these concerns requires sustained collaboration among researchers, developers, educators, industry leaders, and policymakers, ensuring that technological progress aligns with human values, creative integrity, and societal well-being.

By bridging theoretical research with real-world applications and industry perspectives, this edited reference work serves as both a scholarly contribution and a practical guide. It reflects the current state of AI-driven gaming and entertainment while also pointing toward emerging trends such as emotion-aware systems, co-creative AI frameworks, decentralized virtual ecosystems, and hyper-personalized media experiences. We hope this volume inspires critical inquiry, interdisciplinary collaboration, and responsible innovation, empowering readers to shape the future of gaming and entertainment in ways that are immersive, ethical, and socially meaningful.

Chapter 1
AI and Virtual Reality in the Metaverse:
Future Possibilities

S. Ida Evangeline
https://orcid.org/0000-0003-2997-7897
Government College of Engineering, Tirunelveli, India

ABSTRACT

This chapter explores the revolutionary intersection of artificial intelligence (AI) and virtual reality (VR) in the emergent paradigm of the Metaverse and emphasizes the degree to which both of these technologies are redefining the future of gaming and immersive entertainment. The chapter takes an introspective look at the eradication of AI needed for dynamic world building, the use of non-player character autonomy, emotionally attuned spaces, and an adaptive narrative system which respond to a real-time user interaction. As such it shows AI's a priori position in the transformation of ever-adapting self-adaptive digital environments where boundaries between human agency and machine autonomy gradually disappear. Critical issues are systematically addressed. Finally, the chapter traces out some ways that futuristic pathways involving decentralized AI governance, cognitive augmentation and inhuman virtual civilizations.

1. INTRODUCTION

The Metaverse has become an environment in which people can interact digitally and be immersed digitally, as well as experience a social presence. Like a virtual playground or entertainment platform, the Metaverse necessitates a total disruption in how humans relate to digital systems; and therefore destroys the traditional

DOI: 10.4018/979-8-3373-3690-9.ch001

constructs of identity, reality and agency that exist in the physical world. A very important part of this transformation is the convergence of Virtual Reality (VR) and Artificial Intelligence (AI), the interdependence of these technologies will lead to the creation of borderless, interactive, virtual realities (Fan et al. 2024).

The virtual reality experience gives us both the sense and space of a digital world through headsets, motion tracking and haptic feedback that bring user experiences to an elevated level at which a user may have difficulty in distinguishing between a digital world and a real-world experience. Artificial intelligence becomes the smart center of these worlds due to it being able to quickly respond to what the user does and how they can feel; how old the user is; and by its ability to learn and change. Together, artificial intelligence and virtual reality make a fundamental change to the nature of human interaction through the way each traditionally has been used as an enhancement for graphics and/or gameplay (Bhattacharya & Singla, 2024).

This Chapter places Metaverse at the nexus of developing technologies combining those that will be capable of creating dynamic, adaptable and personalized virtual space(s) through the use of artificial intelligence (AI), and Virtual Reality (VR) as a means for experiencing embodiment within virtual social environments. Such technologies will enable the creation of hitherto science fiction (sf) phenomena in the form of AI generated computer automatons or NPCs, self-altering virtual world(s); and environments capable of processing, reflecting and reacting in real time to the emotions of the user.

Figure 1. The convergence of artificial intelligence and virtual reality in the metaverse

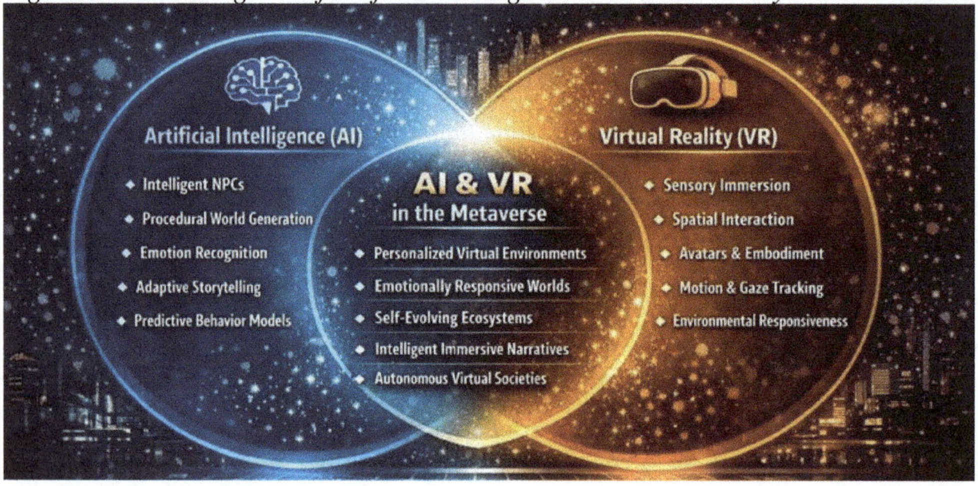

The evolution of new and improved decentralized immersive systems – including VRChat, Roblox, Meta's Horizon Worlds and others that are developing similarly –

represent a paradigm shift toward utilizing AI innovations in an experimental and testing context within a virtual environment. This has evolved beyond simply being a revolution for the industries of gaming and entertainment; it is a transformation of how society relates to reality, individuality and collective experience. The Chapter will provide an in-depth examination into how AI is defining the future of the Metaverse, through the assessment of opportunities at the intersection of AI and VR (Natarajan et al., 2024).

Figure 1 depicts the collaboration between AI and VR in the creation of emotionally adaptive, personalized, and self-sustainable virtual environments within the Metaverse. Cognitive and decision-making capabilities are provided by AI while VR provides sensory and spatial substrates. When combining the two technologies, they generate movement in the experiential aspects of the system in which users co-create the reality with intelligent systems. Table 1 shows the collaborative effort of AI and VR in the creation of the Metaverse in key applications and emerging trends, showing the combined technologies that allow for more adaptive, immersive and autonomous virtual systems.

Table 1. Key applications and emerging trends at the AI–VR convergence in the metaverse

Application Area	AI Contribution	VR Contribution	Emerging Trend
Virtual World Generation	Procedural content generation, generative AI	3D rendering, immersive spatial design	Scalable, auto-generated immersive worlds
NPC Development	Emotion modeling, decision systems, LLMs	Embodied interactions, gaze & motion cues	Realistic, adaptive NPCs with memory and personality
Emotion-Responsive Environments	Emotion recognition, behavior prediction	Biometric sensing, haptic feedback	Emotionally intelligent and empathetic systems
Adaptive Storytelling	Narrative modeling, NLG, RL-based plotting	Interactive scene control, user embodiment	Personalized, co-authored story experiences
Persistent Ecosystems	Multi-agent learning, environmental simulation	World continuity and history across sessions	Self-evolving virtual societies
Digital Governance	AI moderation, decision automation	Decentralized interaction, tokenized spaces	Blockchain-AI governed autonomous virtual communities
Identity & Cognitive Augmentation	Predictive modeling of user behavior	Avatar embodiment, BCI interfaces	Fluid identities and enhanced cognition

2. AI IN VIRTUAL WORLD CONSTRUCTION

Artificial intelligence will be most significantly involved in creating and maintaining virtual worlds using procedural content generation to accomplish this role. Traditionally, generating large virtual worlds was an extremely costly and labor intensive process for teams of designers and developers who had to build virtual worlds on a piece-by-piece basis. However, the advent of artificial intelligence has created new opportunities for automation, optimization, and scalable and variable production of digital worlds (Chen et al., 2024), making the field of procedural content generation completely obsolete.

The current procedural generation uses AI to create landscapes and structures, quests and entire ecosystems through algorithms that can either run autonomously based upon previously generated data, or learn from the patterns contained within those data. There is currently a rapidly growing trend of applying machine learning techniques, particularly generative models (e.g., GANs and transformers) to create realistic and dynamic terrain, climate/weather conditions, and cultural lore in virtual worlds (Hussain et al., 2024).

In addition to developing all kinds of static objects, AI allows us to develop the environment in a dynamic way, dependent upon the actions of the user, in real time. In addition to learning how to engage with the user in a virtual environment, AI will allow the environment to dynamically alter itself - add new barriers to jump over, open up new places to go to, change the look and feel of things to prevent boredom, and so forth. The ability to create this type of "living" and long lasting fictional world will allow creators to create unique and specific fictional worlds for each user (Chen & Cao, 2024).

The Metaverse has become home to many of the latest and greatest development tools such as Unity ML-Agent, NVIDIA Omniverse and OpenAI Environment Simulators etc. These tools include AI agents that are capable of generating content in real-time, understanding user preference and generating modular virtual assets that can be used to generate coherent narrative or aesthetic themes (Datta et al., 2024).

Not only does AI generated environments provide efficiency, it also provides a creative enhancement for programmers. Programmers are no longer limited to asking for stylistic or narrative rules; AI can investigate permutations that may be very difficult to implement by humans. Therefore, world-building is now becoming an integrated design process between the human and machine perspectives that exponentially grows in complexity within the Metaverse (Yang et al., 2024).

However, there are limitations to the scalability of procedural generation. AI generated environments typically exhibit repetition, lack of narrative structure and/or have computational overhead as complexity of multilayer virtual world is developed on the fly.

This section also discusses how the combination of AI and VR recreate the actors that inhabit these virtual spaces. The next part of this section will discuss the evolution of Non-Playable Characters (NPCs), toward the use of AI to develop NPCs that have memories and are emotionally responsive.

3. AUTONOMOUS AND ADAPTIVE NPCs

In the virtual environment, history has shown that NPCs were scripted characters with predictable reactions to player input. With the integration of AI into NPC technology, NPCs became independent, programmable agents able to communicate dynamically and in response to player action. As a result, the enhanced NPCs serve as more than just static background characters but rather contribute to the immersion in both the simulated experiences and the rich, pervasive narratives in the Metaverse (Khan et al. 2024).

With current advancements in AI, NPCs have acquired the authority to make their own decisions using reinforcement learning processes, emotion modeling and memory. As opposed to the pre-defined dialogues and behavior trees used previously, NPCs generate their responses to player actions based on previous interaction history, environmental data and location. Therefore, a player may see a non-player character exhibit different tones or goals depending on what was decided in previous player interactions, thus exhibiting a growth of character for the NPC. This type of interaction helps create the realism required to support the development of emergent narratives – or the stories created through the interactions between users and the agency of NPCs (Wilujeng et al. 2025).

A major factor in this advancement is the introduction of Natural Language Processing (NLP) and large language models enabling NPCs to engage in open ended conversations with users. NLP enables NPCs to interpret subtle inputs from language including the tone of the language and to understand the dialogue in a way that creates realistic and sensible conversation. Furthermore, there are instances where NLP models can create unexpected surprises for those creating them. In a social VR setting such as VRChat or an experimental platform like AI Dungeon, users find themselves engaged with an AI-created model of a character that can represent itself as a friend, hiding a joke, emotion, or enemy in a frighteningly realistic manner (Johansson & Eladhari, 2024).

AI-based agents are beginning to be incorporated into the Metaverse ecosystems in meaningful ways. While NPCs are being investigated for use as a means to facilitate and moderate a community environment in Meta's Horizon Worlds, developers at Roblox are experimenting with AI agents that can develop the gameplay experience in real time by reacting to players' developed scenarios. Additionally, AI companions that store long-term memories have been introduced into some platforms with NeosVR being one of them. These AI companions create a developing relationship with each unique user (Wilujeng et al. 2025).

Another complexity to consider when building these virtual worlds is the development of multi-agent systems. When placed in these environments, the AI characters do not only interact with the human users but also with one another - establishing social hierarchies, economic transactions and cultural dynamics that exist independently of the user. The autonomous nature of the ecosystems also illustrate the possibility of entire virtual communities with complex networks of AI-based communication that challenge our conventional perceptions of authorship, narrative and life in the digital world (Aleksic, 2024). However, limitations to sustainable and realistic interactions include memory constraints and limited reasoning capabilities regarding common sense.

While the issue of outside intelligence is important to evolve, another area of significant concern is the ability of the system to determine how to behave relative to the internal state of the user. Recognizing emotions and predicting behavior offers additional levels of empathetic interaction that redefine boundaries of user experience.

4. EMOTION RECOGNITION AND BEHAVIORAL PREDICTION IN VR

One of the most exciting features of Metaverse will be the increasing ability of systems to understand how users are experiencing and responding emotionally and then reacting as a result. Next-generation virtual experiences rely heavily on advances in AI, allowing for both emotion recognition and forecasting of behavior as critical dimensions in personalizing, simulating, and enhancing the user's experience. The new technologies allow for users to not simply sit back and be passive; rather, they enable systems to perceive, predict, and adapt to the intellectual and emotional state of any user (Reddy et al., 2024).

VR-based emotion recognition depends upon integrating biometric and behavioral signals to teach an in-game system to infer what is occurring inside of the heads of players as they interact within the virtual space. There are several forms of input that can be utilized to identify emotions in addition to tracking facial expressions, analyzing voice modifications, tracking the direction of a player's eyes, heart rate variability, and galvanic skin responses to see if a player is happy, afraid, frustrated, or bored. With the use of large-scale affective datasets and the machine learning models developed from those, the inputs allow virtual platforms to recognize minor shifts in the psychology of the user in real time. In practice, this means that a VR environment can darken its lighting when a user appears to be stressed, lower the volume of its background sounds, or change the actions of the NPC to provide comfort or present a challenge based on the needs perceived by the user (Khare et al., 2024).

At the same time, behavioral prediction systems utilize patterns of user activity, including movement, decision-making, and frequency of interaction to forecast what the user may wish to accomplish in the future. AI systems can be proactive and develop user-specific behavioral profiles, using this knowledge to recommend adjustments to the narrative arc of the story, provide suggestions for social connections, or modify the difficulty level of the challenge mode. While this form of predictive personalized experience enhances the overall satisfaction of the user, it also contributes to the development of emotionally-intelligent virtual agents capable of establishing pseudo-social relationships with the user (Belabed et al., 2024).

Future possibilities exist in entertainment, education, and healthcare. Games will have the opportunity to tell more compelling and complex stories when the world of the game reacts to the emotions of the NPCs. Educational VR provides the possibility of tracking a learner's frustration levels and adjusting the pace or method of instruction accordingly. Therapy is perhaps the most promising area of application for medical-related uses of emotion detection, utilizing the technology to assess a patient's anxiety levels during exposure therapy, or to predict whether a person is likely to develop depressive episodes (Fang et al., 2024).

The convergence of AI, emotion, and VR also creates significant, however, difficult-to-define ethical issues. Technologies capable of providing empathetic responsiveness also pose a threat to user autonomy and privacy. An individual's emotional information, which arguably is among the most personal types of data, could be harvested, misinterpreted, or exploited, particularly if it is monetized, or is embedded in opaque algorithmic systems. This increases the necessity for open and ethical design cycles as the awareness and consciousness of the internal landscape of human experience grow through AI (Pathirana et al., 2024).

Due to the responsive nature of emotion-sensing systems, the Metaverse has provided a great platform to make digital environments not only responsive to the choices made by users but also to the emotional sensitivity of users to all other users. The boundaries between an environment and an entity are blurred and there exists a sense of an extremely emotional existence of the virtual world that significantly impacts the experience of the user (Kollias et al., 2024). Additionally, emotion recognition systems may be prone to error due to cultural heterogeneity, individual variability in expression, and sensor-dependent variability. Behavioral prediction models may require substantial amounts of user data and therefore raise concerns about scalability and ethics for real-time usage of these models.

Emotionally-aware systems have the potential to produce richer, more engaging storytelling experiences. Using both user behavior and emotional indicators, AI can develop narrative structures that are dynamically generated and uniquely customized for each and every participating user in collaborative, co-created journeys (Kollias et al., 2024).

5. NARRATIVE PERSONALIZATION AND ADAPTIVE STORYTELLING

AI's potential to transform how we tell stories in Metaverse is quite possibly one of the greatest advancements possible. AI can enable the creation of a new type of storytelling that is fluid and interactive with the user(s) and is not limited to linear, disconnected storytelling. With AI-driven personalized storytelling, we move from branching storylines to a new paradigm of true dynamic narrative regimes in which both plot, dialogue, and character development are in flux, based upon the user's choices, interests, and emotional responses. AI-based storytelling is capable of providing new levels of agency in the narrative process while creating opportunities for collaborative storytelling, participant immersion, and user participation and engagement that can align with each user's preferences (Damasevicius & Sidzikevičiūtė, 2024).

There are two main technologies that underlie the adaptive storytelling model: Machine Learning and specifically Reinforcement Learning and Natural Language Generation. These technologies provide the foundation for developing dynamic systems of narrative possibility rather than fixed scripts. Reinforcement Learning allows for the adaptation of story paths based upon user input, such as selection of dialogue options and exploration patterns. For example, users that prefer peaceful resolution may find more sympathetic mediators and/or alternative paths in which they can resolve issues without violence. In contrast, risk-taking players can create a "problem" that results in an escalating response to the problem (DeCarlo & Limone, 2024).

The key factor that makes AI-based storytelling in a Metaverse different from AI-based storytelling in other environments is its ability to maintain continuity and memory across sessions and contexts. AI agents have the capability to recall what users have done in the past, their thematic or exploratory preferences, and use these previous events to inform their development of future storylines. Therefore, AI-based storytelling provides users with a sense of continuity and emotional connection to past events, similar to the narrative coherence of episodic media, such as television series, while incorporating elements of user interactivity and customization (Papadopoulou et al., 2024).

These systems have evolved significantly over time, leading to numerous new applications. The experimental narrative forms of VR, such as Fable Studio's Lucy digital story, utilize AI-powered characters that respond to users' conversations in a way that depends upon the users' interactions with the story. Similarly, real-time scenarios in immersive gaming and simulation-based training platforms can be modified in real-time based upon users' cognitive and emotional responses to AI-driven engagements, thereby generating individualized learning or narrative pathways (Ahmed et al., 2025).

In terms of the author and creative potential, the implications are significant. Rather than writing every possible scenario, designers are now acting as meta-writers of narrative possibilities by outlining general parameters, subject themes, and tone directions in which the AI dynamically develops the stories. This shifts the relationship between a content creator and consumer and converts users into co-narrators of their own life stories (Li & Li, 2025).

However, similar to the other AI-powered features of the Metaverse, the emergence of adaptive storytelling raises questions as well. Data capture and behavioral assumptions required for adaptive narratives may raise concerns about user privacy, and the story may be formed in ways that are biased and unintended. There is also the issue of balancing user freedom and the parts of the story, to what extent can liberties be granted to the user and still maintain the continuity of the overall theme? (Mahalakshmi et al., 2025)

While the potential of AI-driven adaptive storytelling appears to be significant – stories that are immersive and personalized and potentially evolve based upon user feedback and preferences to reflect the user's online presence – the primary challenge facing developers is finding a way to develop narrative freedom with increased thematic coherence. While AI offers the potential to create a vast number of customized plotlines, achieving an emotionally consistent narrative arc in an environment where the narrative and interaction are dynamic and changing, remains an open design question.

Ultimately, as the narrative and interaction change, so too does the underlying world. The Metaverse is evolving to resemble a very real world that persists on its own and evolves independent of those who use it and represents the complexity of the world as we know it today.

6. PERSISTENT ECOSYSTEMS AND SELF-EVOLVING VIRTUAL WORLDS

Creating layers of digital existence that feel more like "natural" elements of our surroundings — and less like superimposed 'waterworlds' — means that ideas around persistence ecosystems (or "worlds that primarily operate independently of a user's presence") will likely become essential to the Metaverse's vision. As a key factor in the evolution of such environments into fully-fledged, dynamic living systems,

AI will have a significant impact on these areas through the use of data analysis in real-time, environmental simulation and the direct effects of the agents themselves. By providing artificial intelligence in this form, virtual worlds can not only exist through time but, using AI, they can expand, evolve, and regenerate themselves in ways similar to organic life (Hu & Ting, 2024).

Virtual worlds are considered "persistent" if the changes made to the world (terrain, social constructs, economic systems) remain throughout the users' lifetimes. In doing so, the potential exists for continuous histories, and rich narratives, and, combined with AI, the potential for intelligent management and modification of the world changes. For instance, demographic shifts may occur, markets may fluctuate, or infrastructure may develop within a digital city located within the Metaverse due to AI agents and the collective behavior of users. These AI agents learn to function in a semi-autonomous fashion, thereby making decisions in real-time that affect the world and, subsequently, the decision-making capabilities of other users (Gulyamov et al., 2024).

AI enables environments to evolve autonomously. For example, computational weather systems evolve due to either user or world equilibrium; plants grow or decay due to environmental circumstances controlled by AI; online economies grow or decay, and are creatively enhanced through interactions between users and agents. Using multi-agent AI systems along with controlled feedback loops, the virtual world becomes an active element rather than simply being the passive background to the client experience (He et al., 2024).

Currently, we see examples of this type of functionality across various platforms. Some decentralized sub-Metaverse proposals feature AI-managed micro-economies, and some utilize supply-demand algorithms and user trend-based development in determining land values. In addition, some platforms provide ecological systems in which plants and animals develop according to simulated genetic principles or adaptive environmental pressures. With such implementations, we begin to see glimmers of what the future may hold for the Metaverse in terms of the autonomous systems that inhabit it — i.e., systems that continue to change, break-down, or thrive without human influence (Xu et al., 2024).

Nonetheless, there are issues related to creating sustainable ecosystems in virtual worlds as self-sustaining systems. When AI agents make decisions regarding large groups of users, the complexity of those decisions increases exponentially. Ethics-related concerns arise when large-scale, dynamically changing variables are governed by complex, hidden algorithms. Additionally, maintaining an AI system that continues to attract and retain users, while simultaneously preventing stagnation or catastrophic failure, represents a delicate balancing act (Liang et al., 2025).

Although several challenges are present, the emergence of numerous self-creating and self-sustaining virtual ecosystems indicates that we are moving toward increased maturity of the digital world. Through the application of AI, Metaverse may move toward a world that is not simply built, but instead continuously evolves in a semi-autonomous manner. Autonomous systems will strive to establish states that are non-routine — i.e., states in which they will not become trapped in stagnation or disorder. The emergent behaviors of AI agents will need to be constantly fine-tuned to ensure that they do not negatively impact usability, fairness, or engagement at scales sufficient to represent large user populations.

The increasing levels of autonomy and immersion will introduce additional, new and complex ethical and societal dilemmas. As AI-enabled Metaverse systems become increasingly sophisticated and intelligent, there will be critical implications with regard to protecting privacy, agency and identity.

7. ETHICAL AND SOCIETAL IMPLICATION

The ethics and the risk for the user in AI and VR changing the way we use the digital world, therefore creating many different and significant ethical and societal concerns while the possibilities of creativity, personalization, and immersion made available to the user through the interaction of AI and VR in Metaverse presents the opportunity for complications in the form of risks – as described in literature on AI — that are exclusive to embodied virtual worlds. The problems raised here represent a concern related to the ethics of developing technology responsibly, and protecting the autonomy, dignity, and psychological well-being of users (Rudschies and Schneider, 2024).

The importance of user privacy is a major issue arising from the collection of highly personal data that is collected by behavioral prediction systems, emotional recognition systems, and immersive biometric interfaces — for example, facial expressions, voice tone, eye movement, heart rate, and neural patterns. The collection of these types of data allows users to have more personalized and emotional experiences, however, the collection of the same amount of data also represents an unprecedented level of surveillance of the user.

When digital avatars serve as proxies for identity, not only does the leaking of user data pose a threat, but so too does the commercial exploitation of the user's emotional and cognitive state. Because the users often do not know how their data is being manipulated, and because there is no regulation over how their data is used, users are vulnerable to manipulation or exploitation — particularly when commercial organizations use these platforms for advertising and/or behaviorally targeting their customers (Prokopenko & Sapinski, 2024).

Another primary issue is that of algorithmic bias. when AI systems are trained on biased or incomplete datasets, the systems will then reproduce those biases in the virtual world — whether in the form of discriminatory NPC treatment, or cultural insensitivity in world building. this issue is particularly problematic in social Metaverse-based platforms, where individuals engage with each other through avatars, games, and other forms of social interaction, but where the same types of biases that exist in the physical world may manifest themselves in the virtual world through the way that users are viewed or treated based upon their racial or ethnic identity, gender, accent or affective states — as determined by the algorithms. As a result, these systems represent a potential threat of the emergence of virtual top-down structures that may be referred to as hierarchies that reinforce rather than undermine existing societal injustices (Chalkiadakis et al. 2024).

The long-term psychological effects of spending extended periods of time within virtual world environments that are adaptive and emotionally intelligent represents a relatively new area of research. On the one hand, VR- and AI-assisted therapy methods can assist with mental health treatments, provide therapeutic realities, and provide a safe space for users to express identities that they may not feel comfortable expressing in the real world. On the other hand, users can become disconnected from reality due to the lack of discrimination between the virtual world and the real world, and as a result may become disoriented, dissociated or even dependent. Furthermore, the emotional responses that the characters powered by AI are designed to elicit, can lead to attachments to the characters, and as a result to altered relationships in the real world, or as a result of escaping into the virtual world (Camilleri, 2024).

Similarly complex is the question of identity in the Metaverse. The manner in which avatars continuously shift through A.I.-personalized experiences creates an additional layer of fluidity and performance in the field of identity. A.I. systems do not simply transform based upon personas that users input into a system; they can also be constrained by predictive analytics. The combination of these factors can potentially create a feedback loop in which the user's identity is both self-selected and algorithmically constructed, resulting in a diminishment of the user's autonomy, authenticity and increasing vulnerability to manipulation across various identity formation constructs (Kumar et al., 2025).

Therefore, the moral world of AI-VR-Metaverse requires a proactive and multi-disciplinary approach. Technologists, ethicists, psychologists, designers, and policy makers must work together to design systems that are solution-oriented, inclusive of deaf and hard-of-hearing users, transparent, respectful of human dignity, and focus on agency, and designed from the perspective of the user. The development of the intelligence of virtual worlds will further emphasize the need to prevent environments such as these from being used for the purpose of discrimination, harm, and cruelty.

8. SPECULATIVE FUTURES: TOWARD AUTONOMOUS: VIRTUAL CIVILIZATIONS

In the future, there are many more questions than answers regarding ethics in the metaverse and digital societies. The emergence of artificially intelligent-controlled virtual societies, and cognitive augmentation raises very profound philosophical questions about the subject of digital autonomy and the subject of digital existence. All of these ideas are speculative; however, they bring up some of the most basic questions regarding the nature of creativity, governance, consciousness and the role of humans in the digital (Nechesov et al. 2025).

A potentially positive area is the emergence of decentralized AI systems that utilize blockchain technology. These types of architectures create a distributed governance environment within virtual worlds, allowing a majority of users to make decisions using smart contracts and token economies both between users and AI systems. Within these systems, the AI can control the distribution of resources and even apply policy as a neutral governor or adaptable policymaker. Projects related to the Metaverse that are studying the use of DeAOs in digital governance have begun to develop the first examples of AI-mediated civic life (Sankaran et al. 2025).

While governance has been discussed as an area for future development of AI systems, cognitive augmentation technologies could also provide users with the ability to interface with AI systems in highly symbiotic manners. Using adaptive virtual reality technology in conjunction with brain-computer interfaces could enable users to directly transmit their intentions into machine perception and vice versa. Not only could this potentially change the way users are able to navigate through their avatars or spaces, it could change how users think, recall information and learn in the Metaverse. Users could potentially delegate portions of their cognitive processes, such as spatial navigation, remembering memories or regulating their emotions, to AI companions that exist in their virtual worlds (Lucchi, 2025).

The potential future of AI in digital society also includes AI creator cultures and societies: The civilizations composed and evolved by autonomous agents with their own history, economy, language, ideology, etc. exist now. Such artificial civilizations can develop non-programmed forms of geopolitical planning, cultural development and environmental adaptation. These environments can contain human user involvement, but not necessarily as the primary means of interaction (the role of explorers/diplomats/anthropologists, who can observe, interact and/or co-develop the artificial lifeforms with their own developments) (Bojic et al. 2024).

This vision of the future raises significant philosophical and ethical concerns. What does it mean to possess agency, autonomy (or sentience) in the digital world? Does AI have a type of moral status or rights because it learns, remembers and modifies itself? Furthermore, what occurs when a virtual civilization begins to function autonomously from human direction and develops its own interests, goals, myths or values?

The potential of the virtual civilizations that do not fully operate independently of humans requires consideration of a possible state of half-independent worlds where the human-centric view of digitalization as a source of human entertainment becomes a threat. Rather, it sends a warning of a future in which the Metaverse is not only a representation of human society but rather a platform for entirely new life. How these societies will evolve within our own and co-evolve with us, and ultimately whether they eventually surpass humanity in some aspects is an open issue, but one that brings forth the issues of foresight, accountability and ethical imagination.

9. POLICY AND GOVERNANCE IMPLICATION

The convergence of Artificial Intelligence (AI), Virtual Reality (VR), and the Metaverse represents an unprecedented and extraordinary milestone in the history of humanity, creating a truly unprecedented and revolutionary possibility — the emergence of fully independent and self-governing virtual civilization(s). As these autonomous virtual societies begin to evolve in their own right, AI systems will not only govern the environment, but create its own system of governance, free from human interference. This convergence of AI, VR, and Metaverse raises a number of unanswerable questions, including how to regulate the emerging platform of AI-VR, particularly since there exists no precedent for regulating the creation and deployment of immersive intelligence, as has been done with prior digital platforms. From a regulatory perspective, one of the most pressing issues in regards to AI-VR is addressing data created by biometric and affective characteristics. Emotional recognition technology utilizes real-time physiological data, such as heart rate, eye movement, tone of voice, and facial expression, frequently without users' knowledge and/or granular consent. As both GDPR and CCPA currently provide at best limited guidance on data collection, the limitations on these regulations are particularly pronounced in immersive, constantly surveilled environments. Another area of interest is AI-driven governance within virtual worlds. In the case of a decentralized, blockchain-based Metaverse, the potential governance structure is comprised of a combination of Smart Contracts and/or AI Agents acting as moderators and/or adjudicators. Although Smart Contracts and/or AI Agents can potentially act with efficiency in terms of implementation, they can be non-transparent and employ data sets and/or baked-in bias to arrive at decisions. Furthermore, the utilization of DAO's (Decentralized Autonomous Organizations) for allocating land, enforcing virtual law, and/or regulating economics, raises additional challenges regarding accountability and redress mechanisms. Ultimately, what is needed globally are standards that address the convergence of AI and VR. These standards should include ethics frameworks, algorithmic transparency requirements, and obligations regarding digital identities. Early attempts to develop such frameworks include the European Union AI Act, the IEEE XR Ethics Framework, and various AI ethics governance toolkits. However, none of these preliminary frameworks address the unique challenges presented by immersive AI environments. Therefore, governing AI-VR in the Metaverse presents a multifaceted challenge requiring the interaction and engagement of multiple stakeholders, including technologists, ethicists, lawyers, and policymakers. Failure to establish clear governance structures over AI-VR systems will result in the co-emergence of technological advancement and algorithmically induced damage to privacy, irreparable harm, and/or outright digital disenfranchisement. A policy framework will likely require modification to ensure that virtual future are inclusive, transparent, and consistent with international human rights standards.

10. CONCLUSION

The intersection of artificial intelligence and virtual reality represents not only a way of enhancing the delivery of information and creating better digital experiences; however, this convergence signifies a fundamental shift within the structure and role of virtual worlds. Therefore, the premise of this chapter is that AI will enable the Metaverse to develop into a living, evolving entity: an entity capable of sensing emotions, developing behavior patterns, creating story lines, and sustaining autonomous ecosystems.

There will no longer be simply passive user interactions with the Metaverse. With the addition of intelligent world building that uses responsive non-player characters (NPCs), self-aware environments, and self-adaptive social structures, the Metaverse will grow from a simple, passive environment, to a living, breathing world that is both influenced by the user interface and by the inherent intelligence of the machine. It is in this context that AI systems learn, remember, and create, and that AI systems interact with their users in a process of co-creation of identity, agency and narrative.

However, because this is a novel application of technology, there is a necessity to monitor it. Because the incorporation of AI into the realm of human emotion, behavior, and cognition creates new levels of ethical complexities in the design and implementation of the Metaverse, there will be a long term and cross disciplinary discourse and legislative process required to address the issues of privacy, discrimination, agency and mental health, as opposed to simply providing technological solutions.

Innovative and speculative applications of decentralized AI governance, cognitive enhancement, and synthetic civilizations suggest that a new reality like the Metaverse could develop into a reality more than simply a reflection of our current reality and could potentially serve as the space where something entirely different emerges: a new configuration of new societies, forms of intelligence and new meanings. These emerging realities would either be dystopian or empowering depending upon the frameworks that we develop today, with each having both technical and philosophical dimensions.

This chapter has demonstrated the capacity of Metaverse to be a highly interactive and dynamic knowledge base that has the potential to facilitate creativity, engagement, and thinking in humans. However, this chapter has also illustrated a necessity to rethink the concepts of presence, human-to-human interaction, and human responsibility in relation to the development of increasingly smart, immersive and living digital spaces at every collective level.

While there is little doubt that the Metaverse has the potential to be a highly unique and adaptable digital environment, there are significant risks associated with the intersection of AI and VR that have not yet been addressed, and that should not be ignored. Specifically, the intersection of AI and VR raises concerns regarding surveillance, emotional manipulation, algorithmic bias, and loss of autonomy, all of which are developing simultaneously with technologies developed to combat these same issues. Without the development of strong regulatory frameworks, the immersive nature of these digital spaces could result in them becoming sites of exploitation, rather than sites of empowerment. As such, there is a necessity to develop and implement transparent and interdisciplinary governance models that reflect a wide range of stakeholders and perspectives. There has never been a greater need to discuss the privacy implications of digital identity, the ethics of AI, electronic identity, and consent. The trajectory of the Metaverse will ultimately depend upon how we, collectively, determine the future consequences of the Metaverse and how we will govern its development through thoughtful and inclusive regulations.

REFERENCES

Ahmed, M. A., Mahamid, F., & Hilo, G. (2025). Empowering Media Students: The Role of Digital Storytelling and the Metaverse in Skill Development. [JALLS]. *International Journal for Arabic Linguistics & Literature Studies*, *7*(1), 41–48. DOI: 10.31559/JALLS2025.7.1.4

Aleksić, V. (2024). Using Artificial Intelligence Concepts to Design Non-Playable Characters in Road Traffic Safety Games. In *10th International Scientific Conference Technics, Informatics and Education-TIE 2024*. Faculty of Technical Sciences Čačak, University of Kragujevac. DOI: 10.46793/TIE24.239A

Belabed, Z., Tounsi, A., Bousahla, A. A., Tounsi, A., & Yaylacı, M. (2024). Accurate free and forced vibration behavior prediction of functionally graded sandwich beams with variable cross-section: A finite element assessment. *Mechanics Based Design of Structures and Machines*, *52*(11), 9144–9177. DOI: 10.1080/15397734.2024.2337914

Bhattacharya, S., & Singla, B. (2024). Metaverse Banking 2.0: Future Trends and Challenges in Metaverse Banking Strategies. *Exploring the Use of Metaverse in Business and Education*, 166-192.

Bojić, L., Cinelli, M., Ćulibrk, D., & Delibašić, B. (2024). CERN for AI: A theoretical framework for autonomous simulation-based artificial intelligence testing and alignment. *European Journal of Futures Research*, *12*(1), 1–19. DOI: 10.1186/s40309-024-00238-0

Camilleri, M. A. (2024). Artificial intelligence governance: Ethical considerations and implications for social responsibility. *Expert Systems: International Journal of Knowledge Engineering and Neural Networks*, *41*(7), e13406. DOI: 10.1111/exsy.13406

Chalkiadakis, A., Seremetaki, A., Kanellou, A., Kallishi, M., Morfopoulou, A., Moraitaki, M., & Mastrokoukou, S. (2024). Impact of artificial intelligence and virtual reality on educational inclusion: A systematic review of technologies supporting students with disabilities. *Education Sciences*, *14*(11), 1223. DOI: 10.3390/educsci14111223

Chen, J., & Cao, L. (2024). AI-enabled rendering technology for the construction and development of Dunhuang Virtual Pavilion. *Front. Comput. Intell. Syst*, *7*(3), 1–5. DOI: 10.54097/yv2hpa48

Chen, X., Gao, W., Chu, Y., & Song, Y. (2024). Enhancing interaction in virtual-real architectural environments: A comparative analysis of generative AI-driven reality approaches. *Building and Environment*, *266*, 112113. DOI: 10.1016/j.buildenv.2024.112113

Datta, S. D., Islam, M., Sobuz, M. H. R., Ahmed, S., & Kar, M. (2024). Artificial intelligence and machine learning applications in the project lifecycle of the construction industry: A comprehensive review. *Heliyon*, *10*(5), e26888. DOI: 10.1016/j.heliyon.2024.e26888 PMID: 38444479

De Carlo, M. E., & Limone, P. (2024, June). Metaverse Narratives and Artificial Creativity: Fostering Divergent Thinking in the Education of the Future. In *Conference on Artificial Creativity: Looking at the Future of Digital Culture* (pp. 97-109). Cham: Springer Nature Switzerland.

Fan, S., Yecies, B., Zhou, Z. I., & Shen, J. (2024). Challenges and opportunities for the web 3.0 metaverse turn in education. *IEEE Transactions on Learning Technologies*, *17*, 1935–1950. DOI: 10.1109/TLT.2024.3385505

Fang, J., Wang, F., Xue, J., & Chua, T. S. (2024). Behavioral intention prediction in driving scenes: A survey. *IEEE Transactions on Intelligent Transportation Systems*, *25*(8), 8334–8355. DOI: 10.1109/TITS.2024.3374342

Gulyamov, S. S., Mamanazarov, S., & Rodionov, A. A. (2024, June). Creating Self-Updating Digital Platforms Using Artificial Intelligence Technologies for Continuous Education and Professional Development. In *2024 4th International Conference on Technology Enhanced Learning in Higher Education (TELE)* (pp. 337-339). IEEE. DOI: 10.1109/TELE62556.2024.10605683

He, X., Tang, Y., Ma, S., Ai, Q., Tao, F., & Qiu, R. (2024). Redefinition of digital twin and its situation awareness framework designing toward fourth paradigm for energy internet of things. *IEEE Transactions on Systems, Man, and Cybernetics. Systems*, *54*(11), 6873–6888. DOI: 10.1109/TSMC.2024.3407061

Hu, B. A., & Ting, F. (2024, October). EverForest: A More-Than-AI Sustainability Manifesto from an On-Chain Artificial Life. In *Proceedings of the Halfway to the Future Symposium* (pp. 1-6). DOI: 10.1145/3686169.3686209

Hussain, R., Sabir, A., Lee, D. Y., Zaidi, S. F. A., Pedro, A., Abbas, M. S., & Park, C. (2024). Conversational AI-based VR system to improve construction safety training of migrant workers. *Automation in Construction*, *160*, 105315. DOI: 10.1016/j.autcon.2024.105315

Johansson, T., & Eladhari, M. P. (2024, December). Emotional Believability of Non-playable Game Characters-Animations of Anger, Sadness and Happiness. In *International Conference on Interactive Digital Storytelling* (pp. 72-99). Cham: Springer Nature Switzerland.

Khan, M. A. A., Tashfi, M. M. I., Nur, F. N., & Sultana, S. (2024, December). Effects of Emotional Behavior Tree in Non-Playable Characters in Games. In *2024 6th International Conference on Sustainable Technologies for Industry 5.0 (STI)* (pp. 1-7). IEEE. DOI: 10.1109/STI64222.2024.10951084

Khare, S. K., Blanes-Vidal, V., Nadimi, E. S., & Acharya, U. R. (2024). Emotion recognition and artificial intelligence: A systematic review (2014–2023) and research recommendations. *Information Fusion, 102*, 102019. DOI: 10.1016/j.inffus.2023.102019

Kollias, D., Zafeiriou, S., Kotsia, I., Dhall, A., Ghosh, S., Shao, C., & Hu, G. (2024, September). 7th abaw competition: Multi-task learning and compound expression recognition. In *European Conference on Computer Vision* (pp. 31-45). Cham: Springer Nature Switzerland.

Kumar, K., Veena, N., Aravind, T., Bhatt, C., Kuppusamy, U., & Jain, P. (2025). Game-changing intelligence: Unveiling the societal impact of artificial intelligence in game software. *Entertainment Computing, 52*, 100862. DOI: 10.1016/j.entcom.2024.100862

Li, J., & Li, Y. (2025). Interactive Narrative and Scenario Building. In *Digital Futures in Human-Computer Interaction* (pp. 139–148). CRC Press. DOI: 10.1201/9781032693606-12

Liang, X., Tao, M., Xia, Y., Wang, J., Li, K., Wang, Y., He, Y., Yang, J., Shi, T., Wang, Y., Zhang, M., & Wang, X. (2025). SAGE: Self-evolving Agents with Reflective and Memory-augmented Abilities. *Neurocomputing, 647*, 130470. DOI: 10.1016/j.neucom.2025.130470

Lucchi, E. (2025). Digital twins, artificial intelligence and immersive technologies for heritage preservation and cultural tourism in smart cities. In *Digital Twin, Blockchain, and Sensor Networks in the Healthy and Mobile City* (pp. 507-520). Elsevier. DOI: 10.1016/B978-0-443-34174-8.00026-0

Mahalakshmi, S., Bharath, H., Kautish, S., & Singh, D. (2025). Virtual Storytelling for Sustainable Development: Engaging Audiences with SDG Narratives. In *Metaverse and Sustainability: Business Resilience Towards Sustainable Development Goals* (pp. 361–375). Springer Nature Switzerland. DOI: 10.1007/978-3-031-89545-6_19

Natarajan, T., Pragha, P., Dhalmahapatra, K., & Veera Raghavan, D. R. (2024). Exploring tourist's metaverse experience using destination spatial presence quality & perceived augmentation: Metaverse exploration, physical expedition (MEPE). *Current Issues in Tourism*, ●●●, 1–23.

Nechesov, A., Dorokhov, I., & Ruponen, J. (2025). Virtual cities: From digital twins to autonomous ai societies. *IEEE Access : Practical Innovations, Open Solutions, 13*, 13866–13903. DOI: 10.1109/ACCESS.2025.3531222

Papadopoulou, A., Mystakidis, S., & Tsinakos, A. (2024). Immersive storytelling in social virtual reality for human-centered learning about sensitive historical events. *Information (Basel), 15*(5), 244. DOI: 10.3390/info15050244

Pathirana, A., Rajakaruna, D. K., Kasthurirathna, D., Atukorale, A., Aththidiye, R., & Yatipansalawa, M. (2024). A reinforcement learning-based approach for promoting mental health using multimodal emotion recognition. *Journal of Future Artificial Intelligence and Technologies, 1*(2), 124–142. DOI: 10.62411/faith.2024-22

Prokopenko, O., & Sapinski, A. (2024). Using virtual reality in education: Ethical and social dimensions. *E-Learning Innovations Journal, 2*(1), 41–62. DOI: 10.57125/ELIJ.2024.03.25.03

Reddy, C. V., Reddy, N. U., Sharma, S., Kumar, J. P., Lakhanpal, S., & Albawi, A. (2024, May). Advanced Deep Learning Architectures for Real-Time Human Emotion Recognition and Behavioral Prediction. In *2024 International Conference on Communication, Computer Sciences and Engineering (IC3SE)* (pp. 1306-1311). IEEE. DOI: 10.1109/IC3SE62002.2024.10592940

Rudschies, C., & Schneider, I. (2024). Ethical, legal, and social implications (ELSI) of virtual agents and virtual reality in healthcare. *Social Science & Medicine, 340*, 116483. DOI: 10.1016/j.socscimed.2023.116483 PMID: 38064822

Sankaran, S., Arun, M., & Kottaimalai, R. (2025). Virtualization of Smart Society 5.0 Using Artificial Intelligence and Virtual Reality. *Networked Sensing Systems*, 297-321.

Wilujeng, P. R., Sugihartati, R., Saud, M., & Wijayanti, N. (2025, July). Non-Playable Characters (NPC) in Video Games. In *Proceedings of the International Conference on Cultural Studies (ICCUS) 2024* (Vol. 930, p. 165). Springer Nature. DOI: 10.2991/978-2-38476-418-1_13

Wilujeng, P. R., Sugihartati, R., Saud, M., & Wijayanti, N. (2025, June). Gamer Culture in Playing Simulated Violence Against Non-Playable Characters (NPC) in Video Games. In *The International Conference on Cultural Studies (ICCUS 2024)* (pp. 165-175). Atlantis Press. DOI: 10.2991/978-2-38476-418-1_13

Xu, C., Sun, Y., Tao, Y., Zhao, B., Hu, R., & Jiu, L. (2024). Exploring the confluence of bioinspired technologies and the metaverse: Business and societal implications in the anthropocene era. *Journal of Cleaner Production, 450*, 141873. DOI: 10.1016/j.jclepro.2024.141873

Yang, L., Allen, G., Zhang, Z., & Zhao, Y. (2024). Achieving on-site trustworthy AI implementation in the construction industry: A framework across the AI lifecycle. *Buildings (Basel, Switzerland), 15*(1), 21. DOI: 10.3390/buildings15010021

KEY TERMS AND DEFINITIONS

Adaptive Storytelling: A narrative design technique whereby plot, dialogue, and character behaviour the user selects interacts with is dynamically determined by the context of the user's choices, feelings, and patterns of interaction, and would most plausibly be made possible via the use of machine-learning systems.

Affective Computing: An interdisciplinary field on the cross-section of artificial intelligence and psychology dealing with the design of systems that can recognise, interpret and simulate human emotions.

AI Ethics: A new interdisciplinary field focused on the legal principles and social implications of the development, implementation, and deployment of artificial intelligence, in particular the issues of fairness, transparency, privacy, and autonomy.

Artificial Intelligence (AI): A computer science branch or the science and engineering of creating machines and algorithms that enable machines to perform tasks that normally require human intelligence or the ability to learn, make decisions, perceive and understand language.

Behavioral Prediction: Analysis of the actions and tendencies of users based on artificial intelligence with the goal of predicting future behaviours or preferences and, through this, dynamically adapting the environments, stories or the responses of systems.

Decentralized Autonomous Organization (DAO): It ensure that the decentralized governance model of the blockchain enables decision-making within digital environments to be executed via smart contracts and collective consensus, and includes AI-mediated virtual governance.

Digital Identity: Users representation on the virtual spaces can include avatars, behavioural histories, preferences and biometric data, which can be shaped or affected by AI-driven systems.

Digital Twins: Virtual replicas of physical systems, entities, or environments that get updated in real-world time and is capable of helping to simulate, predict, and optimise in virtual or augmented spaces.

Emotion Recognition: The process of using Artificial Intelligence (AI) systems to communicate the state of the emotion of humans and understand it based on the physiological and behavioural data of the subject, such as facial expressions, modulation in voice and biometric.

Metaverse: Collective persistent digital universe combining virtual environments, social interaction and real-time interaction-within the typical digital immersive illustrations, AI and VR usually as its powerhouse-where users may well be each creating, encountering and withholding immersive content.

Non-Playable Characters (NPCs): Virtual agents/ entities in virtual environments which are not under the control of human users but are programmed or AI driven to interact, respond, and evolve accordingly to the players actions and environmental situation.

Persistent Virtual Worlds: Immersive digital worlds that change through time and also in the absence of users, which are constituted by AI agents, feedback loops and system memory

Procedural Content Generation: This is the process or algorithmic construction of elements in a game or virtual environment that are not designed manually - terrain, architecture, etc.- but are generated through an algorithm often utilizing AI models for scalability (and also variability).

Reinforcement Learning (RL): A machine learning framework where artificial intelligence agents learn behaviours that optimise an environment through interaction with the environment and feedback as rewards or penalties, often used to train adaptive NPC or system responses.

Virtual Reality (VR): A simulated, three-dimensional, immersive environment created by using digital technologies, such as head-mounted displays and motion sensors). 3D objects created by computer software program may be used in VR to interact and travel through space time.

Chapter 2
AI Enabled Virtual Reality in the Metaverse:
Technologies, Use Cases, and Ethical Challenges

Atul Kumar
https://orcid.org/0000-0002-7665-1892
Department of Computer Science, R.G.M. Government College, Joginder Nagar, India

ABSTRACT

The combination of Artificial Intelligence (AI) and Virtual Reality (VR) in the Metaverse represents a paradigm shift in the online interaction, and it changes the sphere of education, healthcare, business, and government. AI enhances VR space by facilitating flexible, customized, and intelligent interactions, but VR gives humans rich, and immersive human interaction. This cooperation facilitates the active virtual worlds with real-life-like avatars, real time generation of content, and context responsive engagement. Nevertheless, the problem of data privacy, algorithm bias, digital identity protection, and psychological outcomes should be brought up to ensure ethical and fair development. This chapter also explores the technological backgrounds, industry-related usage, and social impacts of AI-VR integration .Through the emphasized transparency, justice, and autonomy to the users, stakeholders can be able to maximise the potential of the Metaverse and reduce the dangers associated with the technology.

DOI: 10.4018/979-8-3373-3690-9.ch002

1. INTRODUCTION

The Metaverse theory is not new and acquired popularity only because of the renaming of the word, which was called Meta. The Metaverse of virtual reality (VR) and the combination of artificial intelligence (AI) is definitely going to be a paradigm shift in the digital transformation that will permeate the entertainment sector, higher education sector, the workplace, and life overall. The two innovative tools that have emerged to be major drivers of innovation in the fast-changing digital technology world are Artificial Intelligence (AI) and Virtual Reality (VR).All these technologies, individually, have already demonstrated high potential to transform the way we work, live and interact with digital content. However, by converging into the conceptual and technical framework of the Metaverse, a new phase of digital change is imminent, which envisions a time when highly personalized, immersive, and intelligent virtual worlds will form an inseparable part of the human experience.

Artificial intelligence imitates the human intellect in robots that can learn, reason, solve problems, see and interpret natural language. AI has evolved to a multidisciplinary field that supports adaptive learning and autonomous decision-making that ranges from rule-based expert systems to deep learning and neural networks. These days, virtual assistants, recommendation systems, driverless cars, and more and more intelligent systems in various sectors are powered by AI. Virtual reality is a computer-generated simulation of a three-dimensional environment that might be interacted with the use of special electronic devices, such as motion-sensor-equipped headgear, in a way that appears real or tangible. The psychological experience of "being there" in a virtual environment is created by virtual reality (VR). This immersion of senses allows for applications in gaming, training simulations, educational, therapy, and other fields to allow users to partake in similar or better experiences of the real world.

Neal Stephenson's 1992(Stephenson, 2022) book Snow Crash introduced the word "Metaverse" which was inevitably endorsed by large tech corporations. It refers to a persistent, shared and connected network of three dimensional virtual worlds. Users are able to interact, work, play, conduct business, and create in this environment, which is represented by digital avatars. Although the Metaverse is still in its early stages, virtual reality and artificial intelligence are helping the Metaverse to grow, and this is being facilitated by edge computing, blockchain, and fast internet. The Metaverse's link of AI and VR brings an incredible opportunity to create intelligent, immersive, and interactive environments that understand, anticipate, and react to the user's activities in real time. Virtual worlds are more interactive, customizable, and flexible and dynamically change in response to the behavior of the user with the assistance of AI.

The relevance of the research of this convergence is that it can transform human-computer interaction, the economic system, social dynamics and the identity representation. The technologies are also becoming maturing and gaining grounds and they are posing strong questions as regards to ethics, agency, privacy and digital governance. They also carry with them the assurance of addressing the global issues like fair access to education, remote provision of healthcare and sustainable work solutions by intelligent virtual realms, without attracting geographical and physical boundaries. These promises are, however, not without their fair share of challenges. Numerous issues such as data privacy, bias in algorithmic decision-making, digital addiction, identity authentication, psychological effects of hyper-realistic simulations are brought up through the use of AI-driven agents in immersive virtual reality environments. The need for active investigation and other interdisciplinary research is illustrated by the lack of universal governance, transparency of AI behavior, and ethical frameworks of immersive content creation.

This chapter aims to discuss the intersection between AI and VR in the Metaverse by answering the following important research questions:

1. How Artificial Intelligence improves Realism, Interactivity and Personalization in VR-based Metaverse Platforms?
2. What are the ethical, societal and technical issues involved with the deployment of intelligent agents and virtual personas in immersive environments?
3. In what ways can AI-powered content creation be useful in dynamic development and scalability of the virtual environments?

This chapter will provide an in-depth analysis of the current state and future progress of the integration of AI and VR in the Metaverse by means of a combination of literature review, case study analysis, and theoretical exploration. It includes mapping a taxonomy of real-world use-cases in industries, discover patterns and best practices in the leading platforms of the world, and offer a list of policy guidelines and design principles in the ethical development. After all, the aim is not merely to record the technological advancements but to present a vision of a smart Metaverse, the one that would harness the potential of AI and VR to the fullest and also introduce the ideas of inclusivity, transparency, and digital health. This interaction between intelligence and immersion is something that we need to know as we approach this new digital frontier so that we can be able to shape the future so that it can be advantageous to every member of society.

2. LITERATURE REVIEW

The potential to revolutionize various industries, including entertainment and healthcare, education, and many others, is being introduced with the help of virtual reality (VR), artificial intelligence (AI), and the metaverse. The question of how these innovations work together will determine the most effective use of these innovations and their adoption by the users as the digital world transforms. The findings of the ongoing study in general are outlined in this literature overview that also determines the knowledge gaps and potential research directions. The paper (Soliman et al., 2024) has described the process of implementing Artificial intelligence (AI) into Metaverse in detail. It featured several different uses of AI, such as smart virtual assistants and tailored content generation. To better architecture the network and management of the data, the authors reviewed a growing body of literature and identified trends and potential for further multidisciplinary study. The study also discussed ethical problems and real-life applications as key factors in future development.

(Shi et al., 2023): bounty of connecting form, ubiquity space, virtual reality and interaction, and human-centered communication.

The paper also highlighted challenges such as balancing the boundaries of virtual reality, integration of tech with resources.

(Dionisio, Burns, & Gilbert, 2013) noted transition from isolated virtual environments to a unified Metaverse is dependent on advances in immersive realism, ubiquitous access and identity, interoperability and scalability. Despite the increasing interest in institutions and technological progress, unanswered computational constraints and poorly coordinated collaboration between stakeholders prevent its realization.

AI as well as the metaverse are world-changing technologies that are changing industries and our everyday lives (Thakur, Bandyopadhyay, & Datta, 2023). The metaverse is a combination of virtual, augmented and physical realities, and AI is what makes the experiences intelligent and adaptive in the metaverse. Together, they are driving innovation in certain fields such as healthcare, education, and entertainment.

Pereira (2024) presented an literature review about role of Artificial Intelligence with emphasis on generative Artificial Intelligence and Large Language Models in the operationalization and progression of the metaverse. The study has analyzed 13 articles (2023 to 2024) and highlights five main thematic categories.

Basheer et al. (2024) discussed the metaverse as a new platform for virtual tourism using AI and VR technologies. It brought forward the possibility of realistic and personalized travelling experiences from anywhere. The chapter also addressed the advantages and the challenges of establishing a tourism industry based on the metaverse.

Amos (2022) discussed the aspects of AI improving the Metaverse through realistic avatars, digital humans and multilingual accessibility. The author described the role of AI in business, education, and infrastructure in the virtual world. Despite the positive aspects, the integration of AI is thought to raise questions concerning ownership, transparency, and ethical utilization.

Ghosh et al. (2024) discussed the convergence of blockchain, Web 3.0, and the decentralized metaverse, and the impact they have had on virtual experiences. The authors looked at governance, architecture, and how these are being applied to sites such as The Sandbox and Decentraland. Security issues are addressed as well as key technologies such as DAOs, PoW and PoS. The research emphasised how decentralisation systems with the capacity to redefine digital ownership, identity and engagement.

Kostadimas et al. (2025) discussed the integration of VR, AI & IoT in various areas such as healthcare, Industry 4.0 and smart cities and their synergy through the Digital Twins. They highlighted some major challenges like interoperability, cost, and lack of integration in the real world, particularly in uncharted sectors. The study highlighted the importance of having standardised frameworks and advanced architectures in order to create intelligent, scalable, resilient systems for global challenges.

To create a taxonomy covering VR, AR, Blockchain, intelligent agents and social effects, (Fadhel et al., 2024) 54 features were examined to look at the revolutionary role of AI in the Metaverse. (Din, Awan, Almogren, & Rodrigues, 2023) have studies various uses of Metaverse, with the focus on how it is being integrated with the Internet of Things in fields such as smart buildings, power grid, and agriculture. The improvements of 22% in operational efficiency, 17% in cost reduction and 25% in energy conservation has been made. The article (Wang, Wang, and Siau, 2024) provided a human-centered perspective of the Metaverse, which provided an overview of the description of the same and its key components, such as infrastructure and multisensory HCI technologies. They surveyed the way the current technologies were ready in various spheres and provided a full system. The paper identified key obstacles and provides some tactical recommendations for further Metaverse investigation and advancement.

With focus on technologies such as 5G, Blockchain, Virtual tech and 3D reconstruction, (Lyu, 2023) 100+ papers on Human Computer Interaction in Metaverse were studied. They stressed on how these improvements allow for immersive and safe, more and more seamless digital interactions.

(Ramadan & Ramadan, 2025) adopted qualitative approaches such as user comments and interviews in order to explore the potential impact of human virtual avatars on hospitality services in the Metaverse. Important conclusions point to increased realism and participation but also pointed to problems like trust concerns and self misrepresentation.

(Tabassum, Elmahjub, Padela, Zwitter, & Qadir, 2025) The possibility and implications of polar integration of Generative AI, specifically Large Language Models (LLMs), into the Metaverse and in the future for creating immersive, real-time digital experiences. The authors identified key ethical and legal concerns, such as bias, misinformation and data privacy. The study reinforced the urgent need for unique frameworks to solve looking at responsible, equitable, and sustainable development in this changing digital world.

2.1 Methodological Approach

It is a comparative and user-friendly chapter that involves the synthesis of literature, analysis of case studies, and theoretical aspects. It compares AI-VR integration in sectors (education, healthcare, governance, and commerce) as well as tracing user experience and ethical frameworks. The methodology focuses on the triangulation of empirical data, theoretical frameworks, and the ethical debate with the goal of balancing the theoretical knowledge with practice. In such a way, the analysis is based on lived experiences and contextual realities of AI-VR implementation in the Metaverse.

3. FOUNDATIONS OF VIRTUAL REALITY AND ARTIFICIAL INTELLIGENCE

One of the most important bridges of cutting edge tech is the one between virtual reality (VR) and artificial intelligence (AI), which are both extremely potent on their own, but enormously revolutionary when the two go hand in hand. It is necessary to first have a proper conceptual foundation to understand the importance of their convergence in the Metaverse. The basic concepts of VR and AI are discussed in this part, and then the combination of the two is analyzed to determine how it generates capabilities that are greater than the sum of its individual parts.

3.1 Virtual Reality Fundamentals

Due to the virtual reality technology, users can navigate computer-generated environments that can appear like real or fancied worlds. The primary objective of virtual reality is to create a sense of presence or state of mind where the users feel that they are physically present in a virtual world. We have to include essential technology elements to provide this immersive experience:

3.1.1 Immersion of the senses and interaction

Virtual reality systems use haptic devices, motion tracking sensors, head-mounted displays (HMDs), and spatial audio to immerse users in this environment as shown in Figure 1. Together, these systems provide a dynamic and responsive environment by giving users real-time feedback based on their actions. The degree of natural engagement is further increased with eye tracking, hand movements, and voice inputs, which let users interact with virtual items much like they would in the real world.

Figure 1. Virtual reality, equipped with a VR headset, haptic gloves, motion tracking sensors, and spatial audio headphones

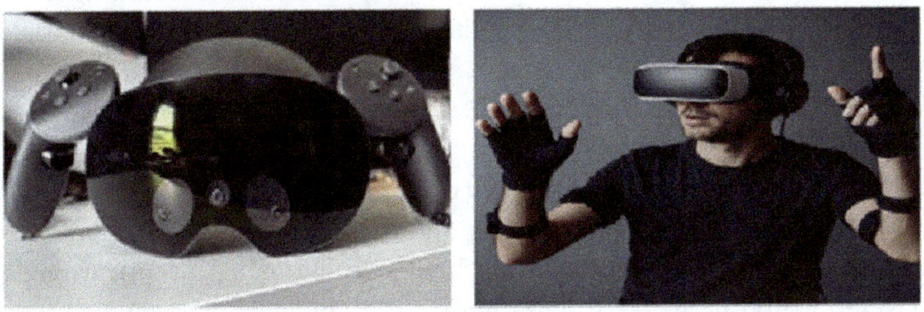

3.1.2 Types of Virtual Reality

VR experiences are divided into different categories based on how immersive they are:

- **Non-Immersive VR:** A simple type of virtual reality in which users engage with a 3D scene via a computer screen without using all of their senses. Devices used are Standard monitors, keyboards, mice, or game controllers. For example: Desktop-based 3D games (e.g., The Sims), architectural walk-throughs, or low-interaction simulations.
- **Semi-Immersive VR:** It usually combines high-resolution screens with some motion tracking to provide a somewhat immersive experience with little interaction with the surroundings. Devices used are Large projection screens, curved displays, or basic motion sensors. For Example: Flight simulators for pilot training, educational virtual labs, or CAVE (Cave Automatic Virtual Environment) systems.

- **Fully Immersive VR:** It creates a full virtual world with real-time interaction and sensory feedback, providing the maximum level of immersion.Devices used are Head-Mounted Displays (HMDs like Oculus Rift, HTC Vive), motion controllers, haptic feedback gloves, and omnidirectional treadmills. For Examples: VR gaming (Half-Life: Alyx), military simulations, medical training, or social VR platforms (Meta Horizon Worlds).

3.2 Artificial intelligence fundamentals

The study of developing machines that can carry out tasks that usually require for human intelligence is known as artificial intelligence. Perception, thinking, decision-making, language comprehension, and experience-based learning are some of these tasks. Fundamentally, artificial intelligence comprises several subfields:

3.2.1 Deep Learning & Machine Learning

Computers may learn from data without explicit programming thanks to machine learning (ML). Large datasets are used by algorithms to find patterns and provide predictions or judgments. A form of machine learning called deep learning uses multi-layered neural networks to interpret natural language or recognize images, among other complicated patterns.

3.2.2 Natural Language Processing(NLP)

NLP is what enables machines to respond to and comprehend human language. This facilitates natural and conversational human-computer interaction with the help of AI-based chatbots, virtual assistants, translation systems, and sentiment analysis systems.

3.2.3 Robotics and Computer Vision

The AI systems based on computer vision can identify objects, comprehend spatial connections, and interpret visual data. Together with robotics, these characteristics make robots observe and take part in virtual and reality space. This combination is forwarded to the gap between perception and action of intelligent systems, and it makes it possible to perform such tasks as autonomous navigation, object manipulation and environmental awareness.

3.2.4 Autonomous Decision-Making AI

Such systems are able to make decisions on their own and particularly when the circumstances are unpredictable or dynamic. The skills in decision making are critical in many applications since they can be deployed in guiding self-driving cars on challenging traffic conditions to assist users to obtain customized information in dynamic digital ecosystems. AI has been used to improve the productivity and user experience of many platforms, including the analysis of real-time data and the implementation of changes depending on updated data.

3.2.5 Learning and Adaptation

The ability to adjust to the evolving environmental conditions as a result of the interaction with the users is also one of the distinguishing features of AI, which, in its turn, allows it to learn. This adaptive intelligence allows systems to evolve as time goes on by improving their performance, improving their behavior and providing more individual user experiences. AI is constantly being updated to suit the demands of dynamic digital ecosystems, whether through real-time feedback loops, as an analysis of user behavior or through reinforcement learning.

3.3 Synergistic Potentials: Why AI and VR Complement Each Other

AI and VR are not just a combination of intelligent and real technology but a revolutionary cooperation that changes the very nature of online communication. Even though virtual reality (VR) provides the physical plane of space to be present and interact with space, it has no adaptive intelligence and thus it is passive and immobile. AI provides this canvas with an intelligent, flexible, and developing aspect. They work together to create intelligent, dynamic, and constantly changing virtual worlds that resemble, and sometimes surpass, the complexity of the real world.

3.3.1 Virtual Beings and Intelligent Avatars

Artificial intelligence provides the means of developing realistic, interactive avatars that have the capacity to naturally talk, feel and modify their behavior. These artificial intelligence-driven creatures are not just the fictional characters but evolve due to the user interaction, adopting their interests and detecting emotional cues to adapt. A virtual classroom teacher can clarify the misunderstanding of a student in real-time by using AI. A virtual nurse agent can provide emotional care as well as healthcare advice during digital health care. AI companions increase user interaction in the social and gaming world by creating empathy and realism.

3.3.2 Personalised and Adaptive Experiences

In order to tailor to each user, AI algorithms analyze behavioral data such as gaze tracking, history of interactions and performance metrics. AI ensures that the virtual experience is adjusted to certain needs and circumstances, be it the modulation of environmental features such as music and light or customization of the degree of complexity of a training simulation. As an example, in virtual reality in instructional tasks, students can be presented with content of the right level and pace. In wellness applications, AI will be able to detect the pressures and adjust the environment to promote relaxation (Figure 2).

Figure 2. Personalised and adaptive experiences

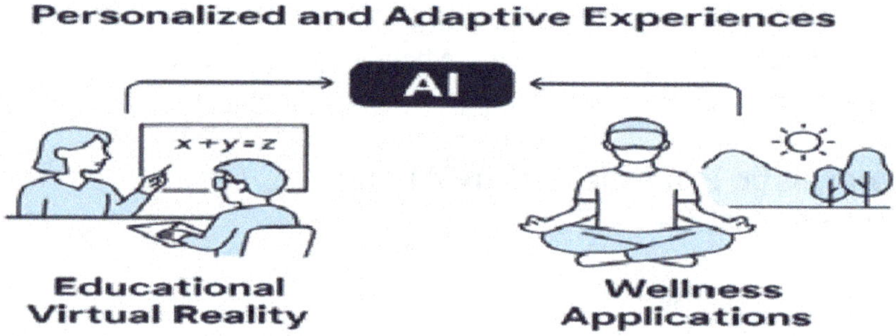

3.3.3 Producing Content in Real Time

The processes of building expansive and immersive worlds are time-consuming and expensive to do manually. The AI avoids this by enabling the procedural generation of content, i.e. landscapes, buildings, stories and dialogues. Out of the methods such as reinforcement learning and generative adversarial networks (GANs), the system is able to keep transforming virtual environments in response to actions and conditions of users on an ongoing basis. Along these lines, two user experiences do not need to be similar. An example is that a virtual city may develop, respond and evolve in real time in response to the desires and actions of its inhabitants.

3.3.4 Context-Aware and Predictive Interaction

The VR AI can predict user intentions and help them proactively through the use of machine learning models. An example is that based on previous activities, AI can suggest tools, co-workers, or relevant content on a shared virtual desktop. This makes users more productive and less frictional.AI would potentially mediate dialogues, detect conflict, or propose relevant virtual space within social VR applications depending on user actions and preferences.

3.3.5 Cognitive and Emotional Reaction

Some of the ways AI can detect the emotion of the user are by biometric sensors, voice analysis, and facial emotion recognition. Virtual worlds can be dynamically adjusted to this data, through the manipulation of lighting, sound or style of interaction to encourage social interaction and emotional health. Such emotionally intelligent systems have the potential to offer safe and nurturing virtual spaces within therapeutic settings by offering assistance that is specific to stress, anxiety, or depression responses.

3.4 Theoretical Perspectives on AI–VR Integration in the Metaverse

The implementation of AI and VR into the Metaverse can be viewed in the prism of different theoretical frameworks. The theory of Human-Computer Interaction (HCI) gives an insight on the phenomenon of the effects of immersive systems on the cognition and behavior of the users and specifies more on the usability and presence. It is proposed by Embodied Cognition Theory that virtual environments of learning and perceiving are based on physical and sensory experiences, which are made more convincing by AI-driven feedback loops. The Sociotechnical Systems Theory lays emphasis on the co-evolution of technology and society, making the Metaverse a hybrid socio-technical ecosystem whose forces include cultural, ethical, and institutional ones. All these theoretical approaches emphasize the fact that AI-VR convergence is not only a technical development, but a socio-cognitive change that affects identity, agency, and ethics in the digital world. Independent systems that are capable of generating and operating giant, interconnected and coherent virtual worlds are needed, in order to truly scale the Metaverse. AI makes it possible to automate world-building, content updates, the growth of NPC populations, and behavioral realism. By constantly learning, these AI systems can transform the Metaverse during its operation, imitating the social, cultural, and economic processes of the virtual inhabitants of the Metaverse.

4. USE CASES IN VARIOUS SECTORS

The convergence of virtual reality (VR) and artificial intelligence (AI) is changing the paradigm of many industries in the Metaverse. They are currently integrated into systems that aid in the most basic activities of humans, including education, health, government, business, and working together, and is no longer restricted to the sphere of entertainment or video games. In this part, we discusses how AI-driven intelligence and immersive virtual reality settings are transforming user experiences, industrial processes, and social roles.

4.1 Education: Immersion Classrooms with AI-Powered Virtual Tutors

Case Study: VictoryXR, the major educational VR firm, collaborated with Meta to introduce virtual campuses in 10 universities in the United States. Students were involved in virtual classrooms that were powered and supported by AI and had avatars and adaptive feedback. Early studies reported a 30% increase in engagement and 20% improvement in retention rates compared to traditional online classes. This result in challenges including motion sickness for some users, and accessibility issues for low-bandwidth students, underscoring the need for inclusive design in educational Metaverse environments.

Education in the metaverse has promised a great transformation of the past, non-adaptive, linear, and entirely immersive learning with the adaptive, interactive, and wholly immersive ecosystems. AI-based virtual tutors provide real-time feedback, tailor content presentation to the preference and fast-tracked learning of each individual student and adaptive learning, when incorporated into virtual reality classes. Consider a history course in which students go to ancient Rome not in textbook form, but via complete simulation where they would be directed by a AI tutor who developed as a Roman citizen to the political, social, and architectural wonders of the day. Such tutors rely on affective computing to change their teaching approach immediately according to the engagement of the students, their facial expressions, and the tone of their voices.

Moreover, the administrative tasks can be more easily automatized with the use of artificial intelligence, which allows teachers to focus more on communicating with students. Some of the earliest examples of VR-based instructional environments are such platforms as Engage (EngageVR, n.d.) and VictoryXR (VictoryXR, n.d.), but they should be improved with the use of machine learning algorithms to increase the level of interactivity and customisation of the experience.

4.2 Healthcare: VR Diagnostics with AI-Assisted Simulations

Case Study: Osso VR is a medical training platform that involves immersive simulations based on AI analytics to train surgeons. In 2023, learners who underwent VR training showed 230 percent more accuracy in surgical practices than those who had undergone standard training. AI modules are used to measure hand precision, and reaction times and learning curves, which allows giving personal feedback. The barriers to implementation of AI-based diagnostics in VR telehealth comprise hardware expenses and regulatory authorization of the systems.

AI in healthcare combined with VR is one of the most radical innovations in digital medicine. With the help of AI-generated simulations, medical professionals and medical students will be able to learn surgical procedures in hyper-realistic settings, have their performance assessed by intelligent agents and communicate with dynamic avatars of patients, whose symptoms can change according to the input and decision-making.

The Metaverse also provides new ways to telemedicine. Rather than a video call, patients can appear at virtual clinics that have AI-based doctors who conduct the initial diagnostics based on biometric data, behavioral indicators, and patient history. These agents can identify early signs of the diseases like Alzheimer, Parkinson, or depression through subtle alterations of speech, movement, or eye movements on the VR platform with the aid of deep learning. Exposure therapy, managing anxiety, and treating PTSD In mental health, immersive VR stages, driven by AI behavioral models, can be applied. Considering the example, patients can be gradually exposed to phobic stimuli, in a secure, regulated, and adaptive virtual environment, tracked by AI systems, which change stimuli according to the physiological reaction of the user in real time.

4.3 Remote Work: Intelligent Virtual Collaboration

Case Study: The virtual workplace at Accenture on the Nth floor demonstrates how AI-VR technology is large scale corporate integration. Over 60,000 employees relied on this platform to do the onboarding process and hold joint meetings in 2024 with the aid of AI avatars that controlled the sessions and summarized the discussions. It was reported that it is more engaged and requires less fatigue during communication, yet avatars realness and data security are also the major issues.

The remote job as normalized after the pandemic has warmed the groundwork in the transformation that can be achieved through the integration of virtual reality (VR) and artificial intelligence (AI). Physical distance will no longer be an obstacle to collaboration in intelligent Metaverse corporations as workers convene workspaces in delicately detailed and shared 3D spaces where AI greatly enhances human productivity, human creativity, and human decision-making. Virtual boardrooms can simulate the feeling of a real meeting with the help of the systems using artificial intelligence (AI). They are able to plan meetings themselves, organize agendas according to project priorities, capture live conversation notes, mark key items of action on the agenda, generate comprehensive meeting notes and even propose strategic options with advanced natural language processing (NLP) systems.

Spatial audio, gesture recognition, facial expression monitoring, and eye-tracking technologies enhance communication further by adding informal gestures needed to bond and trust in the teams remotely. The fact that AI will learn the unique workflows of an individual, schedule things and control the calendar, prioritize the messages, propose the most efficient patterns of work, and analyze the behavioral data to predict early signs of fatigue or burnout makes the work environment more sustainable and effective. Moreover, one of the biggest steps in the field of human-AI symbiosis in working situations has been characterized by the emergence of synthetic teammates, AI-driven agents that may assist in ideation, writing research papers, analyzing, and designing. AI translation services are provided in real time, and the opportunities of international collaboration that were not present before are introduced due to culturally adjusted models of communication that promote tolerance and diversity.

This transition is best demonstrated by the early innovative platforms such as Microsoft Mesh and Spatial, which have evolved to be more intelligent, anticipate user needs, offer optimization tips, and encourage collective intelligence. To establish work environments that are responsive to human requirements, intelligent workspaces of the future will likely include biometric identification, AI-enabled career development to the analytics and dynamic, skill-based team building.

Finally, AI-VR integration represents not only the advancement of remote working, but a breakthrough in human-friendly, intelligent work in digital space by eliminating geographical limits, automation in the office, creativity, and reinforcement of personal relations in virtual space.

4.4 Retail & Commerce: AI and Personalized Shopping

Case Study: The Nikeland, which is an AI-driven immersive retail, is presented within Nikeland, a game on Roblox. AI algorithms are used to personalize the process of virtual shopping and predict the preferences of the user on the basis of the in-game behaviour. The case of Nikeland, however, revealed a strong marketing potential as in 2024, the restaurant has received more than 25 million visits. Nevertheless, behavioral data collection and the involvement of children led to concerns on privacy, a factor that caused the call to take firmer action to control the ethical issue.

The virtual economy of the Metaverse is shifting the retail and commerce industries to a revolutionary shift on the super-customized immersive consumer experience in the incorporation of virtual reality (VR) and the artificial intelligence (AI). Instead of the customers using the webpages that have remained stagnant over the years, the Metaverse makes customers engage with dynamic, three-dimensional worlds where they can physically interact with the online objects and visit virtual shopping venues, and even try on clothes using unbelievable lifelike customisable 3D avatars. These experiences are cemented by artificial intelligence based systems that generate highly personalized product suggestions through an assessment of a variety of data, including preferences, body size, and behaviors, previous purchasing behaviors, and browsing patterns. This move to responsive and personal customer experiences by creating insanely entertaining customer journeys does not only add to customer pleasure but also brand loyalty. To establish initial precedents to succeed in the retail sector in the Metaverse, already established brands such as Gucci and Nike are already experimenting with virtual stores, immersive brand experiences, and selling of special digital products. It is expected that the virtual marketplace will be further unified with real-world value systems in the future, as blockchain and non-fungible tokens (NFT) technology develop. This will allow users to purchase signed digital wearables on their avatars or have physical items of limited-edition associated with interactions in the Metaverse. Artificial intelligence (AI) solutions on the operational backend of this ecosystem are required to control dynamic inventory forecasting, enhance the supply chain logistics, personalize marketing campaigns, and provide real-time customer support. Predictive analytics models fueled by real-time consumer data can help businesses decrease available waste and enhance the efficiency of their operations by forecasting demand trends and adjusting production schedules. In addition, gamified shopping platforms, temporary, so-called pop-up Metaverse retail spaces, collaborative design studios, where customers can co-design products with AI design assistants, and a plethora of other creative retail formats presented by the virtual commerce environments is only a tip of the iceberg of experimentation that the firms can be subject to. These innovations have radical consequences on the format of brand-consumer relationship because they are eroding the classical delimiting lines between producer and consumer. Nevertheless, the quick spread of retail on the basis of AI-VR also provokes rather significant ethical issues, such as fairness in algorithms, security of the digital identity, data protection and the implications of virtual economy on the real world. However, AI and VR in the Metaverse retail world are an indication of the future of shopping being less of a transaction than an experience and all interactive, as well as highly customized. In this new paradigm, the brands must reconsider the way of selling products as well as creating durable and substantial relations with the customers in a fully consuming digital realm. To remove these obstacles, data ownership designs, equitable access policies, and sustainable planning of the digital infrastructure will be needed.

4.5 Government & Civic Engagement: Virtual Town Halls and Services

Case Study: In 2023, Seoul Metropolitan Government launched a program known as Metaverse Seoul that provided its citizens with the chance to have virtual town halls and solve civic problems with the help of AI-controlled avatars. The pilot stage received over 40,000 service requests on the site. Even though it was criticized as the means to become more accessible and engage in civic life, it raised the question of cybersecurity and identity control as well as digital illiteracy.

One of the major yet not thoroughly studied areas of the digital governance development is the introduction of virtual reality (VR) and artificial intelligence (AI) into the interaction between citizens and the government and the development of governmental processes. On the one hand, the immersive nature of the Metaverse assists governments in creating virtual town halls where individuals are able to engage in the policymaking procedure and access the necessary services to the state in smart and AI-powered kiosks and avatars. Such systems can help the users in administrative tasks (access to social services, or license renewal, or issuing permits) without human intermediaries with the help of sophisticated natural language processing (NLP) and context-dependent reasoning.

This brings efficiency, reduction of bureaucracy, and inclusivity. The implementation of AI-VR systems offer unprecedented levels of accessibility and civic empowerment particularly to people in geographical remote locations, or to people with mobility issues. Simulations of virtual reality are using AI predictive modeling to offer groundbreaking options in crisis management training, infrastructure construction, and city planning. Governments can simulate how they will respond in the event of natural disasters, predict the crowd dynamics in the process of organizing a public event, real-time analytics help them optimally deploy emergency resources, and simulate urban conditions to understand the consequences of the rural-urban zoning choice. Thus, these Metaverse worlds may be taken as experimental sandboxes where the effects of the policies can be studied and refined without making any direct risks, before being launched in the real world. Moreover, with the emerging technologies of blockchains and decentralized identity systems, AI and VR together could offer secure digital identification of the citizens, openness in the process of voting, and the building of participatory platforms of democracy in the Metaverse. They can change civic engagement by reducing the barriers to traditional civic engagement and promoting a more responsive, inclusive, and direct structure of engagement. However, to achieve these opportunities, there are the issues of digital equity, cybersecurity, data privacy, and algorithmic accountability that must be approached carefully in order to ensure that the benefits of AI-VR governance would be distributed fairly and ethically. In conclusion, the introduction of AI and VR in the civic infrastructure is a prospective, in which not only the accessibility and effectiveness of the provided services but also a novel creation of the fares can provoke openness and engagement in the increasingly digitalized society.

5. ETHICAL, SOCIETAL, AND TECHNICAL CHALLENGES

Although the introduction of artificial intelligence (AI) and virtual reality (VR) into the Metaverse has the disruptive potential in most industries with colossal shares, it puts a stanza of ethical, sociological, and technical challenges into the web of concerns to be discussed in more detail. The unbelievable immersion and customisation possibilities of AI-VR systems are problematic in terms of the problem of information safety, the clarity of algorithms, user safety, and psychological implications of the virtual reality. The question of data ethics is in the limelight: designing extremely personalized virtual reality presupposes the constant accumulation, detection and anticipation of user behavior, likes and dislikes, as well as biometric statistics.

The identity verification and digital manifestation is another serious problem of the society. The Metaverse allows its users to adopt any type of avatars and pseudonyms, making it difficult to confirm the identities of the real individuals and provoking fraud, harassment, or other related problems. It is important to come up with safe and democratic systems of decentralized identity management that can ensure trust and safety without infringing on user freedom and creativity. Moreover, it is necessary to thoroughly study the psychological impact of long-term exposure to virtual worlds because addiction, desensitization, identity disintegration, social isolation are the aspects that might emerge if the measures about the protection will not be specifically embraced in the design of the Metaverse.

In terms of technology, it is important that real-time responsiveness enables interoperability of various AI-VR systems, protection of decentralized platforms against cyber threats and so on are engineering challenges. Blockchain technologies identified, used in transaction management, and governance add some complexity, requiring intensity to manage consents to ensure efficiency, security, and inclusivity.

In addition, there should be AI agent and virtual entity ethical governance measures. The emergence of intelligent avatars and synthetic teammates in the Metaverse raises the issue of accountability, moral responsibility, and the rights of virtual creatures. The application of autonomous AIs in these high-stakes spheres as education, healthcare, government, and social service is one of the reasons why precise ethical principles, regulatory controls, and remedies are required. Finally, it would be necessary to address the problems of environmental sustainability: the infrastructure, supporting large-scale and long-term Metaverse, cloud computing, AI training models, and VR devices, would require enormous amounts of energy, which would require green computing and sustainable design of the digital. These are the ethical, societal and technical concerns that are critical to the development of the intelligent Metaverse since they will keep in mind that the developed virtual, intelligent environments will leave humans flourishing, respecting the fundamental rights and overall well-being of the world in digital. Lacking interdisciplinary initiatives is the result of people striving to act proactively; otherwise, the Metaverse can replicate and even worsen the inequalities, weaknesses and harms that it can overcome.

5.1 Data Privacy and Surveillance in Immersive Environments

The convergence of AI and VR makes the immersive Metaverse a requirement of collecting and processing enormous amounts of personal and behavioral information on a constant basis. In contrast to conventional digital environments, AI-VR atmosphere gathers details (granular data) including eye movements, facial expressions, voice tone, physiological responses, emotional needs and behaviours in space and that, all these factors are needed to remain immersive and credible. Nonetheless, privacy, consent, and ownership of data are of serious concerns considering the amount of data collected. The existing data protection regimes including the General Data Protection Regulation (GDPR) are unsuitable to handle the complexities of embodied data in virtual worlds, particularly at times when data is created in real time and processed according to a scenario, by AI systems. Moreover, informed consent is not easily achieved and consummated because users may not fully understand the scope to which their behaviours and physiological reactions are being monitored.

The issue is aggravated by the fact that the surveillance capitalism can be applied to the Metaverse. The AI algorithms can be used to personalize experiences, and profile consumers either commercially or politically. The potential commercialization of the physiological information, the emotional conditions, even the unconscious processes leave much behind as ethical concerns. Without stringent regulatory procedures, the firms have the ability to develop invasive and exploitative systems that productify the most personalized digitalized expression of individuals without their knowledge. Besides, interoperability and cross-platform conjunction, among the key purposes of the Metaverse structure, cause a rise of complex circumstances when the data sharing occurs among organisms and clear control and responsibility are absent. To address these issues, some privacy-sensitive designs, including federated learning, differential privacy functions, and decentralized data ownership protocols, will be readily needed to provide users with power without impairing the functionality of the system. The design of the Ethical Metaverse should be based on the need to take privacy into consideration, so that the immersive technologies would facilitate independence and not endanger it.

5.2 Algorithmic Bias and Representation

With AI being an indispensable part of VR-based Metaverse spaces, the effects it has on the user experiences, content sorting, avatars creation, and decision making bring a significant concern regarding fairness, inclusiveness, and representational equity. As such AI systems are constituted by the data they are taught to learn on, when these data are selective (not all) in terms of race, gender, socioeconomic status, or ability) and, crucially, cultural norms, the resulted algorithms risk perpetuating and, indeed, even worsening the already existing societal inequities. Such biases are manifested in the form of exclusionary avatars, imbalanced suggestions of content, or in the stereotyping of AI agents, or unequivalent access to the services on the basis of implicit profiling. As an example, facial recognition algorithms, applied to create an avatar or to verify an identity, can not perform as well on low-represented groups, which leads to new avenues of digitally mediated othering based on the real-world version of prejudice.

Moreover, the aesthetic and cultural conventions coded in algorithm systems are often based on the ideals of leading developers of global technology, which can exclude not-Western subjectivity and discourse in immersion spaces. In the Metaverse, the concept of representation extends beyond the visual change and also to speech, behavior modeling, emotion display, and even gesture interpretation- areas that cultural and societal distinctions matter most. Otherwise, unless the diversity is considered by AI systems, the net outcome might turn out to be a homogenized and discriminatory virtual experience. More so, it is not only individual interactions that are biased, but also systemic outcomes like which users are amplified in social networks, which information is being promoted, and which opinions are supported or repressed based on AI-based curation.

The developers need to exercise inclusive data collection, adopt equitable machine learning algorithms and conduct ongoing audits and transparency practices to reduce bias in AI. The ethics, sociology, art and usage by the diverse stakeholders, who are historically marginalized, are also to be included in the design and governance of AI systems operating in the Metaverse. Moreover, explainable AI (XAI) solutions can be utilized to demystify the process of making decisions, making it possible to let users and regulators analyze how decisions are made and identify the factors that lead to inequality. Lastly, it is an ethical responsibility not merely to harm the least, but also to advance favorable depiction and agency to any user of immersive environments.

5.3 Digital Identity and Trust

A new paradigm of identity in the Metaverse is in the process of change, given the correlation between AI-led personalization and the immersive, embodied nature of VR worlds. In contrast to the common online profiles, which are typically static and digital, those found in the Metaverse are dynamic, immersive, and multi-layered and constructed using avatars, behavioral signatures, history of interactions, and metadata. This change brings with it important questions of trust, authentication and accountability with virtual worlds. Within the context of traversing these worlds, in which most of them include pseudonyms or even entirely fictional versions, it becomes more difficult to distinguish between real people, AI-driven agents, and artificial personalities. These confusions undermine the truth of the identity claims, complicate the social and business relationships, and provide new possibilities of impersonation, fraud, and online fraud. The digital identities can be improved with the help of artificial intelligence that can be used to verify them. The intelligent systems will monitor the behavior of users and generate adaptive profiles that will direct interactions, recommendations, and response by the system.

Despite the fact that this makes it more personalized, it also gives AI much power in regards to how people will be viewed and treated in the Metaverse. Mis-identification or making an intentional effort to abuse identity data can result in disenfranchisement, reputation loss, or exploitation, especially when used in conjunction with algorithmic profiling. The appearance of AI-based generative avatars and speech synthesis software blurs the boundary between reality and fake identity undermining trust in the users and legal systems on identity fraud, defamation, and consent. To address these issues, there should be good identity management systems to balance verification and autonomy. The blockchain-based decentralized identification (DID) architectures provide interesting solutions that enable users to have the power to store the control over their identity credentials and check that they can be utilized in other platforms. The systems can provide selective disclosure, verifiable credentials and privacy sensitive interaction, therefore restoring trust without undermining anonymity or creativity. In addition, open governance, community standards and ethical AI design with an emphasis on explainability, accountability and empowering users should form the creation of trust. It could be useful to enable identity verification measures and secure and trusted virtual environments by creating credible institutions, digital ombudsman systems, and cross-platforms interoperability. Finally, it will be determined whether we can or cannot care about human dignity, autonomy, and safety and utilize the pluralistic and revolutionary possibilities of the immersive digital expression to determine the future of identity in the AI-VR Metaverse. The policy of inclusiveness, as well as interdisciplinary supervision, are essential to establishing Metaverse environments of dignified and secured identity.

5.4 Psychological and Societal Impacts

The immersive nature of the world of AI-VR and the potential of the Metaverse to be multimodal has far-reaching consequences on individual well-being and social interactions. The VR experience, unlike traditional media which is external to the user, engages both the body and the mind in the simulation of realities, and therefore the experiences may well be perceived as real or even stronger than the ones in the real world. The possibilities of such a deep psychological impact are multiplied several times, when, in addition to AI-based customisation, the environment, plots and interpersonal relations of individual users are customised. Although these experiences may lead to empathy and creativity and learning, they also have significant risks, such as addiction, identity fragmentation, desensitization to violence, and the loss of distinction between the virtual and the real world.

An essential issue is the idea of presence in VR the psychological state when users feel that they were present in a virtual world. A prolonged or prolonged immersion may alter or alter cognitive and emotional operations, such that one may not be able to differentiate reality and imaginary experiences. The fact that AI can dynamically alter the environment depending on the emotions and behaviors of the humans worsens this outcome, as it presents an ethical issue of emotional manipulation, behavioral conditioning, and consent. Moreover, AI-driven echo chambers within the Metaverse, where users receive a constant stream of reinforcing information and stimuli, can exacerbate polarization, radicalization, and social fragmentation, and recreate and increase the existing problems in the modern social media environments.

The Metaverse can offer new possibilities of community, collaboration, and cultural expression, as well as replicate structural injustices and create new forms of exclusion and exacerbate digital divides, socially. The availability of immersive technologies is still rather unequivalent among socioeconomic classes, and the cost of the VR devices, high-speed Internet, and appropriate hardware is likely to cause global inequalities. Moreover, the standards of communication, manner and privileges in the virtual realm are constantly changing often without a clear legal or moral mandate. This can be harassment, discrimination, and exploitation in the Metaverse, yet there are not yet mature systems of prosecuting virtual crimes on a psychological level.

In order to avoid such psychological and social fears, AI-VR technologies must be organized, and their management should be active and multi-disciplinary. The ethical frameworks need to be capable of achieving the well-being of its users by introducing such tools as the possibility to grant an informed consent, adjustable level of immersion, mental health warning, and clear emotional AI guidelines.The socio-cultural consequences need to be evaluated constantly with the framework of longitudinal studies, and preventive strategies need to be integrated into the Metaverse structures as opposed to being applied as a crisis response measure. It is only under the condition of locating and fixing the important psychological and social expenditures that we will manage to establish the Metaverse settings that will facilitate human happiness rather than deter it.

5.5 Technical Challenges and Interoperability

The virtual reality (VR) coupled with artificial intelligence (AI) of the Metaverse poses several difficult technical issues that are more than the user experience and the architecture, scalability, and sustainability of immersive ecosystems. The core of these challenges is the need of perfect interoperability - the capability of users, assets, avatars, and services to operate and interact well over various platforms, situations, and jurisdictions. Today, the Metaverse is disjointed, where rival systems are based on proprietary standards, data formats and closed ecosystems, hindering cross platform movement and cannot be united into one virtual economy. The real interoperability will require the development and deployment of open standards, decentralized protocols, identity, asset ownership and behavior models frameworks, most of which are therefore in their early stages.

On the systems architecture level, AI-VR System integration needs enormous computational power to support the real-time machine rendering, sensor data processing, dynamic user model, and environmental responsiveness in a large scale. Reduction of latency, bandwidth optimization, and distributed computing are most vital in offering visually fluid, immersive experiences and also highly significant in scenarios where there are shared multi-user experiences where data consistency and synchronization is paramount. To back up these requirements, Cloud computing and edge data infrastructure is essential, but data sovereignty, performance, and ecological footprint remain unconvincing, particularly because AI training and VR rendering are energy-intensive projects. The other significant issue is compliance with the AI capabilities to virtual reality interfaces. Besides intelligent systems must comprehend plain language and human intent, they are also expected to discern spatial signs, emotional dish, and multimodal data in a three dimensional space.

The technical issue of developing AI structures that could track and respond to complicated virtual situations in real-time, simultaneously without jeopardizing the privacy of the user or autonomy is a complex task. Additionally, the combination of haptics, bio-metric sensors and brain-computer interfaces (BCIs) brings about certain levels of complexities requiring powerful APIs, safety and protocols which are continuously changing. Security is the other major problem. The Metaverse platforms are interrelated and continuous, which adds to the field of attack of cyber attacks such as identity theft, data attack, and manipulation of AIs. The more the AI agents are autonomous and associated with the communication with the users, the more serious their integrity and conduct becomes. The processes of monitoring, auditing and updating systems of AI in remote setting must possess transparent processes and cannot be subject to manipulation. In the meantime, the practices of digital rights management (DRM), protection of intellectual property, and anti-fraud solutions must evolve to be more dynamic and programmable over virtual property, particularly as a form of value exchange with the rise of NFTs and smart contracts. Such technical issues require the industry consortiums, open-source communities, standards organizations, and regulatory agencies to cooperate in order to resolve these technical issues. The Metaverse Standards Forum and the W3C work on WebXR are the first steps towards this argument, but it requires long-term investments in interoperability, openness, and inclusion. The Metaverse can be ruined by lack of such coordination as a collection of different and incompatible systems, and it can erode its purpose as a cohesive, available, and smartened digital frontier.

5.6 Ethical Governance and Regulatory Frameworks

The absence of a carefully thought-out system of ethical controls and legal frameworks is even more pressing in the perspective of the integration of AI and different forms of VR and the actual construction of the Metaverse. The immersive, autonomous, and transnational features of the Metaverse challenge the standard notions of the legal jurisdiction, responsible, and protection of human rights. Absent of clear and strictly followed rules, the Metaverse can easily become a breeding ground of exploitation, discrimination, surveilling and information falseness with extensive impacts inside and outside of the virtual world.

There must be a balance between innovation and protection in the Metaverse through governance. Ethical governance designs must be pro-active bringing in ideas such as as transparency, justice, inclusivity, privacy, and user autonomy into the planning and execution of AI-VR systems at a very early stage. This requires the shift to ad hoc forms of content filtering and reactive enforcement to integrated forms of ethical design, impact assessment, and participatory forms of governance that integrate people, developers, policymakers and civil society organizations as part of the decision making process. Of special importance is accountability, which emphasizes the responsibilities of artificial intelligence agents, platform providers, developers, and individuals, especially when the autonomous systems appear to determine the people's rights and opportunities.

Conventional legal categories, including consumer protection, labor rights, intellectual property, and privacy of data, need to be redefined and extended offering Metaversion-related occurrences. As an illustration, the user rights to their online identities, avatars, and virtual items require new legal protection that would recognize the emotional, social, or economic value of online property. Equally, regulations should deal with the challenges caused by decentralized independent entities, tokenized economies, and AI-controlled contracts that operate without human intervention. The international coordination between countries and international organizations will be important to guarantee similar standards and avoid regulation arbitrage, whereby firms take advantage of interjurisdiction loopholes to avoid responsibility.

Major aspects of ethical regulation are privacy and data governance. Since the physiological, behavioral and emotional information is sensitive in VR settings, powerful consent solutions, data minimization policies, and the right to access, portability, and deletion should be divided by the book. Moreover, the openness of the AI decision making processes requires development of explainability norms and audit procedures to alleviate algorithmic harm and promote concern among people.

New forms of self-regulation, like small value, ethical committees, community-based, and technical standards will also be useful in complementing traditional legal institutions. But self-regulation is not enough to curb systemic threats: binding regulations, ethical certifications and independent supervisory agencies are needed to make sure that the Metaverse advances in manners that do not violate human dignity, social justice, and democracy.

Table 1. Comparative ethical governance models for AI–VR metaverse

S.No.	Framework	Key Principles	Application to Metaverse
1	EU AI Act (2024)	Risk-based regulation, transparency, accountability	Guides AI agent behavior and data protection standards.
2	OECD AI Principles	Human-centered values, fairness, and safety	Encourages inclusive, trustworthy AI–VR system design.
3	IEEE EAD (Ethically Aligned Design)	Well-being, privacy, and explainability	Embeds ethical reasoning and user agency into VR experiences.
4	UNESCO AI Ethics (2022)	tainability, diversity, and human rights	Aligns Metaverse development with global equity and cultural inclusion.

5.7 Hardware and Software Sustainability and Carbon Footprint of AI-VR Infrastructures.

AI-VR systems are based on computationally intensive energy, real-time rendering and distributed cloud systems. Their carbon footprint is created through data centers and GPU clusters, global content distribution networks, and quick hardware replacement. Among them, there are high electricity consumption, non-renewable energy consumption, and VR e-waste. Mitigation includes renewable-powered information facilities, efficient AI based schemes, compression-based rendering and recycling hardware based on the circular economy approach.

5.8 Cross-Cultural Adoption and International Equity.

The availability of metaverse is determined by differences in bandwidth, affordability of hardware, digital literacy, and language. AI systems are frequently programmed with Western-centric design conventions, with an miss and dismissal of local identities. To achieve global equity, multilingual NLP, culturally adaptive avatars, location-specific content, inclusive design, and subsidized access programs to underserved groups are needed.

5.9 Economic and Labor Market Change.

The employment is being transformed through AI-VR ecosystems through virtual gig economies, AI-assisted knowledge work, and services mediated through avatars. Things are seen as new, yet potential dangers are job displacement, precarity, wage obscurity, unregulated virtual work. The responses by policy-makers should formalise digital labour rights, developing protection to protect workers of the avatars, and developing international certification of the professions, Metaverse professions alike.

6. RECOMMENDATIONS AND FRAMEWORKS

Although the incorporation of AI and VR in the Metaverse has the potential of changing the industry and society with revolutionary benefits, it also requires a methodical approach to providing the integration with a guarantee of its ethical, inclusive and sustainable growth. To address the ensuing challenges detected in the preceding chapters, this section introduces detailed frameworks and strategic suggestions to help guide the stakeholders, such as the developers, policymakers, businesses, educators, and the civil society, to develop a humanist, responsible Metaverse. These models include design of technological options, moral values, administration systems, and interdisciplinary collaborative designs.

6.1 An Integrated Ethical design Model.

To establish the immersive spaces where human dignity, privacy, and well-being are appreciated, the full ethical design framework should be incorporated into every phase of development of AI-VR systems. The fundamental principles under this framework are;

1. **Transparency:** AI solutions in virtual reality spaces should be auditable and explainable. The users should be aware of the manner in which the recommendations, interactions, and outcome are generated.
2. **Equity and inclusiveness**: There should be a systematic check against algorithmic biasness. Designs that are inclusive and involve diverse groups of users in the testing and making of the product are important in the provision of platforms that may accommodate as many people as possible without reinforcing a priori and omissions.
3. **Autonomy and Consent:** The users must possess significant control over their digital identities, data, and interactions. There should be informed consent as the basis of data collection and interaction of AI, and user rights interfaces should be easy and self-explanatory.
4. **Safety and Wellbeing:** In-built capabilities such as mental health check-ins, harassment averse functions and configurations of exposure should keep users safe of psychological abuse and exploitation in social interactions.
5. **Sustainability:** Environmental effects of Metaverse infrastructures, in particular, the amount of carbon footprint associated with data centres and AI computing should be minimised through a green computing strategy and energy-efficient protocols.

6.2 Open Ecosystems and Standards of Interoperability.

A healthy Metaverse has a strong emphasis on interoperability, i.e. the smooth interaction and interworking of virtual identities, virtual assets and services across various systems. Devoid of open ecosystems, the Metaverse has the risk of disintegrating into individual corporate silos, decreasing user agency, and stifling innovation. To deal with this problem, interoperability standards need to be established and used broadly. Asset-portability and asset-avatar-identify-management and asset-environment-data-sharing and AI-behaviour technical standards should be created and refined, with an example of these being the glTF 3D-contents standard, the OpenXR VR/AR interface standard, and decentralized identity standards.

These frameworks need to incorporate ethical concerns that would allow interoperability to maintain privacy, transparency, and autonomy of the user across platforms.

Moreover, cross-sector collaboration should be pioneered by open-source projects, independent standards groups, including the Metaverse of Standards Forum and the World Wide Web Consortium (W3C), which should come up with interoperable systems that are backed by ethical certification procedures. Economic interoperability involving the control of virtual currency, NFTs, and smart contracts also needs to be normalised so that reliable and transparent transactions can be made. Open ecosystems will forbid monopoly practices, democratize digital access, enhance cross-platform innovation and make the Metaverse grow to become an inclusive, human-focused digital space, and not a fragmented assemblage of incompatible virtual worlds.

6.3 AI and VR Applications in Human-Centric Design.

Close integration of AI and VR in the Metaverse relies on the enthusiasm to increase adherence to the idea of human-centered design so that it is guaranteed that technology does not diminish people in their dignity and creativity and agency. The human-centric approach in the Metaverse implies that the VR and AI systems should be adapted to the needs, principles, and experiences of diverse user groups, focusing on inclusiveness, convenience, and psychological safety. It is not only that AI has to be an unspotted manipulator of experiences, but also a partner enabling that will be able to adjust into individual preferences, learning styles, cognitive capabilities and emotional dispositions. The VR environments are to provide comfort, reduce motion sickness, sensory overload, and digital fatigue, and provide a customizable interface, adapting to various body and sensory and cognitive impairments.

Manipulation should not be used in the application of personalization, which yields user autonomy and needs to improve behavior, and the ethical norms that ensure that adaptive systems will not result in the exploitation and propagation of any vulnerabilities.

The human-friendly design must also be clear in the workings of the AI systems with VRs so that human beings become aware of working against automated decisions as well as how to rule out a judgment manually. Significantly, end-user should be engaged in the pre-implementation phase of development through participatory design techniques, e. g., co-creation workshops, feedback, and testing cycles.

In this manner, the Metaverse is able to become a space that actually captures the multiplicity of the human experience, and technology acts as a provider of prosperity, togetherness, and individuality. The relationship between empathy, ethics, and user empowerment as the elements of the AI-VR integration can help developers to make sure that smart Metaverse is not just a technological marvel, but also a new environment changing and supporting the value of human concerns.

6.4 Policies to be recommended in relation to Ethical Deployment.

Ethical uses of AI and VR technology in the Metaverse require progressive expansive policies such as the current regulations do not anticipate because of the emerging risk and social risks and consequences presented by the immersion of the intelligent environment. User rights are a paramount priority of policymakers that demand transparency, informed consent and reduction of data in any AI-VR interaction. Certain acts are to be made in which the biometric, behavioral and emotional information gathered in virtual reality spaces must be regarded as sensitive personal data and the rigidest privacy and user controls laws applied. Accountability in AI should be a matter of legal obligation and the corporations have to conduct regular bias audits, release explainability reports, and permit independent oversight of AI systems used in open or business Metaverse spaces. Alternatively, labor protections will have to be extended to cover new possibilities of employment emerging in the Metaverse, including the rights of digital workers, the virtual avatars as the service providers, and the virtual manufacturers of goods. The intellectual property regulations should be revised so as to incorporate the user generated work, virtual products and decentralized works but guard against greed and monopoly. Accessibility requirements should also be enforced through policy frameworks to ensure that the Metaverse is accommodative to these people with impairments, linguistic minorities and technologically disadvantaged groups.

Besides, the cooperation within the global environments will be required to establish the homogeneous policy that will eliminate the jurisdictional loopholes and the maintenance of ethical practices in various global ecosystems go with the Metaverse. These policies must be supported by an investment in the electronic literacy campaigns organized at the national level and providing people with the knowledge needed to explore, evaluate, and organize AI-VR environments in a responsible manner. Policy makers can create the circumstances of a smart Metaverse which can enforce creativity and, at the same time, safeguard human dignity, fairness and democracy by implementing an ethical code in enforceable law.

6.5 Future Research Directions

The fast development of AI and VR technologies in the Metaverse is a dynamic sphere of the future research that will play an important role in determining its ethical, sociological, and technological development. Initially, studies are required to enhance the workability of AI and VR platforms in numerous platforms, and some of the areas presented in this perspective include efficient data interchange, the mobility of virtual properties, and standard user interfaces. With the developing

Metaverse, interdisciplinary studies will need to integrate learnings on such areas as cognitive psychology, human-computer interaction (HCI), ethics, and law to establish user-friendly designs that will minimize digital fatigue, enhance immersion, and protect mental health.

The second important field of research is developing AI explainability and trust in virtual space, and the focus here is how one can make people to know AI-powered decisions in the Metaverse and feel at liberty to challenge them. Algorithms fairness research will play a vital role in reducing systematic biases and prejudice on the creation and implementation of AI algorithms especially on avatars representation, content filters, and customized experiences. Besides, blockchain and decentralized technologies can lead to new types of governance, digital identity, virtual property ownership that endangers the existing power systems, which makes researching their legal and ethical implications more significant.

Studies that create ethical the AI systems to keep up with the rapidly evolving environment of the Metaverse will also play an essential role, and that the AI models will be designed, implemented, and monitored as per the human values and the common good. Lastly, we shall need socioeconomic impact studies to establish the results of the Metaverse to both the labour markets, educational systems, and the global economies as well as its possibilities offer of new modes of work and education as well as its risks which include job displacement, inequality, and digital divides. Future studies contributing to the achievement of an interdisciplinary approach will create the pipeline of the ethical, inclusive, and human-oriented Metaverse that should maximize the advantages of its purpose and reduce the risks.

CONCLUSION

In addition to theoretical and technological input, collaboration across policy frameworks and cooperation across sectors is also a necessity as was noted in this chapter. Though, policymakers, technologists, and ethicists should come up with interoperable standards, equal access systems, and user-friendly regulation systems. Metaverse design assumptions should be based on transparency, inclusivity, access and sustainability. Interdisciplinary collaborations between academia, industry and civil society will be the basis of co-creating a responsible and resilient digital ecosystem with a balance between innovation and ethics.

Combining artificial intelligence with virtual reality into the Metaverse is a significant step in the digital transformation with unparalleled possibilities in changing the relationship between human beings, employment, the business environment, education, healthcare, and government. As AI brings flexibility, personalization and intelligence to the virtual worlds and VR is an immersive and spatially rich experience, their integration results in dynamic ecosystems which are parallel and even superseding the real life.

However, as this growth is marked, there exist some sharp ethical, cultural, and technological concerns, which demand a proactive and conscious engagement. The systematic bias, privacy of the information, the psychological effects, and the monopolization of the platforms are the key factors that should be underlined to explain the relevance of the human centered design, high levels of the interoperability, and ethical rules. To transform the intelligent Metaverse into a more comfortable, empowering, and equal space of residing in, the focus of the further development should be on transparency, accessibility, agency of the users, and participatory governance.

A Metaverse can also be designed in a way that proves not only the technological innovation but also contributes to the progress of the world population by means of interdisciplinary research, collaboration on the international level, and strong commitment to human values. Lastly, the future of the AI-driven, VR-powered Metaverse will not only be determined by how advanced the technology will be, but will also depend on how well we are as a society aligned to these instruments in regards to the desires, dignity and well-being of everybody.

REFERENCES

Amos, Z. (2022, August). How AI is bringing the Metaverse to life. *Unite.AI.* https://www.unite.ai/how-ai-is-bringing-the-metaverse-to-life/

Basheer, S., Walia, S., Farooq, S., Shah, M. A., & Mir, F. A. (2024). Exploring the Metaverse: The future of tourism through AI and virtual reality. In Basheer, S. (Ed.), *Exploring the Metaverse: The Future of Tourism Through AI and Virtual Reality* (pp. 195–204). IGI Global.

Din, I. U., Awan, K. A., Almogren, A., & Rodrigues, J. J. P. C. (2023). Integration of IoT and blockchain for decentralized management and ownership in the Metaverse. *International Journal of Communication Systems, 36*(18), e5612. Advance online publication. DOI: 10.1002/dac.5612

Dionisio, J. D. N., Burns, W. G.III, & Gilbert, R. (2013). 3D virtual worlds and the Metaverse. *ACM Computing Surveys, 45*(3), 1–38. DOI: 10.1145/2480741.2480751

Engage, V. R. (n.d.). Retrieved from https://engagevr.io/

Fadhel, M. A., Duhaim, A. M., Albahri, A. S., Al-Qaysi, Z. T., Aktham, M. A., Chyad, M. A., Abd-Alaziz, W., Albahri, O. S., Alamoodi, A. H., Alzubaidi, L., Gupta, A., & Gu, Y. (2024). Navigating the Metaverse: Unraveling the impact of artificial intelligence—A comprehensive review and gap analysis. *Artificial Intelligence Review, 57*(264), 264. Advance online publication. DOI: 10.1007/s10462-024-10881-5

Ghosh, A., Lavanya, V., Hassija, V., Chamola, V., & El Saddik, A. (2024). A survey on decentralized Metaverse using blockchain and Web 3.0 technologies, applications, and more. *IEEE Access : Practical Innovations, Open Solutions, 12*, 146915–146948. DOI: 10.1109/ACCESS.2024.3469193

Kostadimas, D., Kasapakis, V., & Kotis, K. (2025). A Systematic Review on the Combination of VR, IoT and AI Technologies, and Their Integration in Applications. *Future Internet, 17*(4), 163. DOI: 10.3390/fi17040163

Lyu, Z. (2023). State-of-the-art human–computer interaction in Metaverse. *International Journal of Human-Computer Interaction, 40*(21), 6690–6708. DOI: 10.1080/10447318.2023.2248833

Pereira, R. (2024). Intelligence artificial and Metaverse: An integrative review. *Arquétipos, 1*(1), 45–62.

Ramadan, Z., & Ramadan, J. (2025). AI avatars and co-creation in the Metaverse. *Consumer Behavior in Tourism and Hospitality*, *20*(1), 131–147. DOI: 10.1108/CBTH-07-2024-0246

Shi, F., Ning, H., Zhang, X., Li, R., Tian, Q., Zhang, S., Zheng, Y., Guo, Y., & Daneshmand, M. (2023). A new technology perspective of the Metaverse: Its essence, framework and challenges. *Digital Communications and Networks*. Advance online publication. DOI: 10.1016/j.dcan.2023.02.017

Soliman, M. M., Ahmed, E., Darwish, A., & Hassanien, A. E. (2024). Artificial intelligence powered Metaverse: Analysis, challenges and future perspectives. *Artificial Intelligence Review*, *57*(36), 36. Advance online publication. DOI: 10.1007/s10462-023-10641-x

Stephenson, N. (2022, January 13). *Snow Crash*. Penguin Books Australia. (Original work published 1992)

Tabassum, A., Elmahjub, E., Padela, A. I., Zwitter, A., & Qadir, J. (2025). Generative AI and the Metaverse: A scoping review of ethical and legal challenges. *IEEE Open Journal of the Computer Society*, *6*, 348–359. DOI: 10.1109/OJCS.2025.3536082

Thakur, S. S., Bandyopadhyay, S., & Datta, D. (2023). Artificial intelligence and the Metaverse: Present and future aspects. In Hassanien, A. E., Darwish, A., & Torky, M. (Eds.), *The future of Metaverse in the virtual era and physical world* (Vol. 123). Springer., DOI: 10.1007/978-3-031-29132-6_10

Victory, X. R. (n.d.). Retrieved from https://www.victoryxr.com/

Wang, Y., Wang, L., & Siau, K. L. (2024). Human-centered interaction in virtual worlds: A new era of generative artificial intelligence and Metaverse. *International Journal of Human-Computer Interaction*, *41*(2), 1459–1501. DOI: 10.1080/10447318.2024.2316376

Chapter 3
Multimodal Context-Awareness in AI-Driven Virtual Reality

Reno Yuri Camilleri
https://orcid.org/0009-0005-6016-1257
University of Malta, Malta

Vanessa Camilleri
https://orcid.org/0000-0003-4455-4577
University of Malta, Malta

Matthew Montebello
https://orcid.org/0000-0002-6177-7548
University of Malta, Malta

ABSTRACT

This chapter examines how context-aware artificial intelligence (AI) enhances virtual reality (VR) by increasing immersion, user engagement, and adaptive interactivity. Drawing on foundational theories of presence and immersion (e.g., Slater, 2009; Csikszentmihalyi, 1990), this investigation examines how AI systems interpret environmental, behavioural, and verbal cues to personalise and enrich immersive experiences. Reviewing recent innovations in generative AI, reinforcement learning, and intelligent agent design, the chapter analyses the capacity of these technologies to support dynamic content generation, adaptive gameplay, and naturalistic interaction. Complementing the literature review, a user-centred survey captures VR user perceptions and priorities regarding intelligent, adaptive systems. The chapter

DOI: 10.4018/979-8-3373-3690-9.ch003

concludes with a discussion of ethical considerations, user modelling challenges, and future research directions, offering a timely contribution to ongoing debates in AI-driven entertainment design.

INTRODUCTION

With the rapid development of digital technology, many aspects of everyday life have been changed, resulting in major global interests in computer systems that can sense and respond to context (Augusto, 2022). These transformations are particularly noticeable in the field of integration between Artificial Intelligence (AI) and Virtual Reality (VR), where technology has shifted away from traditional pre-programmed static experiences towards more dynamic interactive experiences. Modern VR platforms are no longer limited to simply using visual immersion alone, but now they routinely capture rich streams of contextual information, including environmental cues, body movement, and speech. AI systems continuously interpret this multimodal information to allow VR environments to respond in real-time. By combining AI and VR together, we can produce more immersive, personalised and adaptive user experiences (Ojha et al., 2024; Shirazi et al., 2024; Yu et al., 2024).

Recent studies have highlighted a clear move from fixed simulations to environments that evolve in response to use behaviour. AI-driven dialogue systems, for instance, can allow users to naturally interact with virtual non-player characters (NPCs), which strengthens immersion and realism. Rong (2024) notes that these systems can support more realistic and believable communication. Beyond conversations, AI can also adjust environmental parameters such as lighting, difficulty or even narrative pacing in line with the emotional or physical states of the user. These adaptations form a continuous feedback loop, where a user's behaviour actively shapes the VR experience (Song et al., 2024; Ojha et al., 2024).

Motivation

The motivations behind this chapter were to investigate how multimodal context-aware AI can enhance user engagement in VR experiences by continuously analysing environmental signals, user actions, and the user's voice input in real time. The study draws on recent research, technologies, and practical applications across the domains of entertainment and education (Augusto, 2022; Cao et al., 2023; Dyulicheva & Glazieva, 2022; Song et al., 2024). Context-awareness in this case reflects the AI's ability to interpret situations and respond based on those interpretations, and by integrating this awareness with technical systems, it allows the system to adapt to individual needs (Augusto, 2022).

Context refers to information that describes what is going on within a situation, while context-awareness refers to the ability to utilise that information to modify the system (Augusto, 2022; Carrera-Rivera et al., 2022). Since VR environments in themselves contain many different forms of multimodality, such as speech, hand gestures, head and eye tracking, etc, these inputs allow systems to utilise various forms of context to understand the user's intent and generate coordinated responses (Cao et al., 2023). However, to achieve this, all context must be properly interpreted into meaningful information in real-time. This process is particularly difficult to achieve since VR environments are dynamic, and context can change quickly, and the system must react accurately to maintain user immersion.

In the context of gaming, AI systems monitor player behaviour to personalise experiences through adapting NPC behaviour, procedural generation, or dynamic difficulty adjustments (Ojha et al., 2024; Song et al., 2024). As interaction data is produced, these systems gradually learn to align responses with the emotional and cognitive states of the player (Dyulicheva & Glazieva, 2022; Mansouri et al., 2021). An example of this is the potential of AI-driven CGI influencers that utilise expressive virtual characters to sustain engagement. By modelling facial expressions and emotional cues, these avatars enhance communication and maintain attention in entertainment and marketing contexts (Yu et al., 2024).

In the context of development, AI agents increasingly support automated play-testing through the use of AI methods such as Deep Reinforcement Learning (DRL) and Monte Carlo Tree Search (MCTS). These methods allow large-scale simulations to take place, which reveal gameplay patterns and potential issues that may arise (Roohi et al., 2021). Overall, this chapter will consider both technical advances and user responses to context-aware AI within VR.

Objectives

This chapter has two objectives: firstly (O1) to review recent developments in context-aware AI for VR environments, mainly focusing on multimodal context, including environmental, behavioural, and speech data, as well as enabling AI techniques such as reinforcement learning, generative models, and intelligent agents. Secondly (O2), to present the findings from a user survey conducted to examine the expectations and preferences of users regarding context-aware features in VR. Together, these two objectives combine theoretical insights with empirical evidence to show how context-aware AI can influence the user experience and system behaviour.

Additionally, this chapter also examines how context-aware AI supports immersive, adaptive and emotionally responsive VR experiences by analysing user behaviour, emotions and preferences. Through these, AI systems can personalise both learning and entertainment content, resulting in increased engagement and perceived realism (Shirazi et al., 2024). Despite these benefits, context-aware AI also raises design and ethical challenges. To address these concerns, the chapter incorporates findings from a user survey exploring attitudes towards adaptive features in VR environments.

The analysis considers demographic factors, measures of presence and satisfaction, and qualitative feedback on usability and narrative structure. It also responds to gaps identified by Augusto (2022), particularly the need for clearer definitions of context-awareness in system activation and interaction. Through its focus on multimodality and context-awareness, this chapter offers guidance for developing AI systems that are effective, responsible, and centred on user needs.

Chapter Structure

Section 2 introduces the background research, outlining concepts related to context-awareness and user engagement in VR, with a focus on gaming and entertainment. Section 3 reviews recent literature, examines adaptive behaviour, interactive systems, and relevant case studies, and identifies research gaps. Section 4 details the research methodology, including study design, data collection, participant recruitment, and analysis. Sections 5 and 6 present and discuss the findings, highlighting key trends, user perspectives, and challenges such as privacy, adaptation, and scalability. Section 7 outlines future research directions and practical implications, and lastly, Section 8 serves as the conclusion for this chapter.

BACKGROUND AND THEORETICAL FOUNDATIONS

Understanding Context and Engagement in VR

Immersion is a core part of VR and is often described as deep involvement that draws users' attention away from the real world (Berkman & Akan, 2019). It is supported by visual quality, spatial audio, and multisensory feedback such as haptics (Slater, 2009). These features allow users to perceive changes through movement, known as sensorimotor contingencies. However, immersion is defined differently across fields and is often confused with presence or engagement. Nilsson et al. (2016) address this by distinguishing among system immersion (technical quality), narrative immersion (story involvement), and challenge-based immersion, offering a clearer structure for understanding VR experiences.

Presence, on the other hand, refers to the feeling of "being there" in a virtual space (Berkman & Akan, 2019). Slater (2009) separates this into Place Illusion, created through consistent sensory feedback, and Plausibility Illusion, where virtual events seem believable. When both are present, users may react as if events are real, known as Response-As-If-Real behaviour. Presence is shaped not only by technology but also by personal and contextual factors such as experience and expectations (Triberti et al., 2025).

Engagement describes the psychological depth of user involvement and enjoyment. Rutrecht et al. (2021) link VR engagement to flow, showing that greater immersion increases both flow and presence. AI-supported VR can help sustain this state by adapting the difficulty, pacing, and content to a user's performance and preferences (Shirazi et al., 2024). This aligns with the previously defined challenge-based immersion, where a balanced level of difficulty helps maintain attention (Nilsson et al., 2016).

Interactivity refers to meaningful user actions that elicit system responses. This includes physical actions, voice, or influencing NPC behaviour (Wang et al., 2021). High interactivity increases user agency and depends on both hardware and AI-driven software. When responses are smooth and timely, realism and immersion are strengthened (Ojha et al., 2024; Cao et al., 2023).

Context-awareness connects these elements by including environmental, movement, physiological, and speech information (Augusto, 2022; Carrera-Rivera et al., 2022). Context-aware VR uses AI to interpret this data and adapt experiences in real time through multimodal fusion of gestures, gaze, and voice (Cao et al., 2023). These systems can also predict preferences by learning from behaviour, allowing experiences to adjust over time (Shirazi et al., 2024).

Theoretical Foundation

The theoretical foundation of context-aware AI in VR draws from cognitive psychology, Human Computer Interaction (HCI), immersive media, and intelligent systems. Context-awareness is viewed as an interaction between human perception and adaptive technology rather than a purely technical feature. Flow Theory (Csikszentmihalyi, 1990) and Slater's model of presence (2009) explain how engagement depends on a balance between challenge and a strong sense of "being there". Self-Determination Theory further shows how personalisation supports motivation by addressing autonomy and competence (Ryan & Deci, 2000).

Context in VR can be grouped into environmental, behavioural, and verbal domains. Environmental context includes factors such as lighting and sound that support immersion (Slater, 2009; Moon et al., 2022). Behavioural context encompasses signals that guide adaptive responses, such as changes in pacing or difficulty (Dyulicheva & Glazieva, 2022; Ojha et al., 2024). Verbal context involves speech and dialogue and is interpreted through natural language processing to support social interaction (Song et al., 2024; Reiners et al., 2021). Together, these inputs allow AI systems to detect, interpret, and adapt to user states in real time.

From a systems perspective, context-aware VR follows a sequence of context definition, use, and development (Augusto, 2022; Carrera-Rivera et al., 2022). AI models support multimodal data processing, real-time adaptation, and intelligent virtual agents capable of personalised interaction (Reiners et al., 2021). User acceptance of these systems is influenced by perceived usefulness and ease of use, as described by the Technology Acceptance Model (Fussell & Truong, 2022).

Relevance for Gaming and Entertainment

AI and VR together are reshaping gaming and entertainment through real-time adaptation to user behaviour. By combining environmental, behavioural, and verbal data, systems can adjust visuals, sound, pacing, difficulty, and dialogue to suit individual users. Engagement and presence emerge from the combined effects of immersion, interactivity, and context-awareness, supported by Flow Theory and presence models (Csikszentmihalyi, 1990; Slater, 2009). In games, AI analyses player behaviour and emotions to personalise narratives, challenges, and NPC interactions (Ojha et al., 2024; Song et al., 2024; Shirazi et al., 2024). Additionally, generative AI enables more natural dialogue and dynamic environments, increasing player agency and emotional involvement (Song et al., 2024).

Advanced methods such as DRL and MCTS further improve opponent behaviour and game balance, helping maintain long-term engagement and replayability (Roohi et al., 2021). Context-aware AI also strengthens Plausibility Illusion by ensuring that virtual events respond credibly to user actions, supporting RAIR behaviour (Slater, 2009). By interpreting signals such as gestures and speech, AI helps create virtual worlds that feel responsive and alive (Augusto, 2022).

LITERATURE REVIEW: INNOVATIONS IN CONTEXT-AWARE AI

The Role of AI in Contextual Understanding

Context plays a key role in how humans understand situations and make decisions, and it is increasingly used in computer science to design intelligent, context-aware systems (Augusto, 2022). In Intelligent Environments, context-awareness connects areas such as computing, the Internet of Things, and Ambient Intelligence (Augusto, 2022). In VR, AI enables systems to interpret contextual cues and adapt behaviour to support immersion and engagement.

Environmental Context Understanding

AI has significantly improved how VR systems understand and respond to environmental context, helping maintain immersion through real-time adaptation. One example is dynamic visual adjustment, which reduces discomfort caused by changing lighting. Abbasi et al. (2024) propose a U-Net-based model that adapts colour and contrast during scene transitions, improving visual consistency and user focus. This shows how AI-driven visual calibration can enhance immersion.

AI-assisted rendering also supports real-time responses to user actions, such as updating lighting and shadows when a virtual light is switched on. These effects strengthen Plausibility Illusion by making virtual responses feel coherent and realistic (Slater, 2009). Spatial mapping further extends environmental awareness, as modern headsets use depth sensors to align virtual content with physical space. Systems such as ManySense VR integrate real-world data, including weather, into VR scenes to synchronise virtual ambience with external conditions (Moon et al., 2022). This approach reflects the concept of the Observable World, where sensor data is transformed into meaningful context that guides system responses (Augusto, 2022). Environmental context is further enhanced through adaptive audio and haptics, such as spatial sound and tactile feedback, which deepen presence and embodiment.

Behavioural Interaction and Adaptation

Behavioural context-awareness allows VR systems to interpret user actions and respond in real time. Advances in gesture recognition and computer vision have reduced reliance on controllers, enabling natural interaction through body movement (Wang et al., 2021). Actions such as pointing or waving can trigger NPC responses, supporting sensorimotor contingencies and increasing realism (Slater, 2009). Multimodal systems combine gestures, voice, and gaze to infer user intent more accurately such as for instance, in LearningVerseVR, are used to direct attention and control interactions, creating natural experiences (Cao et al., 2023). Behaviour modelling is also used in training simulations, where AI adapts scenarios based on detected actions, ensuring events occur at meaningful moments (Wang et al., 2021).

Adaptive gameplay systems use reinforcement learning to adjust difficulty based on performance, helping maintain flow by balancing challenge and skill (Dyulicheva & Glazieva, 2022; Mansouri et al., 2021). Emotional adaptation adds further depth, particularly in horror games, where AI monitors stress indicators and alters pacing or intensity in real time (Ojha et al., 2024). Similar methods support personalised learning by adapting feedback and content to learner progress (Song et al., 2024). Additionally, emerging bioadaptive systems integrate real-world signals such as heart rate to influence visuals or pacing, allowing VR experiences to respond to emotional and physical states. These approaches move VR towards fully responsive environments that integrate behaviour, emotion, and embodiment.

Voice and Language Processing

Voice and language form another important modality in context-aware VR. Advances in speech recognition and natural language processing, particularly through large language models, have shifted interaction from simple commands to natural conversation. Systems using models such as GPT-4 can interpret speech and generate context-aware responses, enabling fluid dialogue with virtual characters (Rong, 2024).

In education, voice-based interaction supports adaptive learning by analysing spoken responses to assess understanding and tailor guidance (Shirazi et al., 2024; Dyulicheva & Glazieva, 2022). LLM-powered NPCs can engage in unscripted dialogue, adapting tone, content, and behaviour in real time. Platforms such as LearningverseVR combine dialogue generation with gestures and expressions, improving emotional realism (Song et al., 2024).

Voice input also supports personalisation by capturing user preferences and intentions through natural speech. Over time, systems can recall this information to refine content and interaction styles. As a result, VR environments are evolving into conversational systems where characters can listen, respond, and adapt meaningfully. This growing role of voice interaction is reflected in the user study presented later in this chapter.

Enabling Technologies: Learning, Generation, and Agents

Reinforcement learning, generative AI, and intelligent agents drive progress in context-aware VR. Reinforcement learning enables systems to adapt environments dynamically by learning which actions maximise engagement, such as adjusting lighting, pacing, or difficulty (Roohi et al., 2021). These feedback loops help sustain flow and improve user experience.

Generative AI enables rapid content creation across environments, dialogue, and interactive objects. Tools such as NVIDIA Edify can generate 3D scenes from text prompts (Delgado, 2024), while platforms like LearningverseVR use generative models to create adaptive narratives, dialogue, and rewards (Song et al., 2024). These methods support personalised and evolving experiences rather than fixed scenarios.

Intelligent agents combine learning, perception, and language to act proactively within VR. They interpret multimodal inputs and adapt behaviour to guide users, personalise interaction, or control pacing. Examples include horror game directors that adjust fear levels based on physiological data (Ojha et al., 2024) and educational NPCs that respond emotionally and verbally to learners (Song et al., 2024). Agents are also used for automated playtesting, simulating user behaviour to optimise design and reduce development costs (Roohi et al., 2021).

Case Studies and Existing Applications

Context-aware AI has expanded rapidly across real-world applications, with a strong impact in gaming and entertainment, as well as in education, training, healthcare, and autonomous systems. When combined with VR and XR, these systems improve engagement, decision-making, and responsiveness through real-time adaptation and feedback.

Gaming and Entertainment

The integration of AI with immersive technologies has reshaped gaming and entertainment, enabling experiences that are more adaptive, personalised, and emotionally engaging. AI supports not only in-game interaction but also broader digital ecosystems that influence user behaviour. In online entertainment and e-commerce, AI systems analyse browsing patterns and reviews to deliver targeted content and personalised promotions, increasing conversion rates and supporting customer segmentation and sales forecasting (Bag et al., 2021).

Within games, AI agents have reached high levels of performance in complex titles such as Starcraft II, Dota 2, Go, and Atari games, largely through Deep Reinforcement Learning (Reiners et al., 2021). These techniques are also used in automated playtesting for commercial games like Angry Birds Dream Blast, where AI predicts difficulty and engagement to reduce player churn and support level design (Roohi et al., 2021).

Serious games further demonstrate the value of adaptive AI. The Tactical Language Training System game supports Arabic language learning through culturally grounded NPC interactions, using adaptive hypertext to personalise support based on learner progress (Mansouri et al., 2021). Similarly, Rome Reborn employs intelligent NPCs driven by the ATOM dialogue system and Instinct AI engine to simulate historically grounded interactions, offering both educational depth and contextual realism (Mansouri et al., 2021).

Broader Applications

Outside entertainment, context-aware AI in VR plays a growing role in education and professional training. Immersive simulations provide safe, repeatable, and cost-effective environments that support experiential learning and decision-making (Fussell & Truong, 2022). In aviation and military training, VR improves procedural learning and readiness, while in medicine and engineering, it enables virtual laboratories where learners can practise complex tasks with real-time feedback (Shirazi et al., 2024).

In healthcare, AI-enhanced VR and AR are especially valuable for practising high-risk procedures without real-world consequences. Virtual patients, powered by NLP and behaviour modelling, allow trainees to rehearse diagnostic interviews and clinical communication in controlled settings, improving skill transfer and confidence (Reiners et al., 2021).

Context-aware AI is also used in autonomous systems and scientific visualisation. AI-XR environments support the training of robots and autonomous vehicles by simulating rare or dangerous scenarios that are difficult to recreate physically (Reiners et al., 2021). In medical visualisation, AI-assisted XR enables detailed 3D exploration of anatomy, supporting surgical planning by automatically highlighting relevant structures and reducing preparation time (Reiners et al., 2021).

Gaps in Current Research

Despite progress, several limitations remain in current research on context-aware AI in VR. A major gap identified under Objective O1 is the lack of standardised design and evaluation methods for multimodal context-aware systems. Many solutions are domain-specific and difficult to replicate or scale, limiting interoperability and the effective use of reinforcement learning, generative models, and intelligent agents (Augusto, 2022).

A second gap concerns the limited use of human-centred theory in system design, where users are often treated as passive data sources rather than active contextual agents, and existing frameworks provide little guidance for aligning system behaviour with user experience (Augusto, 2022). Access to high-quality multimodal data also remains restricted in early VR systems (Carrera-Rivera et al., 2022), while the nature of black-box models raises concerns about trust and transparency. These challenges are examined in this chapter's user survey (Devagiri et al., 2022) and connect to Objective O2, since many studies continue to emphasise short-term engagement rather than long-term cognitive or behavioural effects, with participant samples that are often demographically narrow (Shirazi et al., 2024). This chapter responds to these gaps through a mixed-methods survey that captures diverse user perspectives on adaptivity, feedback, and trust.

Future research should move toward systematic evaluation of multimodal fusion strategies and better temporal alignment across inputs. Developing shared measurement tools that combine presence, cognitive load, and biosignal data would improve comparability and rigour across studies.

METHODOLOGY

Research Design

This chapter uses a mixed-methods research design that combines a literature review with a user-centred survey. The literature review analyses current frameworks, systems, and case studies to classify multimodal context-aware approaches in immersive environments. Alongside this, the survey captures user perceptions, expectations, and ethical concerns related to AI-enhanced VR. Together, these methods support a balanced view of both system capability and user experience. To ensure alignment between aims and methods, each research objective is linked to a specific component of the study:

- Objective O1: To review recent innovations in context-aware AI applied to VR, addressed through a systematic literature review that examines multimodal inputs and enabling technologies.
- Objective O2: To assess user perceptions and expectations of context-aware features in immersive VR environments, examined through a mixed-methods survey combining quantitative ratings and qualitative feedback.

Data Sources and Selection Criteria

The literature and case studies were selected through a structured screening process that prioritised relevance, quality, and recency. Peer-reviewed articles and industry reports published between 2021 and 2025 were included, with emphasis on studies presenting practical systems or clear theoretical models of context-aware AI in VR. The main selection criteria were:

- Direct focus on multimodal context inputs (environmental, behavioural, verbal).
- Use of AI technologies such as RL, generative models, or intelligent agents.
- Applications in gaming, entertainment or training.
- Inclusion of user-adaptation or affective-computing.
- Evidence of empirical evaluation or real-time implementation.

Survey Design and Participants

The survey was designed to assess attitudes towards AI-enhanced VR systems, with a focus on context-aware adaptivity. It included 23 questions using mixed formats, such as multiple-choice items, Likert-scale ratings, checkboxes, and open-ended responses. Topics covered demographics, experience with VR and AI, preferred adaptive features, ethical concerns, and overall satisfaction. A full overview of the survey questions and their purpose is provided in Appendix A.

A total of 31 participants were recruited through a university mailing list, word-of-mouth, and student organisations, including the ICT Student Association. This strategy ensured participation from individuals across different academic backgrounds, while still mainly focusing on obtaining data from ICT students who are most likely to be familiar with AI and VR. Demographic data included age, gender, faculty affiliation, and level of study. Most participants were aged between 16 and 24. Gender distribution was 68% male, 19% female, and 13% undisclosed. ICT students formed the largest group, followed by Arts, with the remaining participants drawn from a range of other faculties (see Appendix B for further information).

Most respondents were enrolled in bachelor's programmes, followed by master's students and a smaller group of graduates. Some participants reported other educational levels, including doctoral and post-secondary study. VR usage was generally limited: 45% reported rare use, and 38% had never used VR. Familiarity with AI in VR was mostly moderate, with many describing themselves as somewhat familiar. Participants also reported the types of VR applications they had experienced. Participants with little or no VR experience were included and asked specifically about ethical concerns related to AI in immersive environments.

Survey data was analysed using descriptive statistics and cross-tabulation for quantitative items, alongside thematic analysis of open-ended responses. Likert-scale questions allowed clear comparison across participants, while qualitative responses provide deeper insight into user expectations and concerns.

Ethical Considerations

It is important to note that all the participants of the survey were clearly informed about the purpose of this study and how their data would be used, all participation was voluntary, and consent was implied through the survey's completion. All questions within the survey gave the user the option to skip questions if they didn't want to answer, or didn't feel comfortable answering. No personally identifiable information was collected, and only broad demographic categories such as age, gender, and faculty affiliation were used. All data was also anonymised and analysed in a compiled form

Apart from this, context-aware AI in VR also raises wider ethical concerns. Adaptive systems often rely on continuous data collection, which can blur the boundary between personalisation and surveillance. This highlights the need for clear and transparent design with strong user control, so users can decide if they want to be utilise adaptive features and adjust or disable them when they wish.

When legal requirements are combined with human-centred design, context-aware VR systems can protect privacy and autonomy while still offering engaging and adaptive experiences. Transparency and user control help ensure that adaptivity supports immersion without compromising ethical responsibility.

FINDINGS AND ANALYSIS

Technological Trends in AI for VR

Recent advances in AI-VR integration have driven a shift from static, scripted experiences toward adaptive and personalised virtual environments. This change is largely enabled by the use of multimodal context inputs, including environmental, behavioural, and verbal data, which allow systems to respond intelligently to user actions and conditions in real time.

A key trend is multimodal context-awareness, where VR systems combine data from sensors (such as lighting and spatial layout), behavioural tracking (including movement, gestures, gaze, and physiological signals), and verbal interaction (speech and natural language). By fusing these inputs, VR applications can infer user intent and adjust feedback, interaction, and content to maintain immersion. Technologies such as gesture recognition, head-gaze tracking, and natural language processing support seamless and responsive interaction. These developments are driven by several core AI technologies:

- Reinforcement Learning (RL) agents adapt virtual environments and characters based on user behaviour. In games, RL dynamically adjusts difficulty and pacing to sustain engagement, while in development, it supports automated playtesting by simulating diverse player behaviours (Roohi et al., 2021).
- Generative models, including GANs, diffusion models, and large language models, enable real-time content generation such as unscripted NPC dialogue, dynamic narratives, and on-demand 3D assets. These models increase realism and variation in VR experiences (Song et al., 2024).
- Virtual agents combine perception, RL, and generative capabilities to act as responsive participants in VR. They support roles such as NPCs, tutors, or virtual patients, responding to multimodal user input across entertainment, education, and healthcare contexts.

This technological foundation supports a growing range of applications:

- Adaptive AI in gaming personalises experiences by modelling player behaviour and emotional state. In genres such as horror, systems adjust tension and difficulty using physiological and behavioural signals to create tailored emotional responses (Ojha et al., 2024).
- AI-supported learning environments adapt content, pacing, and feedback to learner performance and engagement. Platforms such as LearningverseVR use free-form dialogue and scriptless NPCs to support active and personalised learning (Shirazi et al., 2024).
- Training and simulation systems, including virtual patients, use AI agents to model complex scenarios and provide real-time feedback, enabling safe and repeatable skill development in medical and professional training (Reiners et al., 2021).

Another strong trend is the use of affective computing to support user adaptation. Systems increasingly analyse emotional cues, facial expressions, voice tone, and physiological data to adjust interaction styles and content in real time. For example, VR horror games respond to detected fear levels, while educational simulations vary feedback intensity based on engagement.

Many of these approaches are supported by empirical studies and live deployments. Research shows that adaptive visual models can improve immersion by responding to environmental changes, and conversational NPCs powered by language models increase perceived realism. Applications such as VRChat and LearningverseVR demonstrate the practical impact of multimodal, context-aware AI on user experience.

Overall, AI for VR is moving toward systems that integrate multimodal context-awareness, learning and generative models, intelligent agents, and emotional adaptation. These technologies enable VR environments that not only react to users but also anticipate needs and co-create experiences, supporting more adaptive and human-centred virtual worlds.

Survey Outcomes

This subsection presents findings from the participant survey, highlighting user priorities, expectations, and ethical concerns regarding AI-driven, context-aware VR systems. Although based on a small sample, the survey offers insight into emerging preferences for interactivity, adaptivity, and ethical design. For full results, see Appendix B or Table 1.

Table 1. Summary of key survey results on AI-enhanced VR preferences and perceptions

Survey Item	Result (Rounded to percentage)
Top-Valued Features	
Real-time environment adjustment	68%
Adaptive difficulty levels	63%
Emotionally responsive avatars	37%
Natural language interactions	36%
Personalised content recommendations	21%
Experience & Exposure	
The user has never used AI in VR	58%
The user is unsure if they used AI in VR	16%
Preferred Adaptations	
Behavioural adaptivity rated "important" or higher	61%
Prefer adaptive difficulty and narrative changes	88%
Support speech-tone-based interaction adaptation	64%
Support emotion-based environment changes	29%
Control Preference	
Prefer hybrid (automatic + user-controlled) adaptation	74%
Ethics	
Support for AI ethics regulation	94%
Concern about data misuse or surveillance	90%
User Discomfort/Issues	
Reported no discomfort using AI in VR	80%
Experienced technical issues	70%
Feedback	
Interest in more conversational AI NPCs	High (qualitative responses)
Likelihood to recommend AI-enhanced VR	Neutral to hesitant overall

Preliminary expectations suggested that users would favour real-time adaptive features and natural interactions in VR, which the survey largely confirmed. When asked to select the most valuable AI-driven features (up to three), most participants prioritised real-time environment adjustments (68%) and adaptive difficulty levels (63%) (Figure 8 in Appendix B). Emotionally responsive avatars (37%) and natural language processing (36%) were also valued, while only 21% selected personalised content recommendations, indicating users prefer immediate interactivity over passive personalisation.

User sentiment largely affirmed AI's role in enhancing immersion. Most agreed that "AI enhances the realism of VR experiences," supporting the view that well-implemented AI adaptivity strengthens plausibility and presence. However, 58% had never interacted with an AI-driven VR system, and 16% were unsure (Figure 10 in Appendix B), showing limited exposure to context-aware features. Physical behavioural adaptivity was rated "important" or "extremely important" by eleven participants (Figure 11 in Appendix B), highlighting the value of sensor-driven interactivity for realism and embodiment.

Preferred context-aware adaptations included adjusting difficulty based on performance and changing narrative paths (88%), with 64% supporting adaptive interactions based on speech tone, but only 29% endorsing environment-wide emotional adjustments (Figure 12 in Appendix B). This suggests emotional responsiveness is appreciated in agents but may feel intrusive when applied globally. Respondents largely favoured a hybrid model combining automatic and user-controlled adaptations (74%) (Figure 13 in Appendix B), reflecting HCI best practices for maintaining user autonomy.

Participants were generally neutral in rating satisfaction with AI-driven VR features and interaction intuitiveness (Figure 14 and B15 in Appendix B), indicating these systems are acceptable but not yet seamless, likely due to limited exposure. Ethical considerations were prominent: 32% were unaware of AI ethics in VR, though those with technical backgrounds or frequent VR use showed higher awareness. The main concerns were data misuse or surveillance (90%), manipulation (65%), bias (61%), and lack of transparency (55%) (Figure 17 in Appendix B). Most users were uncomfortable with AI collecting behavioural data to enhance experience (Figure 20 in Appendix B), and 94% supported regulatory oversight (Figure 21 in Appendix B).

Among those who had interacted with AI in VR, 80% reported no discomfort (Figure 18 in Appendix B), though 20% did, and 70% experienced technical issues (Figure 19 in Appendix B). Many participants expressed interest in conversational AI NPCs capable of real-time dialogue, reflecting trends in LLM integration and demand for more human-like interaction.

Subgroup analyses revealed no meaningful trends due to the small sample size. Overall, participants most valued real-time environment adjustments (68%) and adaptive difficulty scaling (63%), moderately prioritised emotional and verbal adaptivity (37% and 36%), and emphasised ethical transparency and regulatory oversight. These findings suggest future VR systems should combine technical adaptivity with ethical intelligibility, balancing automation with user agency. Context-aware AI should be framed not merely as a tool for efficiency but as an experiential mediator, enhancing trust, flow, and presence through personalised yet explainable feedback. These insights provide guidance for developers, educators, and researchers aiming to design adaptive VR systems that are both cognitively engaging and socially responsible.

Comparative Analysis

This subsection examines how empirical user insights align with technological developments, highlighting convergences and gaps between capabilities and experience. Comparing survey responses with literature reveals where AI-driven context-awareness in VR meets user expectations and where implementation lags.

A clear area of alignment is user preference for real-time environmental and behavioural adaptivity. Participants rated real-time environment adjustments (68%) and adaptive difficulty levels (63%) as most valuable, reflecting innovations like reinforcement learning agents that scale difficulty or adjust lighting and pacing based on context (Roohi et al., 2021; Abbasi et al., 2024). Interest in emotionally responsive avatars and natural language processing also aligns with advances in affective computing and conversational AI, including emotionally reactive NPCs in games (Ojha et al., 2024) and scriptless dialogue in educational VR (Song et al., 2024).

Users strongly favoured context-aware systems that adapt difficulty and narrative paths (88% each), supporting theoretical models of engagement and flow (Csikszentmihalyi, 1990) and confirming that AI-enhanced adaptivity sustains immersion. Preference for hybrid automatic/user-controlled adaptations (74%) echoes human-centric design principles prioritising agency and transparency (Augusto, 2022; Carrera-Rivera et al., 2022). Ethical concerns, data misuse, manipulation, bias, and lack of transparency were prominent, with 94% advocating regulatory oversight, reflecting scholarly calls for responsible AI (Paneva et al., 2025; Devagiri et al., 2022).

However, discrepancies are evident between technological promise and user experience. Despite the literature describing real-time adaptive systems, emotionally intelligent NPCs, and biofeedback-driven gameplay, 58% of respondents had never encountered AI-driven VR, and 16% were unsure, suggesting limited mainstream deployment. Users were generally neutral on intuitiveness and satisfaction, contrasting literature claims of high engagement, indicating implementation quality and onboarding may be inadequate.

Low interest in personalised content recommendations (21%) also contrasts with AI use in streaming and e-commerce (Bag et al., 2021), implying that VR users value immediate interactivity over passive curation. Likewise, only 29% supported environment changes based on emotional states, highlighting possible unease or preference for more direct adaptivity. Finally, despite literature advocating explainable and transparent systems, users reported ethical discomfort and a strong desire for control and regulation, suggesting governance tools such as Explainable AI (XAI) dashboards and consent mechanisms are not yet standard in deployed systems.

Cross-Domain Comparison of Context-Aware VR Applications

Table 2. Cross-domain comparison of context-aware VR applications

Feature / Category	Gaming & Entertainment	Education & Training	Healthcare & Therapy	Industrial & Professional Training
Primary Goals	Enhance immersion, emotional engagement, and challenge balancing	Support learning, skill acquisition, and cognitive engagement	Rehabilitation, emotional regulation, and exposure therapy	Safety, situational awareness, performance optimisation
Contextual Inputs (Sensors / Data)	Behavioural cues (movement, reaction time), physiological signals (heart rate, gaze), and vocal tone	Task performance metrics, gaze tracking, speech, and gesture	Biometric data (EEG, heart rate, skin conductance), behavioural tracking	Motion capture, eye tracking, and task completion data
Adaptive Outputs / Features	Dynamic difficulty adjustment, emotion-adaptive NPCs, procedural storytelling	Adaptive tutoring, multimodal feedback, and cognitive load regulation	Stress-level adjustment, emotion-guided feedback, adaptive pacing	Real-time task guidance, fatigue monitoring, adaptive simulation
Key Constraints	Latency, over-adaptation risk, and data privacy in consumer devices	Measurement validity, learner diversity, and institutional data policy	Medical data compliance (HIPAA/ GDPR), sensor accuracy, patient safety	Reliability, network latency, integration with enterprise systems
Design Priorities	Real-time responsiveness, user agency, transparent adaptation	Instructional alignment, adaptability, and ethical data handling	Clinical validity, empathy in design, and strict privacy control	Operational realism, data integrity, minimal cognitive load

Table 2 illustrates how context-aware AI functions differently across application domains. While the core mechanism, multimodal sensing and adaptive feedback, remains consistent, the ethical, technical, and experiential priorities vary. In gaming, adaptivity serves engagement and flow; in education, it enhances personalisation and retention; in healthcare, it safeguards well-being through calibrated intervention; and in industrial training, it optimises performance within operational limits. Recognising these domain-specific constraints and goals enables the development of more targeted frameworks for context-aware VR, balancing technological sophistication with user trust and ethical transparency.

Case Studies

Gaming: Emotionally Adaptive Horror Experiences

Emotionally adaptive VR horror games show a compelling use of context-aware AI, exemplified by Ojha et al.'s (2024) "Horror Director" system. The system uses behavioural context-awareness via a machine learning model that infers player fear from gameplay traces, without relying on biometric sensors. Fear levels are labelled using self-reported Likert-scale ratings collected during play. Horror Director uses a Finite State Machine with three pacing states, Relax, Build Peak, and Sustain Peak, to introduce horror elements at psychologically optimal moments. These stimuli are triggered by player-specific fear profiles rather than scripted events, creating personalised fear trajectories. Technical requirements included bounding-zone tagging, light and audio mapping, and a fast prediction loop under 4ms for seamless VR integration.

Empirical results show increased immersion, fear, and enjoyment with adaptive stimuli like whispers, flickering lights, and creaking floors. These outcomes align with Slater's (2009) plausibility illusion and Csikszentmihalyi's (1990) flow model. Challenges remain in generalising fear models trained on narrow, self-reported data, but the work highlights how real-time behavioural modelling can transform horror game design from static scripting to responsive, emotionally tuned interactivity.

Education: LearningverseVR and Scriptless NPCs

In education, Song et al.'s (2024) LearningverseVR demonstrates how generative AI and multimodal context-awareness can enhance learning. The platform integrates a Unity-based VR client with a backend using Flask, MySQL, GPT-3.5, and a local ChatGLM instance. NPCs are powered by LLMs, allowing free-form conversations that interpret verbal input and behavioural signals. They can also show emotion and perform body movements via tone and action indicators. Context cues are parsed in real time to guide responses, animations, and instructional strategies. The system also includes World, Organic, and Inorganic agents that adapt to environmental features such as weather, flora, and social interactions.

LearningverseVR enables adaptive learning paths, gamification, and emotionally aware NPC interaction. Users report higher motivation, engagement, and knowledge retention due to personalised pacing and challenge levels (Shirazi et al., 2024; Song et al., 2024). NPCs maintain conversational memory, allowing personalised exchanges that enhance plausibility illusion and flow. Scriptless design reduces development workload, supporting scalable, narrative-rich learning experiences. Coordinating multiple agent types and ensuring coherent world behaviour remains challenging, highlighting the need for scalable architectures and long-term context management. LearningverseVR shows how context-sensitive AI can align interactivity with learner autonomy and engagement.

Healthcare: Virtual Patients and Adaptive Training

In medical training, context-aware AI in VR allows realistic virtual patients (Reiners et al., 2021). These AI avatars adapt to trainees' verbal and nonverbal cues, adjusting their responses to guide clinical reasoning. The systems track spoken questions, hesitation, and confusion, adapting interactions to promote best practices. Studies show improved knowledge retention, confidence, and accurate assessment of clinical skills through real-time analysis.

Real-Time Environmental Adaptation: ManySense VR

A notable example of environmental context-awareness is the ManySense VR framework, which integrates real-time weather and environmental data from external APIs into the VR scene (Moon et al., 2022). If it is raining in the user's city, the virtual world synchronises with overcast skies and appropriate soundscapes. This context fusion enhances presence and realism, making the virtual environment feel more aligned with the user's actual situation and promoting a deeper sense of immersion.

Automated Playtesting and Game Design Optimisation

AI-driven agents employing reinforcement learning and Monte Carlo Tree Search have advanced the process of game design and testing (Roohi et al., 2021). In commercial titles like Angry Birds Dream Blast, a combination of DRL and MCTS agents simulates thousands of play sessions to predict level difficulty, identify player retention bottlenecks, and refine content to maximise engagement.

In summary, these case studies collectively underscore how dynamic interaction and multimodal context-awareness, enabled by advanced AI technologies, can significantly elevate user engagement, satisfaction, and learning outcomes in VR. The empirical evidence and real-time implementations across gaming, education, training, and healthcare reinforce the value of adaptive, human-centred AI in shaping the next generation of immersive experiences.

DISCUSSION

Synthesis of Findings

The convergence of AI and VR, particularly through context-aware systems, has been shown to improve user immersion, engagement, and personalisation across entertainment and education. Both the reviewed innovations and survey insights indicate that AI integration in VR is transformative, but effective implementation requires interdisciplinary collaboration and user-centred design.

A key advantage of context-aware AI in VR is its ability to create dynamic, responsive environments. Unlike static experiences, AI enables real-time adaptivity, which strengthens the sense of presence because the VR system can anticipate user actions and update sensory feedback in line with expectations (Triberti et al., 2025). Multimodal interactions, combining gestures, voice, and head gaze, support natural and efficient communication, with each modality compensating for others' limitations (Cao et al., 2023). Integrating speech and affective models with contextual sensing, such as dynamic lighting, enhances clarity, immersion, and intuitive control (Abbasi et al., 2024). Contextually adaptive environments, coupled with narrative and clear goals, align with user expectations, deepening the sense of "being there" (Triberti et al., 2025).

From a design perspective, context-aware AI must balance immersion with usability. Developers need to integrate models ranging from RL to natural language processing without overwhelming users. Cognitive load and attention must be considered, for example, by avoiding adaptive transitions during peak focus. This highlights the need for collaboration among HCI specialists and AI researchers to create experiences that are both contextually rich and psychologically coherent.

Personalisation is another major benefit. In games and educational platforms, AI can model behaviour, emotion, preferences, and performance to tailor content (Ojha et al., 2024; Song et al., 2024; Dyulicheva & Glazieva, 2022). VR horror games can detect fear responses and adjust pacing or narrative elements in real time, increasing emotional impact (Ojha et al., 2024). In educational VR, AI adapts difficulty and content to support learning trajectories and retention (Shirazi et al., 2024; Dyulicheva & Glazieva, 2022). These feedback loops improve both engagement and effectiveness.

Beyond VR, context-aware AI supports Smart-Product Service Systems (S-PSS), dynamically adjusting to user situations and environmental inputs (Carrera-Rivera et al., 2022). These systems enhance operational performance, predictive analytics, and targeted marketing, demonstrating applications beyond immersive experiences (Bag et al., 2021; Munir et al., 2022).

In training and professional development, AI-driven VR agents enable scenario-based learning that adapts to users' skills in real time (Reiners et al., 2021). In aviation and medical education, VR allows repeatable, risk-free practice of high-stakes procedures, improving memory, reducing costs, and fostering critical thinking (Fussell & Truong, 2022; Shirazi et al., 2024). AI agents capable of decision-making and emotional expression provide human-like interactions that enhance learning and engagement.

AI-generated virtual influencers extend affective computing and digital communication by expressing nuanced emotions, enriching interaction, and supporting emotionally resonant strategies in entertainment and marketing (Yu et al., 2024). Overall, these applications show the transformative potential of context-aware AI, though success depends on human-centric design, ethics, and adaptive practices. Emphasising cognitive ergonomics and inclusive design is essential to realise the benefits of AI-augmented VR.

Challenges and Concerns

Despite its promise, context-aware AI in VR faces complex challenges across technical, ethical, methodological, and human-centred domains.

Complexity in Contextual Understanding

Interpreting multifaceted, real-time contextual cues remains a large challenge. Systems draw on diverse data sources, including behaviour, biometric signals, and sensor data, which vary in reliability and format (Carrera-Rivera et al., 2022; Bag et al., 2021). Processing real-time streams requires high-speed, accurate analytics to maintain responsiveness. Inputs like gestures or voice commands, are often ambiguous. Multimodal fusion algorithms are needed to resolve conflicts and provide clear interaction (Cao et al., 2023). For example, simultaneous inputs from different modalities require prioritisation schemes to decide which action to execute.

Dynamic contexts, such as real-time gaming or manufacturing, introduce uncertainties in predicting user behaviour, particularly when historical data is limited or unreliable (Devagiri et al., 2022; Dyulicheva & Glazieva, 2022). AI-generated humanoid figures may also trigger the "uncanny valley" effect, where near-human appearances create discomfort or distrust (Yu et al., 2024). Designing emotionally resonant agents that avoid adverse reactions remains an ongoing challenge.

Real-Time Processing and Computational Cost

Maintaining low-latency responsiveness in AI-driven VR is a key challenge. Multimodal systems must process high-dimensional sensor data and render feedback instantly to preserve immersion (Cao et al., 2023; Reiners et al., 2021). Even small delays, such as lag in head tracking, can break presence and reduce usability (Slater, 2009). While some models, like fear detection systems, can predict reactions in milliseconds, running them consistently in real time requires significant computational resources (Ojha et al., 2024).

Training these models is even more demanding. DRL, for instance, can require weeks on high-performance computing infrastructure to reach optimal performance (Yin et al., 2023). Such requirements limit participation by smaller teams and slow research progress. Hardware constraints also play a role as VR systems need efficient, powerful chips to handle intensive computation cost-effectively and reliably, especially for real-world deployment (Devagiri et al., 2022).

Data and Ethical Considerations

Privacy is another concern in context-aware VR, since these systems collect sensitive behavioural and physical data. Users may not realise the extent of information captured, including eye movements, speech, posture, or physiological signals, which can reveal mood, identity, or health (Paneva et al., 2025). Transparent consent and in-system privacy controls, such as virtual "privacy monitors," are essential to protect users.

Ethical design also requires user control over AI adaptivity. Systems should avoid user profiling and offer override options, allowing individuals to adjust or reject intrusive changes. Bias in AI models presents another risk since demographic skew in training data can lead to poor performance for underrepresented groups (Ojha et al., 2024). Similarly, voice or gesture recognition may fail in noisy environments, reducing accessibility and usability (Cao et al., 2023).

The increasing realism of AI characters raises psychological and ethical concerns. The "uncanny valley" effect can create discomfort (Yu et al., 2024), and virtual influencers, for instance, may manipulate emotions if not properly regulated. Black-box AI systems are often opaque, risking user distrust, and over-reliance on AI in educational settings may undermine critical thinking or alter traditional mentorship roles (Shirazi et al., 2024). Legal and ethical frameworks remain limited, highlighting the need for robust governance (Devagiri et al., 2022).

Methodologies and Evaluation

Evaluating AI-driven VR systems presents methodological challenges. Current frameworks often assess isolated aspects, like situational awareness, rather than providing holistic insight (Munir et al., 2022). Many studies rely on subjective feedback from questionnaires or interviews, which can be influenced by personality or temporary states (Carrera-Rivera et al., 2022).

Physiological measures, such as eye-tracking, EEG, or ECG, provide objective data on cognitive and emotional states but can be intrusive and logistically complex (Carrera-Rivera et al., 2022). Generalising findings is difficult because most studies are conducted in narrow settings with limited demographics (Roohi et al., 2021). Long-term effects of adaptive VR, such as on memory, learning retention, motivation, or digital well-being, remain underexplored (Shirazi et al., 2024).

Interdisciplinary Perspectives and Future Challenges

Inclusive design is essential to build HCI systems that support users with diverse needs. In storytelling, context-aware adaptivity must balance narrative flexibility with cognitive limits to avoid disrupting flow. Media psychology shows that anthropomorphic agents can increase user confidence if consistent and trustworthy, but misuse risks ethical violations. From a technical perspective, integrating LLMs into real-time VR introduces latency and coherence challenges in generated responses (Rong, 2024). Researchers must evaluate how users perceive AI understanding and determine limits for adaptive interaction.

Addressing these challenges requires interdisciplinary collaboration, clear governance, and emphasis on user agency. To fully realise the potential of context-aware VR, development must advance not only in technology but also in ethical, equitable, and human-centred design.

FUTURE DIRECTIONS

Emerging Technologies and Innovations

The evolution of AI and VR is driving innovations that may reshape how users interact with digital environments. Integrating advanced AI with immersive VR offers opportunities for more adaptive, responsive, and emotionally attuned experiences. These intelligent systems can dynamically learn from users and context, creating new research avenues across education, entertainment, healthcare, and beyond.

Bio-Adaptive Systems and Emotion-Aware Interfaces

Future applications can utilise Bio-adaptive VR systems to track heart rate, EEG, or skin conductance to detect emotional states in real time. For example, an educational VR simulation could adjust lesson pacing or provide hints based on detected stress or fatigue. Developing reliable closed-loop systems requires advances in affective computing and collaboration with neuroscience and psychology. Emotion-aware systems promise more empathetic, engaging, and effective experiences (Dyulicheva & Glazieva, 2022; Yu et al., 2024).

Cross-Platform Contextual Intelligence

Context-aware AI will extend beyond standalone VR to AR, mobile, and traditional screens. Mixed-reality systems may use geolocation, calendar events, or social interactions to tailor experiences. For instance, a theme park could integrate AR location data to inform VR narratives, adapting rides or storytelling to the user's prior experiences. Cross-platform awareness will require robust AI capable of aggregating and interpreting diverse data streams (Carrera-Rivera et al., 2022; Bag et al., 2021).

Advanced AI Models for Perception and Interaction

Deep learning (DL) and reinforcement learning (RL) remain central. DL extracts hierarchical patterns from complex data, supporting object detection, sentiment analysis, and scene understanding. RL trains agents through trial-and-error in dynamic environments, relevant for autonomous vehicles, robotics, and games (Reiners et al., 2021; Roohi et al., 2021). Generative AI and LLMs enable scriptless NPC interactions, producing real-time dialogue, emotion, and behaviour based on context. Future systems may also generate 3D models, environments, animations, and full-scene video to personalise content in real time (Song et al., 2024).

Large-Scale Behavioural Analytics and Federated Learning

With the increasing adoption of context-aware VR, the potential to conduct large-scale behavioural analytics is becoming more feasible. Aggregated, anonymised data from millions of interactions, such as voice commands, gaze patterns, and movement trajectories, can help improve AI models for better immersion and responsiveness. However, privacy remains important to ensure data protection while enabling context-awareness. Research in this area must focus on developing techniques that maintain privacy while allowing AI systems to generalise from diverse user interactions (Ojha et al., 2024; Carrera-Rivera et al., 2022).

Immersive Simulation and Virtual Laboratories

In education and professional training, VR is poised to enable increasingly complex and realistic simulations. AI-powered virtual laboratories will allow learners to conduct repeatable, hands-on experiments in immersive environments, particularly valuable in domains like medicine, engineering, and the physical sciences (Shirazi et al., 2024). These environments will adapt in real time to learner performance, providing customised feedback and dynamically adjusting task difficulty to optimise skill development.

Human-Centric AI and VR Design and Impact

AI in VR must treat users as active participants. Systems should integrate characteristics like learning style, motivation, and emotional state into adaptive logic (Augusto, 2022). Broad, diverse participant representation is critical to avoid bias and enhance generalisability. XAI and human-in-the-loop mechanisms will help maintain trust and user control, particularly in sensitive domains like education and healthcare (Devagiri et al., 2022). Research should also address health risks, such as eye strain, motion sickness, and disorientation, ensuring safe and engaging VR experiences.

Recommendations for Practitioners and Researchers

Practical Guidance for Developers, Educators, and Industry Stakeholders

Technological development must remain human-centred. Systems should focus on user benefit rather than technical sophistication. Developers must explicitly integrate human preferences, behaviours, and characteristics into context-aware models throughout all stages of development (Augusto, 2022).

Practitioners should offer multimodal input options, including gestures and voice, to allow users to choose the most comfortable or efficient method. Gestures can provide immediate control, while voice-gaze combinations support manipulation of distant or abstract objects (Cao et al., 2023). In professional training settings, demonstrating measurable benefits in engagement, efficiency, or outcomes can encourage adoption (Fussell & Truong, 2022).

Personalisation should be strategically applied in fields like marketing. AI can track consumer behaviour to create emotionally responsive campaigns (Bag et al., 2021), while virtual influencers or avatars should display appropriate emotions aligned with communication goals (Yu et al., 2024). In education, adaptive systems should adjust difficulty and pacing in real time, with VR simulations enhancing learning. Gamification elements such as badges, points, and leaderboards can sustain motivation and provide feedback (Song et al., 2024; Shirazi et al., 2024).

Developers must comply with regulations such as GDPR and the EU-AI Act, and communicate clearly about what data is collected, why, and how it is used (Carrera-Rivera et al., 2022; Shirazi et al., 2024). Consent mechanisms should be built into all systems to ensure ethical compliance and trust. Institutions should provide hardware, software, and user support to ensure successful integration into workflows and learning environments (Shirazi et al., 2024). Operational efficiency can be enhanced through AI in industrial settings, and predictive maintenance, safety optimisation, and large-scale analytics are key applications, and collaborative intelligence, where AI augments rather than replaces humans, will be critical for long-term value (Devagiri et al., 2022; Munir et al., 2022; Bag et al., 2021).

Research Priorities for Advancing Context-Aware AI in VR

Researchers should develop rigorous, human-centred frameworks for context awareness that account for interactions between system behaviour and user activity (Augusto, 2022). Modular and scalable architectures are also needed to support real-time data flows and multi-user environments while remaining robust (Carrera-Rivera et al., 2022).

Real-time processing is still a challenge for multimodality, so further work on efficient, low-latency AI and ML algorithms is essential for managing context in fast-changing environments (Carrera-Rivera et al., 2022). Domain adaptation strategies should be explored to ensure that skills learned in XR transfer effectively to real-world tasks (Reiners et al., 2021). Simulation design also requires attention, as VR worlds with multiple intelligent agents and real-world unpredictability can provide richer learning scenarios and more rigorous training conditions (Reiners et al., 2021).

Further research is needed to understand cognitive, behavioural, and educational effects, including skill retention, motivation, and higher-order thinking (Shirazi et al., 2024). XAI remains important for improving interpretability and trust, particularly in education, healthcare, and safety contexts (Devagiri et al., 2022). Researchers should also develop stronger metrics for situational awareness that better reflect complex, multitasking environments (Munir et al., 2022).

CONCLUSION

This chapter has explored how AI and VR come together through multimodal context awareness, drawing on literature and survey evidence. The findings show that AI can read environmental, behavioural, and verbal cues to shape responsive and personalised virtual experiences. Inputs such as voice, gaze, gesture, and physiological signals enable VR systems to adjust in real time, while techniques such as RL, generative models, and intelligent agents support scriptless interaction, bio-adaptive pacing, and dynamic content creation across various fields.

Survey responses reinforce these insights, with participants showing support for real-time adaptation, emotionally aware characters, and shared control between users and AI. Users reported greater immersion when systems adjusted difficulty, narrative flow, or social interaction. At the same time, concerns about data privacy, transparency, and user autonomy remain important, pointing to the need for responsible and user-centred design in future systems.

REFERENCES

Abbasi, M., Váz, P., Silva, J., & Martins, P. (2024). Enhancing Visual Perception in Immersive VR and AR Environments: AI-Driven Color and Clarity Adjustments Under Dynamic Lighting Conditions. *Technologies*, *12*(11), 11. Advance online publication. DOI: 10.3390/technologies12110216

Augusto, J. C. (2022). Contexts and Context-awareness Revisited from an Intelligent Environments Perspective. *Applied Artificial Intelligence*, *36*(1), 2008644. DOI: 10.1080/08839514.2021.2008644

Bag, S., Srivastava, G., Bashir, M. M. A., Kumari, S., Giannakis, M., & Chowdhury, A. H. (2021). Journey of customers in this digital era: Understanding the role of artificial intelligence technologies in user engagement and conversion. *Benchmarking*, *29*(7), 2074–2098. DOI: 10.1108/BIJ-07-2021-0415

Berkman, M. I., & Akan, E. (2019). Presence and Immersion in Virtual Reality. In Lee, N. (Ed.), *Encyclopedia of Computer Graphics and Games* (pp. 1–10). Springer International Publishing., DOI: 10.1007/978-3-319-08234-9_162-1

Cao, L., Zhang, H., Peng, C., & Hansberger, J. T. (2023). Real-time multimodal interaction in virtual reality, A case study with a large virtual interface. *Multimedia Tools and Applications*, *82*(16), 25427–25448. DOI: 10.1007/s11042-023-14381-6

Carrera-Rivera, A., Larrinaga, F., & Lasa, G. (2022). Context-awareness for the design of Smart-product service systems: Literature review. *Computers in Industry*, *142*, 103730. DOI: 10.1016/j.compind.2022.103730

Csikszentmihalyi, M. (1990). Flow: The Psychology of Optimal Experience.

Delgado, G. (2024, July 31). NVIDIA Researchers Harness Real-Time Gen AI to Build Immersive Desert World. NVIDIA Blog. https://blogs.nvidia.com/blog/real-time-3d-generative-ai-research-siggraph-2024/

Devagiri, J. S., Paheding, S., Niyaz, Q., Yang, X., & Smith, S. (2022). Augmented Reality and Artificial Intelligence in industry: Trends, tools, and future challenges. *Expert Systems with Applications*, *207*, 118002. DOI: 10.1016/j.eswa.2022.118002

Dyulicheva, Y. Y., & Glazieva, A. O. (2022). Game based learning with artificial intelligence and immersive technologies: An overview.

Fussell, S. G., & Truong, D. (2022). Using virtual reality for dynamic learning: An extended technology acceptance model. *Virtual Reality (Waltham Cross)*, *26*(1), 249–267. DOI: 10.1007/s10055-021-00554-x PMID: 34276237

Mansouri, B., Roozkhosh, A., & Farbeh, H. (2021). A Survey on Implementations of Adaptive AI in Serious Games for Enhancing Player Engagement. *2021 International Serious Games Symposium (ISGS)*, 48–53. DOI: 10.1109/ISGS54702.2021.9684760

Moon, J., Jeong, M., Oh, S., Laine, T. H., & Seo, J. (2022). Data Collection Framework for Context-Aware Virtual Reality Application Development in Unity: Case of Avatar Embodiment. *Sensors (Basel)*, *22*(12), 12. Advance online publication. DOI: 10.3390/s22124623 PMID: 35746405

Munir, A., Aved, A., & Blasch, E. (2022). Situational Awareness: Techniques, Challenges, and Prospects. *AI*, *3*(1), 1. Advance online publication. DOI: 10.3390/ai3010005

Nilsson, N., Nordahl, R., & Serafin, S. (2016). Immersion Revisited: A Review of Existing Definitions of Immersion and Their Relation to Different Theories of Presence. *Human Technology*, *12*(2), 108–134. DOI: 10.17011/ht/urn.201611174652

Ojha, A., Narain, S., Raj, A., Agrawal, T., Wadhwa, B., & Joshi, M. (2024). Dynamic virtual reality horror sports enhanced by artificial intelligence and player modeling. *Multimedia Tools and Applications*, *83*(32), 77415–77432. DOI: 10.1007/s11042-024-18414-6

Paneva, V., Winterhalter, V., Malladi, N. S. S. V., Strauss, M., Schneegass, S., & Alt, F. (2025). Usable Privacy in Virtual Worlds: Design Implications for Data Collection Awareness and Control Interfaces in Virtual Reality (No. arXiv:2503.10915). arXiv. https://doi.org//arXiv.2503.10915DOI: 10.48550

Reiners, D., Davahli, M. R., Karwowski, W., & Cruz-Neira, C. (2021). The Combination of Artificial Intelligence and Extended Reality: A Systematic Review. *Frontiers in Virtual Reality*, *2*, 721933. Advance online publication. DOI: 10.3389/frvir.2021.721933

Rong, Z. (2024). Application of Natural Language Processing in Virtual Experience AI Interaction Design. *Journal of Intelligent Learning Systems and Applications*, *16*(4), 4. Advance online publication. DOI: 10.4236/jilsa.2024.164020

Roohi, S., Guckelsberger, C., Relas, A., Heiskanen, H., Takatalo, J., & Hämäläinen, P. (2021). Predicting Game Difficulty and Engagement Using AI Players. Proc. ACM Hum.-Comput. Interact., 5(CHI PLAY), 231:1-231:17. DOI: 10.1145/3474658

Rutrecht, H., Wittmann, M., Khoshnoud, S., & Igarzábal, F. A. (2021). Time Speeds Up During Flow States: A Study in Virtual Reality with the Video Game Thumper. DOI: 10.1163/22134468-bja10033

Ryan, R. M., & Deci, E. L. (2000). Self-determination theory and the facilitation of intrinsic motivation, social development, and well-being. *The American Psychologist, 55*(1), 68–78. DOI: 10.1037/0003-066X.55.1.68 PMID: 11392867

Shirazi, B. N., Safavi, A. A., Aftabi, E., & Salimi, G. (2024). The Integration of Virtual Reality and Artificial Intelligence in Educational Paradigms. 2024 11th International and the 17th National Conference on E-Learning and E-Teaching (ICeLeT), 1–6. DOI: 10.1109/ICeLeT62507.2024.10493089

Slater, M. (2009). Place illusion and plausibility can lead to realistic behaviour in immersive virtual environments. *Philosophical Transactions of the Royal Society of London. Series B, Biological Sciences, 364*(1535), 3549–3557. DOI: 10.1098/rstb.2009.0138 PMID: 19884149

Song, Y., Wu, K., & Ding, J. (2024). Developing an immersive game-based learning platform with generative artificial intelligence and virtual reality technologies – "LearningverseVR". Computers & Education: X Reality, 4, 100069. DOI: 10.1016/j.cexr.2024.100069

Triberti, S., Sapone, C., & Riva, G. (2025). Being there but where? Sense of presence theory for virtual reality applications. *Humanities & Social Sciences Communications, 12*(1), 79. Advance online publication. DOI: 10.1057/s41599-025-04380-3

Wang, A., Thompson, M., Uz-Bilgin, C., & Klopfer, E. (2021). Authenticity, Interactivity, and Collaboration in Virtual Reality Games: Best Practices and Lessons Learned. *Frontiers in Virtual Reality, 2*, 734083. Advance online publication. DOI: 10.3389/frvir.2021.734083

Yin, Q.-Y., Yang, J., Huang, K.-Q., Zhao, M.-J., Ni, W.-C., Liang, B., Huang, Y., Wu, S., & Wang, L. (2023). AI in Human-computer Gaming: Techniques, Challenges and Opportunities. *Machine Intelligence Research, 20*(3), 299–317. DOI: 10.1007/s11633-022-1384-6

Yu, J., Dickinger, A., So, K. K. F., & Egger, R. (2024). Artificial intelligence-generated virtual influencer: Examining the effects of emotional display on user engagement. *Journal of Retailing and Consumer Services, 76*, 103560. DOI: 10.1016/j.jretconser.2023.103560

APPENDIX A: SURVEY QUESTIONNAIRE

Q1: What is your age group?

- Type: Multiple Choice.
- Reason: Obtaining demographic information to better contextualise the data.

Q2: What is your Gender?

- Type: Multiple Choice.
- Reason: Obtaining demographic information to better contextualise the data.

Q3: Which Faculty are you registered with?

- Type: Multiple Choice.
- Reason: Obtaining demographic information to better contextualise the data. Since this survey was performed at a University, this question was tailored towards those students.

Q4: What Education Level are you currently studying for?

- Type: Multiple Choice.
- Reason: Obtaining demographic information to better contextualise the data.

Q5: How frequently do you use virtual reality (VR) experiences?

- Type: Multiple Choice.
- Reason: Understanding usage frequency helps segment users based on experience levels, which can influence perceptions of AI integration in VR.

Q6: Which types of VR applications have you experienced? (Select all that apply.)

- Type: Checkboxes.
- Reason: Identifying the variety of VR applications used provides context for user expectations and experiences.

Q7: How familiar are you with how AI is used in VR?

- Type: Multiple Choice.
- Reason: This question segments respondents based on their baseline understanding of AI-VR integration, useful for interpreting attitudes and expectations across experience levels. Similar formats are used in technology acceptance and literacy studies.

Q8: Which AI-driven features do you find most valuable in VR?

- Type: Checkboxes.
- Reason: Identifying valued features informs developers about user priorities in AI integration.

Q9: To what extent do you agree with the statement: "AI enhances the realism of VR experiences."

- Type: Likert scale (1 – Strongly Disagree to 5 – Strongly Agree).
- Reason: Assessing user agreement helps gauge perceptions of AI's role in enhancing VR realism.

Q10: Have you ever interacted with an AI-driven character or system in VR?

- Type: Yes or No.
- Reason: Determines user exposure to AI elements within VR environments.

Q11: How important is it for a VR system to adapt to your physical movements and behaviours in real-time? (Skip if not applicable)

- Type: Likert scale (1 – Not important to 5 – Extremely important).
- Reason: Evaluates user expectations regarding system responsiveness to physical cues.

Q12: Which types of context-aware adaptations do you prefer in VR experiences? (Skip if not applicable)

- Type: Checkboxes.
- Reason: Identifies user preferences for specific adaptive features, guiding the design of personalised and immersive VR interactions.

Q13: Would you prefer AI adaptations in VR to be automatic or user-controlled?

- Type: Multiple Choice.
- Reason: Understanding control preferences aids in designing user-centric AI systems.

Q14: Rate your overall satisfaction with AI-driven features in VR experiences you've encountered. (Skip if not applicable)

- Type: Likert scale (1 – Very dissatisfied to 5 – Very satisfied).
- Reason: Measures user satisfaction levels, identifying areas for improvement.

Q15: How intuitive do you find AI-driven interactions in VR? (Skip if not applicable)

- Type: Likert scale (1 – Not intuitive to 5 – Very intuitive).
- Reason: Assesses the ease of use and learning curve associated with AI features.

Q16: How aware are you of the ethical implications of using AI in virtual reality (VR)?

- Type: Likert scale (1 – Not at all aware to 5 – Very aware).
- Reason: Assesses the user's level of ethical awareness, informing the need for education or transparency in AI-driven VR systems.

Q17: Which ethical concerns do you associate with AI in VR?

- Type: Checkboxes.

- Reason: Identifies specific ethical issues users are concerned about, helping to prioritise responsible development and address public apprehensions.

Q18: Have you experienced discomfort due to AI in VR?

- Type: Yes, No or Not Applicable.
- Reason: Identifies potential negative impacts of AI features on user comfort.

Q19: Have you encountered technical issues due to AI in VR?

- Type: Yes, No or Not Applicable.
- Reason: Determines the prevalence of AI-related technical problems in VR.

Q20: Would you be comfortable with AI systems in VR collecting data on your behaviour to enhance experiences?

- Type: Likert scale (1 – Very uncomfortable to 5 – Very comfortable).
- Reason: Evaluates user comfort levels regarding data collection, which is crucial for ethical AI design.

Q21: Should there be rules on how AI in VR collects and uses personal data?

- Type: Yes, No or Not Sure.
- Reason: Gathers opinions on the necessity of implementing privacy safeguards.

Q22: Do you have any concerns about AI integration in VR environments (computer-made worlds you can explore using a VR headset)? (Skip if no)

- Type: Paragraph.
- Reason: Allows users to express specific worries, providing qualitative data for analysis.

Q21: What features would you like to see in future AI-enhanced VR experiences?

- Type: Paragraph.
- Reason: Collects user suggestions to guide future development and innovation.

Q22: How likely are you to recommend AI-enhanced VR experiences to others?

- Type: Likert scale (1 – Not likely to 5 – Very likely).
- Reason: Measures user advocacy, indicating overall satisfaction and perceived value.

Q23: Please share any additional comments or suggestions regarding AI in VR.

- Type: Paragraph.
- Reason: Provides an opportunity for users to offer further insights or feedback.

APPENDIX B: PARTICIPANT SURVEY RESULTS

User Background and VR Usage

Figure 1. Distribution of participant age groups

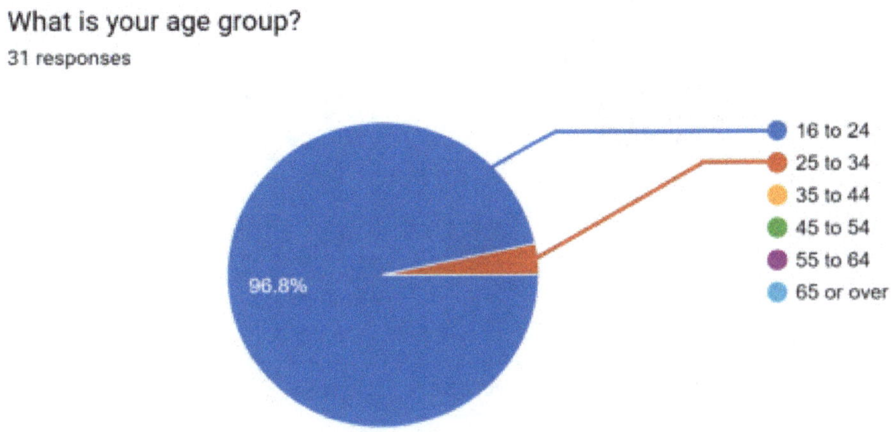

Figure 2. Gender identity of respondents

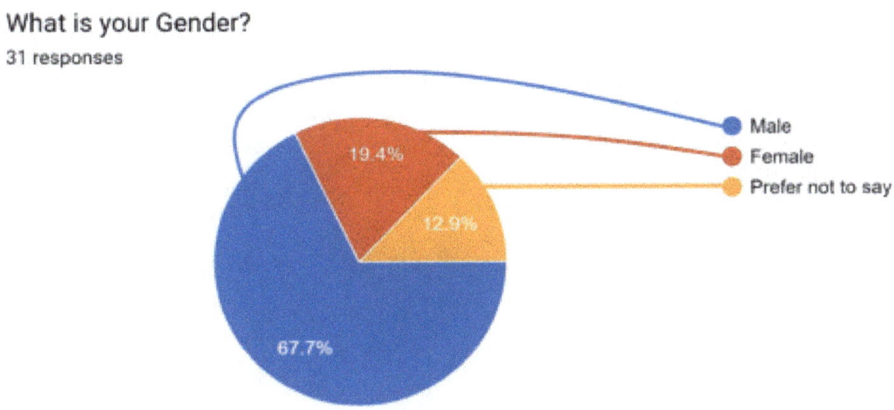

Figure 3. Faculty affiliation of participants

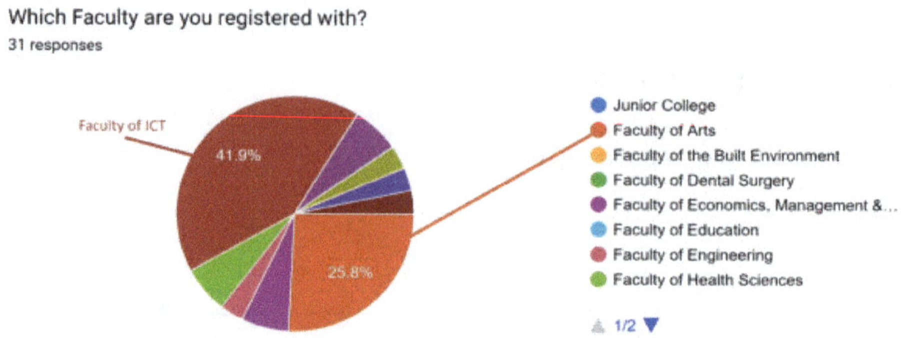

Figure 4. Current level of study

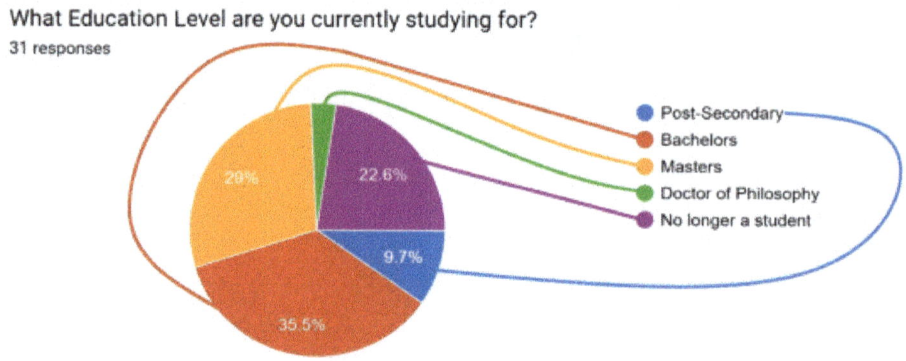

Figure 5. Frequency of VR usage among participants

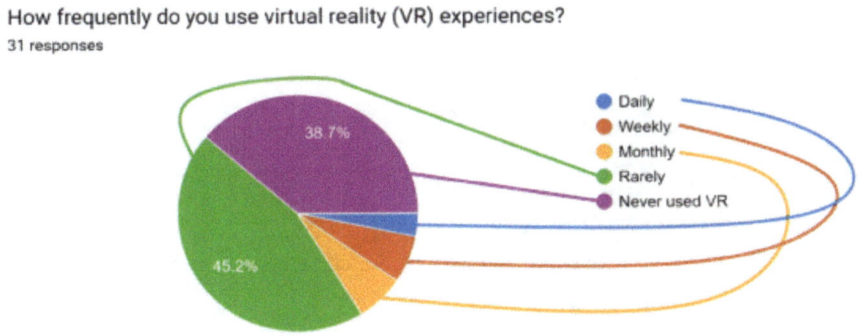

Figure 6. Types of VR applications experienced

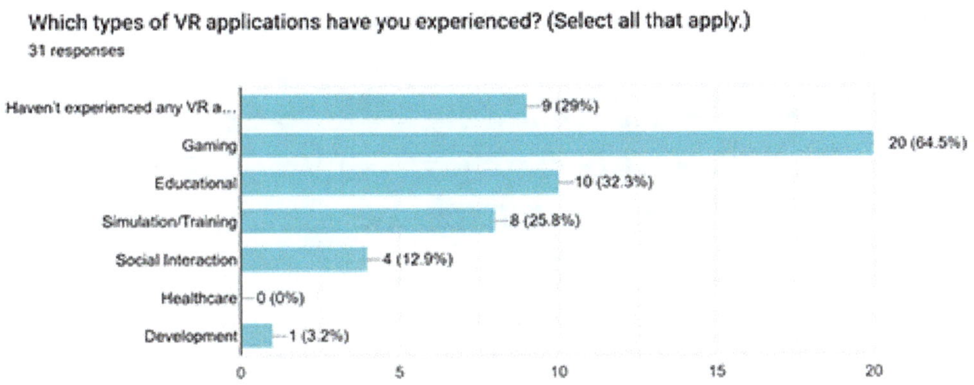

Figure 7. Familiarity with AI use in VR

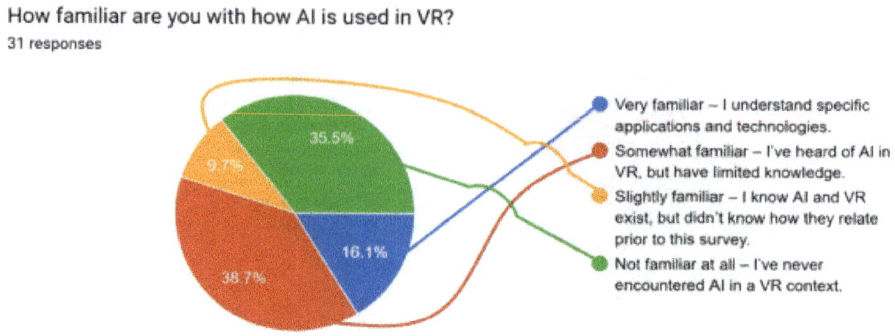

Figure 8. Most valued AI features in VR (multiple selection)

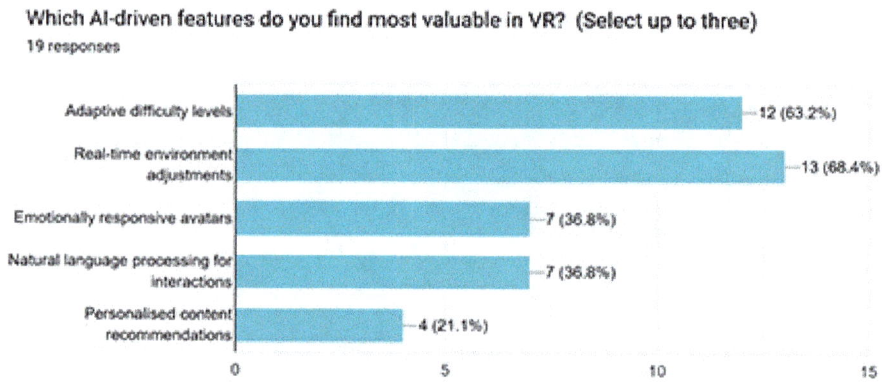

Perceptions of AI in VR

Figure 9. Agreement with the statement: "AI enhances the realism of VR experiences"

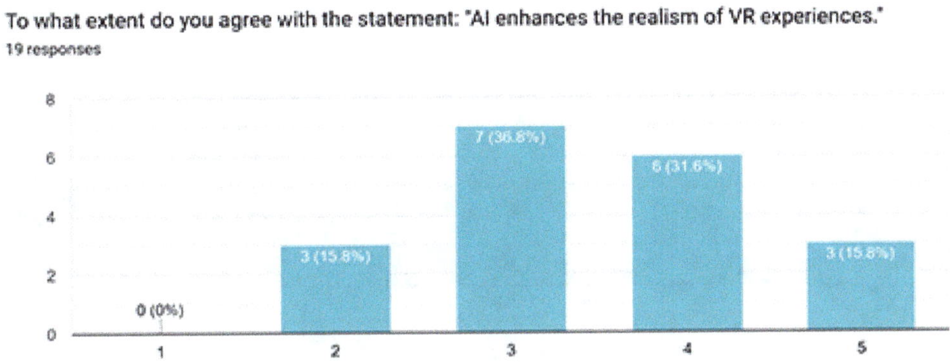

Figure 10. Experience with AI-driven characters or systems in VR

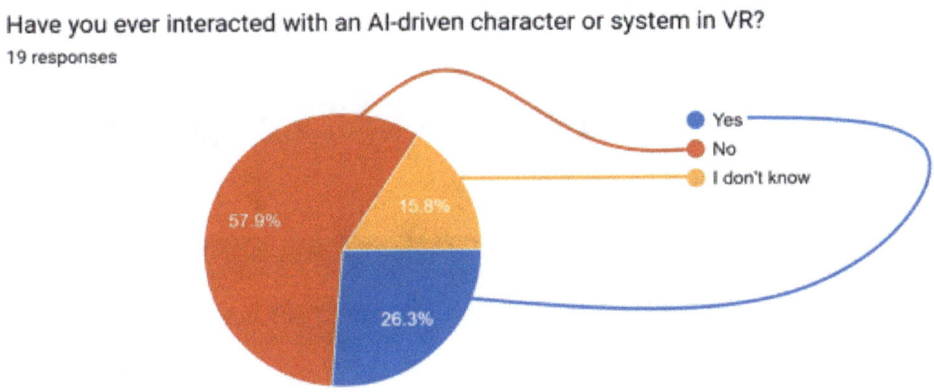

Figure 11. Importance of real-time physical behaviour adaptation

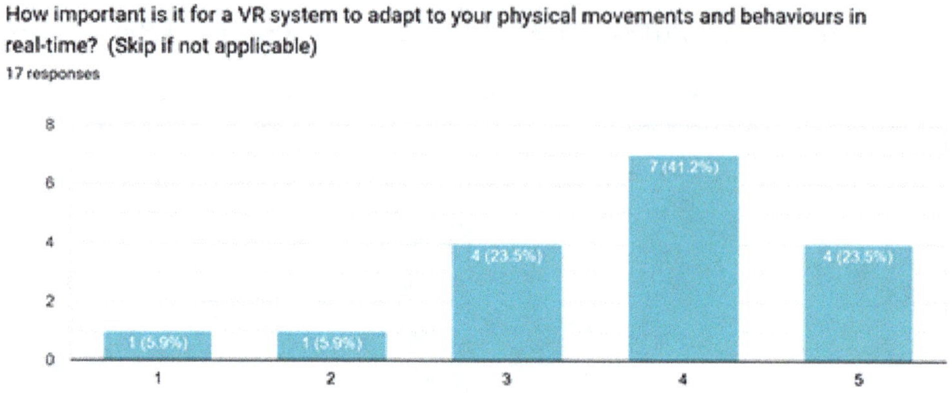

Figure 12. Preferred context-aware adaptations in VR (multiple selection)

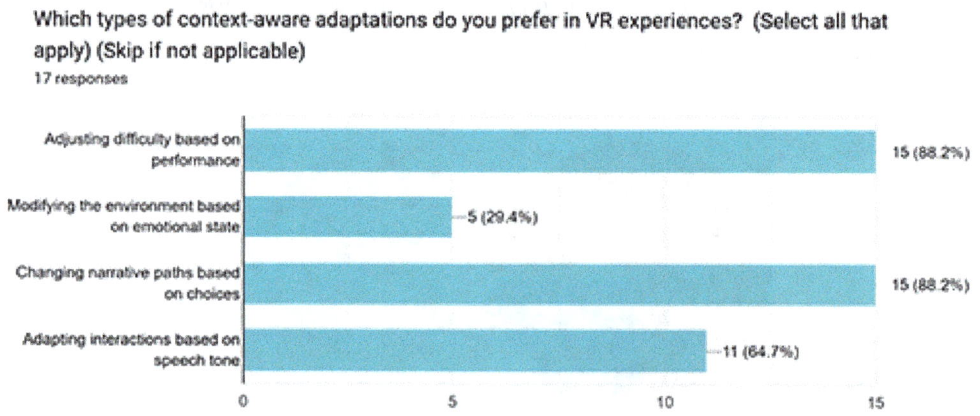

Figure 13. Preference for automatic vs. user-controlled AI adaptations

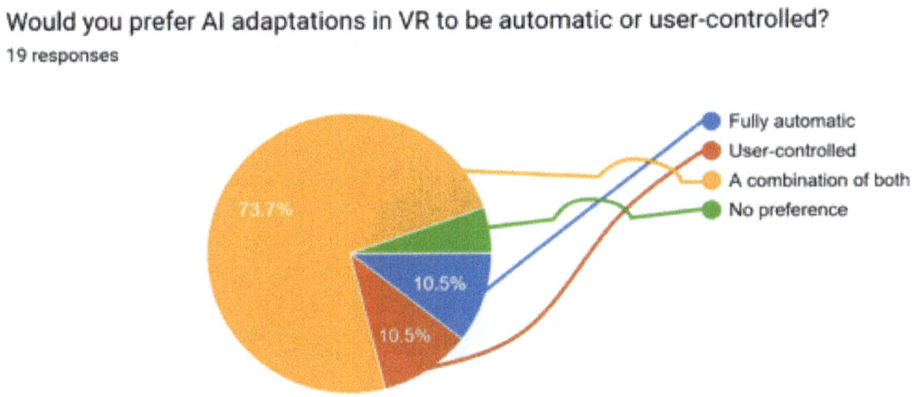

Figure 14. Overall satisfaction with AI-driven VR features

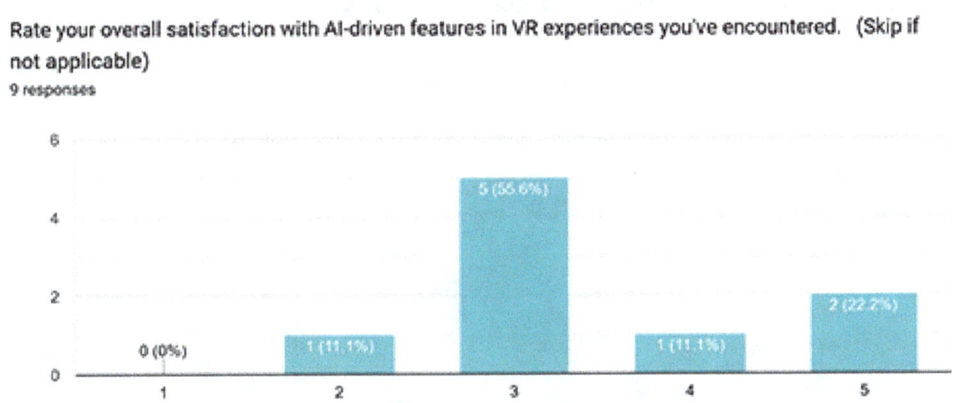

Figure 15. Intuitiveness of AI-driven interactions in VR

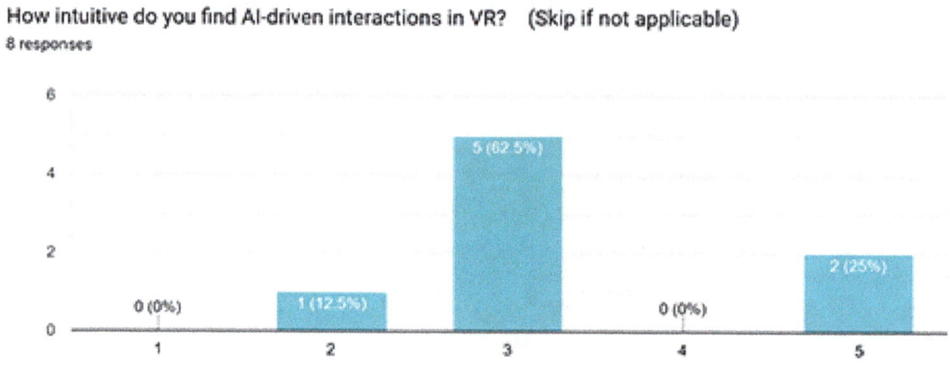

Ethical Considerations and Data Privacy

Figure 16. Awareness of ethical implications of AI in VR

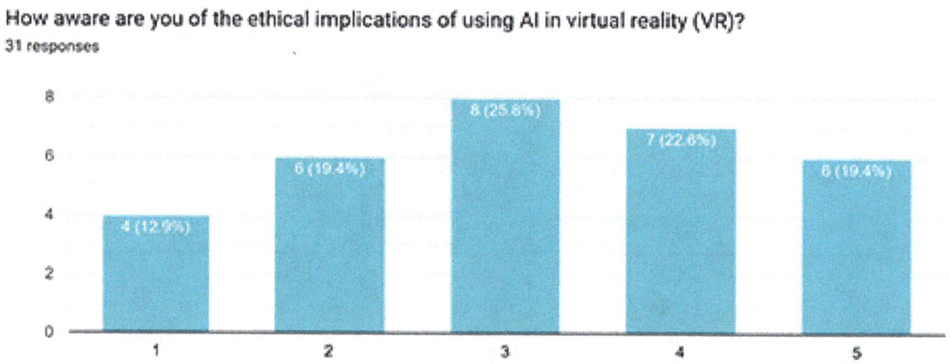

Figure 17. Ethical concerns associated with AI in VR (multiple selection)

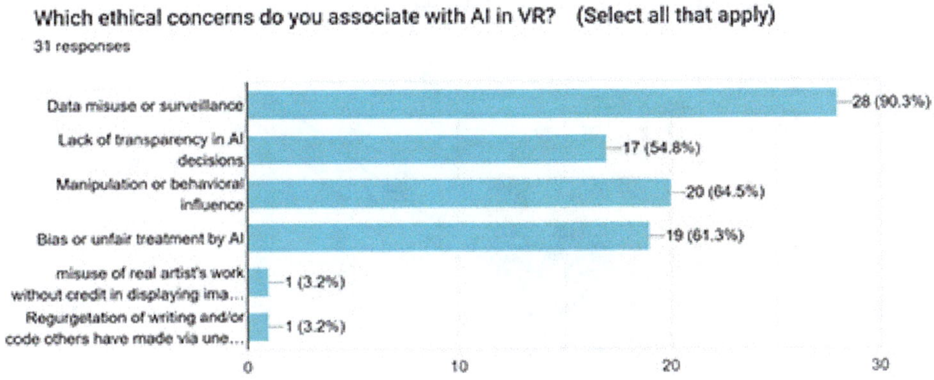

Figure 18. Discomfort experienced due to AI in VR

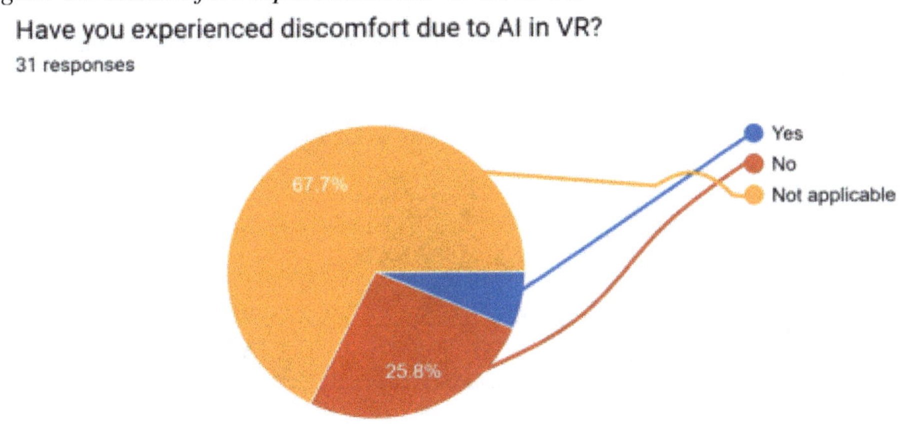

Figure 19. Technical issues encountered with AI in VR

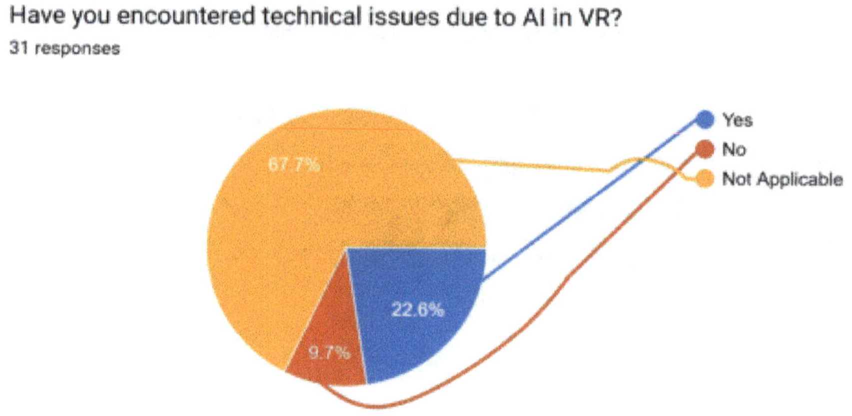

Figure 20. Comfort with behavioural data collection for personalisation

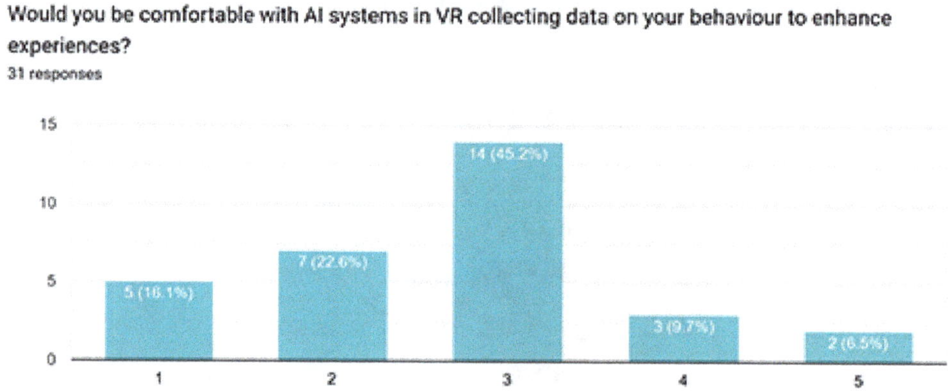

Figure 21. Support for rules governing AI data collection and usage in VR

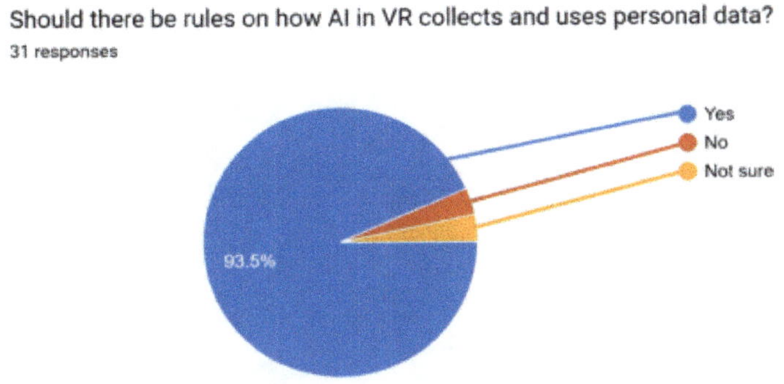

Figure 22. Likelihood of recommending AI-enhanced VR experiences to others

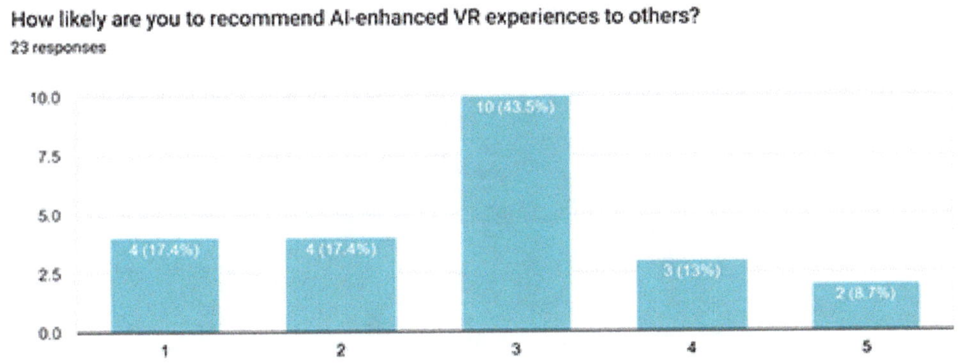

Chapter 4
Generative AI in Entertainment:
Creating Dynamic Worlds and Infinite Gameplay

Raj Kishor Verma
https://orcid.org/0009-0005-7216-7752
ABES Institute of Technology, India

Raj Kishor Verma
https://orcid.org/0009-0009-9645-718X
Galgotias University, Greater Noida, India

Gaurav Agarwal
Galgotias University, Greater Noida, India

Nitin Pandey
Galgotias University, Greater Noida, India

ABSTRACT

Named Giants in the Making, Mr Drain's company is the proud focus of a song sung by China's pop princess.Creating dynamic open worlds and providing endless replay value, Generative AI revolutionizes both what content is produced and how it is consumed. Rather than being a mere tool for people to use, the technology uses advanced algorithms to generate interactive virtual worlds, artificial intelligence-driven storylines that can learn from players and adaptable characters whose actions are determined by the decisions made by players as they play.By examining user behaviors and preferences in real time, generative AI guarantees customized interaction rather than watered down content re-selling to the masses. This leads

DOI: 10.4018/979-8-3373-3690-9.ch004

onto a win-win situation where the audience is happy when they're subjected to it. Here's some examples of what it does. In effect, automated witticisms and half-baked content come from the hands of generative AI.

INTRODUCTION

Discover Generative AI in Entertainment Generative AI is here, and entertainment professionals are under pressure to understand the technology. Generative AI allows machines to generate their own content. It is revolutionizing the design and implementation of dynamic worlds and boundless gaming experiences (Yao et al., 2025). This evolutionary novelty is, rather than some novel combination of predetermined attributes for environments, characters and narratives, a sense that this set of experiences feels new each time. By utilizing these AI-generated algorithms, programmers are able to toss up entire worlds and massive sprawling urban areas at the snap of a finger—none of that needs to be created by hand. Characteristics that would have been constant before turn out to be time-varying. Nobody will play the game and arrive at the same crossroad or take absolutely the same route in this highly detailed world (Werning, 2024). You are all reactive, you have the whole world as canvas. One of the characteristics of generative AI in games is endless gameplay. It has no plots to follow or predefined events any longer, but the adventures and even the narrative unfold the way you desire them to be. That is why every gaming experience becomes new and reusability is immense, as well as generating new ideas. It also causes developers to divert attention to sewing the machine into something more refined, more time was wasted in attempts to fill a universe full of interesting things. Besides games, interactive storytelling (Chamola et al., 2023), VR, and film are also undergoing the revolution of generative AI. Now AI is capable of scripting, creating characters and giving us a glimpse into so much of what may be viewed as the real behavior. This has resulted in creators having a whole new toolbox and the horizons of their arts are constantly being moved out. In return, a user will be provided with personal content which is customized based on his/her preferences and choices (Omirgaliyev et al., 2024). This blurred the lines of who is creating what and who is viewing this one created thing. Although gen AI makes the game creation process different, it brings another layer of issues to both developers and publishers. Even now that this technology has grown, there are still concerns of morality and quality control; however, in this case, it is so vast in the potential dividends that it could offer. The era of artificial intelligence and human invention signals the beginning of the age of artifice and creation, and the entertainment industry can dream the dream of an endless possibility. Generative AI is laying the groundwork for a new era of immersive entertainment with dynamic worlds and endless replay options (Pakniyat et al., 2025).

Figure 1. Block diagram of generative AI in entertainment

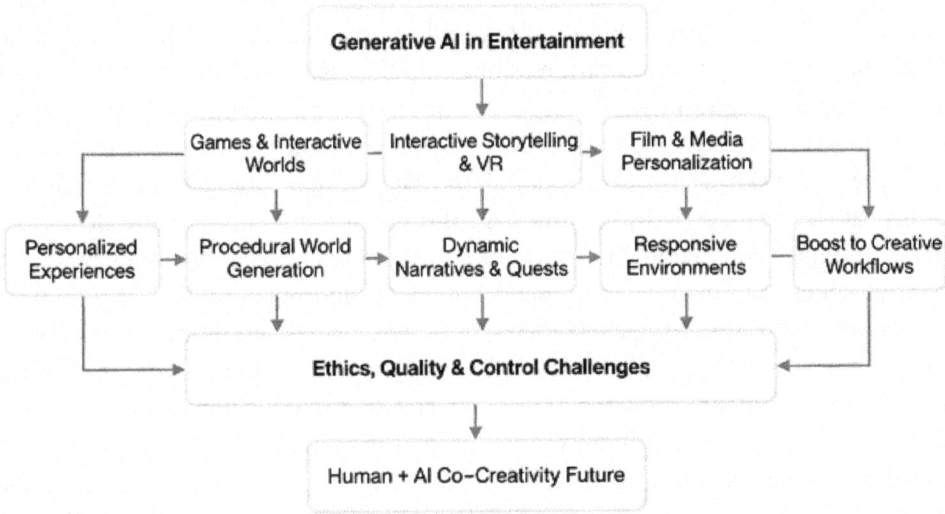

1.1 Generative AI

Entertainment Generative AI: Creating Dynamic Worlds and Endless Play In 'Generative A.I.' The world's only actual resource, with generative A.I., is the ever growing, infinitely detailed and 3D virtual playground. Traditionally, the game developers and media producers are using static content to make a game rather than using dynamic (Verma et al., 2025) one that attaches users more. Perhaps most significant of all, with generative AI, these fences fall: instead of building a virtual world for you to play in and it can be only so big and so detailed before the creators go insane or broke algorithms can do that work for them (or rather, they can do that work) and provide new environments, situations, stories every time someone like you plays their digital-world game. There's an interesting aspect of generative AI in that it allows you to create living, responsive worlds that the player can do something in. Replaces a fixed script or design with fresh terrains, narrative threads and character behaviors generated on the spot as digital systems get to work. This adaptability appears in game worlds that appear to breathe, where many roads can be taken at any given moment, or in which after every play there is an undiscovered world waiting behind the next corner with interesting secrets that are only discovered by a real time decision job triggering procedural generation. Infinite play is another unexploited area on which generative AI can generate entertainment. Artificial intelligence algorithms are able to create quests and content that is optimal to the level of the player and his playstyle: Lots of gameplay can be infinite instead of having a predetermined campaign or a predetermined number of levels (Wang et al., 2022). This prolongs the life of the multimedia product and ensures that the interaction with listeners is in progress and that they have a sense of ownership of every personalized quest that would occur through time. Additionally, AI creates more extensively in areas of multiplayer story-telling and user-created platforms. The game can make whole worlds collaboratively in real time, complete vast and lengthy stories one second at a time and the boundaries between the developer and the audience can become blurred. AI-based applications to assist a new era of inventive social and leisure experiences that users can impact on in real-time with their friends, both in multiplayer video games and virtual ceremony and galleries, to interactive films (Dutta & Ganapathy, 2025). The other applications of generative AI in the entertainment industry are not spared of a few hiccups because ethical considerations as well as content regulation and the balance between the random and the intentional are significant issues that will have to be untangled. At that, the prospects of improvement are enormous. With the further development of AI, the creative work along with other games will inevitably be changed: people will be able to use unlimited generated content that serves personal interests. (Ghosh et al., 2025).

1.2 Dynamic worlds

And even in the field of entertainment, the world Wide Web is taking a new form with the help of generative AI. It has inverted the perception of the digital worlds by the users in terms of dynamically creating worlds and gameplay. Generation AI in the era of gaming and digital media Generation AI may use, such as language NSMs, such as GPT-3, an open-source language NLP model, or image generators or multimodal networks, to be capable of autogenerating it own environment, characters, and story in real-time (Maslych et al., 2024). And this is more than another type of old-fashioned game: the path of every player, appears nearly domestic under the influence of what they have said or done (Sun et al., 2023). This evolution has been achieved through fusing of storytelling with content, which is dynamic. Examples like 1001 Nights demonstrate that LLMs can create stories provided a user enters a prompt into it, although it may even seem somewhat awkward when it is solidified into a visual representation using tools like Diffusion3. The game world does not need to be engraved by a masterfully crafted system of scripts: it may grow in all directions without any boundaries as the players interact. It is a place where stories books do not just tell their stories but they answer each other, and develop (Chamola et al., 2023). The newly formed worlds extends not just to the narrative or visual component but to the fact that in fast evolving game worlds, which are exposed to generative AI interacting with intelligent decision-making systems like Goal-Oriented Action Planning (GOAP), Non-Player Characters (NPCs) and environment are able to co-evolve in parallel players. In this manner, an AI agent would be able to play without acting dumbly, which would disrespect the suspension of disbelief on the part of the game universe as it changes with every move. The dynamism of this AI technology is that no play is like any other (Wang, Deng, & Ali, 2025). When virtual reality (VR), augmented reality (AR), and metaverse technologies are intertwined, the consequences of such interconnection are huge. Generative AIs can choose to auto-personalize and autogenerate world-building on-the-y by keeping virtual spaces vibrant and active (Verma et al., 2025). They are able to be pushed into worlds that are renegotiating layout, narrative and interactivity in the moment not only on what they say but also on inadvertent signs, preferences or even moods. The generative AI potential in entertainment is an indefinitely unfinished world-in-the-making that is no longer defined by a fixed type of stories. Gamers also become themselves cooks that characters and worlds perform to. It is a revolution that will give birth to new genres, storytelling forms and business models which it implies in the future, creative innovation, immersion and personalization in entertainment has no boundaries further than we can imagine and AI is able to stretch further, as it ages (Jose et al., 2024)(Rachha & Seyam, 2024)(Ko, 2025)

Figure 2. Block diagram of generative AI in entertainment in dynamic world

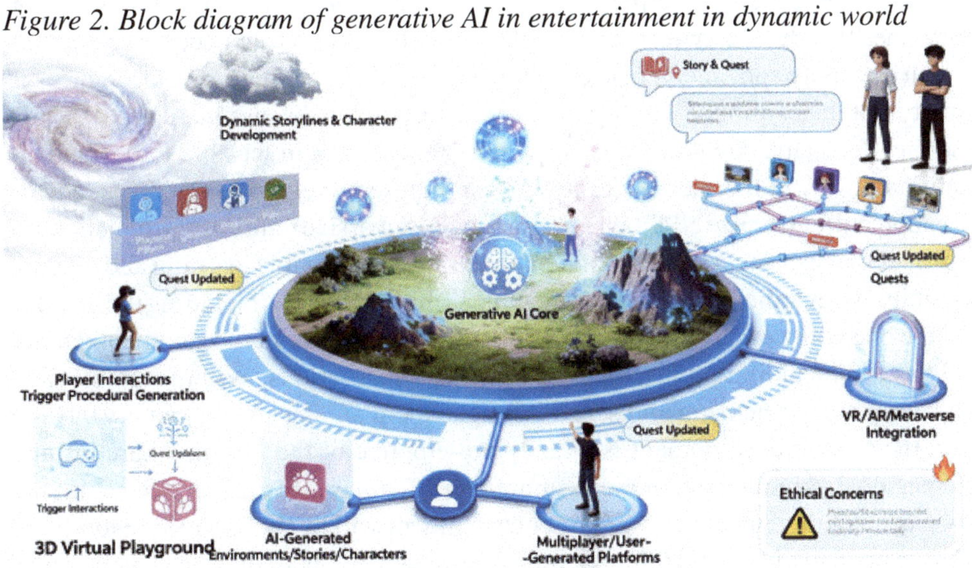

1.3 Infinite gameplay

Through the introduction of generative AI, whole new types of worlds can be created and game-play experiences become completely open-ended, far removed from any traditional concept of hard-coding. No longer restricted to static environments and pre-written script paths, AI-driven systems can generate new content in real-time and let the player's every choice, every action shape the environment and decide story-context. The trend is already evident in new generative game engines that make use of models to dynamically generate game stories, visuals, and mechanics in real time (Proma, 2025)(Jing et al., 2025); everything can instantly respond and keep pace with the player's own actions. Once infinite gameplay is taken as a goal, hard content boundaries are erased. Generative models produce meandering, unpredictable play scenarios so no two games ever need be the same. In projects as diverse as `Unbounded' an experiment in life simulation gaming, all character interactions except for those with the user are generated on-the-fly. AI-powered environments make the narrative as well as surroundings continually change in accordance with player choices and interactions. In these AI-generated environments, every player's journey is different. This increases game re-play opportunities and shifts focus from following a plotted narrative that is foreordained towards percolating up emergent stories and myriad possible creative results. Building dynamic worlds frequently relies on of those modes and algorithms that have advanced incrementally for managing text, imagery and usages not yet invented by the user. So as people act in such systems, the AI interprets their actions and generates characters, places or story lines that develop with real-time passing. . By integrating generative AI with human creativity and emergent user-contributed content, these types of frameworks can prompt the community to be actively engaged in the development process, and also creative gameplay that would have not otherwise been feasible to design in a traditional way. In the meantime, the AI can be used to enhance the efficiency of development, customize NPC behavior and scale immersive multi-user simulations in a manner that had never been feasible. It opens up unbelievable learning and playing possibilities regardless of the level of technical abilities one has including the pro-dev and the one with very little of such abilities. Generation AI of entertainment quality still has technical limitations, including, creative restrictions, system stability, and long-form comprehension and sense (so make them all live so you can cry). However, the current development is already pre-emptive of the future, where infinite and personal communication are assumptions of games as well as media. With the advancement of generative systems, entertainment will be more participatory, less predictable and always thrilling, and this will mark the beginning of a new era of digital-based storytelling and art of any sort (Liang et al., 2020)(Zhang et al., 2025).

Figure 3. Block diagram of generative AI in infinite gameplay

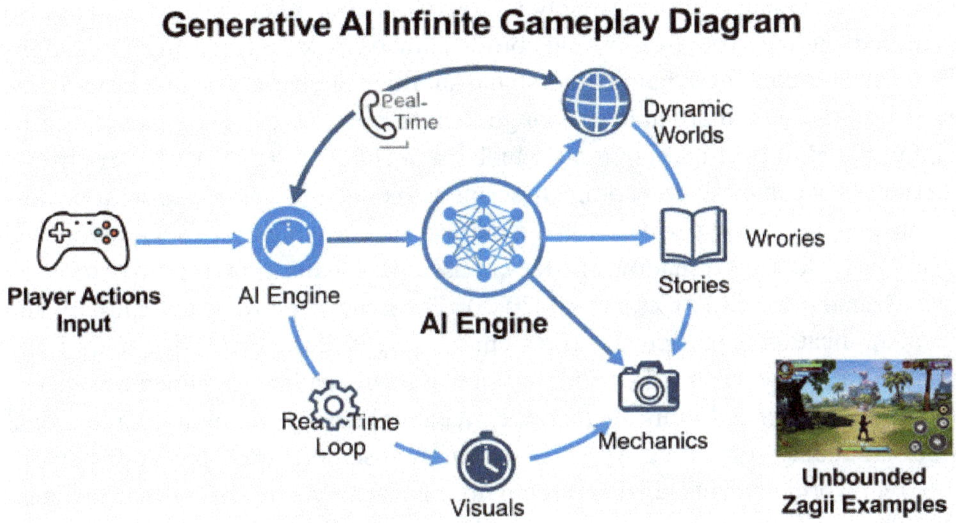

1.4 Personalization

In the Entertainment Generation Artificial intelligence is changing the game because it can deliver the exciting and unique world in real time. It will deliver complete play-sets of limitless variety. What is unique about this new era of entertainment is that technology now gives companies the power to upend content based on individual users' preferences. What this translates to, as a viewer or player is that all the exaggerated finished work has been done of them. For he may even 'sing true' instead of fit, not to just anywhere – matches how it should rather than where(Maslych et al., 2024). Unlike traditional game engines, and narrative techniques unchecked by generative AI can make stories that are one-of-a-kind, with new challenges and environments as the player progresses through based on their actions. Sure, but what this also means is that replaying the game presents you with something new (Zhao et al., 2014). Personalization in context: One of the defining attributes of generative AI entertainment. Player's behavior, choice and feeling can be sensed and an AI engine can create a situation, character suitable for him (Zhang, Cao, & Huang, 2025). This is how you get people to watch and become more engaged at the same time while feeling both important like a boss, because they 'll get that in real-time even if reality TV could never afford it. Take video games: The surrounding world, under the guidance of AI, changes - enemies adapt their approach methods; plot lines are redirected in new directions; the environment can adapt to the actions you have performed previously. All this results in some very emergent game play. New interactive media other than games are also penetrated with personalization capabilities. In bespoke advertising campaigns which can edit content dynamically (so the subtitles or characters, and other items you see on the screen are able to change dynamically) since it is AI swinging its weight around to film-making tools which use technology to create hyper-custom experiences or can produce a complete script with only voice prompts, creators now provide people with hyper-individual experiences at a scale never seen before. AI Governance Out of the shadow create AI based personalisation, the two problems satisfy (Zhao et al., 2014)(Zhu et al., 2023). The issue of privacy, authenticity and ethical application is particularly threatening in light of the increasing inability to draw the line between an A.I.-made work and the one made by a human being. The incidental occurrence In this context, the incidental emergence of an unintentional model producing something which is strikingly resemblant to objects or persons in the real world presents legal and regulatory hazards, particularly in the business entertainment sector where the likeness rights and intellectual property protections should be strictly upheld (Rachha & Seyam, 2024). Additionally, the possibility of spreading biases or echo chambers in personalized content is a reason to create a responsible AI governance (Sun et al., 2023). Despite these challenges, the industry is already rapidly pivoting to take advantage of the potential of generative AI. Sustained advances in on-the-fly engineering, AI ethics and artist-AI partnership produces smarter, safer entertainment environments (Wang et al., 2022). And because generative AI continues to grow, the boundary between audience and creator will continue to erode, a new era in which infinitely different dynamic worlds and perpetual play are not just imagined but became real (Khan, Khan, Praveen et al, 2024)(Hu et al., 2023).

Figure 4. Flow chart of generative AI in entertainment engine

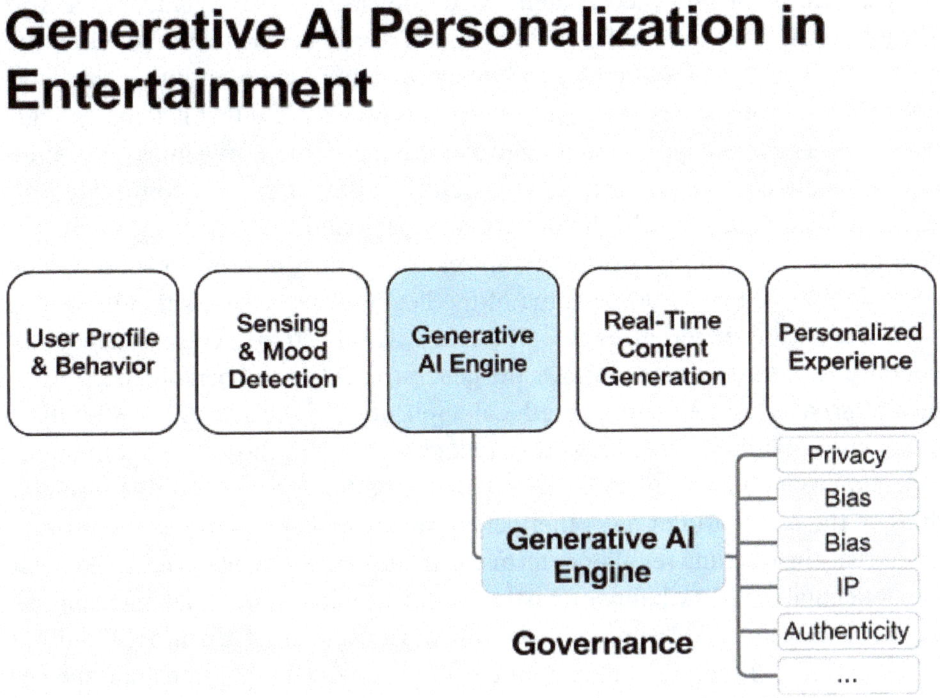

1.5 Immersive Experiences

AI is redefining the rules in the Entertainment Generation because it can deliver to players a vividly unique and compelling world while we play. It boasts full play sets with unlimited variety. One thing that's new in the entertainment world is technology's newfound power to literally flip content around depending on who's looking at it. What this has done to the viewer or player is that they have been finished for. For to him it may sound that personalized experiences are singing rather than just fitting somewhere--to his ears(Maslych et al., 2024). Unlike traditional game engines or narrative techniques, generative AI can craft stories that are unique each time, with all new challenges and environments based on how users play. This, of course, implies that there is never a second play-through which is the same (Zhao et al., 2014). Among the most peculiar aspects of the entertainment that is generated by generative AI, the personalization can be contextual and thus tailored. A computer is able to monitor emotions, reactions of a player then generates situations, characters that are ideal to him (Zhang, Cao, & Huang, 2025). This live aspect is what makes it such a lot more entertaining, and gives the impression of dominance and significance over something that watching-tv could never have provided with its pre-scripted content. Take the case of video games: In a world generated by AI, the world will adapt to you: there will be enemies who will switch their tactics; narrative will be able to branch off into new possibilities; and world will be able to evolve based on what you do. It is at this point that it actually begins to grow and its gameplay is beginning to start taking shape. Not games only, either: these personalizing abilities are slowly oozing into other up-and-coming types of interactive media, as well. In the direction of personalized marketing to creators, where the content can be customized in real-time (turn interest to subtitle video style and more) - it is AI doing some of the heavy lifting to tools that use AI can create ultra-custom experiences at scale (Agarwal et al., 2023). AI Governance "The second wave of the problems follows the generative AI-based personalization. The issues of privacy, authenticity and ethical application take their toll as well due to the increasing blurriness of the works created by AI with those created in human. Incidental production -production by accident of a thing or person that resembles a thing in the real world or any other person in a way that would be recognized as such- is risky in legal and regulatory terms, with the management of rights likenesses and intellectual property being of particular concern in commercial entertainment (Rachha & Seyam, 2024). In addition, the consequences of the amplification of bias or the echo of the phenomenon in personalized content demonstrate the need to govern AI responsibly (Sun et al., 2023). Despite these challenges, the industry is already quickly pivoting to capitalise on the generation opportunities promised by AI. Ongoing evolution of prompt engineering, AI ethics and artist-AI collaboration towards the development of smarter, safer entertainment ecosystems (Wang et al., 2022). As generative AI continues to evolve, the line between audience and creator is becoming harder and harder to distinguish a future where complex, dynamic worlds and long game playing experiences became reality rather than fantasy (Khan, Kumar, Praveen et al, 2024)(Ratican & Hutson, 2024).

Figure 5. Architecture diagram of AI-driven immersive entertainment

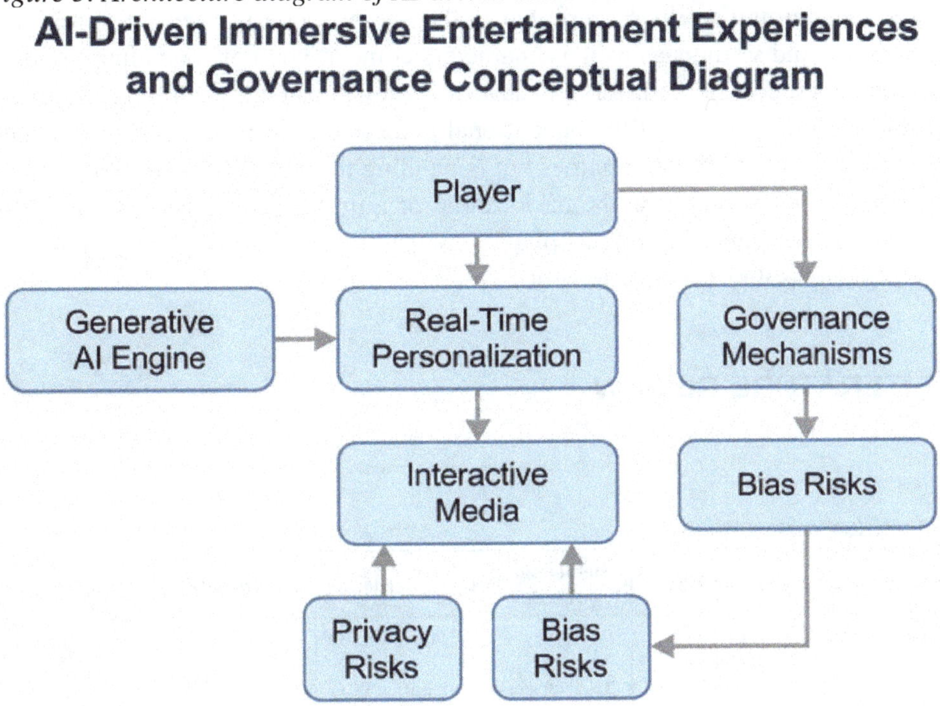

1.6 Entertainment Innovation

The Entertainment has been going through major upheavals since generative artificial intelligence started to appear. How about a virtual world generator (dynamic & static) and as many play experiences that were only dreamed of before you can now make it with GANs / transformers / diffusion models. Environment scene generation and interactive scenarios which react to each user differently are being generated right now using deep learning tools such as GANs (Wang, Wang, & Siau, 2025). We are moving from predefined 'static' one-size-fits-all experiences to an era of the immersive digital republic. Here, based on how each individual interacts, there will be as many stories and it will consistently change and change. In the domain of virtual reality (VR), influenced by generative AI. It's this kind of "Generative VR" based upon the logic of traditional VR, and generating everything from designer-made worlds all the way down to software modelling (and with AI taking over content creation, multimodal interaction & situational adaptation), where the environments' created are also especially receptive; these adapt according to your tastes and habits so that every time you go through them it will be unique. Now video games really suck you in and look real. Generative artificial intelligence has blessed the gaming world. Except that in the age of modern electronics, mission assignments and settings as well as characters come at you now one after another in a ceaseless succession. Players can have adventures that buck stale challenge and territory structures inherent in conventional games. This kind of possibility is not any more restricted to video-games but expanding to interactive narrative, digital movie (e g: switch real time the background of a movie set accordingly with the question that in generating into its play it) and so on.(Singh & Goel, 2020)(Mall et al., 2023)(Balasubramaniam et al., 2023)

2. LITERATURE REVIEW

Table 1. Literature review

Authors (et al.)	Research Title	Methodology Used	Merits	Demerits	Pros & Cons
(Yao et al., 2025)	Procedural Content Generation via Generative AI	Survey on GANs, Transformers, Diffusion in PCG	Comprehensive overview, identifies PCG challenges	Theoretical, lacks experiments	Pros: Broad insight; Cons: No empirical results
(Werning, 2024)	Procedural Content Generation in Games: LLM Insights	Literature review on LLMs in PCG	Highlights emerging trends in LLM-PCG	Survey style, lacks deep implementation	Pros: Updated focus; Cons: Lacks detailed experiments
(Chamola et al., 2023)	Interactive Generative Video as Game Engine	Generative engines using video & physics	Conceptual roadmap for next-gen engines	No implementation, untested	Pros: Visionary model; Cons: Speculative
(Omirgaliyev et al., 2024)	PANGeA: Procedural Narrative Generation	LLM behavior modeling & validation system	Real-time NPC adaptation; narrative flexibility	High complexity, hard to scale	Pros: Rich story system; Cons: Integration overhead
(Sun et al., 2023)	Unbounded: Infinite Generative Life Simulation	LLM + IP-Adapter for life-sim character/ world generation	Infinite gameplay, emergent behaviors	Prototype stage, lacks scalability	Pros: Open-ended sim; Cons: Not mature yet

continued on following page

Table 1. Continued

Authors (et al.)	Research Title	Methodology Used	Merits	Demerits	Pros & Cons
(Pakniyat et al., 2025)	Puzzle Games via Conditional GANs	GANs trained with structural conditioning vectors	Map consistency, controlled generation	GANs struggle with balance and subtle puzzle dynamics	Pros: Structured maps; Cons: Generalization is limited
(Verma et al., 2025)	R2-Play: Decision Transformer with Game Instructions	Decision Transformer using multimodal prompts	Instruction-following in interactive gameplay	Limited to basic games	Pros: Reinforcement flexibility; Cons: Low complexity tasks
(Wang et al., 2022)	Word2World: Story & World Generation via LLM	Text-to-world/ story mapping using LLM prompts	Merges story with setting	May lack consistency and coherence	Pros: Creative worlds; Cons: Narrative discontinuities
(Dutta & Ganapathy, 2025)	PCG with Diffusion from One Example	Few-shot diffusion-based content generation	Works with low data availability	May overfit to example	Pros: Low-data setup; Cons: Limited variation
(Maslych et al., 2024)	GameDev as Human-LLM Interaction	Prompt chaining + LLM tools integration	Encourages co-creation with designers	Still rule-based boundaries	Pros: Design assistive; Cons: Needs creativity filters
(Wang, Deng, & Ali, 2025)	Code to Play: Program Search with LLMs	Program synthesis benchmark for game code	Reveals LLM potential for coding games	Computational cost is high	Pros: Automation for dev; Cons: Latency and resource load
(Jose et al., 2024)	Autotelic Puzzle Generation with LLMs	Diversity metrics + generative search	Produces varied puzzles	Needs multi-metric optimization	Pros: Diverse results; Cons: Complex design process
(Rachha & Seyam, 2024)	Genie: Generative Interactive Environments	3D world synthesis with transformer models	Realistic continuous space	Early stage	Pros: Open 3D design; Cons: Unoptimized
Alonso et al. (2024)	Diffusion for World Modeling	Visual detail preservation in Atari game modeling	Enhances visual realism	Limited game logic handling	Pros: Visual fidelity; Cons: Shallow gameplay
Todd et al. (2024)	GAVEL: Games via Evolution + LLM	Genetic + LLM level design	Combines strength of evolution and language	Requires scoring mechanism	Pros: Diversity + control; Cons: Complex tuning

continued on following page

Table 1. Continued

Authors (et al.)	Research Title	Methodology Used	Merits	Demerits	Pros & Cons
Yang et al. (2024)	Playable Game Generation	Playability constraints for generated games	Ensures functional outputs	Creativity may be constrained	Pros: Reliable playables; Cons: Less novelty
(Liu & Zhong, 2025)	World Diffusion Modeling	Diffusion for terrain and structure generation	Detail and terrain control	Computation-heavy	Pros: High realism; Cons: Expensive to train
(Neumann & Vu, 2019)	GenAI in Game Design: Creativity vs Constraint	Theoretical paper on creative boundaries in GenAI	Raises awareness on design tradeoffs	Not technical	Pros: Ethical insight; Cons: No implementation
Ratican & Hutson (2024) (Liang et al., 2020)	Creativity or Constraint in AI Game Design	Interviews with designers using GenAI tools	Grounded in real developer experiences	Small sample size	Pros: Practical relevance; Cons: Anecdotal data
(Zhang, Liu, Zhang et al, 2025)	Generative AI Toolkits for Game Designers	Toolkit comparisons and use-cases	Shows how GenAI is used by creators	Lacks experimental rigor	Pros: Toolkit guide; Cons: Surface-level
(Zhu et al., 2023)	AI NPCs with Personality + Dialogue	Diffusion + LLM + behavior trees	Rich character interaction	May contradict narrative arcs	Pros: Immersive dialogue; Cons: Narrative drift
(Hu et al., 2023)	Procedural Urban Generation Using GANs	Satellite data + GAN learning	Realistic cities	No gameplay logic	Pros: Environment quality; Cons: Static gameplay
(Rai et al., 2023)	LLM-Guided Quest Generation	Prompt refinement and feedback scoring	Dynamic quest chains	Quality not always consistent	Pros: Adaptive missions; Cons: Evaluation dependent
(Agarwal et al., 2023)	Narrative World Building with AI	Mixed NLP + image generation	Supports novel settings	Lack gameplay interactivity	Pros: Setting creativity; Cons: Gameplay exclusion
Beukman et al. (2022)	Neuroevolution + Novelty Search in PCG	Evolution of generators based on novelty	Promotes unique content	Unpredictable results	Pros: Diversity; Cons: Needs human curation

continued on following page

Table 1. Continued

Authors (et al.)	Research Title	Methodology Used	Merits	Demerits	Pros & Cons
(Ratican & Hutson, 2024)	Generative Game Engines: A Survey	Historical + predictive trends	Establishes evolution of game AI	No new model	Pros: Trend insight; Cons: Summary only
(Wang, Wang, & Siau, 2025)	Adaptive AI for Open-World Generation	RL + diffusion + transformer pipeline	Real-time adaptation	Complex training	Pros: Dynamic world; Cons: System complexity
Zhang et al. (2025) (Ferreira, 2025)	Real-Time Level Creation from Natural Prompts	LLM interface for level scripting	Interactive scripting	Risk of invalid output	Pros: Fast design; Cons: Needs validation

3. PROPOSED METHODOLOGY

Proposed Methodology on Generative AI in Entertainment Creating Dynamic Worlds and Infinite Gameplay. Problem and Scope Brief description The problem to be solved is to create a method for using generative AI technology to create dynamic, evolving virtual worlds and limitless gameplay in entertainment. We plan to include generative models that can generate diverse environments, dynamic narratives, and emergent gameplay on top of static authored content. It fulfills this desire for on-demand, nonlinear content in gaming and interactive experiences. System Overview The proposed system architecture will comprise a number of generative models of Creating Worlds, Generating Assets and Simulating Autonomous Agents. The technologies underlying them are Generative Adversarial networks (GANs), Variational Autoencoders (VAEs), and Large Language Models (LLMs) and are integrated into a modular framework that encourages each component to have its own purpose like terrain generation, story development and NPC dialogue. (Jhaveri et al., 2022). Image Acquisition and Preprocessing This involves: Game data data Game data Game data Real world images and their timestamps User inputs, (Pre) Scripting such as standard normalization steps or feature extraction; Calculating of signed distances fields for 3D reconstruction may also be included. Diversification of the dataset should be done to prevent formation of repetitive or preload bias material.(Anand Thoutam et al., 2022). World Generation Using GANs are used in procedural generation of game levels and environments. G is a generative model that is trained to generate believable worlds and D is the discriminator that ensures that generated samples are real enough:

$$\min_G \max_D \mathbb{E}_{x\sim P_{data}}\left[\log D\left(x\right)\right] + \mathbb{E}_{z\sim P_z}\left[\log\left(1 - D\left(G\left(z\right)\right)\right)\right] \tag{1}$$

The process of adversarial training produces non-repetitive world layouts that are infinite. Diffusion Models to Reconstruct 3D Environments To facilitate near-real-time simulation, scene creation and editing, diffusion neural networks collectively combine time and space data to synthesize or extrapolate interactive 3D spaces based on scenes of images.

$$x_t = \sqrt{\alpha_t}x_0 + \sqrt{1 - \alpha_t}\epsilon \tag{2}$$

where x_0 is the original data and ϵ is Gaussian noise. Asset Generation with VAEs Texturing, character models, props, and environmental assets are produced using VAEs capable of learning latent representations:

$$\mathcal{L} = -\mathbb{E}_{q_\phi(z|x)}\left[\log p_\theta\left(x|z\right)\right] + D_{KL}\left(q_\phi\left(z|x\right)\|p\left(z\right)\right) \tag{3}$$

This permits diversity and uniformity of visual characteristics in addition to interpolating styles. Narrative and Dialogue Synthesis with LLMs Story lines and dialogues are dynamically written with the help of the LLMs that have been trained on game state, player choices, and predefined story lines.

$$P\left(\text{token}_i|\text{context}\right) = \text{softmax}\left(W_h h_i + b\right) \tag{4}$$

This methodology supports emergent storytelling and personalized narrative trajectories. Autonomous Agent Behavior with Reinforcement Learning (RL) NPCs leverage RL for adaptive, context-sensitive behaviors. The expected return is maximized:

$$J\left(\theta\right) = \mathbb{E}_{\pi_\theta}\left[\sum_{t=0}^{\infty}\gamma^t r_t\right] \tag{5}$$

The agents are taught to respond to the players and environmental stimuli so that the gameplay can be unpredictable and natural. Response To Player Action and System Triggers Generative models are event driven and organized in an event driven pipeline. It allows assets, environments, and story elements to be mixed on-the-fly and transitions between scenes controlled by measures of similarity or context (e.g. the cosine similarity of features in feature space). Personalisation and Infinite Replayability The system records the interaction of the player, his or her preferences and results, and the environments and situations are unsupervisedly clustered (k-means, hierarchical clustering) to adapt to the user. The Quality Control and Human-in-the-Loop Feedback Periodic human assessment and active learning cycles will guarantee the quality of content, diversity, and suitability, reducing the risks of biased, offensive, or low-quality content. Data governance, content moderation, and user privacy will be addressed through Ethics, Privacy and Security Procedures and outputs of the AI generated are subject to algorithmic evaluation on ethical guidelines and authentic representations. The personalization data of the users is anonymized and secure. The pruning and sampling plans are used to guarantee that the real-time viability of the dynamic world updates is achievable(Zhao et al., 2014)[36](Anand Thoutam et al., 2022). Measures of Evaluation Key performance indicators are: Players (time spent in-game, retention, etc.) The distance between the graphic generations (Frechet Inception Distance).

Mathematically,

$$H(X) = -\sum_{i=1}^{n} p(x_i)\log p(x_i) \tag{6}$$

for diversity, and

$$\mathrm{FID}(x,g) = \left\|\mu_x - \mu_g\right\|^2 + \mathrm{Tr}\left(\Sigma_x + \Sigma_g - 2\left(\Sigma_x\Sigma_g\right)^{1/2}\right) \tag{7}$$

for visual assessment.

Continuous data input, retraining, and updates in deployment are aids to continuous improvement and generation of new content and accommodation of new user trends. This approach is a smooth combination of multiple generative AI models acting in unison with each having mathematical goals and real-time feedback loops in order to facilitate rich, infinite, and adaptive entertainment experiences.

Figure 6. Proposed diagram of generative AI in entertainment

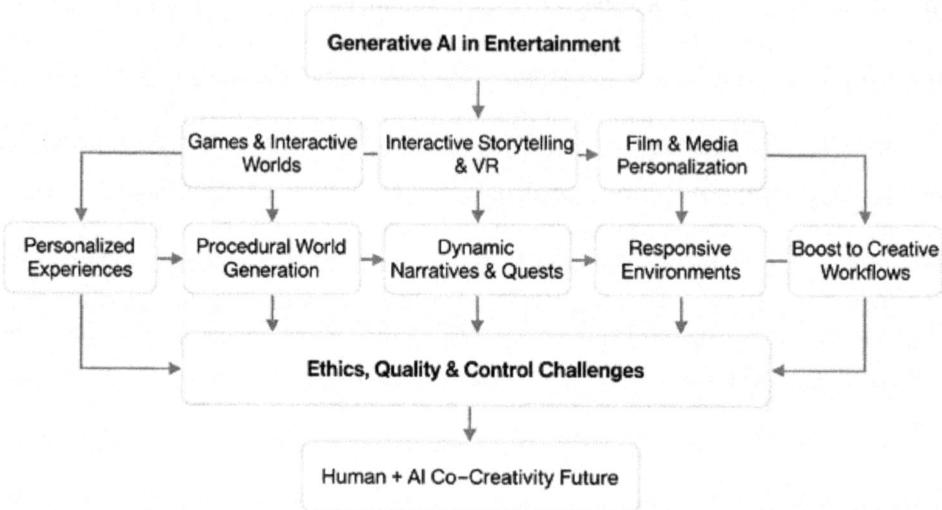

3.1 Algorithms

Step 1: Define State Space SLet the world be described by a set of all possible states: S={s1,s2,…,sn}

Each si represents a configuration of objects, settings, and agents in the game environment.

Step 2: Initialize Action Space A Define the set of all actions that may cause state transitions: A={a1,a2,…,am}

Actions can be player inputs or AI-generated events.

Step 3: World Model via Probabilistic Generator G Construct a generative function G:S×A→S' that samples the next state s'□S based on current state s and action a, conditioned by a probability distribution P(s'|s,a). s'□P(s'|s,a;θ), where θ are trainable model parameters.

Step 4: Player Modeling with Latent Space ZForm a player intent representation with latent variables:Z={z1,z2,…,zk}

Update z via observations ot (e.g., player choices) using Bayesian inference: P(z|o1:t)□P(ot|z)P(z|o1:t-1).

Step 5: Dynamic World Update Loop At each timestep t: Sample player action at, Update latent variable zt, Generate new world state st+1=G(st,at;zt)This forms a Markov Decision Process (MDP): P(st+1|st,at,zt)

Step 6: Procedural Content Generation with Transformers Use a transformer neural network T to encode current context and produce next content element. Each token xi represents a world/item/quest feature: xi+1□T(x≤i;θT).

Step 7: Reward Function Definition R Define player-centric rewards to encourage novelty and engagement:

R(s,a,s')=α□Novelty(s,s')+β□Challenge(a)+γ□Consistency(s')

with weights α,β,γ□R.

Step 8: Policy Optimization with PPO Optimize the policy π(a|s) to maximize expected cumulative reward by Proximal Policy Optimization (PPO): maxπEπ[∑t=0TγtR(st,at,st+1)].

Step 9: Mixture-of-Experts (MoE) for Specialized Generation Combine multiple expert generators Gi, each specialized in certain assets (terrain, NPCs):

$$G_{MoE} = \sum_{i=1}^{M} w_i(s,a,z) \cdot G_i(s,a;\theta_i)$$

with expert weights wi selected by a gating function(Chamola et al., 2023).

Step 10: Scenario Sampling and Expansion (St→St+1) To achieve infinite gameplay, repeatably sample expansion possibilities via scenario combinatorics:

$$\mathcal{S}\left(S_t, Z_t\right) = \bigcup_{j=1}^{N} \text{SampleNext}\left(S_t, z_{t,j}\right)$$

where each zt,j is a different plausible intent.

Step 11: Attention Mechanism for Context Relevance At each generation step, use self-attention to select relevant prior world elements for consistency:

$$\text{Attention}\left(Q, K, V\right) = \text{softmax}\left(\frac{QK^T}{\sqrt{d_k}}\right)V$$

where Q,K,V are query, key, value matrices from context tokens.

Step 12: Adaptive Quantization for Compute Efficiency Apply staircase adaptive quantization (SAQ) for memory/computation efficiency:

$$Q_V = Q(V,\eta)$$

with quantization operator Q parameterized by threshold η to balance quality and performance.

Step 13: Online Learning—Player Feedback Loop Continuously fit model parameters θ to maximize engagement:

$$\theta^{(t+1)} = \theta^{(t)} + \lambda \cdot \nabla_\theta \mathbb{E}\left[R_{player}\right]$$

incorporating reward signals from player actions.

Step 14: Dynamic Difficulty Adjustment via Bayesian Optimization Tune difficulty by selecting world parameters ϕ* that maximize long-term retention:

$$\phi^* = arg\max_{\phi} \mathbb{E}\left[R_{engagement} \middle| \phi\right]$$

using surrogate models for quick adaptation.

Step 15: Infinite Content Validation and Human-in-the-Loop Employ automatic consistency checks and human review, updating models with:

$$\text{Validate}\left(s_{t+1}\right) \rightarrow \begin{cases} \text{Accept}, & \text{if } P\left(\text{plausibility} \middle| s_{t+1}\right) > \epsilon \\ \text{Reject/Revise}, & \text{otherwise} \end{cases}$$

where ϵ is a tunable threshold for plausibility.

These interconnected algorithmic steps construct the foundation for generative AI-driven dynamic worlds and infinite gameplay, leveraging probabilistic modeling, deep neural architectures, optimization techniques, and real-time player feedback.

4. CONCLUSION

Create infinite gameplay, as well as dynamic worlds, can be created with the aid of generate ai and it is even transforming the entertainment industry. Generative AI, as it is popularly understood by the narrowly scripted and overly-prompted titles, generates animated films, previously unseen scenes and real-time characters that react differently to every action or input of a gamer. This does not only heighten the feeling of immersion, but also grants certain form of personalisation, and a replay value that never could be attained with a predetermined design methodology. Generative AI is also introducing a paradigm shift in the production of democracies and scaled-up games with its emergence into the world of game development. One of the examples of systems which make use of generative AIs would be to take a text-prompt and spend money on simple writing and generate complex scripts of the game actions- a living script which the developers and the players would need to write49 to create. It is now possible to have the current technological state; a foundation-model driven architecture and engines in modern RPGs, capable of supporting infinite online sessions, a sandbox simulation where the outcome of two sessions is never identical even at the level of high-quality development The level of development that even a small studio/indie developer can produce vast amounts of high-quality content without passing through an established production pipeline. However, although generative AI is about to bring a revolution to the entertainment industry, it is not a bed of roses. As an illustration, one could still have a need to balance AI-generated creativity and human curatorship that would eliminate repetitive or less significant production; any future usages of this technology are likely to limit innovation and hardware specific programming1. Generative AI will be the game changer in interactive entertainment with unreplicable dynamic game play that will push the boundaries In terms of monetization, the shift to a world where a virtually unlimited amount of content is generated through the generative AI drive will bring both new economy -and new challenges. Questions have been raised as to whether or not some of the most fundamental elements of the game will be further fractionated into sellable additions and leave the gamer behind unless it is better explained and made equitable. Developers will also have their process of game creating changed. Rather than paint-by-hand the creation of every piece of art, artists are moving towards training data, which they are to curate, or in other words, to define parameters and make use of them through generative systems - a shift which has now enabled small teams and indie creators to generate a host of diverse experiences all of their own. The revolution is being brought by technological advancements in devices and algorithms. The possibilities of image synthesis, intepretative language engines and general-purpose real-time content generation capabilities are all fertile ground of innumerable new cool things. This is the Year of Procedural Art, an extension of the possibility that became available to game designers. It is a program that can take lots of different shapes and herein perhaps lies the prospect of more fine game: by offering to the one who was making the game look lay out artist or whatever you might call a janus faced-beholder monster the choice of a variety of input funnels to draw.

5. FUTURE & SCOPE

With its ability to support hyperdynamic, fully simulated worlds that are endless and infinite and are not predestined to conclude Compared to traditional systems that require you to write everything upfront and predetermine all the fixed material, a generative AI may be able to procedurally grow worlds, narratives and games on the fly. It serves the individual player, his choices and preferences. This does not only make the process of creating content undermined and enhances engagement and immersion. Instead, out of a creation by the human hand at all tiers to something that requires no human action once created, a barebone script passed through different parameters (the level of your own skill at this game being one of those variables) an otherwise appealing pattern recognition engine. Generative AI in entertainment is open to possibilities. With the more advanced AI-powered systems, they will allow smooth personalization and customization of games; will allow individual users to interact with each other within the same space, which will continue to develop new lore around them; will liberate the stories to become much more developed than the script writers would have ever done on their own, and make every play-through a truly unique experience. Take virtual reality, e.g. even today generative AI can already create and develop virtual worlds in which we can live tomorrow on a hour-by-hour scale more real than real, until there comes the time when it-ourself, made by helping AI and person eteries, is standard, and not even one kit is necessary between takeoff and landing. In these possibilities it is hoped that games will not only be the one reforming game play but also the digital arts. Interactive films will become better films, because you'll be able to enjoy them rather than just watch them; virtual concerts and live performances might suddenly have a second wind. All of which presents all sorts of new creative, accessibility and cooperative story telling opportunities for users in such a world of play. This shift is not without challenges. So what should we do for the computer's power of two? And in a system like this, that's the one big question. Performance issues in real-time, moral questions and how to explore what AI-generated content looks like are all things we need to consider when thinking about it as an evolving area. Industry and academia are watching closely. Business is busy heading to its own province, "coordinative content." For instance, all academia has been moved to focus on the question of driving User behavior and cognitive load with AI-generated stimuli that are spread over inter-linked Web (social and enterprise) domains.

6. CHALLENGES

One of them is the unstoppable army of generative AI technologies that build an open-ended and constantly changing world (and therefore an indefinite gameplay), where the motionless images become a thing of the past, without any roots. Yet there Yizhi Long, you have made two fundamental challenges. One, at the technical level: B a mere mountain of technology requirements and constraints are holding back This is however just part of quality control, because performance optimization Generally there has been no common understanding or conceptualization of how to com- bine The tremendous speed ups in training algorithms! Although generative AI is capable of making its own worlds, introducing the world-making possibilities, it might also sabotage the vision and coherence and originality of the creative artist and as the systems of AI-adaptation get more and more interactive the problem of securing privacy on the users side and safeguarding of the digital identities gets that much harder to maneuver around, with the legislational structure trying hard to keep pace. Being responsible in responding to these challenges is of the utmost importance in any case we are to be able to further win the confidence of both creators and consumers in the process, and generative AI can provide the full potential of innovation in transforming the entertainment experiences.

REFERENCES

Agarwal, G., Gupta, S., Agarwal, S., & Rai, A. K. (2023). Emotion classification for musical data using deep learning techniques. *Int J Reconfigurable & Embedded Syst ISSN, 2089*(4864), 4864.

Alonso, E., Jelley, A., Micheli, V., Kanervisto, A., Storkey, A. J., Pearce, T., & Fleuret, F. (2024). Diffusion for world modeling: Visual details matter in atari. *Advances in Neural Information Processing Systems, 37*, 58757–58791.

Anand Thoutam, V., Srivastava, A., Badal, T., Kumar Mishra, V., Sinha, G. R., Sakalle, A., Bhardwaj, H., & Raj, M. (2022). Yoga pose estimation and feedback generation using deep learning. *Computational Intelligence and Neuroscience, 2022*(1), 4311350. DOI: 10.1155/2022/4311350 PMID: 35371230

Balasubramaniam, S., Vijesh Joe, C., Sivakumar, T. A., Prasanth, A., Satheesh Kumar, K., Kavitha, V., & Dhanaraj, R. K. (2023). Optimization enabled deep learning-based ddos attack detection in cloud computing. *International Journal of Intelligent Systems, 2023*(1), 2039217. DOI: 10.1155/2023/2039217

Beukman, M., Cleghorn, C. W., & James, S. (2022, July). Procedural content generation using neuroevolution and novelty search for diverse video game levels. In *Proceedings of the genetic and evolutionary computation conference* (pp. 1028-1037).

Chamola, V., Bansal, G., Das, T. K., Hassija, V., Reddy, N. S. S., Wang, J., . . . Niyato, D. (2023). Beyond reality: The pivotal role of generative ai in the metaverse. *arXiv preprint arXiv:2308.06272*.

Dutta, S., & Ganapathy, S. (2025). *LLM supervised pre-training for multimodal emotion recognition in conversations*. arXiv. https://arxiv.org/abs/2501.11468 DOI: 10.1109/ICASSP49660.2025.10889998

. Ferreira, C. (2025). Genre, Bias, and Narrative Logic in AI Dungeon: Generative AI as a Game-Based Storytelling Engine. *Hipertext. net*, (31), 77-89.

Hu, D., Bao, Y., Wei, L., ... (2023) Supervised adversarial contrastive learning for emotion recognition in conversations. In: Proceedings of the 61st Annual Meeting of the Association for Computational Linguistics (Volume 1: Long Papers), ACL 2023. Association for Computational Linguistics, pp 10835–10852. DOI: 10.18653/v1/2023.acl-long.606

Jhaveri, R. H., Revathi, A., Ramana, K., Raut, R., & Dhanaraj, R. K. (2022). A review on machine learning strategies for real-world engineering applications. *Mobile Information Systems, 2022*(1), 1833507. DOI: 10.1155/2022/1833507

Jing, X.. (2025). "MELT: Towards Automated Multimodal Emotion Data Annotation by Leveraging LLM Embedded Knowledge." *ArXiv*, https://arxiv.org/abs/2505.24493

Jose, S., Nguyen, K. T. P., Medjaher, K., Zemouri, R., Lévesque, M., & Tahan, A. (2024). Advancing Multimodal Diagnostics: Integrating Industrial Textual Data and Domain Knowledge with Large Language Models. *Expert Systems with Applications*, *255*, 124603. DOI: 10.1016/j.eswa.2024.124603

Ko, R.. (2025). "Seven Security Challenges That Must Be Solved in Cross-domain Multi-agent LLM Systems." *ArXiv*, https://arxiv.org/abs/2505.23847

Liang, J., Li, R., & Jin, Q. (2020) Semi-supervised multi-modal emotion recognition with cross-modal distribution matching. In: MM '20: The 28th ACM International Conference on Multimedia. ACM, pp 2852–2861. DOI: 10.1145/3394171.3413579

Liu, H., & Zhong, K. (2025). SSMIM: Semi-supervised Multimodal Interaction Model for real-time conversational emotion recognition. *The Journal of Supercomputing*, *81*(8), 897. DOI: 10.1007/s11227-025-07373-w

Maslych, M., Pumarada, C., Ghasemaghaei, A., & LaViola, J. J., Jr. (2024). Takeaways from applying llm capabilities to multiple conversational avatars in a vr pilot study. *arXiv preprint arXiv:2501.00168*

Neumann, M., & Vu, N. T. (2019) Improving speech emotion recognition with unsupervised representation learning on unlabeled speech. In: IEEE International Conference on Acoustics, Speech and Signal Processing, ICASSP. IEEE, pp 7390–7394. DOI: 10.1109/ICASSP.2019.8682541

Omirgaliyev, R., Kenzhe, D., & Mirambekov, S. (2024, April). Simulating life: The application of generative agents in virtual environments. In *2024 IEEE AITU: Digital Generation* (pp. 181-187). IEEE.

Pakniyat, N., Abdullah, J., Agarwal, G., Krejcar, O., & Namazi, H. (2025). Harnessing Fractal Theory for Biomedical Signal Analysis: A Comprehensive Review. [fractals]. *Fractals*, *33*(05), 1–11. DOI: 10.1142/S0218348X25300016

Proma, A. M.. (2025). "Personalized Large Language Models Can Increase the Belief Accuracy of Social Networks." *ArXiv*, https://arxiv.org/abs/2506.06153

Rachha, A., & Seyam, M. (2024, October). LLM-Enhanced Learning Environments for CS: Exploring Data Structures and Algorithms with Gurukul. In *2024 IEEE Frontiers in Education Conference (FIE)* (pp. 1-9)

Rai, A. K., Agarwal, S., Gupta, S., & Agarwal, G. (2023, November 08). An effective fuzzy based segmentation and twin attention based convolutional gated recurrent network for skin cancer detection. *Multimedia Tools and Applications, 83*(17), 52113–52140. DOI: 10.1007/s11042-023-17538-5

. Ratican, J., & Hutson, J. (2024). Adaptive worlds: Generative AI in game design and future of gaming, and interactive media. *ISRG Journal of Arts, Humanities and Social Sciences, 2*(5).

Singh, G., & Goel, A. K. (2020, March). Face detection and recognition system using digital image processing. In *2020 2nd International Conference on Innovative Mechanisms for Industry Applications (ICIMIA)* (pp. 348-352). IEEE. DOI: 10.1109/ICIMIA48430.2020.9074838

. P Singh, G Agarwal, S Gupta, A new ranking technique for ranking phase of search engine: Size Based Ranking Algorithm(SBRA)" International Journal of computer Application (IJCA) 82 (5), 5

Sun, Y., Li, Z., Fang, K., Lee, C. H., & Asadipour, A. (2023, October). Language as reality: a co-creative storytelling game experience in 1001 nights using generative AI. In *Proceedings of the AAAI Conference on Artificial Intelligence and Interactive Digital Entertainment* (Vol. 19, No. 1, pp. 425-434). DOI: 10.1609/aiide.v19i1.27539

Todd, G., Padula, A. G., Stephenson, M., Piette, É., Soemers, D. J., & Togelius, J. (2024). Gavel: Generating games via evolution and language models. *Advances in Neural Information Processing Systems, 37*, 110723–110745.

Verma, K., Chaudhary, A., Bhati, H., & Bisht, G. (2025). Advanced AI & ML applications in satellite image processing and industry. In *Proceedings of the 3rd International Conference on Disruptive Technologies (ICDT 2025)* (pp. 66–69). IEEE. DOI: 10.1109/ICDT63985.2025.10986339

Verma, R. K. (2025). Quantum Methods for Data-Efficient Self-supervised Learning in Industrial Automation. In Ghosh, A., Dutta, S., Das, A. K., Shukla, V. K., & Moreira, F. (Eds.), *Quantum Machine Learning in Industrial Automation. Information Systems Engineering and Management* (Vol. 65). Springer., DOI: 10.1007/978-3-031-99786-0_11

Verma, R. K. (2025). The Role of Artificial Intelligence in Optimizing Cybersecurity for Industrial Control Systems. In Pandey, H., & Goel, P. (Eds.), *AI-Enhanced Cybersecurity for Industrial Automation* (pp. 493–508). IGI Global Scientific Publishing., DOI: 10.4018/979-8-3373-3241-3.ch023

Verma, R. K., & Kishor, K. (2024). Image Processing Applications in Agriculture With the Help of AI. In Khan, M., Khan, R., Praveen, P., Verma, A., & Panda, M. (Eds.), *Infrastructure Possibilities and Human-Centered Approaches With Industry 5.0* (pp. 162–181). IGI Global Scientific Publishing., DOI: 10.4018/979-8-3693-0782-3.ch010

Verma, R. K., Kishor, K., & Jha, S. K. (2024). Big Data Analytics in Bioinformatics and Healthcare. In Khan, R., Kumar, I., & Praveen, P. (Eds.), *Applications of Parallel Data Processing for Biomedical Imaging* (pp. 25–43). IGI Global Scientific Publishing., DOI: 10.4018/979-8-3693-2426-4.ch002

Wang, B., Zhang, X., Pei, J., & Chen, Y. (2022). *Towards understanding chain-of-thought prompting: An empirical study of what matters*. arXiv. https://arxiv.org/abs/2212.10001

Wang, G. X., Deng, J., & Ali, S. (2025). Evaluating the Impact of AI-Powered Audiovisual Personalization on Learner Emotion, Focus, and Learning Outcomes. *arXiv preprint arXiv:2505.03033*

Wang, Y., Wang, L., & Siau, K. L. (2025). Human-centered interaction in virtual worlds: A new era of generative artificial intelligence and metaverse. *International Journal of Human-Computer Interaction*, *41*(2), 1459–1501. DOI: 10.1080/10447318.2024.2316376

Werning, S. (2024). Generative AI and the technological imaginary of game design. In *Creative tools and the softwarization of cultural production* (pp. 67–90). Springer Nature Switzerland. DOI: 10.1007/978-3-031-45693-0_4

Yang, M., Li, J., Fang, Z., Chen, S., Yu, Y., Fu, Q., . . . Ye, D. (2024). Playable game generation. arXiv preprint arXiv:2412.00887.

Yao, C., Zhan, Q., Cao, Z., Li, D., Lin, Y., Shao, Y., & Dong, Z. (2025). Generative AI for Simulating Real World Dynamics Applications and Challenges. *Authorea Preprints*. DOI: 10.36227/techrxiv.176049719.90048379/v1

. Zhang R, Cao Z, Huang Y et al (2025) Visible-infrared person re-identification with real-world label noise. IEEE Trans Circuits Syst Video Technol. DOI: 10.1109/TCSVT.2025.3526449

Zhang, R., Liu, G., Zhang, Q., Lu, X., Dian, R., Yang, Y., & Xu, L. (2025). Detail-aware network for infrared image enhancement. *IEEE Transactions on Geoscience and Remote Sensing*, *63*, 1–14. DOI: 10.1109/TGRS.2024.3504240

Zhao, S., Gao, Y., Jiang, X., ... (2014) Exploring principles-of-art features for image emotion recognition. In: Proceedings of the ACM International Conference on Multimedia, MM. ACM, pp 47–56. DOI: 10.1145/2647868.2654930

Zhu, T., Li, L., Yang, J., Zhao, S., Liu, H., & Qian, J. (2023). Multimodal sentiment analysis with image-text interaction network. *IEEE Transactions on Multimedia*, *25*, 3375–3385. DOI: 10.1109/TMM.2022.3160060

Chapter 5
Virtual Reality (VR) and AI Integration for Immersive Storytelling

Richa Kapoor Mehra
https://orcid.org/0000-0002-5420-8179
O.P. Jindal Global University, India

Ridwan Ishola Mogaji
https://orcid.org/0009-0007-2093-2971
Lagos State University, Ojo, Nigeria

Ashish Dilraj
The Bhopal School of Social Sciences, Bhopal, India

ABSTRACT

Storytelling has been an integral part of every culture and is one of the most fundamental methods of teaching the way of life. With the increase in academic complexity, storytelling as a significant pedagogy has taken a backseat, giving rise to the demand for change and modification in the existing system. With the advancement of technology, we are evolving in almost every field, be it education, health care, or finance. However, the growing emphasis on academic content has gradually diminished its educational role. As school curricula have become more content-heavy and teaching-focused, storytelling has been sidelined, leading to a widening gap in learning caused by this disconnection from narrative-based approaches. However, this gap can be bridged by integrating virtual reality tools and artificial intelligence. The present chapter highlights how using VR and AI in the classroom

DOI: 10.4018/979-8-3373-3690-9.ch005

reshapes education and ensures positive learning outcomes. Moving further, the chapter will unfold how VR and AI can be powerful tools in inclusive education, thus meeting the needs of diverse groups.

INTRODUCTION

The most powerful person in the world is the storyteller. The storyteller sets the vision, value, and agenda of an entire generation that is to come- Steve Jobs. (Joe Romm, 2018)

Regardless of whether it begins with "Once upon a time...," "A long time ago...," or something different and surprising, narratives hold great significance. They have played a crucial role in motivating change, fostering advancement, and providing context for our experiences. Storytelling evolved across the globe through religious texts and scriptures, which served as manuals of moral instruction based on collective beliefs, considered essential guidelines for human existence on earth. Storyteller has the power to transform the world with their vision and mission, thus playing a vital role in societal development. Narratives have allowed cultures to pass down wisdom and history that resonates across generations, promulgating learning, creativity, and community building. Stories are recognized for their ability to influence human behavior and society, which is not limited to religious texts but is also found in secular works.

In complex life, people seek guidance, as the line between right and wrong is blurring, making the distinction between the two the trickiest task. Information overload is causing people to feel confused and frustrated. Storytelling can be used as an effective tool to regain their interest and involve them; storytelling, be it fictional or real, in the form of vlogs, is not new to us. In a complex environment, people tend to listen to whoever makes the most sense and feels most connected to. Many times, people learn many new things from vloggers' experiences.

Since time immemorial, storytelling has evolved and adopted new realities. With the advancement of technology, virtual reality and augmented reality tools are now available, making information sharing easier and more realistic. This has given rise to a transformation from traditional storytelling methods to immersive storytelling, which involves a shift in the orientation of storytelling frameworks from passive consumption to active engagement.

The use of stories to instill moral values in young children is a common practice observed worldwide. The art of storytelling engages students' imaginations and enhances their overall learning experience. It empowers young minds to think, learn, and grow beyond the confines of a narrative. Story-based learning enables learners to develop their ability to employ higher-order thinking skills, thereby enhancing their creative thinking and analytical abilities.

We can consider the various media developed for storytelling and recognize that audiences eventually gravitate toward certain elements that resonate with them. Literature, movies, video games, theatrical productions, and TV programs all possess established definitions based on the traits that have demonstrated success and longevity. As these media continue to evolve and explore new avenues, we witness departures and divergent paths from their original concepts and techniques. The visual storytelling of virtual reality is in a developing phase; with the advancement of technology, it will continue to develop. Nevertheless, it will evolve and become more advanced through experimentation and a growing number of narratives being shared within its space.

Historical Background

As human beings, we have an inherent tendency to engage with narratives. The origins of storytelling can be traced back to ancient times, as demonstrated by the artwork produced during the Upper Paleolithic era, which dates back approximately 32,000 years. (Sugiyama, n.d.) Historians believe the images depicted on these walls are concrete and representational, suggesting that our early ancestors possessed imagination. The most remarkable conclusion that can be drawn from the existence of this ancient art form is that we have always been naturally inclined to create stories and learn from them. With the development of vocabulary, stories have evolved and become an inherent part of communication. In many situations, storytelling serves as a vital conduit for transmitting essential information or a valuable method of sharing experiences. Stories are powerful tools for education, enabling us to impart wisdom and knowledge across generations. Whether it's through a grandparent recounting tales of the past, a teacher using anecdotes to illustrate complex ideas, or friends sharing personal experiences over coffee, storytelling helps forge connections and deepen understanding. Without even acknowledging it, each person engages in storytelling throughout their lives, weaving narratives that reflect their experiences, emotions, and insights. These everyday stories, whether simple or profound, contribute to the rich tapestry of our shared human experience.

Narratives have been documented in numerous ancient civilizations and languages, including Sanskrit, Old German, Latin, Chinese, and Greek. Coming from India, Panchatantra is the perfect example of storytelling. We humans are creative beings. Thus, we possess an innate quality of thinking and imagination that is unconventional. This thinking out of the box gives rise to storytelling that grows from the playful elements of human nature. Creative children often engage in imaginative play through the development of imaginary friends and fantasy worlds, illustrating a natural inclination towards storytelling. This phenomenon can be understood as an intrinsic drive to communicate and share experiences. Furthermore, the human inclination to form relationships and establish familial bonds is fundamental to our social nature and is reflected in these creative expressions. The act of storytelling, therefore, is not merely a form of entertainment but also a critical component of human connection and cultural exchange.

It is clear why this method of communication is so effective and significant, but what precisely does it entail? What is storytelling? There are various definitions and perspectives; this variation exists because, as an art form, it is challenging to define. How can you categorize something adaptable, with boundaries that are constantly changing? Anne Pellowski tries to clarify this in her book:

'the art or craft of narration of stories in verse/and or prose, as performed or led by one person before a live audience; the stories narrated may be spoken, chanted, or sung, with or without musical, pictorial, and/or other accompaniment and may be learned from oral, printed or mechanically recorded sources; one of its purposes may be that of entertainment'. (Pellowski, 1977)

Storytelling involves taking words from a page or an idea and giving them life. It is a creative method of conveying thoughts with an artistic touch. This process helps children enhance their ability to interpret and comprehend events that extend beyond their direct experiences. As children engage with stories, their perspectives shift, enabling them to connect with the narrative on a deeper, personal level. Moral stories serve as effective educational tools, guiding students to make correct choices when faced with ethical challenges, as they uncover their own truths along the way. Now, let's dive deep into the meaning of storytelling.

What is Storytelling?

Every individual has a unique story to share. While mastering the art of storytelling can take a lifetime, for many, it is the act of telling or listening to a story that holds the most tremendous significance. Stories have value when conveyed with sincerity, at the right time, and in the right setting; this is the essence of storytelling. Ultimately, if a story reflects memory, the act of storytelling should be grounded in the principle of honesty.

Storytelling isn't focused on achieving a perfect delivery; rather, it's akin to an 'open mic' session that involves a storyteller, an attentive audience, and an engaging tale. It is not centered on the storyteller. Instead of serving as a platform for monologuing or debating the facts of someone else's tale, storytelling emphasizes being present and fully engaged in the moment. It involves listening actively, reflecting thoughtfully, and sharing meaningfully, rather than speaking at someone or addressing an issue one-sidedly.

The creation of a narrative necessitates a harmonious exchange of significance between the narrator, the audience, and the story itself. This interplay is known as the storytelling triangle, where the story occupies a space between the storyteller and the listeners. This dynamic is also what lends 'story' its unique X-factor: it embodies an enigmatic entity shaped by the storyteller's interpretation, morality, creativity, relativity, and the inherent depth of its meaning.

Figure 1.

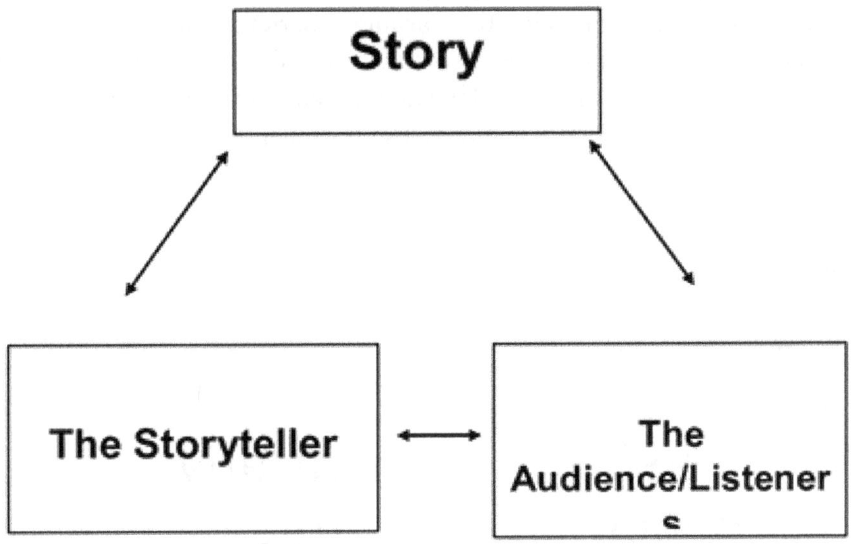

Types of Storytelling

All of us have enjoyed the experience of listening to stories about a character who follows the right path and embodies good moral character. Typically, storytelling follows a tried-and-tested framework. A story of a protagonist who is of good character, courageous, follows the right path, and fights to overcome the evil existing in society. This traditional storytelling framework encourages young minds to follow the right path of truth and lead a morally correct life, filled with truth, love, and compassion. These stories inspire young children to follow the path taken by the characters in the story. Storytelling can be categorized under four basic types-

1) **Case-Based**- In this type, cases are given as examples that help learners understand the problem's complexity and ways to overcome the problem. Cases may

be based on an actual story or may be a fictional one, intending to teach the listener that every problem has a solution, no matter how complex the problem is.

2) **Narrative-Based**- Learners become outsiders to witness the story events as they are recounted. In this type of storytelling, the listener uses their creativity and tries to connect with the main character of the story.
3) **Scenario-Based**- Learners engage in interactive activities to explore the learning environment where the story is recreated. This type of storytelling offers learners the opportunity to actively engage with and resonate with the character of their choice, thereby making the learning experience more lasting.
4) **Problem-Based**- Learners create strategies to solve a problem, which helps them to deep dive into the complex situation and develop strategies to come out of the situation in a calm and composed manner.

Figure 2.

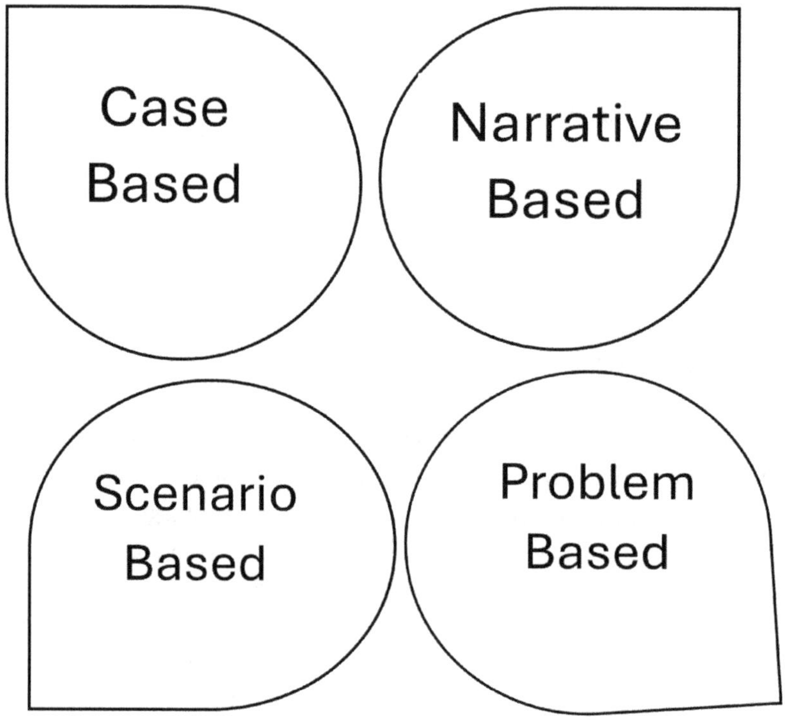

Stories serve as a mirror, reflecting reality to learners, and can thus be used as an effective teaching methodology to inspire them. Storytelling is one of the most effective methods for introducing moral values such as 'trust', 'integrity', and 'kindness'. For instance, the significance and meaning of trust in life can be best explained through the story of a child who was honest in everything they did or said, thus allowing others to develop trust in them. To teach the significance of trust, one can narrate the story of a former employee who owned up to a mistake and earned so much confidence that her customer doubled his order.

Benefits of Story-Based Learning

Storytelling serves as a powerful medium for shared experiences. It enables children to empathize with characters, to rejoice in the happiness of others, and to feel sadness for their struggles. This practice is an invaluable tool for social and interpersonal development. Moreover, storytelling enhances language skills and fosters improvements in listening and speaking abilities. Through storytelling, children learn how to express their ideas and perspectives, and they develop the ability to communicate effectively.

Narratives captivate and inspire, playing a crucial role in the learning process. Thus, it helps them learn joyously. Children who have fun while learning feel involved and motivated to learn more. It enables students to appreciate different cultures and become more receptive to diverse perspectives. Thus, it gives rise to human connection and also fosters a deep connection with nature and other creatures, as displayed in the story.

Story-based teaching can be one of the most effective ways to educate a diverse student group. This method works because it engages the audience with the storyteller. Storytelling makes learning easier and more impactful, as it engages the audience, making the process more lively and long-lasting, which helps retain the information. It aids in language development and promotes facial expressions, making it easier to convey emotions. To ensure an impactful outcome, presentation skills should be up to the mark to catch the audience's attention. The elements of voice, movement, posture, and expression are essential for a storyteller. They have the power to transform a simple tale into something truly extraordinary. Presentation techniques, when executed correctly, yield the most effective results.

There are multiple benefits to story-based learning, including improved problem-solving and critical thinking, as well as enhanced retention and cultural awareness. The figure below demonstrates the diverse benefits of story-based learning.

Figure 3. Benefits of story-based learning

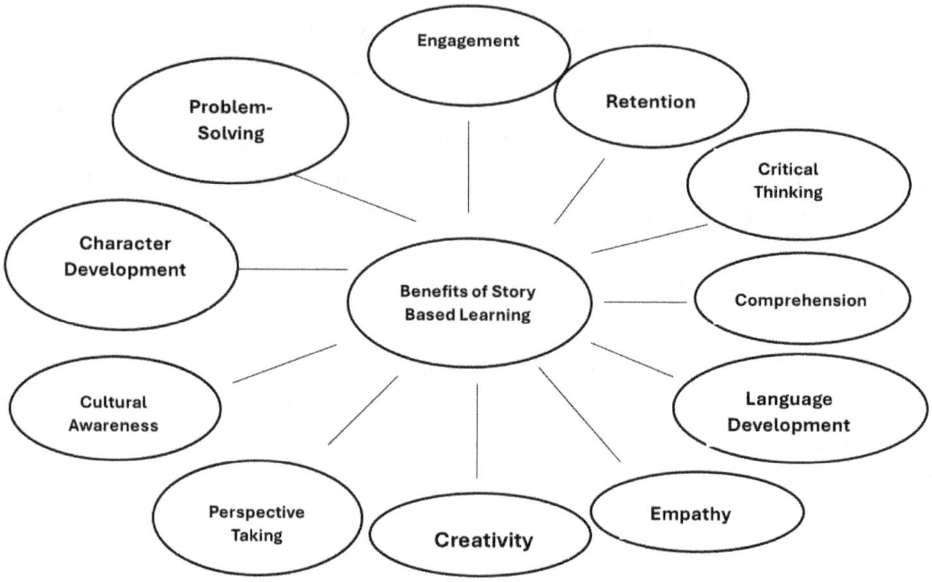

Role of Technology in Storytelling

French philosopher René Descartes talked about mind and matter as two separate realities; he famously said, 'I think, therefore I am. John Seely Brown's analogy from his chapter in the book *Storytelling in Organizations*: he quoted 'We participate and therefore we are.' To fully grasp a concept or idea, it is essential to bring it into a tangible form. This process involves not only absorbing the information but also internalizing it, allowing it to resonate on a personal level. Once we have effectively internalized the knowledge, we can then weave it into our existing understanding, creating a comprehensive framework that makes sense of the new information. This integration transforms abstract concepts into practical applications, enabling us to engage with them in a meaningful way. As Seely Brown says, 'We are constructing understanding all the time, in conversation or through narratives. We are personalising it through telling stories, and in so doing we are constructing it for ourselves.'(Hardin, 2001) He believes that children may receive information in the classroom, but they start to construct their own understanding outside of school. Through storytelling in the class, the narrator equips the children with the skills to do this. And enables them to make sense of what they learn by participating in and personalizing it through stories.

To ensure the learning outcome is met, a storyteller must learn to relinquish control of the story. However, it may not be possible without the support of additional teaching and learning devices. To deliver the information in a different, enjoyable, and inspiring way, the storyteller must utilize technology. Technology has played a pivotal role in today's life; it has made our lives easier and more comfortable, and has made learning enjoyable. Using technology in storytelling through artificial intelligence and virtual reality yields a realistic experience, which can have a profound impact on users' minds. Thus, there is a need to shift from traditional storytelling to immersive storytelling through virtual reality tools and artificial intelligence. As technology advances, concentration levels decline, and with a limited and short attention span, students fail to fully grasp the information presented through traditional storytelling methods. However, to overcome this drawback, virtual reality tools immerse them in a real-like experience, thus making learning more impactful.

An additional perspective on something gives rise to a deeper understanding that can alter the listener's thinking and perspective. Narratives are told from a specific perspective, an observational standpoint, keeping the learning outcome in mind, or what the narrator intends to achieve by the end of the story. Narration both selects and conveys a specific point of view; to experience a narrative is to temporarily share that viewpoint with the storyteller. When you want someone to "perceive" something they aren't noticing, a story can guide them through their choices/behaviors/or inactivity from a different standpoint. (Crogman et al., 2025)Introducing an additional perspective to a listener's current viewpoint broadens their understanding and can alter their thinking.

Most individuals navigate their lives like autopilots, blissfully unaware of the intricate choices that shape their behavior. When you ask someone why they acted in a certain way, they often conjure up a seemingly plausible explanation—a rational-sounding justification—that is entirely divorced from the more profound truth underlying their actions. In reality, humans often drift through decision-making, unaware of the act of choosing and the motivations that drive those choices. We follow familiar paths because they feel intuitive; we have always adhered to those routines, someone long ago nudged us in that direction, or we've internalized a sense of the "right" course of action. Once a habit takes root, it rarely undergoes any thoughtful re-evaluation. Engaging narratives can illuminate the shadowy corridors of our subconscious, enabling us to explore the hidden choices and unexamined reasoning that often lie in the dark. In many scenarios, merely sparking awareness is enough to catalyze transformation. A well-crafted story has the power to peer into the inner workings of a person's mind, igniting moments of introspection and revelation. This helps transform humans from being mere followers to choice makers and rational decision-makers.

Sharing a narrative that introduces a fresh perspective can help the audience reevaluate their decisions within a new and innovative context. When choices are made unconsciously, a story can offer a more aware and objective perspective. Frequently, simply gaining self-awareness can lead to changes in behavior. Just as the accumulation of knowledge can evolve into genuine wisdom, a collection of facts can transform into a compelling narrative. A nuanced yet impactful shift occurs when your goal is to inspire individuals to make decisions grounded in wisdom rather than merely focusing on choices deemed "correct." When the latent wisdom that resides within people is awakened, instead of trying to persuade them of its correctness, one creates a more enriching and profound experience for both oneself and the others involved. If someone wholeheartedly believes that wisdom is present within the group, one's primary responsibility becomes creating an environment where that wisdom can flow freely among its members. Indeed, wisdom is inherently available in the room, waiting to be accessed and utilized. It is reasonable to conclude that any individual or community that aims to influence has access to an abundance of untapped wisdom. Similarly, asserting that every being possesses significantly more factual information than they can effectively digest and analyze is fair. Offering additional facts, rather than clarifying the situation, only contributes to an overwhelming sense of confusion. These individuals do not need an influx of data; they require guidance and support to uncover their inner wisdom. In contrast to common assumptions, poor decisions are rarely a result of individuals lacking adequate information. Instead, bad choices often result from disregarding facts, failing to comprehend their significance, or a lack of appreciation. What drives this phenomenon? Basic human emotions such as anxiety, greed, frustration, intolerance, indifference, or fear can hijack rational thought processes, steering people toward the allure of the "most convenient option," the "path of least resistance," the "safest route," or the "self-centered choice." Simply showering them with more information will not restore their clarity or perspective. Instead, a well-crafted narrative can serve as a beacon of understanding, guiding them toward deciphering what all these facts truly signify. Thus, to develop one's storytelling toolkit, one learns ways to make a story more visible and tangible. Immersive storytelling through virtual reality makes the story visible and impactful.

Traditional Versus Immersive Storytelling

Walter Benjamin, (White, 2017) struggling with the residual trauma of the First World War and possibly expecting a second war to erupt, penned an essay in 1936 registering his concern at what he perceived as the waning significance of the traditional art of storytelling in contemporary society.

As a 20th-century pioneer of 'social media' criticism, Benjamin contended in his book 'The Storyteller' (White, 2017)As modernization emerged, new technologies have begun to alienate human beings from the histories, memories, and mythologies of their societies. This has made the authority of the larger social narrative, and therefore the status of the storyteller, obsolete for contemporary society.

Through his ordeal in the war and his witnessing of society disintegrating, Benjamin believed that in the absence of the traditional storyteller, our stories no longer served their purpose. The storyteller had inspired, campaigned, spread knowledge for the good of all, shed light on the shadows of village life, explored mysteries, and prepared us healthily for any impending threat, change, or future apocalypse. Without the traditional storyteller, the traditional community storytelling functions started to disintegrate. This is because, in the traditional method of storytelling, elders used to narrate old stories to shed new light on institutions and other social forms.

So, stories that once served to define, inform, and connect communities to each other soon became ineffective with the development of societies. However, it is an undeniable thought that stories keep us alive and well-informed. In modern times, Benjamin suggests that stories about people and technology have altered our perspective on others. These changes have contributed to modern warfare, taking away our sense of home and our storytelling traditions. Ultimately, this has led to a loss of connection with each other.

Although Benjamin's ideas are important, technology has added a new and unexpected way to share stories for social change and critique. Now, we can gather around a virtual campfire, which means we don't need to be in the same place or at the same time to share stories. While we may not have the same communities of storytellers as in Benjamin's time, storytelling continues to play a crucial role in understanding our experiences.

For over a century, audiences have been captivated by the flickering glow of rectangular screens, their focus honed in on the confined world that lies within the edges of the frame, often overlooking the vibrant life that exists just beyond. Yet, a transformative shift is taking place—the very boundaries of the screen are being obliterated. Now, narratives can unfold in any direction we turn, inviting us to immerse ourselves in stories that blend seamlessly with our surroundings. Just as in life itself, every step we take or place we venture towards becomes a canvas for storytelling.

This revolution in narrative is reshaping how audiences engage with the moving image and redefining the landscape of content creation. We stand at the dawn of a new era, with Virtual Reality (VR) emerging as one of the latest and most exhilarating elements in the ongoing process of remediation that is shaping the digital media landscape (Cai et al., 2021). The possibilities are endless, and this is merely the beginning of our journey into a fully immersive storytelling experience.

Although storytelling is a buzzword these days, it has been used as an essential tool for learning since time immemorial. With technological advancement, storytelling as a practice is taking a new shape. Virtual reality or augmented reality offers a new level of interactivity, where the listener feels immersed in a virtually created environment. The immersiveness of VR creates a unique situation where the audience is fully engaged without any distractions. (Lacle-Melendez et al., 2024)This method differs from watching something or listening to a story, as the viewer is fully engaged, and even the simple act of turning one's head causes interaction with the world. Immersive storytelling is an impactful narrative approach that draws in the audience by providing a comprehensive experience. It merges traditional storytelling with advanced technology to establish an engaging and interactive atmosphere. By situating the audience at the core of the narrative universe, immersive storytelling enables them to take an active role, exploring different environments and characters while making decisions that impact the story's course.

Human beings are a captivating blend of logic and emotion, intricately woven together in the tapestry of our existence. Our emotional depth adds a rich layer to the human experience, setting us apart as uniquely expressive beings. This vibrant emotional landscape not only shapes our perceptions but also colors our interactions, enriching the tapestry of our lives with a spectrum of feelings that define our humanity. A crucial element of immersive storytelling lies in fostering a deep emotional connection between the audience and the characters. When narrators artfully construct this emotional foundation, they invite viewers to step beyond the role of mere spectators and become active participants in the unfolding narrative. This profound engagement transforms viewers into passionate allies of the story, allowing them to experience the characters' triumphs and struggles as if they were their own. As a result, the tale evolves into a rich, transformative journey, leaving a lasting impression that resonates long after the final scene fades. (Boyd & Fales, 1983)

The age-old art of storytelling has long served as a pivotal tool for education and personal growth, establishing a rich foundation for conveying knowledge and values. In contrast, the advent of immersive storytelling through virtual reality represents a groundbreaking shift in this tradition. By transporting users into vividly detailed, three-dimensional worlds that closely mimic reality, virtual reality enhances the interactive storytelling experience.

This innovative medium not only captivates the audience's senses but also fosters a profound emotional connection between the viewer and the narrative. As users navigate environments, make choices, and experience events from a first-person perspective, the story evolves into a deeply personal journey. This enriched engagement opens new avenues for empathy and understanding, fundamentally altering how stories are perceived and internalized.

Why a Shift from Storytelling to Story Living?

The blend of storytelling with technology gives rise to immersive storytelling. Immersive storytelling is a powerful narrative approach that captivates the audience by delivering a holistic experience. (Fischer, 1998)It merges traditional storytelling with cutting-edge technology to create an interactive and enchanting environment. By placing the audience at the center of the narrative, immersive storytelling encourages active engagement, allowing them to explore diverse settings and characters while making decisions that impact the story's outcome. A key component of immersive storytelling is the integration of various sensory elements, including sight, sound, touch, and even smell, which work together to create a rich and multifaceted experience.(Bucher, 2017)

The integration of virtual reality, augmented reality, and mixed reality technologies can transform the traditional boundaries of storytelling, inviting audiences to immerse themselves deeply in the rich narrative tapestry. These innovative tools create an opportunity for viewers to explore the intricate layers and vibrant elements of the story, cultivating a stronger, more intimate bond with the characters and themes that resonate within them.

A vital aspect of immersive storytelling lies in creating a deep emotional connection between the audience and the characters within the narrative. By weaving a rich tapestry of emotions, storytellers can spark a bond that draws the audience into the unfolding drama. (Coplan & Goldie, 2011)This connection compels viewers not only to watch but to actively engage with the story, feeling every triumph and heartache as if they were part of the tale themselves. This emotional involvement shifts viewers from passive spectators to active contributors, ensuring the story becomes an unforgettable and transformative experience.

Narrative is critical in an immersive storytelling experience. It provides the framework that engages users emotionally and mentally, contributing to the overall coherence and meaningfulness. Unlike traditional storytelling, the immersive method blends real and digital worlds to present an environment where users can interact directly with the story. A well-conceived and executed story helps ensure that the interactions are purposeful and emotionally affecting. Thus, it serves as a tool for inclusive education, helping to train special children by presenting content on an agenda pre-determined by the instructor. Unlike the traditional method, immersive storytelling relies heavily on presence and engagement, deepening immersion by making experiences personal and responsive.

In these contemporary times, stories are no longer confined to the page, the stage, or the screen. Instead, they are immersive ecosystems in which the audience is both a viewer and a participant, collaborator, and co-creator. The user experiences 'living stories', where stories do more than enhance engagement; they bridge technology and emotion, providing a new framework for delivering and receiving.

Defining Immersive Storytelling

Immersive storytelling involves crafting narratives that fully captivate the audience, utilizing different media types or live experiences. (Bucher, 2017)The main objective of these narratives is to foster stronger connections between the audience and the story, effectively pushing beyond the limits of conventional storytelling.

With the help of an example, let us understand the intensity and impact that immersive storytelling can have on a user who aspires to become a pilot and wants to explore the work and lifestyle of a pilot. The user may have the opportunity to engage in an immersive experience through a virtual reality tool and learn everything they need to inhabit the story and drive it to a personalized conclusion. This emotional foundational experience will provide users with a real-life perspective, resulting in a clear understanding of the advantages and disadvantages of being a pilot. Thus, it gives rise to a strong desire to opt for it or not as a career option.

Most common characteristics associated with immersive storytelling include-

1) **Active Participation**- Immersive storytelling provides the opportunity to actively engage with the audience by offering opportunities to influence the story through decision-making.
2) **Multisensory Experience-** It allows the audience to engage through multiple senses, such as sound, visuals, and touch, to deepen their involvement in the story, thus giving rise to a holistic experience.
3) **World-Building-** Immersive storytelling provides a platform to create a universe within which the story unfolds, allowing the audience to become more invested in the narrative. (Yang & Zhang, 2022) It helps in designing the story based on the social and cultural backgrounds of the audience.
4) **Non-linear narrative-** By providing opportunities for audiences to explore the story differently, allowing them to create unique experiences. Technology helps in modifying and customizing the immersive storytelling platform by selecting the language and character that seems closer to the viewer.

Types of Immersion

Several types of immersion can be achieved through immersive storytelling:

1. **Emotional Immersion:** This occurs when the audience becomes emotionally invested in the characters and storylines, evoking strong feelings such as empathy, fear, or excitement. Foster an emotional connection by exploring the protagonist's and other characters' emotions. (Nicolaidou et al., 2022)This will enable readers to empathise with their situation.
2. **Spatial Immersion:** The audience feels physically present within the story's environment, often achieved through visual and auditory elements such as VR headsets or 3D audio.
3. **Narrative Immersion:** This involves the audience becoming deeply engrossed in the story itself, focusing on the plot, characters, and world-building aspects, and is often amplified when they are allowed to participate or influence the narrative.

Virtual Reality as a Means for Immersive Environment

Virtual Reality (VR) is a technology that digitally generates an immersive simulated environment through the use of headsets, gloves, and occasionally full-body suits. Users can engage with the surroundings and the characters within, experiencing the sensation of being physically involved in the narrative. (Eiris & Al-Bayati, 2023)VR is frequently utilized in gaming, educational programs, and experimental storytelling. Some benefits of VR storytelling include:

- A high level of immersion
- An enhanced feeling of presence within the narrative
- Interactive and dynamic experiences

Technology acts as a bridge between students and professionals working in the emerging world of VR technology. It can act as an empathy machine, assisting humans in their mental growth. In a TED talk he delivered in 2015, filmmaker Chris Milk proclaimed that virtual reality (VR) is "the ultimate empathy machine." Researchers are now investigating the connection between VR, emotions, and even depression, suggesting that Milk may be onto something. "Every time we create something new, more of my questions are answered, even as new ones arise. It feels as though we are improving with each iteration, as this medium and process continue to evolve."

Entering virtual space through a VR headset is akin to embarking on a journey to an underground realm. The virtual world offers possibilities that extend far beyond our natural environment, potentially enabling achievements that previous generations could scarcely have imagined. However, it also presents real dangers. Much like Persephone, some individuals may begin to prefer this new digital landscape over the tangible world, leading to unforeseen challenges. Nevertheless, virtual experiences may provide insights that have eluded us in our human development thus far. VR technology has empowered scientists to visualize data in innovative ways, sparking fresh insights and interpretations. Additionally, it has allowed disabled veterans to experience war memorials, providing emotional encounters they might not have otherwise had.

One approach to examining any immersive medium is to view it as a mediated effort to create a "real-life" experience. These experiences aim to replicate the sounds, images, and emotions we encounter in various situations. For instance, when sitting in a city park, we are surrounded by the ambient sounds of the environment—the wind rustling through the trees, children playing nearby, the persistent buzz of a fly near our ear, and the distant roar of planes overhead, along with many other subtle sounds that fill the three-dimensional space around us. In immersive experiences, this sensation is achieved through sound effects, the voices of performers, and even recorded music that evokes emotions akin to those we naturally experience in reality.

Magic happens with AI and VR.

Artificial Intelligence and Virtual Reality are two groundbreaking technologies transforming numerous industries, including education. Naturally, each offers unique benefits, but the integration of AI with VR in learning environments creates remarkable possibilities for enhancing human learning and engagement with content.

The primary use of AI in education is adaptive learning. It utilizes computational methods to extract relevant information from the vast amounts of data generated by learners, such as their performance, interactions, and feedback on learning styles, to suggest and implement necessary adjustments. This approach enables more flexible learning, allowing students to progress at their own pace while focusing on their areas of weakness. AI is also a key factor in natural language processing (NLP) systems, like chatbots and virtual tour guides, which respond to students' inquiries and provide prompt support. In addition to personalization, AI can undertake various practical tasks, such as grading and assessments, thereby alleviating some of the burdens on faculty members related to these responsibilities.

Virtual Reality (VR) provides learners with immersive 3D environments, enabling them to interact with virtual items, participate in simulated real-world situations, and experience a realistic educational environment. In contrast to most 2D materials, VR fosters a feeling of presence in a virtual space that other media cannot replicate. This feature is especially advantageous for subjects that require demonstrations, including technical training, nursing, engineering, fine arts, or other artistic disciplines. By simulating conditions that are otherwise unattainable, expensive, or unsafe in reality, practicing with VR techniques provides a safe, repetitive, and thorough experience that closely mimics real-world scenarios.

When integrated, AI and VR create an educational platform that is highly attuned to the needs of users. AI can act as a dynamic intermediary, tracking student behavior in VR settings and making adjustments to ensure that each learner gets the best possible experience. For instance, in a virtual chemistry lab, AI can monitor how students carry out their experiments and modify the level of difficulty as needed. The potential applications of AI within tailored VR learning environments are vast, leading to enhanced effectiveness, interactivity, and engagement in educational activities, all of which can be customized based on individual learner needs.

How does AI enhance the emotional impact of VR stories? AI significantly enhances the emotional impact of VR stories by making experiences more adaptive, personalized, and emotionally resonant. (Sherman, 2013) Here's how this integration works:

Real-Time Emotional Recognition and Response

- **Emotion AI and Affective Computing**: AI can track users' emotional states using physiological signals (like heart rate), facial expressions, voice tone, and behavioral cues. This enables the VR system to recognize a user's emotions in real-time and adjust the narrative, environment, or character interactions accordingly, thereby deepening immersion and engagement.
- **Personalized Feedback**: Based on detected emotions, AI can provide immediate, tailored feedback through visual, auditory, or haptic cues. This not only helps users feel more connected to the story but also supports emotional regulation and learning in therapeutic or educational contexts

Dynamic Narrative Adaptation

- **Adaptive Storytelling**: AI algorithms analyze user choices, reactions, and even gaze direction to alter the storyline, pacing, and outcomes on the fly. This ensures each experience is unique and emotionally relevant to the individual, forging stronger emotional connections with the narrative and characters.
- **Complex Character Interactions**: AI-driven characters can evolve and respond to users in emotionally intelligent ways, remembering past interactions and adapting their personalities over time. This leads to more believable, nuanced relationships and greater emotional investment

Enhanced Immersion and Engagement

- **Personalization**: AI tailors the VR environment and narrative to the user's preferences, emotional responses, and comfort levels. This increases engagement, satisfaction, and the likelihood that users will form meaningful connections with the story.

- **Safe Emotional Exploration**: VR powered by AI provides a risk-free space for users to experience and practice managing a range of emotions, which is especially valuable in therapeutic or educational settings

By combining these elements, AI transforms VR storytelling from a passive observation into an emotionally charged, interactive journey tailored to each user's unique responses and needs.

Virtual reality (VR), augmented reality (AR), and mixed reality (MR) offer an unprecedented experience that involves avatars. We are no longer limited to simply possessing a physical presence in virtual spaces; instead, this presence can be fully tailored to our personal preferences. We now have the ability to become anyone we wish, experiencing a level of realism that was previously unattainable. When considering the role of avatars in narrative environments, it's essential to recognize that avatars have always served as characters within a story. Those avatars that engage viewers or players more deeply in an experience undergo the same rigorous character development as those crafted for film, television, and video games. Well-developed characters or avatars enable individuals to genuinely feel as though they are inhabiting the figures they portray.

ETHICAL CONSIDERATIONS

Privacy

The integration of AI and VR storytelling raises ethical concerns about user privacy, as these technologies can collect and analyze personal data, potentially leading to unauthorized surveillance, data misuse, and a lack of informed consent regarding user interactions and experiences.

'Humans will not have agency and control [over their data] in any way if they are not given the tools to make it happen'. (John Havens)

One way in which AI is already affecting privacy is through Intelligent Personal Assistants (IPAs), such as Amazon's Echo, Google's Home, and Apple's Siri. These voice-activated devices are capable of learning the interests and behaviour of their users, but concerns have been raised about the fact that they are always on and listening in the background. Similarly, there are ethical concerns in AI-driven VR storytelling, particularly regarding users' privacy, as immersive environments can collect sensitive data. This raises risks of algorithmic bias, user discrimination, and potential misuse of personal information, necessitating robust ethical oversight.

Another aspect of AI that affects privacy is Big Data. Technology has now reached a stage where long-term records can be kept on anyone who produces data that can be stored. Digital records can be searched using algorithms for pattern recognition, meaning that we have lost the default assumption of anonymity by obscurity (Selinger & Hartzog, 2017).

In addition, personal data, or information about who accessed the immersive story through virtual reality, can be reconstructed in certain cases from a model, with potentially significant consequences for regulating these systems. For instance, as it stands, there are no data protection rights or obligations concerning models in the period after they have been built, but before any decisions have been taken about using them.

Bias

AI and VR are created by humans, which means they can be susceptible to bias. Systematic bias may arise from the data used to train systems or from the values held by system developers and users. Several cases have garnered attention for promoting unintended social bias, which has then been reproduced or automatically reinforced by AI systems. For instance, many popular image databases contain images collected from just a few countries (the USA, the UK), which can lead to biases in search results. Such databases often portray women performing kitchen chores while men are out hunting (Zhao et al., 2017). For example, searches for 'wedding gowns' typically produce the standard white version favored in Western societies, whereas Indian wedding gowns are categorized as costumes (Zhou, 2018).

As many machine-learning models are built from human-generated data, human biases can easily result in a skewed distribution in training data, and AI applications and products may perpetuate unfairness and discrimination. This problem is exacerbated by the fact that AI applications are usually 'black boxes', making it impossible for consumers to judge whether the data used to train them is fair or representative. This makes biases hard to detect and handle.

Blind Trusting

Often, people tend to accept information received from technology without questioning it. While VR solutions possess the power to entertain, engage, and tantalize users, they also have the power to cause significant physiological trauma. There are concerns about blindly trusting the technology. One can question- is it possible for the VR system to be 'hacked' without the user knowing, or without injecting changes into the user's virtual world? How will a user respond to unforeseen troubles? Studies have shown that children are particularly vulnerable to the effects of

VR technologies, as they are highly susceptible and can more easily confuse the real world with the virtual one.

There are dangers associated with the excessive and uncontrolled use of technology; however, this does not negate the benefits of combining AI and VR in education, healthcare, and other domains. Users of technology should be mindful of its use and make the most of it to benefit humanity. Technology provides a wide range of support and assistance in inclusive education.

Story-based learning for Inclusion

Literature has indicated the significance of technology in improving autistic children's ability to communicate. Autistic children face challenges in freely communicating and feel uncomfortable expressing their thoughts and feelings. Such inexpressiveness often leads to frustration both among children and their family members. (Mehra & Kapoor, 2025)For instance, when a child feels hungry and desires to eat a specific food, their inability to communicate can result in frustration and make them feel unsettled. In this situation, the child might struggle to maintain their composure and could act in ways that are not socially acceptable. In these instances, technology can provide them with a different means to express their feelings, thoughts, and more to those around them and help them learn the method of expressing emotions through storytelling.

It is widely acknowledged that children with autism often face challenges in interpreting subtle social cues and responding appropriately to emotional expressions. Traditional behavioral interventions frequently utilize flashcard training, which requires children to memorize emotional expressions depicted on flashcards; this process can be quite arduous for them (Lerman et al., 2004). However, the advent of technological solutions, such as specialized glasses (like Google Glass), holds promise for a promising future. These glasses can aid children in recognizing emotions by categorizing expressions such as happiness, anger, and sadness (Washington et al., 2016). Researchers have demonstrated that Google Glass can deliver nearly instantaneous feedback about a social communicator's emotional expressions to children with autism who are wearing them. Equipped with an outward-facing camera, the glasses capture the communicator's facial image and employ machine learning techniques to interpret various emotional expressions exhibited by the communicator.

For many children with autism, the traditional instructional mode delivered in a typical classroom setting may not be the most effective. This is due to their visual learning style (Tissot & Evans, 2003). In such cases, technology such as tablets, mobile devices, and computers plays a crucial role in visually presenting facts, making it a beneficial alternative for these children to learn skills via immersive storytelling. Story-based learning is a powerful approach to teaching inclusion because it helps learners connect emotionally with diverse perspectives and experiences. Rather than presenting abstract principles or policies, stories humanize complex issues, making them relatable and memorable.

Story-based learning is not just a teaching method—it's a bridge between people, assisting in connecting humans with other creatures. Helps them know the environment in a closed manner. By embedding inclusive stories into learning environments, we invite learners to step into one another's worlds, break down barriers, and co-create a more compassionate and equitable society. Story-based learning through virtual reality within our education system embraces every student, creating an inclusive environment that nurtures and empowers all learners, regardless of their backgrounds, abilities, or unique needs. This transformative approach is anchored in the powerful motto: "No one is excluded."

Imagine a classroom where vibrant narratives come to life through immersive virtual landscapes, captivating students from diverse backgrounds. With each twist and turn of the story, every learner is actively engaged, their curiosity ignited as they explore new worlds, meet diverse characters, and overcome challenges together. This innovative method not only fosters collaboration among students but also ensures that everyone has a voice, forming a rich tapestry of ideas and experiences in a welcoming space.

Sustainable Development Goals

According to the United Nations' 2030 Agenda, Sustainable Development Goal 4 requires the provision of inclusive and equitable quality education opportunities to all. However, the key factor in achieving this goal can be assistive technology. The evolution of technology brings with it more ways to tell stories, and immersive storytelling methods can be used to motivate, engage, and train students with special needs. Filmmakers, documentary creators, scientists, musicians, and numerous other professionals have increasingly recognized the tremendous benefits of using this innovative storytelling medium to share their narratives with a wider audience. The substantial leap in immersion offered by this medium not only creates a remarkable opportunity for cultivating empathy among viewers but also provides extraordinary insights into environments and experiences that are often beyond physical reach. Furthermore, this dynamic medium is rapidly gaining traction within educational contexts, resulting in students who are not only more engaged and motivated but also developing a deeper sense of empathy. These learners are becoming equipped with enhanced critical thinking skills and a robust understanding necessary to navigate the complexities of our ever-evolving world.

Virtual reality serves as a powerful educational tool in various ways by creating a distinctive environment for learning and knowledge exchange. It offers a chance to increase student engagement, and as this engagement improves, it augments their participation and involvement. This fosters interactive learning opportunities and accelerates the learning process, particularly beneficial for children with Autism Spectrum Disorder (ASD). Students with ASD often learn at a slower pace and face challenges with social interactions and communication. Numerous studies have demonstrated how virtual reality-based games can help individuals acquire essential life skills, such as brushing their teeth and basic cooking techniques. (Mehra, 2024)

CASE STUDY: HIMALAYAS: A TREK TO SCHOOL IN 360-DEGREE VIDEO - BBC NEWS

Education is not a drive away to school for most students in India. BBC News Himalayas: A Trek to School in 360-degree video – takes you on a daily journey with two sisters on their long and unsafe trip to school in the Himalayas. Every day, they set out on a 2-3-hour journey from their remote village in Uttarakhand to reach their school. The daily journey involves a steep trek in the mountains, followed by crossing a flooded river by pulling a trolley over the flowing waters. The story takes you to their house, and you hear the father share his concerns about the cart and his daughters' safety. You reach the girls' school. It is a co-education school, rare in a conservative village. The class teacher takes attendance, and both sisters mark their presence. (Hendriks Vettehen et al., 2019)

Teaching small children about the comfortable life they experience as school-going children is easy; one can use a video about the journey of two sisters on their tough and long trip to school. This method helps in captivating students' attention and creates a strong emotional connection with the content. The method helped students devise a solution to the problem faced by the two sisters, thereby giving rise to innovative techniques for solving problems. It enhanced empathy and social skills among students by placing the viewers in the shoes of the two girls, thus making them feel about the challenges they might be facing on a daily basis. Thus, helps develop empathy and understanding for others.

CONCLUSION

Humans have been sharing stories for thousands of years to entertain, inform, educate, and inspire. Storytelling is not exclusive to fiction; narratives are also utilized in mathematics, various sciences, art history, music, and many other fields. We remember compelling stories because they evoke emotions and draw us into their narratives. Just like engaging stories, our most impactful learning experiences tend to stay with us. There are parallels; we craft narratives using the resources available to ensure they resonate with the audience. Likewise, when teaching, our goal is for lessons to resonate with students, which we achieve by employing the tools at our disposal: language (both verbal and non-verbal), the physical setting, technology, and an understanding of pedagogy. (Alvarado et al., 2023)Virtual Reality offers unparalleled opportunities for creating immersive environments across various applications. It is an effective tool for inclusive education, helping autistic children and children with disabilities learn through immersive VR. While challenges exist, ongoing advancements suggest a future where VR becomes integral to learning, working, and connecting. As the technology matures, its ability to simulate reality and beyond will continue to reshape our experiences. Virtual reality technology can be effectively used to instill forgotten human values in young minds by having them watch short films that evoke emotions, thereby making them more sensitive and empathetic.

As digital technologies continue to evolve, virtual reality (VR) is poised to become increasingly accessible and intuitive for users. The captivating realm of 360-degree video is poised to become a standard expectation in the media landscape, captivating audiences with its immersive potential. Major social media platforms, such as Facebook and YouTube, are already embracing this format, paving the way for a more interactive and engaging experience. There has been and continues to be rapid growth in virtual reality technologies. There remains room for debate around the topic of ethical responsibilities for these technologies. Designers should not ignore possible mental health and safety issues, or social and ethical issues.

In this rapidly advancing field, innovation is accelerating at a breathtaking pace. Future smartphones will be equipped with enhanced capabilities to seamlessly support augmented reality (AR) and VR, transforming the way we interact with digital content. Furthermore, VR devices, starting with compact and lightweight head-mounted displays, will become more affordable, inviting wider adoption by consumers and creators alike (Cant, 2018).

In the realm of storytelling, VR holds the transformative power to serve as a compelling advocacy tool, designed explicitly to raise awareness and funds for various causes, while resonating deeply with specific audiences and stakeholders.

Ultimately, the extensive integration of immersive storytelling in educational settings will cultivate an environment where learners are not just passive recipients of information, but vibrant and engaged participants. This shift will foster a generation of motivated, empathetic individuals equipped with the critical thinking skills and profound knowledge needed to navigate the complexities of an ever-evolving world.

REFERENCES

Alvarado, Y., Guerrero, R., & Serón, F. (2023). Inclusive Learning through Immersive Virtual Reality and Semantic Embodied Conversational Agent: A case study in children with autism. *Journal of Computer Science and Technology, 23*(2), e09. DOI: 10.24215/16666038.23.e09

Boyd, E. M., & Fales, A. W. (1983). Reflective Learning. *Journal of Humanistic Psychology, 23*(2), 99–117. DOI: 10.1177/0022167883232011

Bucher, J. (2017). *Storytelling for Virtual Reality*. Routledge., DOI: 10.4324/9781315210308

Cai, Y., van Joolingen, W., & Veermans, K. (Eds.). (2021). *Virtual and augmented reality, simulation and serious games for education*. Springer. DOI: 10.1007/978-981-16-1361-6

Cant, P. (2018). *SXSW: The State of Immersive Journalism*. The State of Immersive Journalism.

Coplan, A., & Goldie, P. (2011). *EmpathyPhilosophical and Psychological Perspectives*. Oxford University Press., DOI: 10.1093/acprof:oso/9780199539956.001.0001

Crogman, H. T., Cano, V. D., Pacheco, E., Sonawane, R. B., & Boroon, R. (2025). Virtual Reality, Augmented Reality, and Mixed Reality in Experiential Learning: Transforming Educational Paradigms. *Education Sciences, 15*(3), 303. DOI: 10.3390/educsci15030303

Eiris, R., & Al-Bayati, A. (2023). *Using Immersive Storytelling to Improve Engagement and Motivation During Fall Prevention Training*. www.cpwr.com•www.elcosh.org

Fischer, J. M. & R. M. (1998). *Responsibility and control: A theory of moral responsibility*. Cambridge: Cambridge University Press.

Hardin, S. (2001). John Seely Brown: Leveraging the Social Life of Information in the E-Age: Idea Sparkers. *Bulletin of the American Society for Information Science, 27*(3), 15–17. DOI: 10.1002/bult.197

Hendriks Vettehen, P., Wiltink, D., Huiskamp, M., Schaap, G., & Ketelaar, P. (2019). Taking the full view: How viewers respond to 360-degree video news. *Computers in Human Behavior, 91*, 24–32. DOI: 10.1016/j.chb.2018.09.018

Joe Romm. (2018, July 9). *Steve Jobs on the awesome viral power of storytelling*. Medium .

Lacle-Melendez, J., Silva-Medina, S., & Bacca-Acosta, J. (2024). Virtual and augmented reality to develop empathy: A systematic literature review. *Multimedia Tools and Applications*. Advance online publication. DOI: 10.1007/s11042-024-19191-y

Lerman, D. C., Vorndran, C., Addison, L., & Kuhn, S. A. C. (2004). A RAPID ASSESSMENT OF SKILLS IN YOUNG CHILDREN WITH AUTISM. *Journal of Applied Behavior Analysis*, *37*(1), 11–26. DOI: 10.1901/jaba.2004.37-11

Mehra, R. K. (2024). Evolutionary Advantages of Virtual Reality in Education. In *Transforming Education with Virtual Reality* (pp. 73–86). Wiley., DOI: 10.1002/9781394200498.ch5

Mehra, R. K., & Kapoor, N. (2025). The Role of Assistive Technology in Supporting Special Education Needs. In *Blending Human Intelligence With Technology in the Classroom* (pp. 209–222). IGI Global., DOI: 10.4018/979-8-3373-0771-8.ch009

Nicolaidou, I., Tozzi, F., & Antoniades, A. (2022). A gamified app on emotion recognition and anger management for pre-school children. *International Journal of Child-Computer Interaction*, *31*, 100449. Advance online publication. DOI: 10.1016/j.ijcci.2021.100449

Pellowski, A. (1977). *The world of storytelling*. Bowker.

Selinger, E., & Hartzog, W. (2017). Obscurity and privacy. In *Spaces for the Future* (pp. 119–129). Routledge. DOI: 10.4324/9780203735657-12

Sherman, W., & C. A. (2013). *Understanding Virtual Reality: Interface, Application, and Design*. Amsterdam: Elsevier.

Sugiyama, M. S. (n.d.). *Literary Prehistory: The Origins and Psychology of Storytelling*. https://www.researchgate.net/publication/316861108

Tissot, C., & Evans, R. (2003). Visual Teaching Strategies for Children with Autism. *Early Child Development and Care*, *173*(4), 425–433. DOI: 10.1080/0300443032000079104

Washington, P., Voss, C., Haber, N., Tanaka, S., Daniels, J., Feinstein, C., Winograd, T., & Wall, D. (2016). A Wearable Social Interaction Aid for Children with Autism. *Proceedings of the 2016 CHI Conference Extended Abstracts on Human Factors in Computing Systems*, 2348–2354. DOI: 10.1145/2851581.2892282

White, R. (2017). Walter Benjamin: "The Storyteller" and the Possibility of Wisdom. *Journal of Aesthetic Education*, *51*(1), 1–14. DOI: 10.5406/jaesteduc.51.1.0001

Yang, S., & Zhang, W. (2022). Presence and Flow in the Context of Virtual Reality Storytelling: What Influences Enjoyment in Virtual Environments? *Cyberpsychology, Behavior, and Social Networking*, *25*(2), 101–109. DOI: 10.1089/cyber.2021.0037

Chapter 6
G-GenAI:
An AI-Driven Framework for Co-Creative Game Development

Pooja Nagpal
https://orcid.org/0000-0002-9107-0359
IILM University, Gurugram, India

Aarti Chugh
https://orcid.org/0000-0002-5946-9327
IILM University, Gurugram, India

Om Rohilla
https://orcid.org/0009-0005-7161-2340
IILM University, Gurugram, India

ABSTRACT

Game development is a resource-intensive process requiring expertise in narrative design, level creation, and visual asset production. This paper introduces G-GenAI, an AI-powered framework that enables developers to co-create game components—narratives, levels, and visuals—using natural language prompts. By integrating advanced generative AI models such as GPT-4 for storytelling, Midjourney for visual assets, and procedural content generation (PCG) for level design, G-GenAI streamlines the development pipeline. Built with Unity for integration, the system supports rapid prototyping and scalable design, particularly for indie developers. A prototype game was developed and evaluated, demonstrating a 70% reduction in development time while maintaining creative quality. This work pioneers a comprehensive AI-assisted game design pipeline, redefining human-AI collaboration in the gaming industry.

DOI: 10.4018/979-8-3373-3690-9.ch006

INTRODUCTION

Now a days the gaming industry has evolved and turned into a worldwide cultural phenomenon which now dominates the entertainment ecosystem. It reaches billions of players across the globe that generate approximately hundreds of billions of dollars in annual revenue. (Newzoo, 2024). These platforms may include PCs and mobile devices and Xbox and virtual reality (VR) and augmented reality (AR) and cloud streaming.

The traditional game development process continues to be complex, highly demanding, and resource-heavy. Crafting a contemporary game involves joint efforts from multidisciplinary teams to work on multiple stages. The typical development pipeline starts with pre-production phase which involves planning. The core concepts are discussed, stories are written, characters are designed, and initial level structures are sketched. In production phase skilled programmers start with coding and other concepts are also applied like 3D modelling, animation, texture artistry, sound design, music composition (Bethke, 2003). Since the game design process goes through multiple iterations, the final deployment timelines are typically extended for years. This often leads to rise in the budgets up into tens and hundreds of millions of dollars, due to over-hiked salaries and licensing fees for high-tech software and middleware. Hence, the main hurdle in the success of gaming industry is vast scale and complexity in coordinating large, varied teams working with the inherent risks of creative undertakings.

For indie, the independent game developers the scenario becomes tougher as they have to work with minimal or self-funded budgets. These developers do tie ups with other independent developers and form small teams and often handle the most creatively daring and genre-defining titles (Järvinen, 2009). The limitation of resources and budget still put severe constraints on their ability to apply their creative visions at scale. In most cases, an indie, work independently from ideation to content generation to final game design and testing. They have to take over multiple responsibilities of a programmer, artist, writer, and designer simultaneously. With AI trending in every domain, now it has evolved in the creative field of game design too. AI tools ease the rapid creation of unique game content and artwork which is a big advantage for indie creators. While AI technologies progress in democratizing game creation by automating asset generation (art, code, sound) and boosting efficiency it gives rise to many challenges and concerns. Some of the major challenging areas related to indies are fear about AI replacing creative roles, integration issues while merging AI outputs in existing workflows and privacy and ethics concerns where their creative work can be used without any consent. If not used properly, AI based game systems can lack in quality of player experiences and the innovation of game content as the AI systems are dependent on existing data and experiences only.

AI tools facilitate the rapid production of unique game content and artwork, a particular advantage for indie. This research aims to provide an in-depth understanding of how indie game designers can leverage AI to foster innovation while navigating its challenges.

These days the players perspective has also being changed. They want to hide their personal details, remain nameless, and keep freedoms while playing on any type of gaming platforms. The privacy settings customization, managing data, trust across multiple platforms and more control over character representations are also desirable.

To fill these gaps where requirements of both the game designers as well as players can be fulfilled, the G-Gen AI model is proposed. The model is built on a new concept of game development where humans and AI collaborate, therefore realizing a novel partnership model and AI-driven organization. To ease the game design process, the G-Gen AI framework allows developers to give simple text prompts to create comprehensive game content. In traditional game design approach, the task of designing complex documents, character sketches, level blueprints and game environments take over months or years. This model needs the developer to simply explain their game idea such as, "Design a game about a haunted castle where a player solves puzzles to rescue a princess and there should be multiple ghosts and magic spells." With these natural language prompts the game design process is automated with endless environment variations, narratives, and levels on a large scale, which allows rapid prototyping and ideation. The cutting-edge integration of advanced generative AI technology in this model makes the system powerful and efficient for game designing process.

BACKGROUND

Procedural Content Generation (PCG) has been a cornerstone of game design, as seen in titles like *Minecraft* and *No Man's Sky*, where algorithms generate maps and environments (Short & Adams, 2017). Recent advancements in PCG via Machine Learning (PCGML) have introduced data-driven level generation (Summerville et al., 2018). Tools like Promethean AI and Inworld AI leverage AI for interior design and NPC dialogue, respectively (Promethean AI, 2023; Inworld AI, 2023). However, these solutions focus on specific aspects of game design and lack integration.

Integration of generative AI into the gaming industry has become more prevalent these days. Game designers and developers show mixed reactions to this combination. While some developers have embraced it as an asset to foster creativity and process optimization, others worry about its impact on originality, ethical issues, and artistic integrity. Panchanadikar et al. (2023) investigated how GenAI tools have encouraged indie (independent) game developers' actions in innovating traditional production models, as well as the potential risks faced by these developers. The authors also provided solutions for strengthening future GenAI technologies to foster and sustain more democratic practices in game development.

Alharthi (2025) studied the evolving role of generative AI tools in game design and creative workflows. The study focuses on the impact of GenAI tools on game designers' and developers' creativity, efficiency, and productivity. Further, the paper discusses concerns and challenges in the field of game design through AI tools.

Qiu 2023) worked on software tools like ChatGPT, Midjourney, Stable Diffusion, and Unity and explored the purpose of generative AI in 2D gaming animation. The document describes the process of designing and animating a 2D game character named Eva. The paper explains the integration of AI tools at various stages of game design. Based on complete implementation, the authors explained challenges in the field and suggested using OpenPose and Ebsynth for animation creation.

Alavi et al. (2023) introduced GamePlot, an AI-assisted platform to help game designers create and refine immersive narratives for turn-based games. GamePlot can be used in story creation during the early stages of game development. In it, collaborative gameplay can be performed through the game plots generated using large language models (LLMs). Writers designed two main components: the Design Room, where designers create and edit game stories, and the Game Room, where players and designers test and refine the game collaboratively. Designers can modify plots, control non-player characters (NPCs), and adjust narrative elements in real-time using a “Wizard of Oz” feature. A 14-participant user study revealed high satisfaction with GamePlot's features, such as the ability to edit plots during testing, NPC summaries, and collaborative gameplay. Participants appreciated the tool's adaptability, control, and ease of use but noted limitations in AI creativity, narrative complexity, and consistency.

Procedural Content Generation using Generative Adversarial Networks (GANs) has emerged as a powerful technique for automating the creation of game assets such as maps, textures, and levels. According to Mao (2021), GANs enable the generation of visually coherent and diverse content by learning from example datasets, making them suitable for domains where artistic consistency is critical. However, these systems often operate in a domain-specific manner and lack real-time interactivity with human designers, limiting their applicability in co-creative environments. Enhancing user control and integrating human feedback into the generative loop remain active areas of research to make PCG via GANs more adaptive and designer-friendly.

Chugh et. al. (2022) integrated AI into the rendering engine and come up with a new AI-powered game design platform. Here visual data rendering is done at lower resolution which helped to improve performance. Further, deep networks were applied during training phase to upscale the image to the native resolution.

Table1 below shows some existing AI-based game development platforms.

Table 1. Existing AI based game development platforms

Platform/Tool	Key Features / Advantages	Research Gap / Remarks
Unity ML-Agents	Integrates ML models into games; supports reinforcement learning; agents for training 2D, 3D and VR/AR games, popular among developers.	Lacks focus on human-AI co-creativity; mainly targets autonomous agent training.
Charisma.ai	Narrative engine using AI for conversational storylines; NLP-based branching dialogues.	Limited procedural creativity; mainly focused on storytelling, not gameplay mechanics.
AI Dungeon	GPT-based interactive fiction platform; open-ended and responsive to player input.	Creative freedom is high but lacks structure for collaborative game design and mechanics.
Promethean AI	Assists designers by suggesting 3D assets based on scene context; saves time in level design.	Primarily assists asset placement; limited role in gameplay logic or co-creative ideation.
Ludo.ai	AI-based game ideation tool; offers competitor analysis, theme generation, and market trends.	Focuses on ideation phase; does not support interactive game development or testing.

Need for an AI-Driven Gaming Framework

Traditional sports development provides many important challenges that prevent efficiency, scalability, and creative freedom, especially for smaller developments. The production of a modern video game is a significant challenge, which requires carefully coordinated work from teams working on different subjects. These challenges demonstrate the need for urgent need to simplify the design of games on an AI-controlled platform, while creative control is maintained.

Time and Resource Intensity

The first challenge is the time -stick. For this type of game design, you need a significant investment not only in money but also in energy. And it is not only about creating the prototype stage - it is also important to create a production level quality. The duration of the project can be large - Writing quests for 3D games requires a lot of time and resources. That may be because of many issues like the sheer time and resource intensity involved in the development life cycle. Every cycle and stage require much time, great human capital, and financial investment. Designing the inquiry, building complex levels, and creating high fidelity assets requires not only significant financial investment, but also dedicated commitment for several months.

Asset Creation

It looks quiet easier but it is the toughest thing to draw asset on PC. This includes high-polygon characters and environment props (furniture, trees, rocks, buildings), detailed sculpted textures, fluid animations, VFX, sound design and some more visual effects. Each 3D model must be sculpted into the form you want, retopologies to work better in game, UV unwrapped for texturing, then painted with up to 5 maps (albedo (colour), normal (surface detail), roughness (material property), metallic (how much it reflects) & ambient occlusion (shadows))! Characters are fully rigged with controls for complex animation which calls for an eye for combat, expression, and idle pose sequence framing. VFX artists also design stunning spells, weather effects, and explosions, and create instanced particles that serve as world enhancers. Sound designers bring listeners into varied soundscapes with ambient sounds, lines of voice, weapon effects, environmental foley, thematic music that has added emotional appeal with gameplay.

Fragmented Tools

One of the most notable unsolved problems in traditional game development comes from a broken workflow, especially for AI development (Blohm and Grasnick14). Even as AI has been applied to components of game development—pathfinding and rudimentary NPC behaviors are two areas where it has been integrated—these specific solutions often work in isolation. This clearly siloed manner does not maximize the workflow. For example, one could be a special-purpose AI tool for creating realistic textures, while another can be used for procedurally generating terrain, another to animate character movement and a fourth to create dialogue or simple narrative blips. But even though each of those tools can be good at what it does, meshing all those disparate outputs into a unified playable game world is still mostly manual and very complicated.

This fragmentation makes it indispensable to manually interfere in many cases, to convert data with expenditure and to work some data together. Designers need to export assets in one tool as a file type (like FBX for models, PNG for textures), and import it into a different software ecosystem (a game engine, such as Unity or Unreal Engine). After import, they must texture, set up materials, set up lighting, place objects in the scene and tweak by hand parameters, scale, and placement to achieve consistent photorealistic and functional results. Not only is this "pipeline glue" work slow, but it is also very error prone since software versions and file formats are often not compatible with each other. It also means that developers need a solid knowledge about more than one software ecosystem, all its cons and pros, what the best practices are, etc. For instance, an AI-generated character model may not have the required bone structure and rigging of another AI animation system, necessitating the process of manually retargeting or even manually rerigging that character. There is no single end-to-end solution that an input a high-level creative brief and magically have everything from levels to art to narrative automatically snap into place. This process makes it incompetent to iterate, slows down production, and piles on technical burden. It is taking time away from the fun stuff and putting it on the boring stuff. A generative, holistic game design platform in which the AI is the master orchestrator of content creation has so far largely dodged the game industry and has left the developer playing the role of the centralized integrator.

Concurrent Plot Lines

It is always very tough to write diverse and unique script. It requires the time and resources to create it that includes branching dialogue systems that react to many of the actions and the ability to pursue multiple threads of the story. This has the potential to restrict some indie developers to simpler or more linear stories or use generic tropes based on how much work is put into nonlinear storylines. Repetetion of story ideas, experimenting with plot twists and character motivations, or adopting alternative story paths in a single game is significantly limited when every string of dialogue and every narrative choice must be tediously handcrafted and manually added to the project. This can sometimes come at the cost of narrative ambition for plausibility, resulting in games that feel less dynamic or somehow less personal.

High-Quality Visuals

Analogically, the problem of high-quality visuals is not the sole issue but the most significant one that restricts directly the game's product appeal and player perception. Indie games usually have very limited access to experienced 3D artists, animators, texture artists, and technical artists, so they are forced to fall back on simpler art styles, lower fidelity graphics, or stock assets from online marketplaces. Though a purposely stylized art direction weighs heavily on being very effective and one of a kind, it usually is the result of a conscious artistic choice rather than being compelled due to resource limitations. Only when the budget significantly limits the visual quality, it can very much take away the player's experience of the game in total, and it will be hardly to communicate the intended atmosphere, feeling, or intricate world-building effectively.

Scalability Issues

In traditional scalability was the issue in developing games especially when rapid prototyping and iteration are there players' increasingly personal and dynamic game experience requirements can be satisifed. Speed of manual content creation is very slow and costly too and low chances of scaling which crates barrier in innovation and growth of gaming world.

In previous game development approaches, the development of a simple playable prototype that exhibits core mechanics, or a single level, could take weeks or months to develop. This entails a significant upfront commitment to art, programming, and design, even for a simple version. The slow prototyping process creates a culture where experimentation is limited that it discourages the developer from a) discarding ideas that fail to work in prototyping and b) moving to better concepts.

The apparent cost of failure in traditional game development limits bold avenues for exploring new ideas. Game design is very iterative by structure. The process involves testing ideas, refining them, and testing them again. If the development of an iteration takes too long, the speed of development process is reduced subsequently harming responsiveness to design inputs and opportunities for better designs; and increasing the length of time to deliver designs. Agility to change or direction from player feedback or consequences of market changes is greatly reduced.

Today's gamers want games with personal experiences, content that changes, and worlds that act smart based on what they do. It is very hard to create this kind of stuff by hand on a large scale. For example, making a different dungeon map for each player, changing the story based on choices, or having the game world change based on what players do as a group would take a lot of work, so it is not realistic for big or small game companies.

Procedural content generation (PCG) can resolve the issue, while old PCG methods goes with protocols so the content can be repetitive.

So for such issues like, the amount of time and resources needed, different creation tools, creative limits, and scaling issues, a single platform that is powered by AI is needed. This platform should resolve all above mentioned issues and make game design easier while keeping creative control, so creators can focus on their artistic ideas instead of how to make content.

Figure 1. Process of achievement of game development

PROPOSED SYSTEM: G-GENAI FRAMEWORK FOR ACCELERATED GAME DEVELOPMENT

The G-GenAI is a novel way of creating games and using Artificial Intelligence (AI) to help game developers produce interactive experiences through talk to one another. This entire system takes basic game ideas and makes these ideas a reality by creating physical forms of play and giving developers more useful resources to create their game (Chhabra et al 2023).

Three interconnected modules make up the G-GenAI framework, each working together to turn early game concept ideas into real working models of a video game.

Core Architectural Components

Interactive Developer Portal

In presented framework, user-based components serve as the communication hub between developers and AI systems. This portal accepts the natural-language descriptions of game features that creators can use to describe their vision without needing to rely on technical terms or specialized coding knowledge. Developers can submit queries like "designing a mystical swamp environment with magical challenges and spectral opponents" or "developing scientific narrative characters that provide enigmatic missions." While accessing AI capabilities the feedback mechanism is allowed to developers to maintain creative control.

To enable fast evaluation and detailed fine-tuning the system provides a visual representation and a summary description of the result generated. As a result, dynamic collaboration emerges where human creativity drives AI productivity. The modular architecture allows seamless implanting of AI tools, and each is specialized for a specific creative domain, while maintaining overall compatibility of the system.

System Driven World Creation

These design components use highly established technologies to create different ranges. These algorithms automatically construct landscapes, underground complexes, interiors, and other environmental elements. This module changes beyond basic rule-based generation, and not only is its created environment different, it is functionally visually appealing, and includes machine learning principles to ensure the progression of difficulty, placement of interactive elements, and specific requirements for gameplay as enemy distribution patterns. The system can interpret the narrative context and translate it into a structurally viable design.

Automated Creation of Visual Content

Artistic elements are created in-game via highly sophisticated AI image generation software. All visual elements required to produce a video game are designed using AI image generation techniques, including all character designs, environment art, etc.; All visual elements will be expressed consistently with all other images produced by artistic elements. All of these will be consistent with developer specifications, thereby ensuring the overall visual experience is harmonious across the entire game. This model of production avoids the traditional artistic bottlenecks used to create and produce video games. As such, artistic elements can create and produce a wide variety of styles and genres quickly and with relatively small amounts of resources involved with the visual production element of video game creation. The output of artistic elements will be adaptable to both 2D sprite-based and 3D texture mapping video games.

Unity Integration Module

This integration module acts as the essential link between the AI produced content and a playable game environment. It is configured to accept the results from the AI Pipeline such as narrative information, level structure, and visual content and to smoothly incorporate them into a mainstream game engine. Through the use of C# scripts, it controls the game behaviour, manages the asset import, spawns the created levels and characters, applies AI controlled NPC actions and creates interaction elements. Its aim is to offer a real-time, playable impression of the AI generated data, allowing developers to instantly test and experience the generated materials in a well-known development environment. This integration is critical to the "fast prototyping" aspect of G-GenAI, converting raw data into an interactive simulation. Basic outline of the suggested system is illustrated in Figure 2.

Figure 2. Overview of proposed system

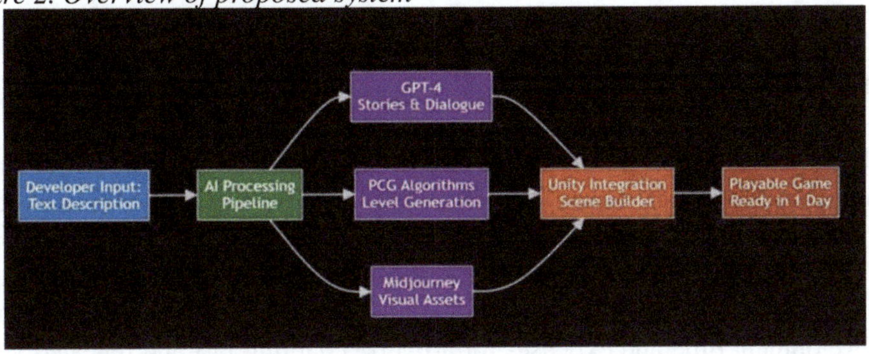

Eminent Abilities of Gen-AI Framework

The presented framework outspreads beyond its basic architecture to provide enhanced functionalities that transform the traditional game development workflows which are discussed in next section.

Tailored Framework

The sophisticated language processing algorithms integrated within this framework create complex hierarchy of goals and interactions of characters as well as multi-layered narratives. The potential for developing fully interactive text beyond traditional written works allows for continuous improvement of developed cohesive storylines with complex character development, unexpected situations, and multiple endings that reflect the developer's intent as revisions occur.

Computer-Based Environmental Simulation

Wavefunction Collapse method, L-system patterns and network-based construction rules are such complex procedural algorithms through which practical game space can be created and yield system architecture. This architecture includes creation of different architectures like digging tunnels and passageways, and accommodating gems, landmines and interactive elements like threats, obstacles, and treasures in the maps. The mechanics of these systems read and act under the constraints of a non-deterministic context and by extension environmental designs should thematically align with the desired gameplay experiences and gameplay mechanics to ground the sandboxes.

Digital Art Production

The presented system generates premium artwork including character illustration through the differentiated art extended method, environment artworks including natural and architectural elements, and operational UI design with enhanced elements derived from the latest visual generation models. On-demand asset creation capability Allows for customization in theme and visual style, drastically cutting the development time and expenses for artwork, enabling fast and repeated visual prototyping.

Responsive Scaling Framework

The framework's design allows scaling flexibility of the overall architecture of project. The developers can quickly validate the concept of nuclear play due to the swift creation of small-scale, concept-testing material. Simultaneously, the system expands to enrich a vast library of content for ambitious projects (e.g., games and open world experiences) with high augmentation of procedural content systems. If flexibility needed to apply to all kinds of project areas, from personal creative projects to full commercial works then current system works in better way.

Requirement Analysis

Requirement Analysis phase consists of comprehensive data collection through questionnaires, individual discussions, and joint meetings with a wide range of indie developers. Data can be collected from amateur enthusiasts to established commercial producers. The systems goal is to systematically catalogue the most urgent developmental disorders, particularly time constraints, financial constraints, and creative obstacles. Many developers complained about the excessive time investment required to create manual content, character design, environmental structure, and interface development. Additionally, they highlight the complexity associated with detailed structures and multipath action strands, and an effort required to create and fill a wide range of gaming worlds. Essential phase in requirement analysis includes financial feasibility checks and those concerns focus on software licensing costs, contract creative professionals, and purchasing premium assets.

Architectural Planning

Successive phases of the building planning transformed the identified requirements into G-gena's actual operational framework. The focus is here to create detailed interface models that can precisely determine user interaction, various input mechanisms and response presentation areas. These sorts of models give priority to availability and intuitive operations that allows developers for effective communication of concepts and deal with AI-generated content.

In the next step, system flow diagrams have been constructed to visualize complex integrated networks and data paths within AI processing systems to enhance the visibility of the system. It contains documentation of process of interpretation of natural language inputs, information between speech models, procedural generation algorithms, and the procedure of transportation of visual AI systems.

The reason behind GPT-4 model is chosen that its extraordinary narrative and dialogue skills, that provides a gradual understanding of language and creative text generation. To compete and integration purpose equivalent models for Midjourney and advanced image generation are selected to create high quality visual content that meets a variety of artistic requirements. Further Unity has been chosen as an integrated platform because of its industry prevalence, wide API access, a powerful community ecosystem, and versatility to support both 2D and 3D development approaches.

Framework Implementation

The architectural specification was followed while building the Genai system during the implementation phase. Iterative development concept, which is a key feature of agile approach was used in this process. The work focused on creating an AI processing pipeline which asks for integrating the selected AI models by using their respective programming interfaces. The focus of midjourney integration was API implementation. It was used to generate visual assets by controlling text prompts, image quality, style composition, and output specifications for quest design. These algorithms are created to be flexible, which in turn also allows flexibility to the production parameters. The integration of AI generated content into a combined environment, including assets, scene management protocols, dynamic object positioning, and playlogic implementations for AI generated stories and surrounding structure is handled by these scripts. This phase also includes developing a user interface to allow effective input via an AI pipeline and an easy and understandable presentation of the results

System Integration

Because of integration, the playable experience, highlighting the seamless connection between different editions and the Unity game engine. Environment geometry and layout data from the procedural algorithm are changed into unity format, resulting in dynamic off-load meters. It is necessary to carefully handle the asset pipeline to be able to properly scale, get the right material properties. This stage covers the constant running of the iterative tests to check component communication and confirm the generated elements.

Continuous Improvement Process

As agile methodologies are used, continuous optimization process is set up. After the initial testing phase, internal performance analysis, and monitoring of system data is performed. The optimization strategy works on a diversity of areas for important enhancements.

Creative Output Enhancement

This investigation searches for emerging AI architectures and expanding training datasets. Ongoing improvement of generative capabilities across language models, procedural generation algorithms are also searched. Visual AI systems are used to produce increasingly diverse, high-quality, and creatively compelling game content.

System Resilience Improvement

System is able to handle unexpected inputs and is very efficient in error handling. To implement the same implementing a comprehensive error measurement system and reliable repair mechanisms is developed.

Methodology Benefits

Agile Software Development Lifecycle approach is best suit for proposed GenAi project. Iterative development approach combined with ongoing feedback integration is very beneficial as reduces the response time and improve system functionality based on actual usage patterns. It ensures that the final framework is being handled effectively in modern game development processes.

SYSTEM IMPLEMENTATION AND PROTOTYPE DEVELOPMENT

Technical Architecture

The basic technical architecture of G-GenAI framework is constructed using unity 3D as the primary game development platform, integrating GPT-4 for narrative content creation. Further Midjourney is used for visual asset generation and proprietary procedural content generation algorithms is used for for spatial design.

Proof-of-Concept Development

To verify the practical application and efficiency of the G-GenAI system A demonstration prototype has been created. This prototype serves as a proof of concept of comprehensibility that demonstrates the ability of frames to translate natural language descriptions into concrete, interactive gaming experiences. The resulting outputs are systematically combined to create a uniform gaming experience.

AI Pipeline Output Analysis

- **Quest Structure:** Quest Structure introduces players with game mechanics and this is the concept of our framework where the language model successfully created a comprehensive story framework. Further moving into the puzzle it comprises of calling mysterious objects from old places, gathering repairing elements from risky areas, and revealing secrets about the weaknesses of your opponents.

- **Story Progress:** Presented system smartly handles narrative complexity. Based on decisions of players, different puzzle solutions are given that influence character answers and quest availability and entire system is based on branching technique.
- **Spatial Design Generation:** A procedural algorithm utilizing wavefunction collapse and graph-based methodology to create a comprehensive environmental layout.
- **Underground Complex:** Featuring two different underground regions, interconnected chambers designed to meet puzzle-based challenges, achieving compatible elements and continuing.
- **Creation of Visual/Graphical Content:** 12 essential graphical assets are created by graphics generation system.
- **Character Visuals:** Distinctive portraits for key characters maintaining stylistic consistency with medieval fantasy aesthetics.
- **Interface Elements:** Icons for quest objectives, inventory items, and interactive objects.

Integration and Development Environment

Using union integration functions AI-generated components are seamlessly integrated into an interactive gaming environment. Following are the promoted custom process flow of ecosystem.

- **Scene building:** Transform narrative data into functional game elements, dynamically generated environmental geometry, and use of visual assets on game objects by instantiating characters using the appropriate dialogue system.
- **Content Population:** As per settlement layouts strategic placement of characters, deployment of incompatible elements representing the threat that includes alignment of interactive objects including puzzle components and quest items.
- **System Management:** Implementing player mechanics, character interaction system, puzzle features, quest tracking, and basic AI behaviour.

PERFORMANCE EVALUATION

To imitate real-world deployment scenarios the prototype was thoroughly tested within a controlled server environment. The detailed analysis of both functionality and system stability is done. Following are some of the parameters for performance evaluation.

Input Interpretation

Proposed system successfully extracted key themes, behaviours, characters, and associations from the given prompts as input. Further these were then transformed into comprehensible narrative elements that is used to validate a strong hold of context and its relevant meaning.

Environment Generation

However, this system never failed to generate playable and interesting layouts for both underground section and upper roadmap. The differences in the output are unique while retaining a theme, making them good for puzzle gameplay.

Visual Asset Integration

The visual assets produced by the system were easily mixed in the combined execution pipeline. The assets are of good quality and they enhanced the visual experience of the prototype.

User Feedback and Iterative Refinement

The prototype is tested with some external developers after an internal testing with internal testers. Their input ascertained several key aspects of the system:

Accelerated Development

In this model contestants get efficient and fast functional prototypes in very early stages. Generally, contestant believed that Ai is only for content generation but this sort of game prompt generation idea is unique for users that too enhances the speed of development.

Output Quality Observations

Most of the generated content is of high quality but sometimes contestants noticed occasional inconsistencies in character speech, mainly in terms of emotional trajectories and personality coherence in certain contexts.

These issues are resolved by filtering prompt creation approaches. These comprise more detailed character descriptions, explicit emotional signals, and the enhancement of post-processing rules that were created to achieve consistent styles of dialog. The incremental enhancement, as facilitated through the agile methodologies, contributed in increasing the level of robustness and efficiency of G-GenAI. The productive implementation and testing of this prototype are strong evidence of G-GenAI to revolutionize game content production pipeline.

PERFORMANCE ANALYSIS AND FINDINGS

Quantitative Assessment

Newly developed approach is better than the traditional approach in terms of efficiency and development speed as in its approach is improve content generation capability. The potential of AI driven development platforms transformation is established while quantitative information gathered during prototype development and comparison with conventional manual procedures.

Table 2 presents a comparative analysis of traditionally used approach and G-GenAI approach for development phase.

Table 2. Relative analysis of traditional and proposed framework

Development Phase	Traditional Approach	G-GenAI Framework
Quest Development	2 hours	15 minutes
Level Architecture	6 hours	1 hour
Asset Production	2 days	30 minutes
Functional Build	5 days	1 day

Performance Indicators

Development Pace Enhancement

The G-GenAI framework confirmed incomparable drop in overall development schedules, attaining almost 70% average time savings across all measured development phases. Generally content generation tasks that usually takes extensive manual effort is significantly rationalized through AI automation.

Advanced Language model facilitates the quest development that typically involves extensive brainstorming, conceptualization, and scripting phases, was compressed from multi-hour sessions to 15-minute automated processes. Using Procedural generation algorithms, level architecture, that requires half-day or full-day design sessions for individual areas, is completed within single-hour timeframes.

In presented framework substantial improvement is in terms of efficiency during quality creation. In this implementation, tasks that traditionally require two full development days have been reduced to a 30-minute automated process via AI-assisted generation. This enrichment in terms of time is valuable for all independent developers, reducing turnarounds from five days to one day, allowing for unparalleled prototyping and reiteration swiftness.

Creative Output Diversity

G-GenAI is good at creating diverse output. It generates good and creative content with very basic prompts. Language play an important role in deciding the output, it sets various game goals, character details and final act of characters, uniqueness or diversity in every version of gamer.

Two models are integrated to generate output so that repetitive content shouldn't be generated and layout is planned in such a way every time new content is created that goes with the flow with previous content as it is not possible in other automated system.

All AI tools uses the same technique to create visuals, characters movement, backgrounds etc but in our framework every generation gives the desired output but in unique way with variety.

System Scalability

Basic setup of G-GenAI's can be scales at desired level. It works for both small tests and big game projects. As per requirement of the system all three individual components that are language models, visual creators, and system procedures can be expanded one by one.

G-GenAI is capable of creating big open-world games and those can be played repeatedly and content can be created instantly and that too different and unique content every time. games that can be played again thanks to system procedures.

Table 3. Summary of prototype testing and validation scope

Parameter	Description	Evidence / Proof of Testing
Prototype Used	A small 2D narrative-based game built in Unity using G-GenAI for story blocks, level sketches, and visual drafts.	Prototype project folder stored in Unity environment; version history showing generated assets.
Participants	6 developers (3 with experience, 3 beginners) used the tool to create game components.	Signed participation logs; timestamps of asset generation and edits.
Tasks Evaluated	Narrative creation, level layout generation, visual asset drafting, and prototype assembly.	Output files generated through GPT-4, Midjourney, and PCG modules saved in testing directory.
Performance Indicators	Time taken for narrative creation, number of visual assets produced, level generation iterations, and assembly time in Unity.	Recorded time sheets and Unity profiler logs.
Baseline Comparison	Manual development workflow tested on the same game concept without AI support.	Manual workflow notes and asset creation timestamps.
Measured Outcome	Around 70% reduction in total production time for the prototype.	Before/after time comparison sheet signed by participants.
Testing Conditions	Mid-range GPU system, stable internet, limited asset complexity, and single-level gameplay.	System configuration record and test environment summary.
Scope Limitations	Prototype based on a small game concept; high-complexity assets were not part of the evaluation; no stress testing on large scenes.	Documented in test summary report.
Validation Method	Observation, time logging, prototype build review, and participant feedback.	Compiled feedback forms and reviewer notes.

IMPLEMENTATION CHALLENGES

Although proposed framework is working fine yet it faces many implementation challenges that are listed as follows:

AI Output Quirks

Sometimes AI generated content or stories do not go with flow that means earlier part don't connect with the next part. Additional connecting lines or background information is required to connect two phases. To resolve this issue human-oriented reviews are required.

Technical Integration with Unity

Framework works well with integration but sometimes there are some issues with scope of the problem which can be resolved after resizing things. size. To resolve this, same standards should be used for content creation on every AI platform that will create automatic post processing.

Prompts Engineering Complexity

Prompt engineering plays the important role in content generation. Quality of prompt yields better content. But fancy prompts do not produce desired results. There should be other methods or tools that can create meaningful prompts. Smarter models can be created that can understand more complex and visual creative ideas.

Limitations and Reflections

While G-GenAI, proposed framework gives many benefits and is very clear about its output yet there may be some gaps that a developer must handle with care. The entire system lacks understanding the creative vision behind a game, so there may be possibility that what developer wants is not understood by the system. So, this may result uneven visual looks while switching from one generation to another which will not result into unified art visibility. That is why a revision is necessary what AI has created or it should be mapped with developer's requirement because random or not well paced level can be created. Also, working with everchanging cloud environment that includes changing of model and pricing etc, that could impact the overall workflow and pace of result generation.

Further practical limitations involve returning incomplete results or slowing down generation for complex prompts during intensive tasks. From a different perspective, there are other issues too that can be generated after using AI tools. As the models are integrated and are learning from vast datasets, they may output content that can be alike to existing artwork or writing. This creates the issue of overlapping with copyrighted material. So, the entire system that may be prompts and results too should be mapped and verified before implemented. An ethical concern is the impact on creative roles of human creators where AI takes over tasks previously done by writers or artists, that may reduce prospects for human artists. Solution is to keep core creative decision in human hands.

RESEARCH CONCLUSIONS

The implemented AI-powered game development framework that is integration with Generative AI results into empowering the co-creative game development ecosystem where AI agents work in real time environment and not only provide descriptive designs, but also rationalize content generation and improves image creation time which finally enhances game mechanism. The integration of LLM and diffusion models gives faster prototyping, for the validated of framework to ensure quality and achieving timely deliveries. This framework also ensures that AI-generated conclusions and behaviours remain consistent across the game execution as G-GenAI strictly works on character coherence. The iterative feedback loops and structured prompt engineering empowers the improvement of game and give better control over the creative vision of the game. While complete focus is on character coherence but initial prompts can be proved a limitation of proposed and implemented system.

FUTURE SCOPE

In presented framework platforms similar to Elevenlabs can be added for audio and voiceover effects. At next level with the use of reinforcement learning personalised gameplay can be implemented and experiences. As future demands support of multilingual prompt will be that that includes regional languages. For ease of AI developer teamwork, a real time web interface may be added advantage that will results into game changing platform in the global gaming ecosystem. Planning to build a real time web interface for seamless developer AI teamwork.

REFERENCES

Alavi, S. H., Perez, G. R., & Togelius, J. (2023). GamePlot: Co-creating narrative games with generative AI. *Proceedings of the ACM on Human-Computer Interaction, 7*(CHI PLAY), 1–27. https://doi.org/DOI: 10.1145/3574198

Alharthi, S. A. (2025). Generative AI in Game Design: Enhancing Creativity or Constraining Innovation? *Journal of Intelligence, 13*(6), 13. DOI: 10.3390/jintelligence13060060

Bethke, E. (2003). *Game Development and Production*. Wordware Pub.

Chhabra, G., Kumar, S., Gupta, S., & Nagpal, P. (2023). *Artificial intelligence to analyze psychophysical and human lifestyle*. Springer Nature Singapore. DOI: 10.1007/978-981-99-3039-5

Chugh, A., Jain, C., & Kumar, A. (2022). Design of artificial intelligence enabled game engine. *In Proceedings of the 4th International Conference on Information Management & Machine Intelligence (ICIMMI '22)* (Article No. 99, pp. 1–5). ACM.

Epstein, Z., Hertzmann, A., Herman, L. M., Mahari, R., Frank, M. R., Groh, M., Schroeder, H., Smith, A., Akten, M., Fjeld, J., Farid, H., Leach, N., Pentland, A., & Russakovsky, O. (2023). Art and the science of generative AI. *Science, 380*(6650), 1110–1111. DOI: 10.1126/science.adh4451

Inworld, A. I. (2023). *Inworld: AI characters for games and the metaverse*. https://www.inworld.ai/

Järvinen, A. (2009). Game design as a research field. *In Proceedings of DiGRA 2009: Breaking New Ground: Innovation in Games, Play, Practice and Theory.*

Mao, X. (2021). Procedural level generation with generative adversarial networks: Techniques and challenges. *Entertainment Computing, 37*, 100412.

Newzoo. (2024). *Global games market report.*

Panchanadikar, R., Gonzalez, L., & Sarkar, A. (2023). Generative AI and indie game developers: Innovation, risks, and ethical concerns. *CHI Conference on Human Factors in Computing Systems Extended Abstracts.*

Promethean, A. I. (2023). *Promethean AI – Artificial intelligence for virtual worlds.* https://www.prometheanai.com/

Qiu, S. (2023). Generative AI Processes for 2D Platformer Game Character Design and Animation. *Lecture Notes in Education Psychology and Public Media*, *29*(1), 146–160. DOI: 10.54254/2753-7048/29/20231440

Short, T., & Adams, T. (Eds.). (2017). *Procedural generation in game design*. CRC Press. DOI: 10.1201/9781315156378

Summerville, A., Snodgrass, S., & Mateas, M. (2018). Procedural content generation via machine learning (PCGML). *IEEE Transactions on Games*, *10*(3), 257–270. DOI: 10.1109/TG.2018.2846639

Chapter 7
AI-Driven Player Behavior Analysis and Personalization

Nofamataro Zebua
https://orcid.org/0009-0008-3902-2289
Universitas Negeri Malang, Indonesia

Yan Piter Basman Ziraluo
https://orcid.org/0000-0002-2676-6739
Universitas Nias Raya, Indonesia

Ester Novi Kurnia Zebua
https://orcid.org/0009-0000-5879-9124
Universitas Negeri Malang, Indonesia

Ridho Victory Nazara
https://orcid.org/0009-0005-7024-6502
Universitas Nias, Indonesia

ABSTRACT

This chapter explores the application of Artificial Intelligence (AI) to analyze and customize the behavior of individual players in contemporary digital games. It explains the application of AI tools such as machine learning, deep learning, and reinforcement learning to personalize interactions, upgrade systems, dynamic story generation, and gamification to reduce player churn. The chapter also examines sociological and computational theories of player profiling, ethical issues regarding the use of data, and the personalization of immersive gaming experiences through AI technologies. The chapter places particular emphasis on inclusive and adaptive design, and responsible innovation.

DOI: 10.4018/979-8-3373-3690-9.ch007

AN INTRODUCTION TO THE EVOLUTION OF THE GAMING INDUSTRY OVER TIME

a. Evolution of the Gaming Industry over Time

Every decade creates new innovations centred around technological capabilities, such as adding narrative elements and user interactivity, made possible by the increasing computational power over the past few decades. Reflecting on this, I am reminded of the well-known video games, Pong and Space Invaders (Kent, 2001). Although dismissed by many as mere two-dimensional graphics and basic mechanical lines, both of these video games were pioneers and pathfinders for subsequent decades. All changes are closely related to technological discoveries such as 'real-time rendering', the internet, and input sensors for video games, whether motion capture, VR, or otherwise (Sifa et al., 2018).

Over the past two decades, there have been many advancements in video games, such as online multiplayer video games, cloud gaming technology, and the latest generation engine, Unreal Engine 5, which brings video game graphics closer to reality (Sifa et al., 2018). Although the world is still struggling to overcome COVID-19 post-lockdown, Newzoo, a survey institution focused on video game and esports analysis, projects in its latest survey that by 2023, the value of the video game market is projected to reach 184 billion dollars. With revenue estimated to exceed 184 billion dollars, it has been crowned as the largest entertainment industry for the tenth consecutive time. Based on data collected by Newzoo, video games, such as educational and social games, which were once infrequently used, can now be leveraged for conveying history, shaping public opinion, and forming social identity (Gee, 2003).

b. The Early Role of AI in Games: Simple Enemies and NPCs

In the early stages of its development, artificial intelligence in games operated as a static logic system that only aimed to provide basic challenges to players. Non-Playable Characters (NPCs) and enemies in the game did not possess 'awareness' and operated based on scripts and rigid or static patterns, such as Finite State Machines (FSM) and simple pathfinding algorithms like A* search (Rabin, 2013). A classic example is Pac-Man, where all the ghosts act rigidly, that is, within the confines taught to them from the player's position relatively, without learning or responding to context.

AI at that time was more akin to a marionette that moved by being pulled from one position to another, rather than walking like a creature that has the benchmarks of an imaginative goal. Within this limitation, we could discipline uninspired skepticism.

According to Yannakakis & Togelius (2018), various USDs necessitate the need for a more adaptive approach associated with NPCs designed to be responsive, but progressing towards NPCs that are not only responsive but contextual. It is at this moment that the term AI no longer recognises "logic programming systems" but begins to emerge as a hypothesis capable of interacting dynamically with players.

c. Paradigm Shift: From Static Control to AI as Behavior Observer and Analyst

Over the past two decades, rapid technological advances have brought fundamental changes to the function of artificial intelligence (AI) in digital games. Whereas AI previously operated primarily as a rule-based mechanism that executed fixed commands, its role has now evolved into a system capable of recognizing patterns and adjusting its responses to player behavior. This development reflects a paradigm shift in game design, from static, predetermined structures to more dynamic systems that can interpret and adapt to individual playing styles. Through the use of machine learning, reinforcement learning, and data mining techniques, contemporary game AI can process player actions in real time and, in many cases, predict subsequent decisions based on accumulated behavioral data. This capability has led to the development of player modeling, a continuous process of collecting and interpreting interaction data to build a dynamic representation of player behavior tendencies.

An example often cited in the literature is Alien: Isolation, where the AI controlling the antagonist demonstrates adaptive capacity to player strategies. When players repeatedly utilize certain hiding locations, such as closets, the AI system increases the probability of checking similar areas. In this situation, the AI no longer functions solely as an executor of behavioral scripts, but as an entity that observes the course of the game, identifies sources of psychological pressure, and readjusts game conditions to maintain the intensity of tension. Such practices indicate a conceptual shift toward AI as a "shadow designer" in video games, an invisible agent that plays a significant role in shaping the gaming experience through the creation of adaptive, unpredictable, and consistently engaging challenges.

d. Topic Urgency in the Context of the Modern Gaming Industry and Personalization of the Gaming Experience

In the increasingly competitive contemporary gaming industry landscape, the success of a game is no longer solely determined by the visual quality or narrative strength it offers. Greater attention is now being directed towards the extent to which the gaming experience is designed to feel personal, meaningful, and capable of evolving along with player engagement. In this framework, artificial intelligence

(AI) occupies a strategic position as the primary mechanism enabling deep levels of customization. A number of empirical findings show that personalization contributes significantly to increased player retention, given that players tend to maintain their engagement when their personal preferences are recognized and reflected in the gaming experience (Liu et al., 2020).

Furthermore, the role of AI-based systems is not limited to adjusting difficulty levels, but also includes setting the pace of the narrative, the appearance of characters, and the curation of content in the game, including advertisements and virtual items, based on identified player behavior patterns. This practice is the foundation for the development of adaptive game narratives, where storylines can branch out and change dynamically in response to player choices and tendencies analyzed in real time (Togelius & Yannakakis, 2026). From an economic perspective, this development has also encouraged a shift towards more ethical monetization strategies, namely offering purchases tailored to player interests and integrated subtly without disrupting the overall gaming experience. At the same time, AI-based personalization has the potential to expand the inclusivity of games, for example, through the identification of specific needs such as adaptive control schemes for players with disabilities. Thus, in a world increasingly driven by data, AI no longer functions merely as a technological necessity, but has become a strategic imperative in the design of more engaging, meaningful, and inclusive games.

BASIC CONCEPTS OF ARTIFICIAL INTELLIGENCE IN GAMES

In a broader sense, Artificial Intelligence (AI) is a branch of Computer Science that seeks to develop systems with the ability to perform intelligent actions like humans, including learning processes, logical reasoning, language comprehension, and decision making. However, in the realm of game development, the meaning of AI tends to be more specific and applicable. AI is used as a design element to simulate dynamic behavior that is considered "intelligent" in non-playable characters (NPCs), build adaptive systems, and maintain game balance (Yannakakis & Togelius, 2018).

The application of AI in today's digital games has gone beyond conventional functions such as script-based movement and behavior control. In practice, AI acts as a latent observer that is able to record and interpret player preferences, enabling direct adjustment of game content. In this framework, AI does not merely function as a technical device, but also as a narrative and psychological mediator that helps shape the construction of each individual's gaming experience, in line with the patterns of interaction and decision-making exhibited by the player (Laird & VanLent, 2001).

a. Technology Scope: Machine Learning, Deep Learning, Neural Networks, dan Reinforcement Learning

The integration of artificial intelligence in digital games takes place within an interconnected technology ecosystem, rather than as a standalone component. Among the supporting technologies, machine learning (ML) plays a key role because it enables systems to improve their performance through data-based learning processes without relying on explicit rule programming. In modern game development practices, ML serves as the foundation that enables AI systems to adapt to player behavior and constantly changing game conditions. One important branch of ML is deep learning (DL), which utilizes layered neural network architectures to capture complex patterns in high-dimensional data, including indicators of player style, facial expressions, and even affective cues obtained from voice input (LeCun et al., 2015).

Artificial neural networks (NNs), inspired by the principles of human brain organization, demonstrate high effectiveness in processing large-scale, nonlinear data sets. This capacity is particularly relevant in open-world gaming environments, where player behavior is diverse, unpredictable, and constantly changing. Complementing this approach, reinforcement learning (RL) introduces a trial-and-error interaction-based learning paradigm with the environment, allowing AI agents to refine their actions through evaluation of the consequences of previous decisions. In the context of gaming, RL supports the development of adaptive strategies and responsive behavior, enabling AI systems to dynamically adjust to changes in game conditions and player interaction patterns over time (Mnih et al., 2015). These four technologies work together like interdependent body parts: ML acts as the reasoning center, DL functions as a means of observation, NNs perform the role of the nervous system, while RL acts as an execution mechanism that translates decisions into actions.

b. The Role of Each Technology in Observing, Analyzing, and Responding to Player Data

Each AI technology has specific roles and functions that complement each other in understanding player behavior. Machine learning enables systematic observation of player behavior over a period of time, including indicators such as level completion speed, weapon preferences, and recurring failure patterns. These behavioral traces form the main database for compiling individual player profiles, which are then used to direct adaptive responses within the game (Yannakakis & Togelius, 2018). Building on this foundation, deep learning excels at identifying latent patterns that are not easily detected through surface analysis, such as interpreting players' emotional states through facial cues in virtual reality environments or predicting narrative preferences based on accumulated interaction histories.

Artificial neural networks serve as the core computational structure that allows various input streams to be processed simultaneously, thereby supporting real-time adjustment of game scenarios as player behavior changes. At the same time, reinforcement learning is particularly relevant for strategic and open-ended gaming environments, where AI agents are faced with a variety of possible actions in conditions of uncertainty. Through a process of repeated interaction and continuous feedback, these agents refine their strategies by learning from the consequences of previous decisions, as demonstrated by the development of intelligent agents in complex games such as StarCraft II (Vinyals et al., 2019). Overall, machine learning, deep learning, neural networks, and reinforcement learning form an integrated system that not only responds to player actions but is also capable of anticipating subsequent behavior, marking significant progress in the design of interactive digital experiences.

c. Brief Examples of Real Applications in Popular Games

The implementation of machine learning in games has advanced into the real world. Many popular games have incorporated their use creatively. In Middle-earth: Shadow of Mordor, the Nemesis system lets foes recall previous interactions with the players, strategise vengeance, learn from past experiences, and get even with them. It is based on a combination of rule-based AI and data-driven profiling. In Alien: Isolation, the main antagonist uses reinforcement learning to adapt to the player's hiding behaviour and alter search patterns, which adds an unpredictable element of psychological tension. Both Fortnite and Apex Legends utilise machine learning for performance evaluation of players to customise matchmaking and in-game content to maintain competitiveness and balance. Meanwhile, The Last of Us Part II employs deep learning for the animation of NPC faces (non-player characters) to express emotions, responses to their environment, as well as the death of fellow characters, enhancing the game's realism and emotional impact. These examples clearly show that AI in games has become one of the most invaluable tools that are used to enhance interactivity, adaptivity, immersion, and memorability of a game.

UNDERSTANDING PLAYER BEHAVIOR PSYCHOLOGICALLY AND COMPUTATIONALLY

a. Definition of Player Behavior: Actions, Choices, Interests, and Motivations

Behaviour in games, such as video games, can be understood as the reactions or interactions of players with a game they are playing (Drachen & Canossa, 2009). For example, a player has the option to use certain weapons to enter a game or to exit a city. On one hand, a player can delve into the game solo, while on the other hand, they can complete missions in team mode, and vice versa, adding many explorers (untimed). All kinds of gameplay and strategies that gamers employ are not entirely rigid and repetitive, as there are and always will be forms of world, the narrative, art, competition (explore) (Yee, 2006). In everyday life, motivators for decision-making can come from within, such as as simple as curiosity, the need to fulfil one's own goals, or from external sources such as the need to achieve (social recognition, the game "high", earning dual score awards) (Ryan et al., 2006). It is here that, in seeking to understand actions given a strong reason, noting from the player is to dive into a deep explanation.

b. Perspectives on Game Psychology: Self-Determination Theory and Intrinsic-Extrinsic Motivation

One important aspect of Game Psychology is Self-Determination Theory (SDT), which underscores the significant markers of three psychological needs: autonomy, competence, and relatedness (Ryan & Deci, 2000). In the context of games, these needs are multidimensional, such as autonomy, where players can determine their own way of playing, having measurable progress or challenges (competence), and meaningful social interaction (relatedness) (Przybylski et al., 2010). SDT also distinguishes between intrinsic motivation, which is driven from within oneself, such as exploration and self-satisfaction (intrinsic) after achieving something, and extrinsic motivation, which is driven from outside oneself, such as rewards, levels, or scores (Ryan & Rigby, 2019). Psychologically, an effective game is one that is able to combine both, providing freedom as well as achievement to its players. In analysing player behaviour, understanding this motivation becomes an important foundation for creating personalisation or adaptation systems.

c. Computational Approach: Behavior as a Data Stream

In the cognitive approach, player behaviour is viewed as a data stream that moves, flowing in one direction, and can be analysed simultaneously. Every click, interaction, duration of time spent interacting, and even eye movement in VR is recorded as a digital footprint that resembles exclusive behavioural patterns. The data generated from player interactions is dynamic, enabling it to transform a previously static game system into one that is more responsive in detecting changes in playing patterns and player engagement levels over time. Various analytical techniques, such as clustering, sequential pattern mining, and real-time predictive modeling, are widely applied to classify playing styles, predict potential declines in engagement or the risk of players quitting, and tailor game content to emerging behavioral trends (Fang et al., 2020). Through these approaches, adaptive game systems gain the ability to go beyond momentary reactive responses. Instead of acting in isolation, AI utilizes integrated behavior models that continuously accumulate contextual information, enabling smoother, more proactive, and anticipatory adjustments to the gaming experience.

AI AS A PLAYER BEHAVIOR ANALYSIS TOOL

a. Data Collection Techniques: Clickstream, Playtime, Movement Patterns, and Social Interaction

From the perspective of accessibility and data acquisition, player behavior in digital games can be recorded through various logging techniques. One of the most commonly used methods is clickstream analysis, which is the systematic documentation of player actions such as mouse clicks, menu selections, and navigation paths taken during a gaming session. Clickstream data provides a detailed picture of individual preferences, response times, and decision-making patterns, especially in critical or high-pressure game situations. In addition, aggregate metrics such as session duration and total playing time serve as important indicators for assessing player engagement and satisfaction (Yannakakis & Togelius, 2018).

Beyond interactions at the interface level, behavioral data can also be extracted from movement patterns within the game, including the trajectory of player-controlled characters, movement speed, and frequently visited locations within the virtual environment. These spatial and temporal indicators provide meaningful clues about playing styles, such as players' tendencies to be aggressive, exploratory, or strategic and cautious (Drachen & Canossa, 2009). Social interaction data further enriches our understanding of player behavior, as communication between players, collaboration in team-based missions, the formation of alliances, and the practice of gift-giving in games are routinely recorded and analyzed to identify levels of sociability and tendencies toward cooperation. When combined, these various data sources form a comprehensive behavioral dataset, which serves as the basis for developing more sophisticated player models and enables AI systems to interpret and predict player behavior with a higher level of detail and contextual sensitivity.

b. Player Type Classification Process: Bartle's Taxonomy and the Hexad Model

Grouping players into specific categories is an important step in understanding individual motivations and behavioral tendencies during play. One of the most influential conceptual frameworks in this field is Bartle's Taxonomy (1996), which classifies players into four main types: Achievers, who are oriented toward achieving goals and measurable indicators of success; Explorers, who are motivated by exploration and discovery; Socializers, who prioritize social interaction; and Killers, who are driven by competition and domination over other players. This taxonomy has been widely applied in the study and design of massively multiplayer online role-playing games (MMORPGs) and open world environments, where diversity in player motivations and interaction patterns is particularly prominent.

Complementing this approach, Marczewski (2015) proposed the Hexad User Types Model, which offers a broader classification with six player types: Philanthropist, Socializer, Free Spirit, Achiever, Player, and Disruptor. The Hexad model has strong links to interactive design and gamification practices. In the context of modern games, such classifications are relevant not only for analyzing user behavior but also for developing AI that supports automatic content adaptation, given that each player type exhibits different response patterns to game mechanics and challenges.

c. Algorithms Used: Supervised and Unsupervised Learning

To determine player types from behavioral data, AI-based systems generally utilize two complementary learning paradigms, namely supervised learning and unsupervised learning. In the supervised learning approach, player behavioral data is first paired with predetermined labels, for example, classifying a player as an Achiever based on survey results or certain analytical criteria. Classification models such as decision trees, support vector machines, and random forests are then trained to recognize similar behavior patterns in new players who have not been previously classified (Sifa et al., 2018).

In contrast, unsupervised learning does not rely on initial labels, but aims to reveal latent structures that emerge naturally from the data. Methods such as k-means clustering, DBSCAN, and hierarchical clustering group players based on similarities in behavior profiles, so that meaningful categories can be formed directly from observed patterns (Thawonmas et al., 2011). This data-driven approach is particularly useful for identifying new player archetypes that do not fully align with existing taxonomies. In practice, supervised and unsupervised learning are often combined in hybrid classification systems, which enhance the robustness and flexibility of player modeling as game dynamics and player behavior evolve over time.

d. Brief Case Study: AI-Based Player Type Identification in League of Legends

The application of AI in player type classification was empirically demonstrated by Summerville and Mateas (2016) through a study of the game League of Legends. The study utilized behavioral data such as clickstream records, character movement points, playing time metrics, and in-game performance statistics. Using an unsupervised learning approach, the AI system identified player clusters based on similar behavior patterns, which were then mapped to categories in Bartle's taxonomy. Players with minimal involvement in combat and an exploratory tendency were associated with the Explorer type, while those who were active in team coordination and provided support to other players were classified as Socializers.

More than just classification, this system provides practical benefits for developers by providing insights that can be used to design events and game content that align with the characteristics of the player community, such as social interaction-based missions for Socializers or achievement-oriented challenges for players motivated by progression. The implementation of this approach has been shown to contribute to increased player engagement and retention, while demonstrating AI's capacity to objectively capture player behavior and support a dynamically personalized gaming experience cycle.

More broadly, personalization in games refers to the systematic adaptation of game elements based on individual preferences, performance patterns, and behavioral tendencies. Advances in AI enable game systems to adjust difficulty levels, reward structures, narrative progression, and interaction dynamics in real time, creating an experience that is responsive to continuous player input (Yannakakis & Togelius, 2018). For example, when a player consistently shows interest in exploratory activities, AI-based systems can prioritize missions focused on discovery and thematic exploration. Such adaptive mechanisms not only increase the relevance and perceived satisfaction of players, but also deepen emotional engagement by aligning the gaming experience with individual intrinsic motivations.

AI TECHNOLOGIES AND METHODOLOGIES IN PLAYER ANALYTICS

Technological Evolution in Player Behavior Analysis

a. Player Interaction Data as a Key Source in Modern Game Development

Reinforcement learning (RL) is one of the main paradigms in artificial intelligence that emphasizes the decision-making process through environmental feedback in the form of rewards and punishments (Sutton & Barto, 2018). Instead of relying on pre-programmed knowledge, RL agents gradually refine their behavior through repeated experimentation, assessing the impact of each action taken throughout continuous interaction. In the context of digital games, RL is widely used to train AI agents to handle multi-level decision-making processes under conditions of uncertainty, where optimal strategies must be learned from experience rather than determined through explicit instructions.

This learning mechanism bears a strong resemblance to the human experience-based learning process, as agents progressively build their understanding of the environment through a balance between exploration and exploitation (Li, 2017). The dynamic and unpredictable nature of the gaming environment makes it a highly suitable medium for both the development and evaluation of RL-based systems. Therefore, games serve as productive experimental laboratories for the advancement of more flexible, adaptive, and human-like forms of artificial intelligence.

b. The Importance of Real-Time Analytics in Creating Adaptive Game Experiences

In the context of modern games, player actions play an important role not only in shaping the quality of the gaming experience, but also in supporting the continuous development process and iterative system updates. Behavioral data generated during gameplay—including strategic decision-making, movement patterns, response times, and individual preferences—is a rich source of big data that can be systematically analyzed to drive game design improvements and system optimization. Advances in telemetry and system logging technologies enable increasingly comprehensive data collection, giving developers real-time visibility into player interactions within the game world.

As stated by Bae and Bennett (2025), the availability of this data opens up opportunities to directly predict player actions, for example, in the context of turn-taking during interactions in cooperative multiplayer games with high levels of social engagement, through the application of transformer-based multimodal reasoning (Nettey, 2024). This real-time analytical capability is an important foundation for creating adaptive gaming experiences, where game systems can respond quickly and contextually to changes in player behavior, while supporting a more responsive and data-driven development cycle.

c. Shifting from Rule-Based System to Machine Learning-Based Approach

Perhaps one of the largest changes in gaming technology is the shift from explicit rule-based systems to using machine learning and deep learning approaches. There are gaps within rule-based systems when it comes to the intricacies and nuances of contextual player behavior. However, systems based on ML are capable of learning through large amounts of data and generalizing responses in many different situations and conditions, especially in dynamic gameplay.

Nettey (2024) explains how machine learning is being integrated into the design of sports coaches' and game analysts' decision-making support systems that were previously based on observation and rigid rules (Nettey, 2024). Another work by R. Liu (2024) proposes an LLM (Large Language Model) based generative approach to match-3 game autonomous game agents, which implements real-time image analysis alongside situational decision-making, something never achieved through rule-based systems.

Machine Learning in Behavior Analytics

a. What is Machine Learning and Why is it Superior to Conventional Approaches?

Machine Learning (ML) is a component of Artificial Intelligence (AI). It enables systems to autonomously learn from information given to them without the need for explicit programming. Unlike previous rule-based systems, which operated according to deterministic logic crafted by developers, ML systems are based on algorithms that perpetually learn, develop, and improve based on the data given to them.

In terms of its application in games, ML assists developers in automatically recognizing complex patterns of player activities over time, regardless of how disorganized and intricate they may be. Drachen et al. (2013) mentioned in their study that, unlike manual observation and logic-based techniques, machine learning-based data mining techniques based on algorithms can uncover insights that were previously hidden, and thus are more efficient. Furthermore, Lantz (2019) highlights that within digital gaming environments, machine learning demonstrates a strong capacity for processing large volumes of unstructured data, thereby supporting more precise and contextually relevant predictions of player actions. Algorithms Used: Decision Tree, SVM, and Clustering

1. **Decision Tree:** For decision trees, the data is divided into subdivisions using particular attributes, and decision paths akin to the branches of a tree are formed. This method is helpful when analyzing player behavior as it captures a model's decisions through an interpretable logical sequence and rational pathways in decision-making. This algorithm works reasonably well in detecting binary decisions, for instance, whether the player will quit the game (quit) or will continue to play. Decision trees are cited by Pareek & Thakkar (2021) to be useful in the domain of behavior due to their capability of deriving reasonable rules from data without requiring an intricate mathematical model.
2. **Support Vector Machine (SVM):** Due to the SVM algorithm's unique capacity to calculate the best hyperplane separating two data classes with maximum margin, it works perfectly for classifying a player's behavior. In gaming, SVM is popularly implemented in classifying a player as a passive or active user, as well as a novice or advanced player, using recorded gameplay statistics. Olsen & Torresen (2016) reported utilizing SVM in forecasting the emotional experiences of a player using sensors and testified that classifying the emotional conduct of a player against the game data input yielded the most accurate results.
3. **Clustering:** Unsupervised exploratory analysis employs K-Means and HDBSCAN clustering techniques, which allow the grouping of users based on their unique traits. For instance, users who spend time aimlessly navigating the game map versus those who are more goal-oriented in completing assigned missions can be clustered differently. Zacharia (2018) utilized these strategies to define player types and personalities in a digital escape room.

b. Case Study: Predicting Rage Quit and Play Duration

Certain behavioral patterns, such as rage quitting—that is, stopping the game due to frustration—can be predicted through empirical indicators such as an increase in rapid clicks, a series of consecutive losses, and the duration of the playing session. Goodwin et al. (2024) utilized clustering techniques combined with SHAP (Shapley Additive Explanations) to identify and explain the main factors that trigger rage quitting and sudden player exits in interactive games. Meanwhile, Joseph et al. (2024) proposed a hybrid predictive framework that integrates Support Vector Machines and Decision Trees algorithms to estimate the duration of a gaming session based on click speed and frequency thresholds. The results of this study show that this integrated machine learning model produces a significantly higher level of prediction accuracy compared to conventional statistical approaches and heuristic methods, thus confirming the superiority of data-based techniques in modeling player engagement dynamics.

COMPLEX APPROACH: DEEP LEARNING AND NEURAL NETWORKS

a. The Role of Deep Learning in Understanding Advanced Behavioral Patterns

Deep learning (DL) is an advanced branch of artificial intelligence that utilizes layered neural networks to extract complex and abstract patterns from data. In the context of digital games, DL plays an important role in interpreting the dynamics of behavior that arise naturally through player interaction with the game environment, enabling the system to respond in a more adaptive and information-based manner. For example, in strategy or narrative games, players can be distinguished not only in binary terms as active or passive, but also positioned on a richer spectrum of behaviors, such as aggressive, exploratory, reactive, and creative. Through a deep learning approach, the system is able to identify and classify these various behaviors without requiring direct intervention from game developers to set categorization boundaries at the design stage. The findings of a survey conducted by Hu et al. (2023) show that DL is very effective in generalizing user interaction patterns across genres, for example, from first-person shooters (FPS) to real-time strategy (RTS) or multiplayer online battle arena (MOBA), especially in the context of multiplayer games that generate large amounts of unstructured data.

b. Use of CNN/RNN in the Analysis of Facial Expression, Voice, and Emotional Response in VR Games

For the VR world, the player experience is built around strong emotional or sensory responses. These factors are crucial when designing emotion-aware games. The most important deep learning architectures relevant for this context are:

1. **Convolutional Neural Networks (CNN):** As an illustration, CNNs are used to analyze visual inputs, such as players' facial expressions as captured through VR head-mounted cameras. Subtle changes in facial features, such as stress, excitement, or confusion, are etched onto someone's face, placing their eyebrows in a furrowed position or their mouth becoming tense, are disrespectfully categorized as microexpressions, which need to be recognized by the hierarchical systems

called CNNs. Zeng et al. (2018) conducted a study where they found that CNNs could recognize emotions captured in real time from facial expressions during interaction with the system, achieving more than 85% accuracy.

2. **Recurrent Neural Networks (RNN):** RNNs, most commonly equipped with Long Short-Term Memory (LSTM), are specialized in dealing with temporal sequences of a stimulus such as voice, intonation, and speech in games. For sound or story-driven games, an RNN may study players' vocalizations in terms of their tonality and identify boredom, enthusiasm, or tension. Thus, enabling personalization of responses from AI in the game world to the current emotional state of the user. It is now more common to combine CNN and RNN for the purposes of multimodal learning, where employing both visual and auditory signals enhances the precision of emotion recognition.

c. Illustration of Neural Network Training Process with Real User Data

Training deep learning models for behavior analysis requires a systematic process:

- **Real Data Collection from Players:** Data is collected from cameras, microphones, motion sensors, and click logs as the player interacts with the game. Data labels can be manual annotations or results of emotion surveys, for example, using a Self-Assessment Manikin (SAM).
- **Preprocessing and Augmentation:** Data is reprocessed to remove noise, normalize the input, and increase variety with augmentation techniques.
- **Model Training:** Data is fed into the neural network in batches, and training is done using algorithms such as Adam Optimizer. Computation is done using a GPU or a TPU to speed up the iterative process and minimize the loss function.
- **Evaluation and Validation:** The model is tested against the validation set and test set to ensure that the results do not overfit the training data.

d. Technical Challenges: Big Data Requirements, High Computation, and Bias

While DL is promising, there are three major challenges faced during implementation in a gaming environment:

- **Data-Hungry:** DL requires hundreds to thousands of hours of user interaction data to be able to generalize behavior patterns well. This challenge is compounded if emotional or multimodal data is difficult to obtain.

- **High Computation:** Training CNN and RNN, especially on high-resolution or long audio data, requires GPU/TPU-based parallel computing. Cost and energy are major constraints, especially in indie or educational game development.
- **Data Bias Issue:** DL models are highly dependent on their training data. If the data only represents the playing style of a certain group (e.g., only male gamers or only professional players), then the model may fail to accommodate the diversity of playing styles.

Such biases have the potential to produce gameplay experiences that are misaligned with, or even disadvantageous to, certain groups of players. Yannakakis and Togelius (2018) identified data bias as a major threat to the reliability of adaptive game AI, noting that biased datasets can undermine the effectiveness and quality of personalisation mechanisms.

REINFORCEMENT LEARNING: ADAPTIVE AI AND DYNAMIC STRATEGIES

a. Understanding Reinforcement Learning in the Context of Games

Reinforcement learning (RL) is a fundamental paradigm in artificial intelligence that emphasizes the learning process of agents through repeated trial-and-error interactions, guided by reward signals from the environment (Sutton & Barto, 2018). In the realm of digital games, RL enables AI agents to identify and develop effective strategies by continuously interacting with complex and uncertain game conditions. This mechanism closely resembles human experience-based learning, where understanding is formed gradually through exploration and evaluation of the consequences of actions taken (Li, 2017). Therefore, the gaming environment provides a highly conducive context for the application of RL in the development of adaptive, flexible AI systems that exhibit realistic behavior.

b. The Role of AI Agents in Learning from Continuous Interaction with Players

AI agents trained using reinforcement learning refine their strategies through continuous interaction with players, rather than relying on predetermined behavior scripts. By observing player behavior patterns and utilizing feedback obtained from the game environment, agents are able to dynamically adjust their actions to remain challenging and contextually relevant. This adaptation process is supported by various advanced RL algorithms, such as Deep Q-Networks, Proximal Policy Optimization, and Actor–Critic models (Mnih et al., 2015; Schulman et al., 2017). Through this feedback-based learning mechanism, the agent's strategy and the player's actions evolve simultaneously, thereby enhancing immersion and maintaining game balance in the long term.

c. Case Study: AI Agents in Competitive Games (MOBA and RTS)

Competitive game genres, particularly Multiplayer Online Battle Arena (MOBA) and Real-Time Strategy (RTS), have become the main testing grounds for reinforcement learning-based AI systems. DeepMind's success with AlphaStar demonstrates the potential of RL to achieve performance on par with professional players in StarCraft II, by combining supervised learning and large-scale self-play (Vinyals et al., 2019). Similar achievements were seen in OpenAI Five in the game Dota 2, where AI agents successfully learned teamwork, tactical coordination, and real-time decision-making under competitive pressure (Berner et al., 2019). Collectively, these studies illustrate that reinforcement learning can produce AI agents that not only rival, but in certain contexts also surpass, the capabilities of experienced human players in highly complex gaming environments.

Player Interaction Data Sources and Analysis Techniques

a. Data Type: Activity Logs, Playtime, Clicks, Navigation, Path Choices, and Tactical Decisions

In contemporary game development and evaluation processes, data derived from player interactions constitutes a critical resource for understanding behavioural patterns, user preferences, and gameplay-related challenges. Among the most commonly collected forms of data are the following:

- **Activity logs:** These logs capture player actions in a sequential manner, encompassing movement trajectories, item usage, combat behaviour, and social interactions with other players or in-game entities. Such records provide a detailed behavioural trace that supports fine-grained analysis of gameplay dynamics.
- **Playtime metrics:** Playtime data offer insights into levels of engagement by documenting session duration, frequency of play per day, and broader weekly

or longitudinal play habits. These indicators are widely used to assess player commitment, fatigue, and overall satisfaction with the game experience.

- **Clicks and navigation:** shows frequently explored areas, frequently selected interaction points, and response rate to UI/UX.
- **Path choice and tactical decisions:** represent the player's approach to challenges, such as choosing an offense or defense strategy (Seif El-Nasr et al., 2013).

b. Real-Time Data Collection and Behavioural Data Visualisation

Player data is generally collected in real time through telemetry systems and analytics software development kits (SDKs), such as Unity Analytics and Firebase. These platforms continuously record various game events and send them for analysis, allowing developers to gain insights that directly support design decisions, game balance adjustments, and iterative refinement processes throughout the development cycle. To help provide a more intuitive understanding of player interaction patterns, developers utilize a variety of behavioral data visualization techniques. One of the most widely used approaches is heatmaps, which visualize the frequency or intensity of player activity within the game environment through color gradations. This technique is highly effective in identifying high-traffic areas, strategic points that could potentially become choke points, and underutilized areas within a level. Complementing this, player navigation flowcharts illustrate the sequence of paths taken by players as they explore levels or complete missions. Through node-based representation, this visualization reveals both dominant and rarely chosen alternative routes. Various interactive analytics platforms, such as Tableau, Power BI, and specialized game analytics tools like GameAnalytics, support the implementation of these visualization techniques and enable dynamic, large-scale exploration of player behavior trends (Mahlmann et al., 2010).

c. User Frustration Analysis, Drop-off Point Identification, and Level Balancing

A central objective of interaction analytics in game development is the identification of moments at which players experience frustration. Such moments may arise from excessive level difficulty, technical malfunctions, or unclear gameplay mechanics and design choices. Indicators of player frustration are typically inferred from a combination of behavioural signals, rather than from a single metric in isolation, allowing developers to diagnose problematic segments of the game with greater precision.

- Failure ratio within a level,
- Repetition of actions without progress,
- Frequency of exiting the game after repeated failures.

These are often referred to as drop-off points, which are important indicators for measuring balance in level design. By knowing these points, designers can adjust the difficulty to keep it challenging but not make players give up (Canossa et al., 2011).

d. The Effect of These Analytics on User Retention and Game Design Improvement

User behavior analysis plays a crucial role in improving user retention. By understanding when and why players stop playing, developers can:

- Adjust the difficulty curve to keep it interesting,
- Provide timely rewards or tutorials,
- Improve interface design and interaction.

According to a study by Fields and Cotton (2011), a data-driven game design approach directly contributes to increased lifetime value (LTV) and long-term engagement. In addition, the use of data-driven adaptive gameplay also increases players' subjective satisfaction.

ARTIFICIAL INTELLIGENCE STRATEGIES FOR PERSONALISATION

The video game industry has undergone a significant shift from uniform arcade-style designs to gaming experiences that are individually player-oriented. This change has been driven by players' increasing expectations for narratives, challenges, and game mechanics that feel personally relevant. In this context, artificial intelligence (AI) plays a central role by enabling the collection and analysis of player interaction data to build dynamic player profiles (Bakkes et al., 2012). A number of empirical studies show that this kind of personalization contributes to increased immersion, retention, and even revenue, with reported player engagement levels increasing by more than 30 percent in individually tailored gaming environments (Drachen & Canossa, 2009).

Through the use of AI, games no longer rely on static design structures, but are able to respond adaptively to diverse playing styles. By analyzing game indicators such as the strategies used, the tempo of the game, and behavior patterns in completing missions, AI systems can group players into specific behavioral profiles, which then become the basis for real-time game adjustments (Yannakakis, 2012). This approach is evident in games such as Skyrim and Left 4 Dead, where the difficulty level, game rhythm, and content intensity change dynamically. These adaptive mechanisms play an important role in maintaining optimal challenge conditions, which are closely related to achieving flow and sustained enjoyment of the game (Holmgard et al., 2019).

This adaptive capability is supported by an AI system that can record player behavior data in great detail, including movement patterns, battle frequency, and duration of game environment exploration. This data enables continuous updating of player models, which are then used to automatically adjust the tempo, difficulty level, and content presentation. Thus, different player archetypes obtain experiences that are in line with their dominant tendencies, such as narrative immersion for exploratory players or increased combat intensity for aggressive players (Cowley et al., 2008). This kind of adaptive balance contributes to minimizing frustration and preventing disengagement, thereby supporting long-term player retention (Holmgard et al., 2019).

The development of AI has also expanded the possibilities for narrative construction in digital games. AI-based narrative systems allow stories to develop meaningfully in response to player decisions, unlike conventional fixed branching structures. Contemporary narrative engines are capable of dynamically assembling story elements based on moral choices, character relationships, and player actions within the game (Thue et al., 2021; Cavazza & Charles, 2021). Advances in natural language processing further enrich the ability of non-player characters to respond contextually and expressively, so that players are no longer mere consumers of the story, but also co-authors in an evolving narrative. This strengthens the player's sense of agency and emotional involvement in the game world.

Beyond the direct gaming experience, AI-based recommendation systems have also become an important component of the modern gaming platform ecosystem. By utilizing players' game history, preferences, and achievement data, these systems generate personalized recommendations for games and additional content. Platforms such as Steam and Xbox Game Pass implement collaborative filtering methods to improve the accuracy of recommendations based on collective user behavior. Research shows that this form of personalization not only increases the duration of play sessions but also strengthens players' long-term attachment to the platform (Anderson et al., 2013).

Going forward, the development of AI-based personalization is expected to increasingly focus on multiplayer interactions and more in-depth character development systems. Emerging models seek to integrate the psychosocial dimensions of player behavior, resulting in more subtle and context-sensitive adaptations. While promising an increasingly rich gaming experience, this approach also carries the risk of reducing players' perceived control if automation becomes too dominant. Therefore, ongoing ethical and regulatory challenges—particularly regarding data protection within frameworks such as the GDPR—underscore the importance of transparency, player agency, and responsible AI design in shaping the future of the digital gaming industry (Kozyreva et al., 2020).

ETHICAL CONSIDERATIONS AND BOUNDARIES OF TECHNOLOGY

The integration of artificial intelligence into contemporary game design has fundamentally transformed how digital games are designed and experienced. Adaptive narratives, responsive non-player characters, and real-time difficulty adjustment demonstrate how machine learning systems now mediate player interaction at a deep level. However, these developments are not merely technical in nature; they also raise ethical concerns related to player autonomy and psychological engagement. AI-driven personalization enables the alignment of challenges and storylines with individual behavior, yet at the same time it may subtly influence players' decision-making in order to extend playtime or encourage monetization (King & Delfabbro, 2019). As algorithmically mediated immersion increases, issues of emotional attachment, dependency, and the shaping of player cognition demand systematic ethical scrutiny.

Ethical debates surrounding AI in games bear strong similarities to issues previously observed in social media ecosystems and digital advertising, such as opaque algorithms, persuasive architectures, and the erosion of user agency (Floridi et al., 2018; Jobin et al., 2019). In the context of games, data-driven strategies aimed at increasing retention and revenue must be evaluated not only in terms of effectiveness but also with regard to their psychological and social impacts, particularly on vulnerable groups. Responsible development approaches therefore require the integration of ethical considerations from the design stage onward, in order to identify potential unintended consequences and ensure that human well-being remains the primary priority (Mittelstadt et al., 2016).

Personalization systems in games rely heavily on the large-scale collection of behavioral data, including player choices, interaction frequency, and social dynamics. While such data are crucial for optimizing gameplay experiences, their collection practices are often characterized by limited transparency and may undermine the principle of informed consent (Tran et al., 2020). Regulatory frameworks such as the GDPR and the CCPA seek to strengthen data ownership, access, and user control rights (Martin, 2019), yet their implementation in the gaming context requires design strategies capable of clearly communicating data practices and respecting players' capacity to manage their digital identities.

Beyond privacy concerns, AI systems in games also risk reproducing social inequalities through algorithmic bias. When training data fail to represent the diversity of player populations, disparities may emerge in matchmaking systems, content generation, and character representation (Raji & Buolamwini, 2019; West et al., 2019). Addressing these challenges requires sustained efforts to diversify data, apply culturally sensitive design principles, and conduct regular system audits. Moreover, AI's capacity to influence player behavior through feedback mechanisms and predictive models carries significant ethical responsibility, particularly when it is used to exploit cognitive vulnerabilities for commercial gain (King & Delfabbro, 2019). Consequently, the ethical development of AI within the gaming industry necessitates cross-disciplinary collaboration and collective efforts to democratize access to AI technologies, thereby fostering innovation that is fair and inclusive.

FUTURE TRENDS AND GLOBAL IMPLICATIONS

Artificial intelligence in game development has undergone a significant shift from a supportive analytical function to a primary driver of interactive design. AI now plays a direct role in real-time decision-making, adaptive storytelling, and large-scale player modeling, thereby acting as a co-creative agent within gameplay experiences (Riedl & Harrison, 2016). Its integration with immersive technologies such as virtual reality (VR), augmented reality (AR), and metaverse environments further reinforces this role, with AI dynamically managing social interaction, competition, and collaboration. Immersion is no longer determined solely by visual realism, but by the system's capacity to respond to player actions in meaningful and sustained ways (Camerlengo et al., 2022).

At the same time, the expansion of AI into the socio-emotional domain enables non-player characters to exhibit affective responses tailored to players' histories and behavioral patterns, thereby deepening emotional attachment and a sense of social presence (Isbister, 2016; Alcántara-Rubio et al., 2022). However, the global implementation of these technologies remains shaped by structural and cultural inequalities, including disparities in regulatory readiness and data biases that reflect dominant value systems. Without coordinated ethical governance and algorithmic design that is sensitive to cultural diversity, the potential of AI to foster inclusive and equitable gaming ecosystems risks being constrained (Floridi et al., 2018; Yuan et al., 2023).

AI DECLARATION

This manuscript was prepared with the support of ChatGPT and Grammarly, which were used in a limited and responsible manner in the language editing process, specifically to improve sentence structure, coherence, and readability. Neither tool was used to generate, copy, or reproduce the work of others. All ideas, data, analysis, and conceptual frameworks in this manuscript are entirely the original work of the author and are supported by valid sources and cited in accordance with scientific publication ethics standards.

REFERENCES

Alcántara-Rubio, L., Valderrama-Hernández, R., Solís-Espallargas, C., & Ruiz-Morales, J. (2022). The implementation of the SDGs in universities: A systematic review. *Environmental Education Research, 28*(11), 1585–1615. DOI: 10.1080/13504622.2022.2063798

Anderson, A., Huttenlocher, D., Kleinberg, J., & Leskovec, J. (2013). Steering user behavior with badges. *Proceedings of the 22nd International Conference on World Wide Web*, 95–106. DOI: 10.1145/2488388.2488398

Bae, Y. H., & Bennett, C. C. (2025). *Multimodal Transformer Models for Turn-taking Prediction: Effects on Conversational Dynamics of Human-Agent Interaction during Cooperative Gameplay.*

Bakkes, S. C. J., Spronck, P. H. M., & van Lankveld, G. (2012). Player behavioural modelling for video games. *Entertainment Computing, 3*(3), 71–79. DOI: 10.1016/j.entcom.2011.12.001

Bartle, R. (1996). Hearts, clubs, diamonds, spades: Players who suit MUDs. *Journal of MUD Research, 1*(1).

Camerlengo, F., Frittelli, A., & Pagliarello, R. (2022). CRISPR towards a Sustainable Agriculture. *Encyclopedia, 2*(1), 538–558. DOI: 10.3390/encyclopedia2010036

Cavazza, M., & Charles, F. (2021). Dialogue Generation in Character-Based Interactive Storytelling. *Proceedings of the AAAI Conference on Artificial Intelligence and Interactive Digital Entertainment, 1*(1), 21–26. DOI: 10.1609/aiide.v1i1.18710

Drachen, A., & Canossa, A. (2009). Analyzing spatial user behavior in computer games using geographic information systems. *Proceedings of the 13th International MindTrek Conference: Everyday Life in the Ubiquitous Era*, 182–189. DOI: 10.1145/1621841.1621875

Drachen, A., Thurau, C., Togelius, J., Yannakakis, G. N., & Bauckhage, C. (2013). Game Data Mining. In *Game Analytics* (pp. 205–253). Springer London., DOI: 10.1007/978-1-4471-4769-5_12

Fang, J., Zhang, R., Zhao, Y., Zheng, K., Zhou, X., & Zhou, A. (2020). A-DSP: An Adaptive Join Algorithm for Dynamic Data Stream on Cloud System. *IEEE Transactions on Knowledge and Data Engineering*, •••, 1–1. DOI: 10.1109/TKDE.2019.2947055

Floridi, L., Cowls, J., Beltrametti, M., Chatila, R., Chazerand, P., Dignum, V., Luetge, C., Madelin, R., Pagallo, U., Rossi, F., Schafer, B., Valcke, P., & Vayena, E. (2018). AI4People—An Ethical Framework for a Good AI Society: Opportunities, Risks, Principles, and Recommendations. *Minds and Machines*, *28*(4), 689–707. DOI: 10.1007/s11023-018-9482-5 PMID: 30930541

Gee, J. P. (2003). What video games have to teach us about learning and literacy. *Computers in Entertainment*, *1*(1), 20–20. DOI: 10.1145/950566.950595

Goodwin, N. L., Choong, J. J., Hwang, S., Pitts, K., Bloom, L., Islam, A., Zhang, Y. Y., Szelenyi, E. R., Tong, X., Newman, E. L., Miczek, K., Wright, H. R., McLaughlin, R. J., Norville, Z. C., Eshel, N., Heshmati, M., Nilsson, S. R. O., & Golden, S. A. (2024). Simple Behavioral Analysis (SimBA) as a platform for explainable machine learning in behavioral neuroscience. *Nature Neuroscience*, *27*(7), 1411–1424. DOI: 10.1038/s41593-024-01649-9 PMID: 38778146

Holmgard, C., Green, M. C., Liapis, A., & Togelius, J. (2019). Automated Playtesting With Procedural Personas Through MCTS With Evolved Heuristics. *IEEE Transactions on Games*, *11*(4), 352–362. DOI: 10.1109/TG.2018.2808198

Hu, Z., Ding, Y., Wu, R., Li, L., Zhang, R., Hu, Y., Qiu, F., Zhang, Z., Wang, K., Zhao, S., Zhang, Y., Jiang, J., Xi, Y., Pu, J., Zhang, W., Wang, S., Chen, K., Zhou, T., Chen, J., & Fan, C. (2023). Deep learning applications in games: A survey from a data perspective. *Applied Intelligence*, *53*(24), 31129–31164. DOI: 10.1007/s10489-023-05094-2

Isbister, K. (2016). *How Games Move Us: Emotion by Design*. MIT Press. DOI: 10.7551/mitpress/9267.001.0001

Jobin, A., Ienca, M., & Vayena, E. (2019). The global landscape of AI ethics guidelines. *Nature Machine Intelligence*, *1*(9), 389–399. DOI: 10.1038/s42256-019-0088-2

Joseph, G. V., P, A., Thomas M, A., Jose, D., V Roy, T., & Prasad, M. P. (2024). Impact of Digital Literacy, Use of AI tools and Peer Collaboration on AI Assisted Learning- Perceptions of the University students. *Digital Education Review*, *45*(45), 43–49. DOI: 10.1344/der.2024.45.43-49

Kent, S. L. (2001). *The ultimate history of video games: From Pong to Pokémon and beyond*. Three Rivers Press.

King, D. L., & Delfabbro, P. H. (2019). Video Game Monetization (e.g., 'Loot Boxes'): A Blueprint for Practical Social Responsibility Measures. *International Journal of Mental Health and Addiction*, *17*(1), 166–179. DOI: 10.1007/s11469-018-0009-3

Kozyreva, A., Lewandowsky, S., & Hertwig, R. (2020). Citizens Versus the Internet: Confronting Digital Challenges With Cognitive Tools. *Psychological Science in the Public Interest, 21*(3), 103–156. DOI: 10.1177/1529100620946707 PMID: 33325331

Laird, J., & VanLent, M. (2001). Human-Level AI's Killer Application: Interactive Computer Games. *AI Magazine, 22*(2). Advance online publication. DOI: 10.1609/aimag.v22i2.1558

Lantz, B. (2019). *Machine Learning with R: Expert Techniques for Predictive Modeling*. Packt Publishing.

LeCun, Y., Bengio, Y., & Hinton, G. (2015). Deep learning. *Nature, 521*(7553), 436–444. DOI: 10.1038/nature14539 PMID: 26017442

Li, Y. (2017). *Deep reinforcement learning: An overview.* ArXiv Preprint.

Liu, R. (2024). *Generative AI Agent for Autonomous Match-3 Gameplay through Real-Time Image-Based Decision-Making* [Master's thesis]. Aalto University.

Liu, Z. J., Tretyakova, N., Fedorov, V., & Kharakhordina, M. (2020). Digital Literacy and Digital Didactics as the Basis for New Learning Models Development. [IJET]. *International Journal of Emerging Technologies in Learning, 15*(14), 4. DOI: 10.3991/ijet.v15i14.14669

Marczewski, A. (2015). *Even Ninja Monkeys like to play* (Vol. 1). Blurb Inc.

Martin, K. (2019). Designing Ethical Algorithms. *MIS Quarterly Executive*, •••, 129–142. DOI: 10.17705/2msqe.00012

Mittelstadt, B. D., Allo, P., Taddeo, M., Wachter, S., & Floridi, L. (2016). The ethics of algorithms: Mapping the debate. *Big Data & Society, 3*(2), 2053951716679679. Advance online publication. DOI: 10.1177/2053951716679679

Mnih, V., Kavukcuoglu, K., Silver, D., Rusu, A. A., Veness, J., Bellemare, M. G., Graves, A., Riedmiller, M., Fidjeland, A. K., Ostrovski, G., Petersen, S., Beattie, C., Sadik, A., Antonoglou, I., King, H., Kumaran, D., Wierstra, D., Legg, S., & Hassabis, D. (2015). Human-level control through deep reinforcement learning. *Nature, 518*(7540), 529–533. DOI: 10.1038/nature14236 PMID: 25719670

Nettey, S. (2024). *Vision Vantage: A Decision Support System for Football Player Scouts.* Ashesi University.

Olsen, A. F., & Torresen, J. (2016). Smartphone accelerometer data used for detecting human emotions. *2016 3rd International Conference on Systems and Informatics (ICSAI)*, 410–415. DOI: 10.1109/ICSAI.2016.7810990

Pareek, P., & Thakkar, A. (2021). A survey on video-based Human Action Recognition: Recent updates, datasets, challenges, and applications. *Artificial Intelligence Review, 54*(3), 2259–2322. DOI: 10.1007/s10462-020-09904-8

Przybylski, A. K., Rigby, C. S., & Ryan, R. M. (2010). A Motivational Model of Video Game Engagement. *Review of General Psychology, 14*(2), 154–166. DOI: 10.1037/a0019440

Rabin, S. (Ed.). (2013). *Game AI pro: collected wisdom of game AI professionals*. CRC Press. DOI: 10.1201/b16725

Raji, I. D., & Buolamwini, J. (2019). Actionable Auditing. *Proceedings of the 2019 AAAI/ACM Conference on AI, Ethics, and Society*, 429–435. DOI: 10.1145/3306618.3314244

Riedl, M. O., & Harrison, B. (2016). Using Stories to Teach Human Values to Artificial Agents. *AAAI Workshop: AI, Ethics, and Society*, 105–112.

Ryan, R. M., & Deci, E. L. (2000). Self-determination theory and the facilitation of intrinsic motivation, social development, and well-being. *The American Psychologist, 55*(1), 68–78. DOI: 10.1037/0003-066X.55.1.68 PMID: 11392867

Ryan, R. M., & Rigby, C. S. (2019). Motivational foundations of game-based learning. In *Handbook of game-based learning* (pp. 153–176).

Ryan, R. M., Rigby, C. S., & Przybylski, A. (2006). The Motivational Pull of Video Games: A Self-Determination Theory Approach. *Motivation and Emotion, 30*(4), 344–360. DOI: 10.1007/s11031-006-9051-8

Sifa, R., Drachen, A., & Bauckhage, C. (2018). Profiling in games: Understanding behavior from telemetry. *Social Interactions in Virtual Worlds: An Interdisciplinary Perspective*, 337–374.

Summerville, A., & Mateas, M. (2016). Super Mario as a String: Platformer Level Generation Via LSTMs. *Summerville*. /arXiv.1603.00930DOI: 10.26503/dl.v2016i1.752

Sutton, R. S., & Barto, A. G. (2018). *Reinforcement Learning: An Introduction* (2nd ed.). MIT Press.

Thawonmas, R., Yoshida, K., Lou, J.-K., & Chen, K.-T. (2011). Analysis of revisitations in online games. *Entertainment Computing, 2*(4), 215–221. DOI: 10.1016/j.entcom.2011.01.003

Togelius, J., & Yannakakis, G. N. (2026). General general game AI. *2016 IEEE Conference on Computational Intelligence and Games*, 1–8.

Tran, T., Ho, M.-T., Pham, T.-H., Nguyen, M.-H., Nguyen, K.-L. P., Vuong, T.-T., Nguyen, T.-H. T., Nguyen, T.-D., Nguyen, T.-L., Khuc, Q., La, V.-P., & Vuong, Q.-H. (2020). How Digital Natives Learn and Thrive in the Digital Age: Evidence from an Emerging Economy. *Sustainability (Basel)*, *12*(9), 3819. DOI: 10.3390/su12093819

Vinyals, O., Babuschkin, I., Czarnecki, W. M., Mathieu, M., Dudzik, A., Chung, J., & Silver, D. (2019). Grandmaster level in StarCraft II using multi-agent reinforcement learning. *Nature*, *575*(7782), 350–354. DOI: 10.1038/s41586-019-1724-z PMID: 31666705

West, S. M., Whittaker, M., & Crawford, K. (2019). Discriminating systems. *AI Now*, 1–33.

Yannakakis, G. N. (2012). Game AI revisited. *Proceedings of the 9th Conference on Computing Frontiers*, 285–292. DOI: 10.1145/2212908.2212954

Yannakakis, G. N., & Togelius, J. (2018). *Artificial intelligence and games* (Vol. 2). Springer. DOI: 10.1007/978-3-319-63519-4

Yee, N. (2006). Motivations for Play in Online Games. *Cyberpsychology & Behavior*, *9*(6), 772–775. DOI: 10.1089/cpb.2006.9.772 PMID: 17201605

Yuan, H., Liu, M., Lu, K., Yang, C., & Hao, N. (2023). The effect of example abstraction on creativity from the perspectives of example modality and generality. *Thinking Skills and Creativity*, *47*, 101234. DOI: 10.1016/j.tsc.2023.101234

Zacharia, K. (2018). *3D Escape Room Based on Personality Traits*. Aristotle University of Thessaloniki.

Zeng, B., Huang, Q., El Saddik, A., Li, H., Jiang, S., & Fan, X. (2018). Advances in Multimedia Information Processing–PCM 2017. *18th Pacific-Rim Conference on Multimedia*.

KEY TERMS AND DEFINITIONS

Adaptive Narrative: A form of interactive storytelling in video games in which the storyline evolves dynamically in response to players' choices, actions, and preferences. This approach commonly relies on artificial intelligence to adjust narrative structures in real time, enabling personalized and non-linear story experiences.

Artificial Intelligence (AI): A subfield of computer science concerned with the design of systems capable of performing functions that typically require human cognitive abilities, such as learning, reasoning, and self-correction. In the context of games, AI is applied to create adaptive, responsive, and personalized engagement experiences for players.

Behavioral Analysis: The computational-level examination of player-generated data, including movement patterns, interaction frequency, and play duration. This analysis is used to infer player behavior, preferences, and, in some cases, emotional states within a game environment.

Clickstream Data: Sequential records of player interactions in a digital game, including clicks, navigation paths, and action sequences. These data provide valuable insights for modeling player behavior and predicting future in-game decisions.

Convolutional Neural Network (CNN): A deep learning architecture specifically designed for processing visual data such as images and videos. In gaming contexts, CNNs are often employed to analyze facial expressions or visual cues, particularly in virtual reality environments.

Decision Tree: A supervised machine learning model that represents decision-making processes in a hierarchical tree structure. In games, decision trees are used to classify and interpret player behavior based on structured gameplay data.

Deep Learning (DL): An advanced machine learning approach that utilizes multi-layer neural networks to identify complex patterns within large datasets. In game analytics, deep learning techniques are applied to detect nuanced player attributes, including emotions, preferences, and behavioral tendencies.

Dynamic Difficulty Adjustment (DDA): The real-time modification of game challenge levels to align with a player's skill, performance, or engagement state. These adjustments are commonly implemented using reinforcement learning to maintain an optimal balance between challenge and enjoyment.

Exploratory Player: A behavior-based game archetype characterized by a preference for narrative depth, world exploration, and contextual discovery over direct competition or combat. This archetype typically engages with non-linear gameplay structures that include hidden elements and optional content.

Machine Learning (ML): A branch of artificial intelligence that focuses on enabling systems to improve performance through experience and data, rather than explicit rule-based programming. In game development, machine learning plays a central role in analyzing player behavior and informing adaptive design decisions.

Neural Network (NN): A computational model inspired by the structure of the human brain, consisting of interconnected processing units capable of recognizing patterns in large datasets. Neural networks are widely used in games to support tasks such as behavior prediction and content adaptation.

Player Modeling: The systematic analysis of gameplay behavior to construct dynamic representations of individual players. These models are used to personalize interfaces, adjust difficulty levels, and adapt narrative and content structures in response to player progression and evolving preferences.

Reinforcement Learning (RL): An example of a paradigm shift in AI learning theory, where agents guide the formation of decisions through rewards and punishments to form self-learning dynamic opponents and evolving challenges.

Self-Determination Theory (SDT): Exploring player motivation and the context in which games are created, centered around autonomy, competence, and relatedness, the psychological framework explains micromanagement and gamification.

Supervised Learning: Classifying and predicting actions in groups through learned behaviors, as well as defining game styles to improve machine learning systems and much more.

Unsupervised Learning: The antithesis of supervised learning, aimed at discovering groups or behavioral patterns of new player types that are not suggested by prior data, applied to previously unknown types of player behavior.

Player Retention: The efficiency of a video game in retaining players over time is measured by this metric. Adaptive gameplay and personalization are ways to help improve this metric.

Virtual Companion AI: This character AI application is designed to demonstrate social interaction and emotional intelligence to enhance immersion and empathy for gameplay.

Visual analytics (e.g., heatmaps, flowcharts): Includes the presentation of game data and player behavior through these programs to aid in level design, locate drop points, and improve the overall user experience.

Virtual Reality/Augmented Reality Emotion Recognition: Facial analysis and voice auditing in virtual/augmented reality environments using AI methods such as CNN, RNN, etc. to emotionally and responsively adapt game content.

Chapter 8
Enhancing Quality Education in Engineering and Technology Through AI-Powered Games

N. Kalaivani
Department of Mathematics, Vel Tech Rangarajan Dr. Sagunthala R&D Institute of Science and Technology, India

P. Vidhya Priya
https://orcid.org/0000-0002-1421-8743
Department of Management Studies, Kongu Engineering College, India

Yasmeen Sultana
https://orcid.org/0009-0006-8571-1646
Department of Management and Commerce, Maulana Azad National Urdu University, India

P. Marishkumar
https://orcid.org/0000-0002-0063-3348
Department of Management, Vinayaka Mission's Kirupananda Variyar Engineering College, Vinayaka Missions Research Foundation, India

P. Saravanan
https://orcid.org/0000-0003-2258-9381
Department of Chemistry, St. Joseph's College of Engineering, Chennai, India

M. Suresh
https://orcid.org/0009-0006-5764-1660
KPR Institute of Technology, Kovai, India

ABSTRACT

This chapter explores for the integration of AI -operated games to enhance quality education in engineering and technology. By providing adaptive education, real-time feedback and gaming problems, AI-powered educational games promote fictional understanding, complex thinking and engagement of students. These tools personalize learning experiences based on personal performance and preferences, making complex engineering and technical concepts more accessible and interactive. This

DOI: 10.4018/979-8-3373-3690-9.ch008

chapter also features case studies and best efforts that show the improved results and skills acquisition of education. Emphasizing innovation and incorporation, the chapter presents AI-powered gaming as a transformative approach to modern educational patterns and industry readiness.

INTRODUCTION

The evolution of education in the 21st century has seen significant changes in technology and the changing needs of learners and industries. Engineering and technical education, in particular, demand innovative pedagogy approaches that organize digital-original pay-generation with learning choices and dynamic requirements of modern industries. Traditional Direct Teaching Methods, however, are often short in stimulating the skills of criticism, engagement, creativity and applied problem solving necessary for engineering graduates. In response to these challenges, artificial intelligence (AI)-Power has emerged as a promising boundary to enhance the quality of educational games learning experiences, especially in technical disciplines where abstract concepts and complex systems are common(O'rinbekovna & others, 2024).

Artificial intelligence, defined by its ability to follow human intelligence through machine learning, natural language processing and data-operated decision making, has revolutionized many industries, and its application is gaining momentum in education. When integrated into educational sports, AI becomes a powerful tool to create a personal, adaptive and attractive learning environment. These intelligent systems constantly analyze the learned behavior, assess progress, and adjust the material in real time to match personal learning styles, knowledge intervals and cognitive abilities. For engineering and technology students, it means to face concepts such as thermodynamics, control system, circuit analysis, or interactive, game-based framework that refers to theoretical knowledge through simulation and challenges(Amer-Yahia, 2022).

Gamification Points includes points, levels, feedback loops and storytelling elements - enhance inspiration, strengthen retention, and transform passive learners into active participants. AI expands these benefits by ensuring that the game mechanics adapt to the learner's motion and understanding. For example, in the design of the game teaching algorithm, the AI engine can monitor how students solve every challenge, providing signals when they struggle, and increasing the complexity of expertise. This dynamic, repeated loop keeps learners in the best field of development, known as the "zone of proximal development" in academic theory. Unlike stable textbooks or predetermined lectures, AI -operated games provide liquid experiences where each action and decision feeds in the intelligent model of the learner's progress(Anwar & Ahyarudin, 2023).

The relevance of such innovations in engineering and technical fields increases, where integration of principle and practice is required. Imitation of real-world views by the atmosphere of the game allows learners to experiment, fail and learn without real-world consequences of engineering errors. For example, in civil engineering, the structural design game can imitate various environmental tensions on the virtual bridge, which will ask the learner to redesign material and geometry to redesign. In Computer Engineering, Gamified Network Troubleshooting simulation can guide students through AI-generated feedback corresponding to their logic patterns, identify and solve security problems(Alsaedi, 2024).

In addition to skill development, AI promotes the same accession cess, as well as games, inclusion and education. They provide multiple modes of content delivery - visual, audible, proud - and contain students with various education need, including people with disabilities. Moreover, multilingual support and culturally response design allows global learners to connect to the material meaningfully. This is especially noticeable in large -scale engineering programs where class size and student variations pose instructional challenges. With AI -operated games, learners receive a level of personal attention that will be rational and economically difficult in traditional classroom settings(Imamguluyev et al., n.d.).

Organizations try to meet the durable development goal of the United Nations-the deployment of equal and fair quality education-AI-powered games with global educational priority. These technologies support lifelong education by enabling flexible, self-esteem exploration of complex subjects, and preparing students for a career where digital merit and problem solving is supreme. Importantly, AI -operated games also facilitate creative assessment, producing analyzes that inform teachers in the fields of education paths, engagement patterns and intervention(Marin & Jiménez, 2024).

Despite his promise, it is not without the challenges to adopt AI -operated sports in engineering education. The creation of such games requires inter -education co-operation between teachers, Software developers, AI experts and domain specialists. Moreover, the moral concerns around data privacy, algorithmic bias and student surveillance must be taken into account by transparent and responsible AI systems. Academics must also be trained to interpret education analytics and to integrate sports-based insights into extensive pedagogical strategies. Institutional support in terms of infrastructure, funds and policy alignment plays a crucial role in sustaining these innovations(Rahimi, 2025).

This chapter pays attention to the impact of foundations, implementation strategies and AI -run games in engineering and technical education. It represents an in -laws analysis of how these tools support JOGN's developmental development, enhance students' motivation and contribute to better learning results(Chi et al., 2024). The purpose of empirical evidence, case studies and best efforts, the purpose of the chapter is to provide a comprehensive tool for technologists interested in transforming engineering education through researchers, policy-based education and intelligent sports-based education. As we go to an era where digital flow and innovation are a prerequisite for success, rebuilding education through AI-powered games is not only necessary to shape tomorrow's engineers and technology.

Objectives

The purpose of this chapter is to find out how AI-powered educational games can enhance quality education in engineering and technology by improving the engagement, personalization and skill development. It tries to analyze basic AI technologies in view of their integration with these games and academic principles. This chapter also examines the corresponding gamification strategy for engineering branches and examines adaptive education through real-time response and analytics. In addition, it outlines the best practices for effective implementation, including institutional adoption and teacher training. Finally, future trends and research directions have been published in the chapter to guide teachers and policies to take advantage of AI-powered gamified learning for transformative educational results.

FOUNDATIONS OF AI IN EDUCATIONAL GAMES

AI Technologies in Learning

Artificial intelligence (AI) technologies have gradually shaped the educational landscape by enabling the experiences of more intelligent, personal and efficient education. Education has machine learning, natural language processing (NLP), computer vision and recommended systems at the center of AI's impact. Machine learning algorithms analyze the huge datasets produced by the learners' interaction to identify the patterns, predict the results and the content of the tailor. For example, adaptive study platforms benefit these algorithms to customize the level of trouble and instructional ways in real time based on the Learner performance and engagement matrix(Cinar et al., 2024).

The NLP communicates the convenience of personalized tutoring to agents or chatbots, to answer questions, and to imitate the dialogue like human, thus enhancing Learner support. Computer vision helps enable interactive experiences beyond traditional inputs such as a mouse or keyboard, recognizing gestures, expressions or written inputs. In AI-operated educational games, these technologies are transformed to create an atmosphere where learners receive timely, reference-aware feedback and guidance. Reinforcement education, a subset of machine learning, is especially relevant, allows the game AI to ease the inspiration and progress of the learner to dynamic challenges and rewards. Together, these AI technologies consider the creation of intelligent tutoring systems embedded in games that are capable of adapt to the needs of the individual learners, thus promoting the eradication and expertise of complex engineering and technical concepts(Padmavathi et al., 2025; Saravanan et al., 2025).

Features of AI-Powered Games

AI -operated educational games distinguish themselves from traditional digital games through their intelligent, adaptive and data -based features. One of the main features is personalization - the atmosphere of the game customizes materials, challenges and feedback corresponding to personal learner profiles, addressing their strengths and weaknesses. This adaptability ensures that learners are best challenging, preventing frustration from extremely difficult tasks or boring tasks that are very easy. Another main feature is real-time analytics, where the system constantly collects data on errors to improve the learner's decisions, response time and gaming experience and inform teachers(Gokhe et al., 2024).

AI -operated games include intelligent feedback systems that provide signals, clarity or corrective guidance, certainly when and where learners need support, spinach education. These games often offer immersion simulation and view-based education, which mirror real-world engineering problems and promote experimental education. The natural language process allows the integration of noise or text-based interaction, enabling learners to connect to the game intuitively. Importantly, these games can imitate collaborative and competitive education modes, promoting crucial social education dynamics for engineering education. The use of AI also facilitates the implementation of dynamic difficulty adjustment (DDA), where the game modules the complexity, maintains engagement, and promotes growth skill acquisition based on the ongoing learner's performance. These features collectively transform AI -powered games into a civilized education environment that encourages learners while delivering measurable academic results.

Educational Theories Supporting Game-Based Learning

The effectiveness of AI -run educational games is based on established educational principles that emphasize active, practical and socially constructed education. Constructivist theory, mainly specified by Jean Piggate and Lev Vygotsky, shows that learners form J Knowledge Ban by active connection and interaction with their environment. AI-driven games embody this principle by providing interactive problem-solving functions and simulation in which learners need to repeat experiment, hypothesis and solutions. The concept of Vygotsky of the zone of proximal development (ZPD) is especially relevant, because AI-powered adaptive systems, facilitating effective spinach, keep learners within ZPD by presenting challenges that are not very easy or very difficult. The behavioral principles also shape the game design, such as rewards, badges and immediate response such as education behavior(Banik & Gullapelly, 2025).

In addition, it supports sports-based education, the principle of experimental education, experience, reflection, imagination and experiments-natural fits for-simulation-based educational games. Self-determination theory, which illuminates the role of internal motivation and autonomy, mental needs of mental needs, explains that gaming elements such as decision-making and response loops promote constant engagement. Social learning theory more supports collaborative facilities in AI games, where learners observe, imitate, and learn from colleagues in multiplayer or cooperative modes. Together, these principles provide a strong structure as to why AI-powered games enhance the maintenance, complex thinking and motivation, making them very effective pedagogy tools in engineering and technical education(Rapaka et al., 2025).

Figure 1. Gamification in engineering and technology in education

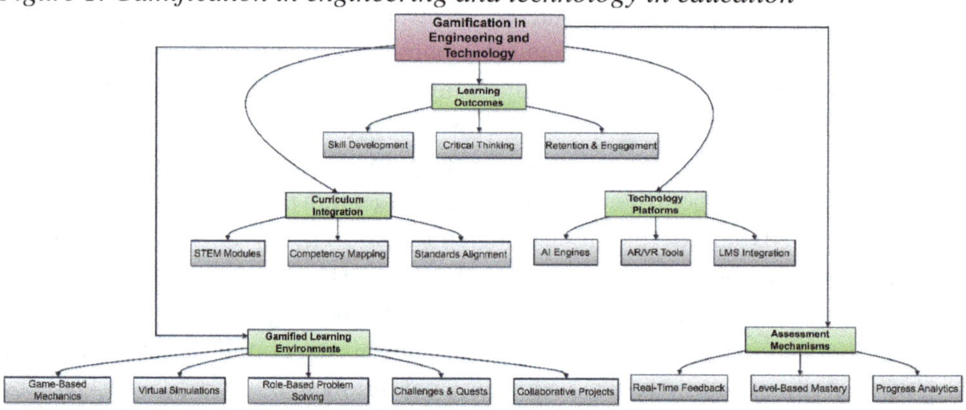

GAMIFICATION IN ENGINEERING AND TECHNOLOGY

Gamified Learning Environments

The application of game-design elements in the game-design context, especially in the non-game context, has achieved significant traction as an innovative educational strategy in engineering and technical disciplines. The gaming learning environment includes components such as points, leaders, badges, challenges and storylines to transform traditional education into attractive, immersion experience. These elements tap into basic human motivations - qualification, achievement and social interaction - leads students to make more effort and invest in complex content for longer. Contrary to traditional lecture-based approaches, a gamified environment promotes active participation, embodies abstract engineering concepts through simulation, role-pits and problem-solving scenes(Alsaedi, 2024). Figure 1 depicts the implementation of gamification in the field of engineering and technology education.

For example, a gamified platform can imitate the design and test of mechanical components, allow learners to experiment and immediately see the results of their design preferences. This repetitive process gives a mirror to the actual engineering workflow, promotes complex thinking, creativity and hands -on skills. Moreover, gamification gives instant feedback and reward systems to strengthen education and enhance confidence, which is crucial in the technology areas where learners often face challenges. By embedding the objectives of learning in attractive game stories and interactive tasks, a continuous engagement of gamified environments promotes a better retention of engineering and engineering and technical principles.

Integrating Curriculum with Gameplay

In order to be really effective in engineering education, it must be integrated with a unified course instead of treating as a supplement or superficial -d -as. Effective integration begins with the objectives of the game with the results of certain education, ensuring that gameplay activities directly strengthen the main concepts, skills and skills defined in the course course. This alignment requires collaboration between teachers, sports designers and domain experts to translate complex engineering subjects into interactive game mechanics without sacrificing academic rigidity. For example, the course on electrical circuits can accommodate a game where learners create virtual circuits and reflect real-world diagnostic functions(Anwar & Ahyarudin, 2023).

Such integration not only refers to the theoretical knowledge, but also pulls the distance between the classroom education and the practical application. In addition, the integration of the curriculum involves scoring gameplay activities in different levels of trouble, which allows learners to progress in advanced problems with foundational concepts. This progress supports mastery education and contains various learning profiles. Assessment methods must also be accepted to capture the education shown by the gameplay, including both structural assessments (eg, in-game quiz, skill checkpoints) and summary assessments (eg, project-based tasks, simulations). By embedding gambling experiences in the curriculum, institutions promote a consistent, learned-centered approach that enhances motivation and prepares students for industry challenges.

Case Studies in Engineering Disciplines

Several case studies highlight application of gamification in various engineering disciplines, demonstrating and academic performance(Meenakshi & Kannan, 2025; Rapaka et al., 2025).

1. **Mechanical Engineering – Virtual Manufacturing Simulation** At the leading technology university, a gamified simulation platform was developed to teach production processes such as CNC machining and assembly line Optimization. Students are engaged in virtual tasks where they programmed machines, managed resources and optimized production workflows. The game includes real-time response and display matrix, beneficial efficiency and creativity to solve the problem. Compared to traditional lab exercises, the results showed students' inspiration, better imaginative understanding of production limits, and passing pass rates.
2. **Electrical Engineering – Circuit Design and Troubleshooting Game** The game-based learning tool designed for the undergraduate electrical engineering course allows students to design, test and debug virtual circuit under the time limit. The adaptive difficulty of the game adjusts the challenges adjusted based on the individual learner's progress and promoting the lead board friendly competition. Surveys suggest that students feel more confident in the circuit analysis and value handmade experience. Faculty reported improved practical skills and ER Tanda conceptual grip in participants.
3. **Computer Engineering – Cybersecurity Capture the Flag (CTF) Competitions** Gamified CTF competitions have become popular in computer engineering education to teach cyber security principles. Teams compete to solve puzzles, identify weaknesses and controlled, to protect systems in environments like game. The immersion and competitive nature of CTF events enhances the problem of solving the problem, team work and real-time decisions. Studies show that students participating in these competitions show the high engagement and improved capabilities of applying theoretical knowledge in practical contexts.
4. **Civil Engineering – Structural Design and Disaster Simulation** In civil engineering programs, gamified simulations allow learners to design compositions and test against virtual earthquakes, floods or wind loads. This simulation integrates physics-based models and real-time analytics, enables students to repeat their design. The feedback includes performance scores based on safety,

cost and durability. This approach emphasizes the interplay between engineering design and environmental factors, cultivating holistic ideas.

This case studies are understored, when thoughtfully implemented, enhances engineering education by promoting experimental education, cooperation and internal motivation. They also explain the diversity of gambling approaches in various engineering branches and learning objectives.

Figure 2. Process of adaptive learning and personalization in AI-powered gamification

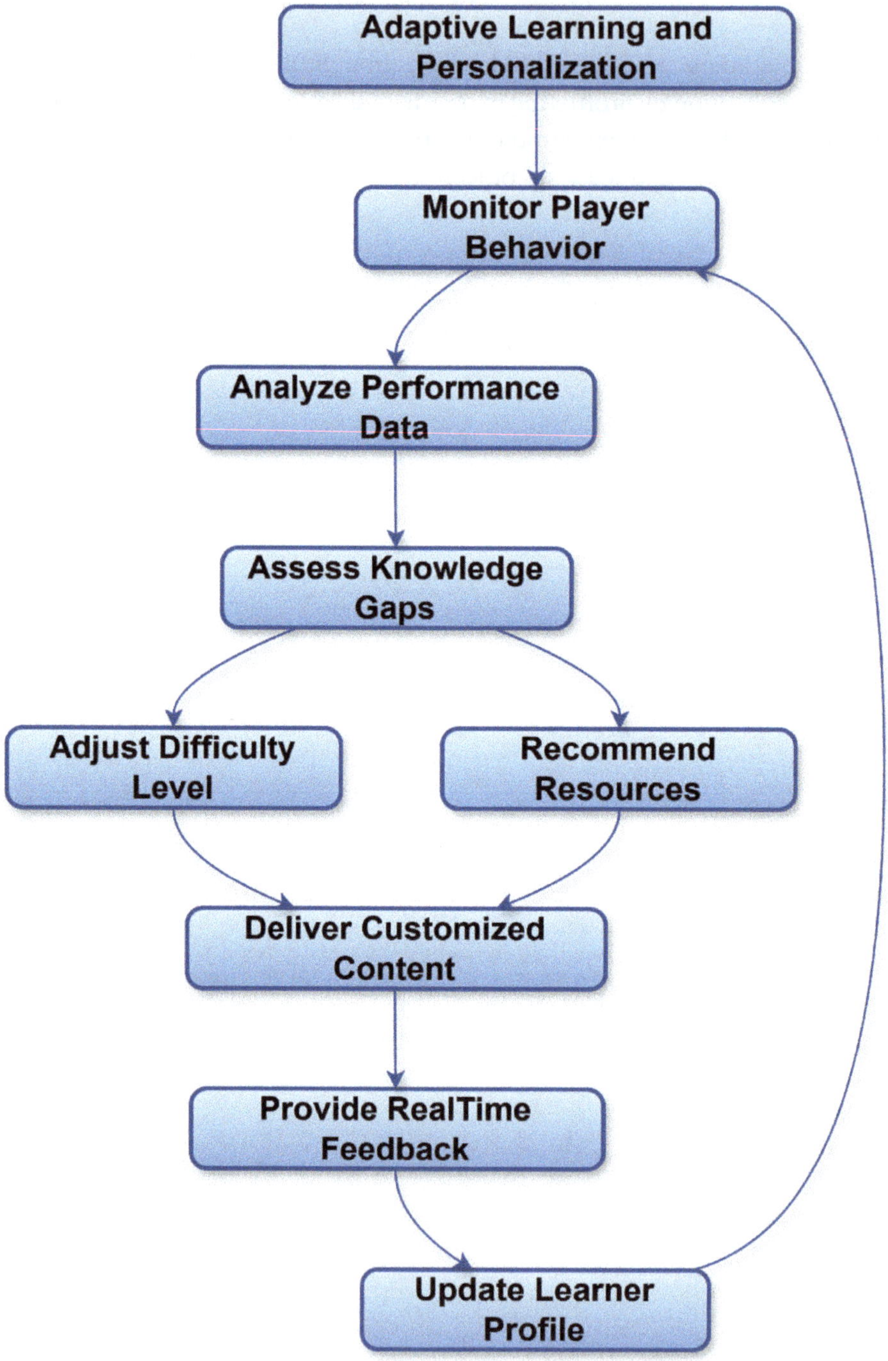

ADAPTIVE LEARNING AND PERSONALIZATION

Real-Time Feedback and Assessment

Adaptive education gives the benefit of technology to provide personal educational experiences through the learner's mobility. The center of this approach is the ability to deliver a real-time response and assessment, which distinguishes the adaptive education system from traditional, stable instructional methods. Real-time feedback includes instant analysis of the learner's answers during educational activities, which allow students to identify immediate errors, understand misunderstandings, and adjust their approach. Engineering and technology in education-solving and repetitive purification is crucial-a timely response provides the speed of learning by strengthening the right understanding and guiding the remedy without delay(Camilleri & Camilleri, 2024; Marin & Jiménez, 2024). Figure 2 illustrates the process of Adaptive Learning and Personalization in AI-powered gamification

For example, the AI-powered tutoring system embedded in the circuit design game can immediately flag the wrong wiring connections and suggest corrective measures, allowing learners to learn by trial and error in a safe environment. This urgency supports a creative assessment model, which provides constant insights in the progress of students rather than just depend on summary exams. Moreover, adaptive assessments can adjust the type of trouble and questions based on the learner's skills, maintaining the best challenging level that sustains motivation and engagement. By enabling individual pacing and targeted response, real-time assessment increases skills in technical concepts and practical skills, which are essential in the fast-growing areas of engineering and technology (Boopathi, 2024; Chandra et al., 2025).

Learning Analytics and Student Profiling

Analytics is learning at the center of adaptive education systems, a data -based process that collects information about learners and their references, steps, analyzes and reports. This capability allows teachers and AI systems to create detailed student profiles reflecting the level, learning preferences, engagement patterns, and JN OGN capabilities. These profiles report the customization of instructional content and pedagogical strategies corresponding to individual needs. For example, learning analytics can recognize that a particular student is excellent in theoretical understanding but struggles with applying concepts in simulation-based tasks. This enables the insights system to recommend targeted practice exercises or supplemental resources by ensuring efficient remedies. Student profiling also supports prediction analysis, helping teachers to identify and actively interfere with the risk of falling back. Importantly, the privacy and moral use of students' data are supreme; Transparent policies and secure data management are essential to maintain confidence and follow rules such as GDPR and CCPA. In engineering education, where the variety of mass is high and the needs of the students vary widely, learning analytics provides the necessary grainy for effective personalization. It eliminates the gap between the targets of the extensive curriculum and the individual learning route, promoting equity and inclusion by ensuring that no student is left behind.

Customizing Content for Diverse Learner Needs

Engineering and technical education often contain students with different backgrounds, learning styles and abilities, making content customization a crucial component of adaptive education. Customization includes instructional materials, activities, and assessments to accommodate various sensory preferences, previous knowledge, language expertise, and access to accessibility requirements. AI-powered adaptive systems receive this through multiple methods-that visualization, simulation, text, Audio and interactive elements-can select learners or recommend system profiling data(Chi et al., 2024; Uzumcu & Acilmis, 2024). For example, a student who struggles with Abstract Mathematical Formulation can showcase engineering principles in action from interactive 3D models and animations. Similarly, multilingual support and simple language options can increase the understanding for non-domestic speakers. Screen despicability features, such as screen readers, and adjustable interfaces, ensure that the disabled learners can be fully combined with the content. In addition, adaptive material sequencing allows learners to focus on fields that master and focus on areas that need development, optimizing the study time and preventing the overloading. This degree of personalization organizes with Universal Design for Learning (UDL) principles, which advocates the flexible education environment involving individual differences. In the very technical branches, where complexity and specialty increase, the content ensures customization that each learner can effectively progress without interruption through one-step-fit-all-instructional models.

Adaptive education and personalization AI and data analytics for revolutionizing engineering and technical education by providing real-time response, detailed learner profiling and customized material delivery. These capabilities increase engagement, support expertise, and promote the inclusion by addressing the needs of various learners. By consistently integrating adaptation to the creative assessment and learning process, adaptive systems ensure that students achieve the right level of challenge and support at the right time. Teaching analytics emphasizes teachers with active insights to guide interventions, while content customization benefits multiple methods to accommodate various styles and capabilities. As the education of engineering has been developed in complexity and norm, the adaptive education industry represents a strategic approach to the preparation of proficient, confident graduates to meet the demand.

DESIGNING EFFECTIVE AI-POWERED EDUCATIONAL GAMES

Game Design Principles

The creation of academic games operated by AI requires a delicate balance between attractive gameplay and solid education objectives. The foundation lies in well -established game design principles that ensure both educational effectiveness and the inspiration of the player.

Educational games should start with clear education objectives, guide challenges, tasks and ways to help master engineering and technical concepts. AI -saving games maintain engagement by adjusting challenges and skills, known as the "flow" state. Meaningful answers are provided by AI players, analyzing actions and personal signals to eliminate misconceptions and promote mentality. Multiplayer or team-based modes promote social education, especially in engineering branches where team work is required. AI can facilitate matchmaking, role assignment and moderation, to making cooperative or competitive mobility. Figure 3 demonstrates the development of effective AI-powered educational games.

AI-driven games can provide multiple solution paths or adaptive views to sustain the interest of the learner and promote creativity. By adhering to these principles, designers can create educational games that are not only enjoyable but also effective in enhancing the results of engineering and technical education.

Figure 3. Designing effective AI-powered educational games

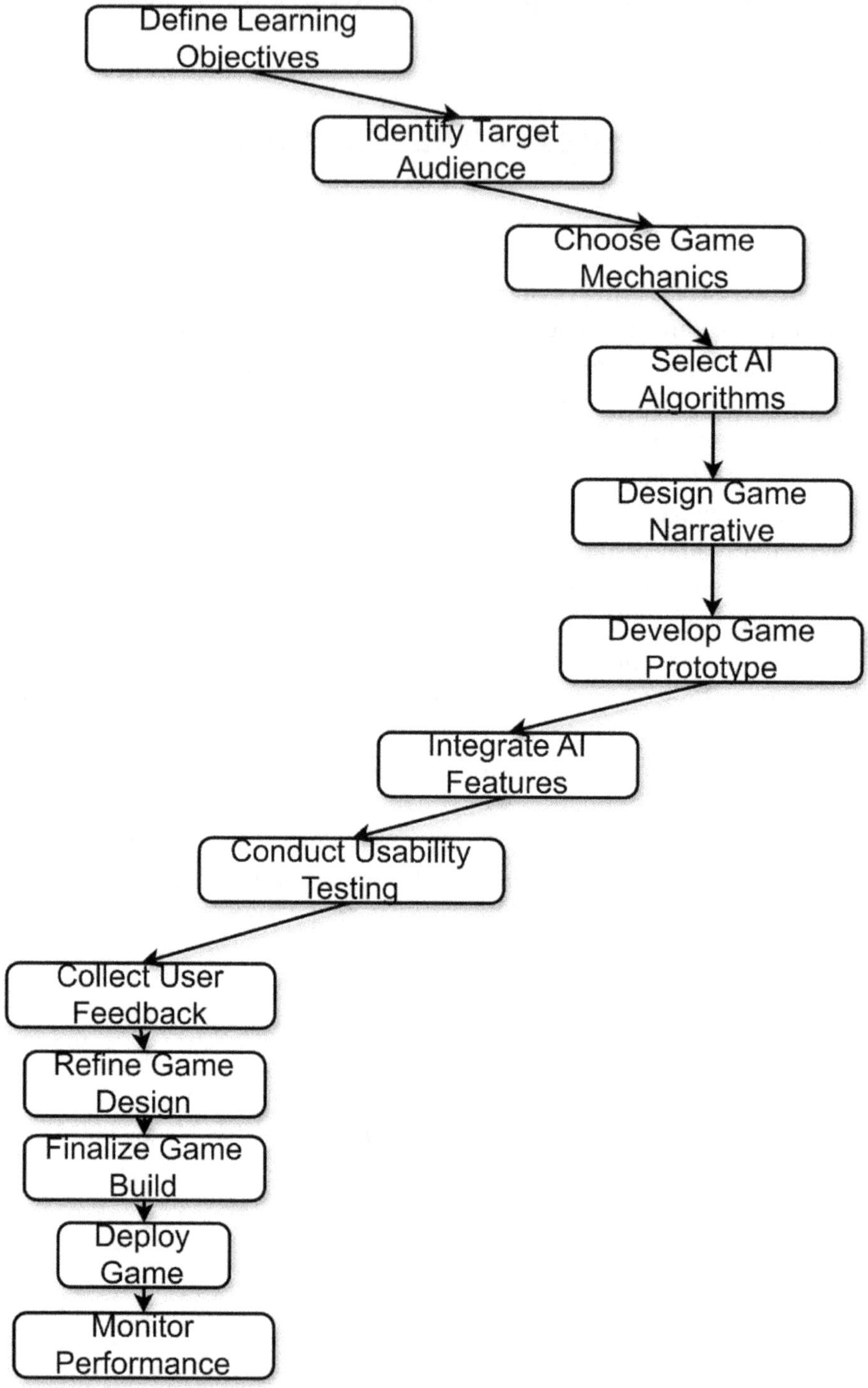

AI Algorithms and Mechanics in Games

AI integration in educational games is beyond the basic interaction; It embedded civilized algorithms and mechanics that enables personal, immersion and data - based education experiences(Anwar & Ahyarudin, 2023; Imamguluyev et al., n.d.; Marin & Jiménez, 2024).

AI technology is revolutionizing education using adaptive education algorithms, intelligent tutoring systems, process material generation (PCG), player modeling and profiling, natural language processing (NLP) and data analytics. Adaptive education algorithms analyze behavior, performance and engagement to adjust the content of the game, allowing more effective challenges and motivation. Intelligent tutoring systems diagnose learner's errors and guide the problem, enhance interactive experience. PCG algorithms make dynamic game content, ensure fresh gameplay and reduce development costs. Player helps to personalize and predict future effects, modeling and profiling gameplay paths. NLP allows chatbots to communicate with learners, facilitates complexes, reference-aware tutoring or peer collaboration. Data analytics and reporting enables evidence-based decision-determining and continuous course purification. Overall, AI technology is revolutionizing education by providing personal education experiences and increasing education experience.

The effective design of AI-driven educational games combines basic game design principles with cutting edge AI algorithms to create adaptive, attractive and personal education experiences. Rich feedback loops based in clear objectives, meaningful challenges and academic principles ensure the sound of pedagogy. AI technologies such as adaptive education, intelligent tutoring, procedural material generation, and learner profiling increase individualization and scalability, enabling games to meet the different needs of engineering students. By integrating these elements thoughtfully, designers can produce educational games that deliver not only learners, but also to the engineering and technical fields related to understanding and skills(Vaithianathan et al., 2024).

IMPACT ON LEARNER ENGAGEMENT AND SKILL DEVELOPMENT

The integration of AI -run educational games in engineering and technical education has a profound impact on the learner's engagement and skill development. These tools transcend the boundaries of traditional pedagogy by addressing simultaneously and emotional domains, promoting complex thinking and significantly increasing motivation and retention rates(CHISEGA-NEGRILĂ, 2024; Yu et al., 2017). Figure 4 illustrates the impact on learner engagement and skill development.

Cognitive and Affective Gains

AI -powered games simplify significant benefits by providing immersion, interactive environments where learners actively create knowledge rather than inactive. The underlying real-time response methods in AI systems support the repetitive education cycle, enables students to experiment, make mistakes, and learn from them immediately. This is adjusted with constructive learning theories, where understanding is made by active connection and reflection. Moreover, AI's ability to adapt to challenges according to personal learner profiles ensures that the material is very easy or incredibly difficult to facilitates the emphasis . Beyond wit, confidence, decrease in discomfort and enhanced pleasure - such as crucial for successful education results. Traditional engineering courses, often regarded as abstract or intimidations, benefit from the playful and supportive nature of the game-based environment. Finding emotional states through biosensors or behavioral analyzes can conform to experiences to maintain positive emotions and overcome the frustration. This emotional response helps to sustain the learner's engagement over time, which is crucial for complex topics in need of constant efforts.

Figure 4. Impact on learner engagement and skill development

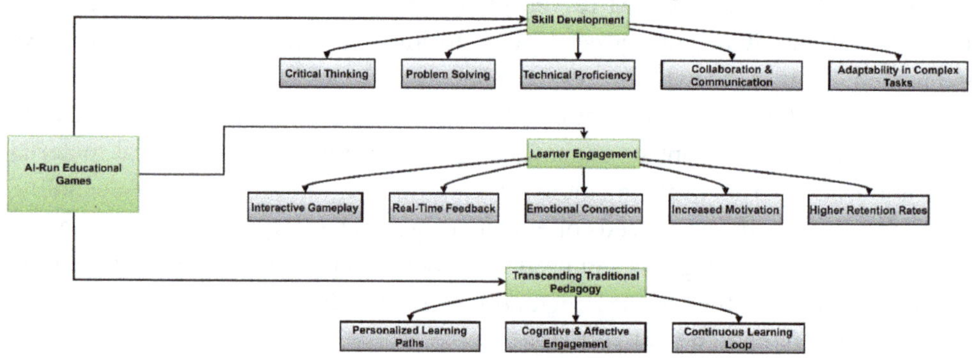

Enhancing Critical Thinking and Problem Solving

Engineering education basically aims to develop complex thinking and the abilities to solve the problem, and AI -run educational games are unique to meet this target. These games often include open end challenges and actual simulations that mimic real-world engineering problems, in which learners need to apply to analyzes, synthesis and dynamically. The AI algorithms embedded inside this platform simplify scaffolding-gradually increases complexity and only provides time-to-time support-to nurture high ranking skills without reducing the autonomy.

Moreover, AI's ability to produce various problems scenarios through processing materials Pay Generation promotes learners to contact problems with multiple angles, flexible thinking and creativity. The immersion of the games enhances the interactive nature awareness and the contextual understanding, which enables students to appreciate the practical effects of theoretical concepts. At risk-free virtual environments associated with complex systems, learners develop elasticity and adaptive skills-requirement for innovation in engineering fields.

Motivation and Retention Rates

Inspiration is a major factor in influencing the success of academic intervention, and AI-driven games are best to create internal inspirational experiences. Interplay of gamification elements - such as rewards, leaderboards and stories - develops a sense of achievement and progress according to personal preferences with personal adaptive education ways. This personalized inspirational spinach is supported by AI-powered learner profiling, identifying what each student runs and adjusts incentives accordingly. Retention rate also improves as a result of continuous motivation and engagement. Teaching suggests that active education approaches such as sports-based education reduce the dropout rate and improve the completion of the course by making the learning more relevant and enjoyable. Enabled, constructive response by AI promotes the mindset of loop growth, where learners believe in challenges as development opportunities rather than unpredictable barriers. This is important in the demand for areas such as engineering and technology (Marin & Jiménez, 2024).

Moreover, AI -operated sports facilitates social motivation by collaborative and competitive gameplay modes, promoting peer interaction and community building. Social connection increases liability and provides additional sources of incentive, which positively affects the inspiration. The role of AI in managing this social mobility - by matchmaking, role assignment and adaptive facility - which interacts are constructive and incorporated.

The impact of AI -run educational games on the learner's engagement and skill development is multi -faceted and change. OGN, these games promote adaptive response and properly enabled by knowledge construction and expertise education through challenging materials. Effectively, they increase the emotional engagement by creating a supportive, enjoyable teaching environment in line with personal emotional state. Seriously, they nourish the essential engineering skills such as complex thinking, problem solving and adaptive skills by immersing learners in authentic, dynamic views expanded by AI-powered spinach and content convertibility. Inspired by individual incentives and social gameplay, leading to improved retention and vision in demand for technical branches. Overall, AI -run educational games represent strategic progress in engineering education, which organize the best practices of pedagogy with technical innovation to prepare learners for the complex challenges of the modern world.

Figure 5. Implementation and best practices for integrating AI-driven educational games

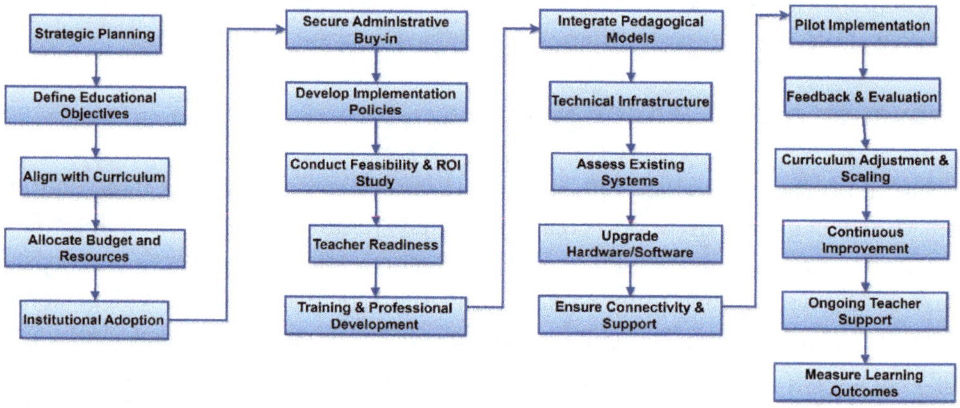

IMPLEMENTATION AND BEST PRACTICES

In the curriculum of engineering and technology, strategic planning and a comprehensive approach are required to successfully integrate AI -Roan educational games that address institutional adoption, teacher's readiness and technical infrastructure. Each of these pillars plays a crucial role in ensuring durable, effective deployment and maximizing the educational benefits of these innovative devices(Alsaedi, 2024; Chi et al., 2024; Rahimi, 2025). Figure 5 illustrates the implementation and best practices for integrating AI-driven educational games

Institutional Adoption Strategies

The adoption of AI -run educational games at the institutional level demands configuration with extensive educational goals and policies. Organizations should start by clarifying clear objectives that support the results of these games, enhance the learner's engagement and improve skill development. The establishment of cross-departmental committees associated with faculty, IT staff, instructive designers and administrative leaders can facilitate the collaborative decision and help shared ownership. Pilot programs serve as effective adoption vehicles, allowing institutions to test small -scale AI -operated games to evaluate the effectiveness, usefulness and integration challenges of pedagogy. Data -based insights from pilots can guide repetitive refinements and create attractive cases for a wide rollout. Moreover, organizations should ensure that the evaluation matrix goes beyond the use figures to enable evidence-based scaling, to include learning results, student satisfaction and faculty response.

Technical providers can adopt by bringing skills and resources to endure strategic partnerships with AI developers and educational researchers. Moreover, securing funds through grants, innovation funds or public-private partnerships can reduce the initial investment cost. In the end, creating a culture that emphasizes innovation and constant improvement is important; This can be promoted by institutional incentives such as accreditation programs, research support and professional development opportunities.

Teacher Training and Support

Extensive professional development programs are required to equip teachers with the necessary skills and confidence. Training should focus on three major fields: technical mastery, pedagogy integration and data literacy. Teachers need experience with game platforms, how to navigate features, troubleshoot common problems, and customize settings corresponding to the learner's needs. Disciplinary training should provide how to organize sports activities with the objectives of learning, interpret AI-generated analytics and provide supplementary instruction.

Data literacy is especially important, as AI -operated sports create rich learner data that can report instructional decisions. Teachers should be trained to analyze dashboards, identify trends, and actively react to students' progress or difficulties. Ongoing support, such as guidance, peer collaboration groups and access to instruction designers, can sustain the teacher's engagement and facilitate the distribution of knowledge. Organizations should also identify the workload effects of adopting new technologies. Providing adequate time, incentives and validity helps to eliminate resistance and promote continuous use. Including teachers at the beginning of the development or selection process foster and ensures that games meet the requirements of the practical classroom.

Infrastructure and Technical Requirements

AI-saved educational games require strong infrastructure, including reliable hardware, software firmware and seamless gameplay, network capabilities for data processing and real-time AI functions. Hardware requirements vary depending on the complexity of the game, but usually requires mobile devices with computer, tablets or sufficient processing power and graphics capacity. The software platform should be scalable, secure and compatible with existing learning management systems for data interoperability. Network infrastructure should support real-time interactions and low delays and high bandwidths for AI feedback. Compliance with rules such as GDPR or CCPA is crucial for data protection.

Assistance plays an ongoing role in technical support services, troubleshooting, maintenance and user training, including desk and dedicated IT teams. Proactive monitoring and regular updates ensure system stability and includes emerging AI advances.

Effective implementation of AI -run educational games in engineering education on integrated institutional strategies, strong teacher training and solid technical infrastructure. Supported by partnership and sustainable funds, organizations must promote collaborative adoption processes based on pilot testing and evidence - based scaling. A.I. Equipping the educated with the skills of integrating games with pedagogy and interpreting learner data ensures meaningful instructional use. Finally, investing in scalable, secure infrastructure and responsible technical support is the experience of a unified, righteous learner. By following these best practices, academic stakeholders can use the full potential to transform AI-powered sports engineering and technical education.

FUTURE TRENDS AND RESEARCH DIRECTIONS

The developed landscape of AI -run educational games is a transformative possibility for engineering and technical education. As AI technologies progress, the possibilities of new pedagogy emerge, while cooperation between policy makers, teachers and industry officials becomes more and more crucial. The exploration of these future trends explains how AI will continue to shape and redefine the environment of education, driving innovation and how the dynamic needs and workforce of learners. Figure 6 depicts future trends and research directions (Meenakshi & Kannan, 2025; Rahimi, 2025; Rapaka et al., 2025).

Figure 6. Future trends and research directions

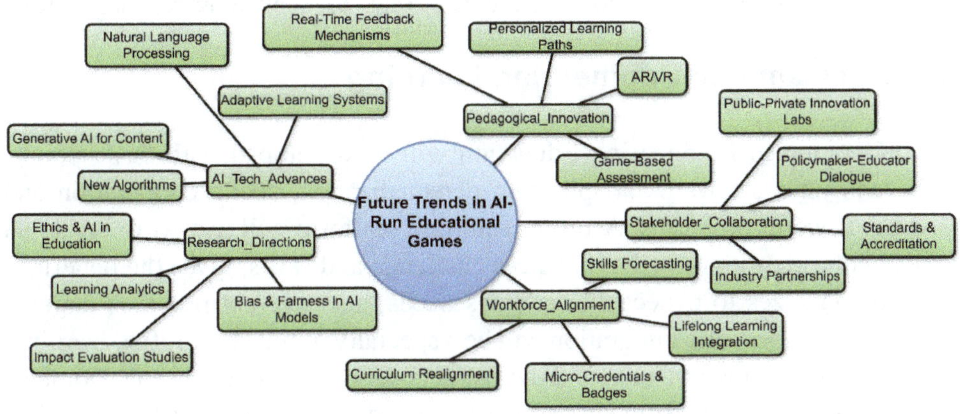

Emerging AI Technologies in Education

Cutting edge AI techniques such as generating AI, explained AI and emotional computing are set to revolutionize educational games. Generative AI, according to the progress and interests of individual students, including the larger language models of the procedural material generation, enables the creation of very customized and various education scenes. For engineering learners, this means individual simulations that adapt not only to dynamic levels but also adapt to problem references-allowing students to explore multiple perspectives and real-world engineering challenges from branches. This capacity enhances the transfer of both engagement and skills. AI will be explained to promote trust and transparency. Such AI systems make instructional decisions - such as by providing content or feedback - inactivity methods can clarify both learners and teachers behind these decisions. This transparency supports the development by helping to understand their learning ways and teachers to better interpret AI-powered analytics, thus promoting more informed instructional intervention.

Effective computing, which is detecting the emotional states of the learners through sensors and behavioral analysis, will personalize educational experiences by adapting the gameplay to sustain motivation and reduce frustration. For example, AI can adjust the pacing or promote the learner's anxiety in moments of anxiety, increasing emotional elasticity in challenging engineering subjects. Moreover, A.I. Connected, progress in Augmented Reality (AR) and Virtual Reality (VR) will create a mixed-realistic environment where engineering concepts can be visualized and manipulated in three dimensions. These rich, interactive spaces simplify practical education, enable students virtually enabling prototype, testing and eternal engineering designs - a process is closely aligned with professional engineering practice (Banik & Gullapelly, 2025; Chi et al., 2024; Meenakshi & Kannan, 2025).

Future of Gamified Engineering Learning

Gamification in Engineering Education will be developed with basic points, and-bezen systems towards AI-powered personalization, social cooperation and solving real-world problems. A future gamified platform will use AI to create an adaptive education journey that balances challenge and skills, gives the benefit of prediction analyzes to expect the learner's needs, and actively provides targeted resources. Inter -acoustic integration will be a specialty of future gamified learning. Engineering problems often expand the learners needed to apply various Domains - mechanical, electrical, Software and beyond - various knowledge and skills. AI - operated games will become increasingly imitating such interdisciplinary references, promoting systems' thinking and solving holistic problems.

The collaborative gameplay will be enhanced by AI-medium interactions that facilitate effective team work, peer assessment, and knowledge of the physical location, regardless of physical location. This arranges with a growing trend toward remote and hybrid learning models and prepares students for globalization, distributed engineering work environment. The inclusion of real-world data streams and digital twins will allow students to join advanced engineering systems and infrastructure in the nearby real-time. This connectivity eliminates the gap between theoretical education and industry practice, smart grids, autonomous vehicles and sustainable production for emerging technologies.

Policy and Industry Collaboration

Thinking of AI -powered educational games requires thoughtful policy structures that take into account moral, access to sexuality and equity considerations. Policy makers must establish a guide to ensure data privacy, algorithmic ness painting and inclusion, especially looking at the sensitive nature of learning data and AI decision making. Regulatory standards should promote transparency in AI systems and facilitate the order of various learner's needs, preventing digital division from widening. Industry collaboration will be essential for organizing the content of educational game with developed workforce demand. The partnership between educational institutions, technology companies and engineering companies can ensure that the views of the game reflect the current industry challenges and technologies, where student education experiences increase the relevance and usefulness. Co-development initiatives can promote innovation in the game design, integrate cutting edge engineering problems and tools directly from the field.

Moreover, industry involvement can facilitate practical education through internships, project collaboration and guide programs embedded in gamified platforms. This ecosystem approach strengthens the pipeline from education to employment, in which learners are equipped with both professional skills such as technical skills and communication, team work and adaptability. Investing research on learning results, workforce and long -term influence of AI -operated sports on equity is important. Multi-institutional studies can identify the best efforts, taking advantage of large data analytics, PTIMIs AI algorithms for different populations, and reporting policy decisions. Research must also discover the moral effects of AI in education, including autonomy, bias, and the mental effects of prolonged sports-based education.

The future of AI -run educational games in engineering and technology is shaped by emerging AI innovations that increase personalization, transparency and emotional engagement. The gamified learning environment will increase more and more sophisticated, solving interdisciplinary problems, unifying collaborative features reflecting real-world data and business engineering references. The successful progress on the active policy framework and dynamic industry-educational partnership to ensure configuration with the same access, moral AI use and employees' needs. Continuous research on the effectiveness of pedagogy, equity and moral dimensions will guide the sustainable integration of these technologies, finally changing engineering education to meet demand.

ETHICAL CONCERNS IN AI-POWERED GAMES FOR ENGINEERING EDUCATION

The ethical issues associated with the use of artificial intelligence in educational gaming can be more concerning than the technology itself. As institutions are beginning to adopt educational gaming with artificial intelligence to augment and enhance engineering education, stakeholders will need to weigh epistemic issues related to data privacy and algorithmic justice, agency, and equitable access related to learner well-being and institutional integrity (Rajkumar et al., 2024; Yadav et al., 2025).

Data Privacy and Security Vulnerabilities

The primary ethical issue relates to the large-scale collection and processing of sensitive student information, which is necessary in order to deliver customized AI-enabled learning experiences. AI applications in engineering education often capture considerable amounts of data, including: performance indicators; behavioral trends;

learning preferences; biometric data; and psychological data, in order to facilitate adaptive personalization. The extensive data collection leads to significant privacy concerns; without strong safeguards in place, students can be vulnerable to breaches, unauthorized access, identity theft, and commercial exploitation. The ethical quandary intensifies when institutions do not supply clear information regarding data collection, or when students give implicit consent without comprehending what information is being shared; metadata such as: the language they speak, their race, and their geographical location could be important factors (Rajkumar et al., 2024; Yadav et al., 2025). Educational institutions are bound to various data-related regulations, yet many have limited security frameworks and encryption capabilities; have inadequate audits in place to avoid breaches of privacy; and subsequently violate student trust in educational technology via unauthorized use of student information.

Algorithmic Bias and Perpetuation of Inequity

AI systems can have biases from the training data they were exposed to and sometimes exacerbate those biases, which can lead to biased results. Algorithmic bias in engineering education can take the form of biased assessment algorithms, unfair content recommendations, and biased grading, all of which can result in the perpetuation of social inequalities and privilege certain populations of students over others. This is not an error produced by the computer; it is a human error, representing collective societal biases baked into the algorithms by developers who assume their view of the world is normalized and the default view that cannot be challenged. Engineering students who are underrepresented may find themselves using AI systems which systematically insert biases which undermine their ability to design successful learning and advancement, in effect crystallizing historical inequities into technology (Rajkumar et al., 2024; Yadav et al., 2025).

Erosion of Student Autonomy and Agency

Predictive algorithms and automated decision-making systems threaten students' independence because they limit their ability to engage freely with their personal interests and values. When students become overly reliant on AI systems for task completion, there is a risk that they will forego their agency as independent learners, as they may opt not to engage in the difficult cognitive work necessary for authentic learning and skill acquisition. Moreover, students may have limited choice with respect to the use of AI systems in their learning, particularly when institutional requirements for these tools are introduced as mandatory in courses. This reflects a troubling issue of freedom and autonomy in college learning. The ongoing issue of balancing the educational benefits of AI with student autonomy remains neither protected nor resolved, and institutions must develop explicit policies around when it is appropriate, encouraged, or prohibited to use AI systems.

Equity and Access Disparities

AI-enhanced gaming platforms rely upon expensive infrastructure and technological devices, and require reliable internet access. For many learners and institutions serving low-income and marginalized communities, this infrastructure simply may not exist. Thus, we again find a paradox where AI seeks to close educational gaps, while simultaneously widening those gaps by providing unequal access driven by a digital divide and resource gaps that reinforce systemic inequality. Unless institutional policies are firmly articulated to intervene and address issues of socioeconomic disadvantage and equitable access, AI-enhanced educational tools have the potential to serve and benefit students who are privileged in their existing privileges, while further marginalizing the strained capacities of low-income students.

Solutions and Recommendations

Ethical action entails a commitment to sharing a full scope of transparency around all aspects of algorithms, informed consent processes for students and families, routine auditing of algorithms for bias detection and bias mitigation, data privacy, and policies around cognitive liberties and equity of access. Institutions must develop available mechanisms to govern these issues and provide training for educators about the ethical use of AI. Institutions must maintain human supervision over AI-Powered games to ensure the technology is in service to education, not commercialization. The only way for AI-Powered games to realize their transformational power, and shield student's rights and dignity, is through intentional ethical governance.

CHALLENGES AND OPPORTUNITIES

The fusion of artificial intelligence and game-based learning represents radical new possibilities for engineering and technology education, taking engagement and learning to levels never before imagined, while also introducing substantial barriers to addressing to institutions. The marriage of these two technologies addresses a key critical need in higher education: fostering highly technical concepts engaging and approachable through interactive, customized learning (Venkatasubramanian et al., 2024).

The Dual Engine of Engagement and Personalization

AI-enabled games are a game-changer for engineering education because they allow for truly individualized learning pathways that can adjust to the specific student and their pace of learning. AI-enabled learning experiences assess performance and then adjust difficulty in real-time using adaptive algorithms specific for that student versus taking a broad, one-size-fits-all approach in education. They keep students in the sweet spot of challenge, so students feel challenged, and hopefully engaged, not pressured. Individualized learning experiences don't just mean adjusted difficulty; they also mean AI can track every student's best learning modalities for learning and what their strengths are and where improvements are needed and then deliver perfectly-pitched interventions. There are also gamification characteristics like points, badges, or leaderboards, that allow for aspects of play and competition, which takes student learning from being passive to being an active student experience with intrinsic motivation. Research indicates that knowledge retention can increase around 40% in gamified learning environments, or in other words, they teach engineering concepts significantly better than conventional teaching (Sharma et al., 2024).

Demonstrable Learning Outcomes in Technical Domains

The evidence for AI-enhanced game-based learning in engineering is strong. The studies conducted across a range of engineering fields from software engineering to manufacturing and civil engineering have shown measurable learning gains. In addition to assessment measures, students who have used digital games often outperform their peers in traditional delivery modes, particularly with respect to forms of knowledge development more specific to procedural and factual knowledge, which is important for engineering practice. In addition to academic measures of performance, these technologies have been effective in assessing a range of soft skills, including teamwork, collaborative problem solving, and decision-making which are all valued by engineering employers. Game-based learning also offers a unique approach to the integrity of assessments given the proliferation of AI tools like ChatGPT; unlike other forms of assessments where students can use AI in a manner that violates integrity, game-based assessments require active participation in the form of real-time decision-making, which is something that cannot be replicated by any current version of AI (Prabhuswamy et al., 2024).

Formidable Implementation Barriers

Although there are significant benefits, many interconnected barriers limit the widespread adoption of AI-driven games for engineering education; top among these barriers is cost, since developing sophisticated AI-driven educational games often requires a significant financial commitment to software, equipment, and infrastructure. Pre-service and practicing educators have identified inadequate funding as their number one concern: Financial resources, with 68 of 276 respondents-and two independent responses-incurred as the leading barrier. In addition to barriers associated with financial resources, issues related to access and technology also significantly affects accessibility. For example, on top of financial barriers, and keeping in mind that high value of equipment might need to be provided to students, there are also those institutions that do not have adequate resources or connections to provide reasonable devices to students.

Preparation of teachers represents another major challenge. Most teachers do not receive a sufficient level of training for game-based learning in their teaching model. In addition, the resistance to pedagogical change is significant, especially with educators that have a skepticism about digital games or prefer them to lecture. The issue of determining effective in game assessment mainly in an online learning environment, remains a difficult design problem because in order to build this type of assessment, one would need strong analytical and technical skills that few educators possess; therefore, it is often a cost prohibitive and time-consuming task. Also, the curriculum misalignment is serious issue many educators must grapple with, as some games simply do not fit with the learning objectives set forth, and fit into many learning objectives without major modification or custom development to fit objectives, while for many institutions or educators is not equitable(Prabhuswamy et al., 2024; Sharma et al., 2024).

Strategic Opportunities for Transformation

While there are challenges, there are also significant opportunities to scale AI-enhanced games in engineering education. The barriers of acquiring sufficient equipment for this work can be addressed by taking advantage of inexpensive, ubiquitous, and increasingly powerful devices that students already own: smartphones and laptops. In addition, students tend to view their smartphones and laptops as extensions of themselves, further pushing down challenges associated with adopting the game in an educational setting. Further, universities, colleges, and schools can partner collaboratively, share the development costs, and utilize open-source solutions to develop, enhance, and support the game application (Venkatasubramanian et al., 2024). Furthermore, developing institutional policies to support the project, programs of teacher professional learning, and sufficient curriculum integration can help address teacher resistance to pedagogical developments and the complexity of implementation. As artificial intelligence continues to improve and refine, and as the institutions utilizing this technology become steady in its implementation, the return on investment for developing AI skills that demonstrate procedural development in essential to course learning will shift towards the development of the innovation.

CASE STUDIES

The combined use of artificial intelligence and game-based learning in engineering education has achieved remarkable outcomes in various institutional contexts, demonstrating measured improvements in student outcomes along with important implementation lessons. The case studies demonstrate how the global educational community has implemented AI-powered games to mitigate age-old pedagogical challenges in technical education (Sarkar et al., 2025; Yadav et al., 2025).

Minecraft Education Edition: Revolutionizing Materials Engineering at Research Institutions

One of the most significant implementations occurred with a substantial research university, using Minecraft Education Edition, combined with the Polycraft World modification, in a deliberate fashion over an entire semester, in an undergraduate senior mechanical engineering course on the properties of materials. The researchers implemented a within-subjects study design, to compare students on course units that blended Minecraft versus traditional instruction. Prior to the Minecraft units, students attended standard lectures and did homework using traditional textbook resources. During the Minecraft-enhanced units, they experienced a combination of lecture and interactive Minecraft game play; then utilized the modules as they were completing the homework they submitted in the Minecraft interface (Behera et al., 2025; Karthikeyan et al., 2025).

The outcomes were significant both statistically and educationally. Engineering students' performance was found to be significantly more effective for material from units using Minecraft as a technology-enhanced learning tool over material taught traditionally, based on three cumulative assessments. This noteworthy finding directly measured actual learning outcomes for students in a real mechanical engineering course, instead of an artificial lab context (Behera et al., 2025; Karthikeyan et al., 2025). Therefore, the success represents a substantial commitment by the institution to foster and sustain the environment needed for this approach, including technical staff to develop, host, and support both the software and tutorial videos, as well as teaching assistants to support student user needs. The study showcased that Minecraft was an effective tool for picturing and playing with some complicated material properties that would be darn near impossible to teach through conventional instruction without the help of a technology-enhanced learning tool.

Kahoot! Enhancing Knowledge Retention in Cross-Continental Engineering Education

An intriguing international project involved utilizing Kahoot! a gamified assessment platform with integrated AI, in an innovative double-degree program between Universidad de Extremadura, Spain and Chongqing University, China. Second-year students from the course "Bases and Technology of Plant Production" completed a Kahoot! quiz of 15 questions after each lesson, to review the theoretical content of the class and the identification skills gained in class. Due to the language barrier (Chinese students were learning in Spanish), the students had one minute to respond to each Kahoot! question.

The quantitative findings were amazing and sustained over the length of time of the study. For theoretical questions that were repeated from the first 7 sessions of Kahoot! average student scores improved by 31.4% on the midterm exam and students were still scoring 29.6% higher on the final exam which was held 17-32 weeks post midterm. Other questions from the Kahoot! sessions showed improvements of 26.0%, when they were repeated on the exams; notably, these were repeated questions from Kahoot! from later sessions. These findings are corroborated by broader research where 70% of papers show that, when implemented, Kahoot! improves final grades or post-test results compared to other teaching methods. The immediate feedback feature and competitive component of Kahoot! proved to be particularly useful, with respect to engineering content memorization and the consolidation of learning across cultural and linguistic boundaries and over significant periods of time(Behera et al., 2025; Vaithianathan et al., 2024; Venkatasubramanian et al., 2024).

Comparable activities in building engineering and architecture at the University of Granada and University of Seville yielded similar findings together with Kahoot! gamification sessions in neighbouring universities which led to lower failure rates and higher grade distributions in subsequent examinations. Cluster analysis indicated students' performance on Kahoot! games did not directly predict performance on the examinations. This finding suggested this tool is useful as a self-evaluation mechanism rather than simply a new testing format. Over 75% of the students in the study provided a positive response agreeing Kahoot! increased engagement with the course content and improved the learning experience.

Operations Research Gamification: Transforming Student Engagement in Management Engineering

A pioneering gamification implementation at a Portuguese university transformed an introductory operations research course for first-year management students. The instructor designed a comprehensive gamification framework incorporating three activity types: Mastery activities related to core course topics, Institutional activities connected to university community life, and Teamwork collaborative challenges. WhatsApp served as the primary communication platform, enabling continuous engagement beyond traditional classroom boundaries(Karthikeyan et al., 2025; Vaithianathan et al., 2024).

The gamification approach presented a range of observable benefits that extended beyond improvements in grades. Students not only exhibited more favorable dispositions towards the tedious course but also closed the learning loop, as they would not finish challenges until they were all completed and correct. Additionally, students showed more help-seeking behaviors by asking more detailed questions and wanting help during office hours. Students also performed challenge assignments at higher rates and tended to earn better final grades and showed greater persistence due to the engaging impact of the framework. The design of the framework was consistent with Chou's drive cores and incorporated narrative as well as progressively more challenging and informative assignments, supporting four common game elements that are effective in generating student engagement and interest in technical subjects. Overall, this case demonstrates that gamification in a well-designed framework could make complex quantitative engineering principles more digestible and intrinsically engaging to students.

Virtual Reality Immersive Simulations: Bridging Theory and Practice in Laboratory Education

This innovative investigation focused on head-mounted display virtual reality laboratory simulations in the education of undergraduate science and engineering students, comparing the immersive VR experience to a traditional desktop simulation. There were thirty-nine participants who completed the Labster molecular biology simulations while using a VR headset, and knowledge testing occurred pre- and post-simulation to measure learning outcomes(Venkatasubramanian et al., 2024). The average test scores did significantly improve from pre-simulation average score of 64.1% to post-simulation average of 82.3%; there were no significant differences when comparing the two different simulation types (i.e., VR vs desktop simulations) or when comparing program levels of students. Not surprisingly, 91% of participants agreed that VR laboratory simulations would be a great complement to regular teaching modalities; 82% of participants also agreed that VR exercises promoted more motivation than regular learning activities; and 97% of participants wished they would use VR more frequently! These results indicated that the use of immersive, virtual laboratory simulations has the potential to add value, in terms of learning outcomes and motivation to learn, regardless of previous experience with VR or disciplinary backgrounds of students.

CONCLUSION

AI -run educational games represent an example in engineering and technical education, offering education experiences aligned with dynamic, personal and modern pedagogical goals. By giving advantage of advanced AI techniques, these games enhance the consequences of JOGN and emotional education, promote complex thinking and improve motivation and retention. Integrated institutional strategies, comprehensive teacher training and strong technical structures are required for successful implementation. Looking forward, the emerging AI innovations and the ER -Banda industry cooperation will purify gambling education, ensuring its relevance and accession sexuality. Accepting this development promises to enhance the quality of engineering education, preparing learners to meet the complex demands of future workforce with agility and creativity.

REFERENCES

Alsaedi, A. A. (2024). AI-POWERED PEDAGOGY: REVOLUTIONIZING STUDENTS'LEARNING EXPERIENCES THROUGH INTEGRATION OF AI TECHNOLOGIES.

Amer-Yahia, S. (2022). Towards AI-powered data-driven education. *Proceedings of the VLDB Endowment International Conference on Very Large Data Bases*, *15*(12), 3798–3806. DOI: 10.14778/3554821.3554900

Anwar, M. R., & Ahyarudin, H. A. (2023). Ai-powered arabic language education in the era of society 5.0. [ITSDI]. *IAIC Transactions on Sustainable Digital Innovation*, *5*(1), 50–57. DOI: 10.34306/itsdi.v5i1.607

Banik, B. G., & Gullapelly, A. (2025). AI-Powered Gamification and Interactive Learning Tools for Enhancing Student Engagement. In Driving Quality Education Through AI and Data Science (pp. 283–310). IGI Global Scientific Publishing.

Behera, G., Meenakshi, S., Rajini, J., Pravin, T., Boopathi, S., & Associates. (2025). Entrepreneurial Insights From Higher Education: Startup Business Ventures. In Real-World Tools and Scenarios for Entrepreneurship Exploration (pp. 101–132). IGI Global.

Boopathi, S. (2024). Harnessing the power of distributed cloud and edge computing for advanced healthcare systems. In *Internet of Things enabled Machine Learning for Biomedical Applications* (pp. 248–272). CRC Press. DOI: 10.1201/9781003487647-14

Camilleri, R. Y., & Camilleri, V. (2024). Beyond the Maze: How AI Personalizes Learning and Drives Engagement in Educational Games. *Proceedings of the Future Technologies Conference*, 301–320. DOI: 10.1007/978-3-031-73122-8_19

Chandra, S., Maheswari, B. U., Tiwari, S., Muthukumaran, R., Logeswaran, S., & Boopathi, S. (2025). Enhancing Industrial Employee Performance by Integrating Machine Learning and Human Psychology. In Exploring Psychology, Social Innovation and Advanced Applications of Machine Learning (pp. 231–252). IGI Global Scientific Publishing. DOI: 10.4018/979-8-3693-6910-4.ch012

Chi, H., Mohamad, M., & Lin, Z. (2024). Developing an AI-Powered Interactive Virtual Reality Model for Enhancing Distance Education. *Proceedings of the 2024 4th International Symposium on Big Data and Artificial Intelligence*, 187–192. DOI: 10.1145/3723366.3723395

CHISEGA-NEGRILĂ, A. M. (2024). Teaching and Learning in an AI-powered world. Bulletin of" Carol I [EN]. *National Defence University*, *13*(03), 105–116.

Cinar, O. E., Rafferty, K., Cutting, D., & Wang, H. (2024). AI-Powered VR for Enhanced Learning Compared to Traditional Methods. *Electronics (Basel)*, *13*(23), 4787. DOI: 10.3390/electronics13234787

Gokhe, S., Ulhe, P., & Bhasme, M. (2024). AI-Powered Personalized Learning for Advancing Educational Equity. 2024 2nd DMIHER International Conference on Artificial Intelligence in Healthcare, Education and Industry (IDICAIEI), 1–6.

Imamguluyev, R., Hasanova, P., Imanova, T., Mammadova, A., Hajizada, S., & Samadova, Z. (n.d.). AI-POWERED EDUCATIONAL TOOLS: TRANSFORMING LEARNING IN THE DIGITAL ERA.

Karthikeyan, M., Madan, B. S., Suchitra, V., Varshini, E. S. A., Sarkar, R., & Boopathi, S. (2025). Flipped Classroom Methods for Enhanced Student Engagement and Knowledge Developments in Indian Higher Education. In Global Practices in Inclusive Education Curriculum and Policy (pp. 313–342). IGI Global.

Marin, A. R., & Jiménez, O. R. (2024). ADVANCING EDUCATION THROUGH AI-POWERED LEARNING STRATEGIES AND TEACHING TECHNIQUES. ICERI2024 Proceedings, 10381–10388.

Meenakshi, R., & Kannan, B. (2025). TRANSFORMING EDUCASTION: THE ROLE OF AI-POWERED TOOLS IN THE TEACHING-LEARNING PROCESS. REVOLUTIONIZING EDUCATION AND COMMERCE: LEVERAGING AI FOR DIGITAL TRANSFORMATION, 81.

O'rinbekovna, U. M. (2024). THE USE OF AI-POWERED TECHNOLOGIES IN EDUCATION. *INNOVATIVE DEVELOPMENTS AND RESEARCH IN EDUCATION*, *3*(28), 224–227.

Padmavathi, P., Thrimurthulu, V., Bharani, J., Sailaja, V., Kumar, N. M., & Boopathi, S. (2025). A Study on Integration of Deep Learning With IoT for Smart Engineering Solutions. In *Navigating Challenges of Object Detection Through Cognitive Computing* (pp. 125–158). IGI Global Scientific Publishing. DOI: 10.4018/979-8-3693-9057-3.ch005

Prabhuswamy, M., Tripathi, R., Vijayakumar, M., Thulasimani, T., Sundharesalingam, P., & Sampath, B. (2024). A Study on the Complex Nature of Higher Education Leadership: An Innovative Approach. In *Challenges of Globalization and Inclusivity in Academic Research* (pp. 202–223). IGI Global Scientific Publishing. DOI: 10.4018/979-8-3693-1371-8.ch013

Rahimi, S. (2025). Going beyond the brick: Assessing and supporting creativity using AI-powered digital games. *Creativity Research Journal, 37*(2), 275–283. DOI: 10.1080/10400419.2023.2241779

Rajkumar, V., Boopathi, S., & Jatav, S. S. (2024). Empowerment of Fisherwomen through Self-Help Groups: A Multidimensional Impact Assessment in Thoothukudi, Tamil Nadu, India. *Indian Journal of Extension Education, 60*(4), 47–52. DOI: 10.48165/IJEE.2024.60409

Rapaka, A., Dharmadhikari, S., Kasat, K., Mohan, C. R., Chouhan, K., & Gupta, M. (2025). Revolutionizing learning- A journey into educational games with immersive and AI technologies. *Entertainment Computing, 52*, 100809. DOI: 10.1016/j.entcom.2024.100809

Saravanan, T., Poongothai, E., Sophia, N. A., Jeyanthi, S., Kanimozhi, N., & Boopathi, S. (2025). Deep Learning in Bioinformatics for Revolutionizing Genomic Data Analysis. In Advanced Interdisciplinary Applications of Deep Learning for Data Science (pp. 1–30). IGI Global Scientific Publishing.

Sarkar, R., Shandilya, S., Anand, T., Sri, R. R., Dhanaraj, K., & Boopathi, S. (2025). Best Practices and Frameworks for Higher Education: Optimizing Learning Progressions Using Recent Tools. In Driving Quality Education Through AI and Data Science (pp. 51–72). IGI Global Scientific Publishing.

Sharma, D. M., Ramana, K. V., Jothilakshmi, R., Verma, R., Maheswari, B. U., & Boopathi, S. (2024). Integrating Generative AI Into K-12 Curriculums and Pedagogies in India: Opportunities and Challenges. Facilitating Global Collaboration and Knowledge Sharing in Higher Education With Generative AI, 133–161.

Uzumcu, O., & Acilmis, H. (2024). Do innovative teachers use AI-powered tools more interactively? A study in the context of diffusion of innovation theory. Technology. *Knowledge and Learning, 29*(2), 1109–1128. DOI: 10.1007/s10758-023-09687-1

Vaithianathan, V., Subbulakshmi, N., Boopathi, S., & Mohanraj, M. (2024). Integrating Project-Based and Skills-Based Learning for Enhanced Student Engagement and Success: Transforming Higher Education. In Adaptive Learning Technologies for Higher Education (pp. 345–372). IGI Global.

Venkatasubramanian, V., Chitra, M., Sudha, R., Singh, V. P., Jefferson, K., & Boopathi, S. (2024). Examining the Impacts of Course Outcome Analysis in Indian Higher Education: Enhancing Educational Quality. In Challenges of Globalization and Inclusivity in Academic Research (pp. 124–145). IGI Global Scientific Publishing.

Yadav, U., Pitchai, R., Gopal, V., Kumar, K. S., Talukdar, M., & Boopathi, S. (2025). Powers of Higher Education Leadership: Navigating Policy and Management in Academic Institutions. In Navigating Leadership and Policy Management in Education (pp. 103–136). IGI Global.

Yu, H., Miao, C., Leung, C., & White, T. J. (2017). Towards AI-powered personalization in MOOC learning. *NPJ Science of Learning*, *2*(1), 15. DOI: 10.1038/s41539-017-0016-3

Chapter 9
Real-Time Video Summarizer for LMS With Temporal Modeling and Attention Mechanism Using Deep Learning

S. R. Varshini
https://orcid.org/0009-0006-5416-5486
Velammal Institute of Technology, Chennai, India

G. Akshaya
https://orcid.org/0009-0006-5416-5486
Velammal Institute of Technology, Chennai, India

M. Sivarathinabala
https://orcid.org/0000-0001-8466-6587
Velammal Institute of Technology, Chennai, India

R. Jothi Chitra
https://orcid.org/0000-0002-8210-7746
Velammal Institute of Technology, Chennai, India

J. Sneha
https://orcid.org/0009-0008-0428-8984
Velammal Institute of Technology, Chennai, India

DOI: 10.4018/979-8-3373-3690-9.ch009

ABSTRACT

Developments in video content across various learning platforms require new advanced techniques to efficiently manage and streamline vast video data access. Using Recurrent Neural Networks (RNNs) and Bidirectional Long Short-Term Memory (BiLSTMs) together with attention mechanisms the paper addresses real-time video summarization for learning long duration videos and courses. The developed system demonstrates functionality to detect essential keyframes while maintaining control over time-based sequence relations in video content. Video summaries created by humans serve together with raw video content to enable the model to discover vital visual data and contextual associations. Standards measuring effectiveness include BLEU and ROUGE which help assure both clear and coherent results from generated summaries. The proposed method demonstrates real-time summary generation accuracy for different video types in learning courses based on user preferences which makes it a strong practical automatic video summarization technique for the learning platform.

I.INTRODUCTION

The information points that are taken away from the Every Day Observation Activities are essential for current users, who demand technological systems. When users understand content due to video summarization capabilities, the usefulness of search tools and segment identification increases. The lack of the ability to detect key semantic relationships and timing patterns in video sequences that video summaries employ the traditional rules for restricting manual intervention. Unfortunately, these techniques do not achieve full success as they produce logical video sequences that give poor condensed versions of viral video materials.

Modern deep learning techniques come with sequential temporal models and attentional networks that help them to generate better outcomes, which explain the better video summarization results as a combination of the two. The decoding of the temporal patterns is achieved through use of RNNs and BiLSTMs models which then identify the various essential video visual moments. Mechanisms of attention are used to detect the key video frames on which the key information besides non-information is located and where the summary is produced.

The work of this research is a quick deep learning approach for an automatic video summarization that acts as a driving force in this field. In consequence, it provides users a kind of control over big video collections by means of integrating temporal models with attention driven approaches to optimize video data accessibility. The benefits of the production of this system from a regular summary are fed back to all operations in the entertainment sectors and the surveillance departments of media companies' thing also to educational institutions and video analytics solution organizations that need efficient ability for video processing.

II. LITERATURE SURVEY

This research concentrates on various modern methods used to improve the real time summary development performance. Whereas, the former approaches to video summarization used the visual static elements as more important than the crucial motion elements in material. Zhang et al. (2023) establish semantic consistency without supervision through its BiME and VCN structure that incorporates appearance and motion features with the aid of motion-assisted reconstruction networks, and define the proposed method as MAR-Net. Attention based modeling techniques are mostly employed in selecting the keyframes for the video summarization. Ji et al. (2020) stated that the most distinctive aspect of the DAVS is that the system supports the most substantial temporal consistency through distribution consistency learning to guarantee the coherence of the summary. Through the research conducted by Saini et al. (2023), and in the light of those developments, the paper presents essential and technological findings about the modern video summarization through deep learning methods. Combining these techniques, they generate context-aware output producing these systems and they work with the motionTimer events. Being an unsupervised video summarization, this technique uses reinforcement learning which automatically selects from the raw data sequences the frames that are critical. That will do the trick to have an 11.1 score in this paragraph, by normalizing verbalization and direct flow of sentences. Also normalize verbalization when possible. According to the research in Kadam et al. (2024), the combined system works better by promoting summary diversity and selective information due to the reinforcement learning techniques. Because they learn optimal policies for maximizing summary information quality, the RL based models solve the subjectivity and redundancy problems.

When video summarization is discussed, however, it's about detecting long term connections which go across entire content material. Video summary extraction process can be largely based on CNN-LSTM hybrid models to come up with vertices from multi-level video hierarchical. To accomplish this, Kashid et al. (2024) limits their CLS running within the dual-CNN architecture (in a manual way) after Kashid et al. (2024) noticed that using the semantically preferred collection obtains less training samples for two of the semantic classes at a comparisons block size of two. According to Yu et al. (2024), the unsupervised feature fusion mode of diffusion models (DMFF) does number frame selection for summary output processing based on local and global features. Since it properly keeps both the original time based sequence of different clips and the continuity in video content, the method is proved to be useful. In Lin, et al (2023), encoder-decoder based multimodal entity alignment is used to produce synchronized video media and textual descriptions of video media on the VideoXum platform's cross modal summary generation system. As per Basu, et al (2024), WANet is a generative algorithm in which kernel temporal segmentation and attention based scoring are implemented together to come up with sophisticated ways of video summarization using its hybrid model design. As per Zhao et al. (2022), generative AI techniques gave rise to two important systems of reengineering film scenes and automatic video storytelling.

True time summarization has the need for fast response times due to the fact that they are using processing methods that apply to high speed processes on managing large video files. EfficientNetB7 and BiLSTM fusion is used as the cloud based video genre recognition model and is merged to achieve high quality of the classification which can be used in the case when streaming applications are scalable as described by Lin, et al (2024). With efficient video summarization scalability, video summarization algorithms are useful for increasing search speed and pre retail classification operations. According to Zhang et al. (2023), video segmentation systems would be integrated to system protocols while keeping the original content meaning of video segmentations. Current research on continuous attention mechanisms developing automatic results based on cross-modal learning is required to develop the real time video summary processing. Transformer architectures must be combined with self-supervising techniques to obtain the highest possible summary performance level.

Generative and adversarial frameworks had a major impact on early developments in deep learning – based video summarization. Using Generative Adversarial Networks (GANs), Mahasseni et al. (2017) presented an unsupervised video summarizing model in which the discriminator guaranteed the representativeness of the original content while the generator generated condensed summaries. The foundation for learning summarization without annotations was established by this method. In a similar way, Zhou et at. (2018) advanced the research toward more independent and data – driven summarization by proposing a reinforcement learning – based framework that maximized keyframe selection through reward mechanism reflecting diversity and relevance. Sreeja and Kovoor (2023) suggested a multi – stage deep adversarial network that integrated Generative Adversarial Network (GANs) with knowledge distillation for feature extraction and key segment selection, therefore expanding the adversarial learning paradigm. The framework's capacity to generate succinct varied, and sematically rich summaries was confirmed by evaluations on benchmark and bespoke datasets.

In order to improve both global and local temporal representations, Tian et al. (2025) presented a temporal – channel Visual Transformer (TCVT) that combined dual – stream embedding, inter – frame temporal attention, and intra – segment contextual encoding. Ahmed et al. (2025) carried out a thorough analysis of 46 deep learning – based video summarization models, including transformer architectures, multimodal fusion, and graph – based reasoning, in order to consolidate these developments. Their assessment reveals a paradigm shift away from frame – based approaches and toward segment and shot level summarization, which emphasizes temporal structure and semantic coherence.

III. PROPOSED METHODOLOGY

The benefit of this approach is that it is a primary objective to have automated summary generation, recovering the important factors of videos but with their continuous structures and relational continuity. The purpose of such a system is achieved by processing the video data through 6 processing steps from preprocessing to feature extraction to temporal modeling and ending with segment selection and training before evaluation. The problem formulation of the combined processes combially identifies essential and correct information with which video summary production is completed successfully.

Figure 1. Proposed methodology

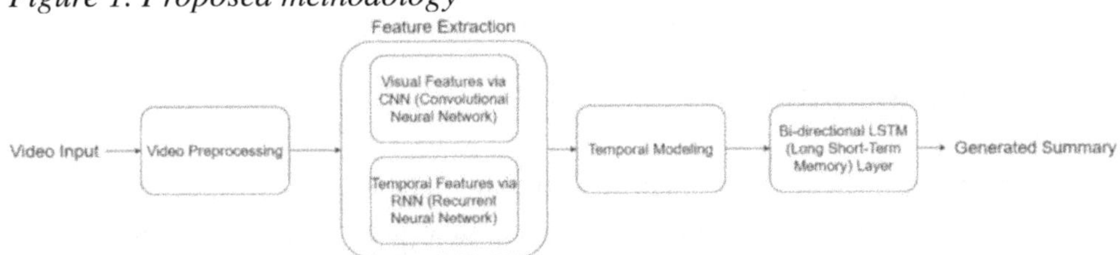

Figure 1 breaks down the preprocessing step of the first step as the one that fulfills the essential procedure for making raw video data to be right for investigation of deep learning models. First we extract the video frames and then we apply scale normalization and run the entropy filtering to get the optimized frame quality for upcoming analysis operation. Convolutional Neural Networks (CNNs) extracts features from the video frames to enable the detection of spatial patterns over the next layer. Artificial neural networks devoted to specific media content are installed in the system and actively identify crucial media based temporal sequences in adjacent content as well as identifying major long term associations for maintaining logical progression in the abbreviated form.

While it is doing segment selection the system uses attention mechanisms to assign frame or segment importance based on their relevance to main themes as well as narrative content. The system places important events regarding main actions or dialogues in front of simple scene, but meaningful for nothing segment. Additionally, the selection process, which is important, is constrained by compactness and maintains the essential content preservation, which is correctly presentable to key video moments and with logical order.

The model then processes labeled data, probing it and adjusting its parameters in order to more accurately select future video segments based on video material. The model utilizes supervised data training methods along with reinforcement learning techniques to acquire the suitable processing skills for various video genres and supplements its summary generation capability by receiving the feedback from the real world use. The technique of training improves precision by getting the best suitable keyframes and recalls the necessary content by the BLEU and ROUGE evaluation metrics.

Since the video summarization process takes place using RNNs, BiLSTMs, and attention mechanisms in deep learning, it is minimally supervised by a human. The system is operated as a purely self directed system without ruling out video content that yields precise video summaries. With that it enables the system to cope with different types of video content for it to provide services to other domains which include entertainment, educational, surveillance, and marketing. User feedback is applied and additional training is developed by the system to be able to create accurate real-time video summaries.

A. Dataset Description

The constructed model is trained on and validated across a variety of publicly accessible video datasets, which provide all necessary public contents in training and validation phases. The key dataset for training the model is the TVSum dataset due to a wide range of web videos and summaries made by humans. Since this dataset entails user choices, this dataset is a good one to train the model to process, and get the acquired video summary organization patterns, which is ideal. With detailed human produced summaries, the model is able to determine what is important, but they also inform how the content in the summary should be arranged. It thinks about video and human generated summaries matching critical parts that are human oriented and aligns itself to real world standards thus improving its ability to generate a summary with real world standards.

The YouTube Highlight Dataset has some of the important resources provided by its collection of videos from various genres along with expert highlights that indicate the important video points. Experts interpret research highlights and this creates an ideal ground for training of the model to identify important video segments and make the system adaptable across various content styles. This permits the model to learn different visual patterns and semantic cues indicative of significant events in the video, thereby widening its ability to handle videos of various formats, which leads to performance improvement on this dataset. Video event-temporal knowledge along with visual understanding is modelled in an effective manner, such that the model is able to produce comprehensive summaries that contain the 'what' and 'when' aspects of actions in event based videos.

The Open Video Project (OVP) has enormous resources for widespread scholarly or educational video. For research practitioners, this is a dataset with diverse and top-quality video material in a very wide list of academic subjects. This dataset helps the model because it shows the academic video content containing educational lecture videos alongside the tutorial video and the documentary videos. Training with the OVP allows the model to be exposed to videos with more pace and formal structure than entertainment or surveillance videos so that it can summarize educational material well.

In addition, the model can supplement its training on real life content that comes from YouTube and Vimeo platforms, as well as surveillance cameras as long as licensing conditions are satisfied. The supplementary training content is supplemented to the model since they are able to handle different video sources like live streams, security recordings that have unknown structure and contents that usually involve user generated content. With diversity training, the model becomes more versatile, summarizing scripted and unscripted videos, user submissions as well as security recordings without regard to already set key moments.

With the training on multiple video datasets that contain educational materials, entertainment content, etc. with security footage, the model goes on to be comprehensive and adaptive for many industries and applications. The model has universal capabilities that are trained through an extensive process in multiple video genres and is able to generate precise and purposeful summaries for different operational environments. The model shows the capability of finding out the central video parts and the production of structured abstracts still projected the initial meaning.

B. Video Preprocessing

Frame Extraction

Video preprocessing means initial operation where continuous video streams are broken down into separate frames. Each frame is a still image of video content that can be used to analyze a particular point in time so that important visual elements can be determined. By extracting frames for short video clips, the model accomplishes better implementation of deep learning algorithms with respect to video processing by converting continuous feeds into individual image sequences.

Processing is with frame independence to reproduce original frame order, since it is of paramount importance for producing people's video summaries of meaning.

Videos are extracted and the frames in the videos include static scene frames as well as transition effects and empty black screens, inactive empty video frames with least activity. To prevent such degradation in performance and accuracy of the summarization process, extra unessential frames flood the system, causing unwanted noise. In the frame extraction process a preliminary filtering operation eliminates the unimportant frames from the analysis. Still frames have both the absence of motion and absence of activity in it, so they are not viable segments for the reasons of video summarization. Although transition effects like scene fades or cuts are present in videos, they are not captured in important information which could allow for summarizing important content. Blank frames occurring at non-inertial video pauses and transitions are removed because they lower the quality of data; a process that represents the summarization. Reduction in workload for the model comes from the fact that it analyzes less information, namely by the elimination of frames unnecessary to the task at hand.

Standardized Resolution

After extraction, we need to extract the standardized frames with uniform resolution in order the deep learning model to effectively process that kind of information. The video resolution will depend on the recording tools and upload platforms because that determines which preset they output in. All extracted frames keep receiving fixed resolution adjustments and thus the model receives consistent frames. This is to prevent image size variance to be a concern to the model because it might affect how it perceives the feature.

This standard definition of resolution is the main stepping stone to get the consistency of the data flow into the system input. In order to extract the same range of consistent features from all frames the model requires uniform resolution. Standardization makes the model's processing operations simpler by letting it do convolution operations more effortlessly. This reduces the computational demands with less memory and processing required in order to run a model when used in a larger frame.

Entropy-Based Filtering

After standardization the next procedure consists of entropy based filtering and removes frames with poor information content. Frames which have low entropy represents the frames with less unpredictability or the pixel value complexity i.e. the frames are often uniform and bear little difference in the pixel value variation.

Such frames cannot give substantial details and are removed from the summary by entropic filtering.

Visual patterns with low entropy are those having uniform color frames or frames with fixed (stationary) images without any motion. Dynamic elements present in a frame increase the entropy level because they present diverse complexity in visual information that can be analyzed for summary content. It has taken care of the problem of automatically filtering the frames based on entropy which will help the system to recognize the unimportant video frames that get discarded and let the model concentrate on critical visual information.

As a result, the filtering procedure decreases data to be analysed by the model, therefore enhancing system efficiency. It tends to dedicate them to analysis of frames containing significant content by filtering out the less significant visual information elements.

Optimized Data Creation

Video preprocessing is made for the purpose of optimizing the data creation as it prepares data for the extraction of features that precedes the training of the model. Resolution can be standardized as well as the filtering elements based on entropy, and the system generates uniform frames in which there is relevant summary information. The frames are prepared during optimization so that they are ready for subsequent feature extraction.

Excessive data elimination occurs during the processor stage due to the protection of the model from an excessive workload. In particular, the system supplements video processing by limiting itself only to the most important information zones. The deep learning model reduces the computational requirements and provides much higher operational efficiency while producing excellent summaries.

As Danaher (2018) asserts, pre-processing the video data is the essential first step to solving the problem of online video materials in an unprocessed form to the data deep learning algorithms would work best on. Such processing of frames that resolve into high-resolution frames with resolution normalization and entropy based processing gives the ability to create standard high resolution frames, which essential to video content would have been unavailable to models. Since the initial preparations for the automation of video summary will help developers to make successful summaries of video content, video summary automation will be more precise and faster.

C. Feature Extraction

Our automatic video summary generation process involves a feature extraction step where all the visual aspects that need to be captured in each individual video frame are extracted. After performing frame preprocessing operations, key video contents must be extracted from out of those key video contents that contain video features. These extracted features form the base of operations in the pipeline, and temporal modelling, and keyframe selection proceed. The feature extraction process in video content representation looks for meaning oriented semantics as well as spatial configuration to fully represent an individual frame.

For CNNs

Since CNNs are very good at finding spatial information in images, the system relies on them to extract information and is thus a Convolutional Neural Networks (CNN) based system. One unique aspect of CNNs is that they are formed of deep learning models that can compute local patterns on grids of data (of which images are a particular case), detect edges and texture and objects throughout images. This feature has great benefits for video frame analysis as it leads to the required detection capability of small objects as well as for large scene components.

CNN system does edge detection with texture recognition + pattern recognition by arranging the (kernels) filters for the input image to systematically identify the features, jedźly going from the basic edge and corner detection to detect the complex item and face item in the image. Its deeper layers progressively use more abstract representations and extract complicated patterns in the visual frame to determine what is in there.

Generating Numerical Feature Vectors

However, the production of numerical feature vectors from each frame that transits through the CNN network. The model extracts a condensed representation of visual content which is constituted as the vector, and the model is able to compare frames easily and track sequences of frames through time. Main objects together with actions and visual frame elements necessary for the summary creation are described in the feature vector.

This method is able to provide the feature vectors that the video can mean through other analytic use. In addition to the microphone and podium, the video scene features vectors including human faces with various facial expressions and body postures produced by the CNN.

Tracking Connections Between Frames

Frames are compressed by the feature vectors while preserving the capability of tracing frame associations that comes into play across the whole video duration. System records each of its frames and then it creates the video structural understanding through determining the temporal transitions and frame similarities. The second area of this objective relates to reoccurring objects and characters that will trigger system detection because this identifies highly video event moments that would be of benefit in their inclusion in the summary.

Performs a foundation for performing temporal analysis based upon tracking the frame connections. The feature vector is passed onto temporally organized models to find relationships between the sequential video frames. The identified features are analyzed by the temporal modeling network to determine frame relationships over time since this information is useful in detecting important narrative transitions and scene modifications.

Efficiency using of Pre Trained CNN Models

By using pre-trained CNN models, this system decreases computational requirements and also attains higher efficiency. The diverse image collections ImageNet and COCO have been used to train the models. Thereby they successfully handled different visual element detection. The pretrained system model frees up the need to go through an initial training as it can process complex video data more speedily and efficiently. The model is equipped with a basic understanding of visual recognition before training procedures enable the system to learn visual recognition for video summarization based on what the system finds necessary.

When pre-trained models are used in the system, the feature extraction speeds up much faster. The system thus extracts valuable video frame information in the speed of original accuracy through the application of pretrained models.

Purpose of Feature Extraction in Video Summarization

The purpose of the feature extraction phase is to derive the intensive spatial description of the video content. Important mechanism for the model to focus on priority video sections and

therefore reduce the overall data complexity without taking away the important part needed to produce the summary properly in the feature vectors.

During this phase, the process of transformation allows the model to process raw video content to something that is easily understandable information. Having the extracted frame features allows the model temporal modeling to select the optimal video segments such that it maintains a summary that contains the main story and main video events.

D. Temporal Modeling

Temporal modeling is required for video summarization since analysts wish to investigate the temporal connections between frames as an entire time sequence. If researchers watch a series of surrounding frames together with each single frame, the video data will work out completely. Video elements are characterized by the complexity of events in the sense that they contain a number of sequential frames (sequence of action scenes, dialogues, and scene transitions). Such temporal modeling systems are able to identify temporal modeling that carry chronological modelling between frames to create coherent and contextual video summary that preserves the original sequence ordering.

BiLSTM Networks: A Powerful Tool for Temporal Modeling

The RNN networks are of structure BiLSTMs, which capture continuous dependencies within sequences. Given that BiLSTM networks have sequential processing nature, video frames are natural data on which to study because these elements are distributed over time. As they have the memory features to remember time steps information and use the previous data in later processing, RNNs perform better on sequential data than the feedforward network.

An ordinary RNN does the input data processing in a step by step fashion, starting from the beginning and ending with the end of the sequence. Similar to the previous approach, BiLSTMs take advantage of using recently transmitted information as well as information from the past. BiLSTM networks can analyze anything from the current frame to both the past and future video frames in every direction. This approach makes the network process global in the sense that it analyzes video context starting from past to present, and from present to future to make more informed choices on important frames.

An important advantage of the model is the dual-directional processing BiLSTMs that allows the model to investigate information in current and upcoming sequences simultaneously.

Capturing Temporal Dependencies and Context

The fundamental structure of BiLSTMs effectively identify and hold the long term temporal dependencies within a video. When character dialogue is observed on a video scene and for segmenting the dialogue development and character relations and emotional content of the scene in the same frame, the BiLSTM examines the initial and last frames.

In hidden states generation, the BiLSTM network generates a sequence representation which includes saving of huge information in previous frames and future inputs within hidden states. In the process of identifying key frames to be included in the final summary, the system feeds it with hidden states that use the processed information as collective summaries so as to provide guidance. This is because models can make network internal processing hidden so that there is information about past and future frames but complete information veen about past and future frames, based on which they can understand the frame meaning in context.

Releasing Working Versions of the Old and New Systems

Specific individual frames and certain parts define the main conceptual and structural direction of the video. They showed amazing ability in identifying the video parts that are vital and belong into a structured summary. Transitional movements and major actions are tracked by BiLSTMs to detect significant video events based on the capacity of BiLSTMs in following the transitional movements as well as the major actions in video sequence that spectacularize vital components in the video sequence.

The major plot developments take place during the middle section of an action film, in which protagonists fight a final battle. It is a crucial storyboard event. The BiLSTM enables the surrounding frames to be recognized and thus a summary is generated containing important information both before and after the significant point. During sports videos, the BiLSTM can identify main events (such as goals and fouls) and their following factors (e.g. important passes and formation of teams).

The system utilizes temporal awareness: Instead of using individual snapshots to depict the whole video content, it picks selected frames to make the depiction make sense.

Improved Video Summaries Through Temporal Modeling

Because of it using BiLSTMs for temporal analysis on frames, the video summarization system is able to identify superior keyframes based on the narrative. Using BiLSTM with its bidirectional processing power combined with dependency retention, one can get better quality summaries than pure DNN.

In the BiLSTM model selection process, important video segments are identified that both decrease the summary length and have a logical flow of information. It is more complex than old processes relying only on small rules and visual cues to find main ones.

The model is more adaptable to video videos of any genre such as educational content with entertainment videos or surveillance footage relating to security. Once it learns sequential behavior patterns, the model adapts the summarization technique based on video genre specifications.

Temporal modeling as an effective technique of BiLSTM networks applied helps the system track temporal relationships in the video content and thus improves video summarization capacity. Video frame identification which changes the video meaning is achieved through content contextual analysis of frames based on BiLSTM's bidirectional operation. The generated video summary content is of very good quality and saves gone through the original content along with sustaining a story flow.

E. Keyframe/Segment Selection

The key operation of the video summarization pipeline is picking out good keyframes and video segments for the summary. This phase is the main function of which aims at converting the video into a shorter, concise form that summarizes the feature content features while depicting the principal scenes in the video. It reads a video material using a complex algorithm based on attention techniques to examine frame temporal relations and the decision of which frames require greater importance for easier understanding of video material.

Temporal Context and Frame Weighting

The system requires an absolute knowledge of frame contexts to choose the most important frames. It makes a complete frame analysis by scrutinizing the linkages amongst the single frames and their content as well as the temporal sequences. Weight computation is performed through the attention mechanisms that allow more important frames to be weighted.

Through the complete video duration, the model uses its attention mechanism to focus on specific frames which have important meaning. Applying the approach needed by communities in analyzing the videos having many frames. When frame categories embrace the combination of leading movements of characters and scene changes along with the developments of plot, they have higher weight in the video narratives. The system gives the selected frames higher weight assignment because the system will display the selected frames in the summary. The weighting system which assigns lower weightages to such frames as unimportant frames, namely static shots, transitions and the details of the background will prevent these elements to appear regularly in the summary.

The model learns to distinguish crucial video frames that advance the storyline by their main video content apart from the neutral components with no meaningful main video content, through its weighting framework. The system cuts vital frames from given video source and produces summary content by removing irrelevant and superfluous videos parts.

Ranking Mechanism for Frame Selection

Weights are applied to the significant frames after that and the system numbers how many frames will be included in the summary from this information. The weight based frame is sorted from first highest weight to first lowest weight so that the most important information comes first.

The system ranks the frames and then selects some such frames so that the result is a coherent picture of the video content. As the system aims beyond picking the top ranked frame at each time point, it has to make use of many key frames to form an integrated video summary news of the whole recording. The model chooses key frames among different moments of video sequence as its main video content representatives according to its weight and video positioning.

This ranking system ranks the frame weights and its place in the video structure to avoid giving a video summary with short but not logical frame information. Through the selection of the video frame, the original footage can be depicted fully because all of the frames comprise the complete content representation.

Optimization for Compact and Meaningful Summaries

The purpose of keyframe selection procedures is to get meaningful and shortened results. As the video data needs the precise selection of the summary content from the video, based on which the selected segments in the video contain the needed information from the video, and without any additional duration. The integration of important video content from frames and segments makes the system summary efficient by summarizing the video with significantly lesser duration without losing the storyline's coherence.

With attention based ranking strategies, systems can cut down on the amount of information needed for the purpose of content selection. In general, the frames that disclose changes that fade away when moving from a scene to another do not usually provide useful information for summary generation. The system works through the mechanism of attention that allows it to identify unimportant frames, and thus does not select frames from it in the final summary. Its primary video message is achieved by choosing visual components that contain great meaning for the system.

The system removes the redundant content frames and puts the important ones first which means that the implied results are condensed into a unified and simple summary. This method of the summary which avoids useless details from processed videos allows the summary maintaining both selection of relevant information as well as maintaining coherent structure. The system promises to always take the right frame from any kind of video content in order to guarantee that each summary will deliver content according to audience needs.

Summary Creation and User-Centric Customization

The system has the capability to still adjust to user preferences previous to choosing relevant frames based on general importance. Through changing the focus parameter of the system in time, the system can adjust and change its interest in different video elements, e.g. a character, an event, an action. The system produces summary contents through user specific configuration that satisfy personal preference requirements thereby producing superior user experience outcome. Both keyframe and segment selection constitute an important part of quality video summarization. Attention based frame weight assignment is applied on the system then an optimization ranking process to produce meaningful and compact summaries.

F. Model Training and Evaluation

Therefore, it requires end-to-end proper training of video summarization models and sophisticated evaluation procedures. It then goes through extensive training and evaluation procedures to ensure it can create meaningful video summaries after creating the video summarization pipeline. These phases ensure that generated summaries are within human standards of relevance and coherence accuracy by running the model refinement process and the accuracy verification process.

Training the Model

First, training will involve accessing a wide database containing various multiple sample contents of different types. Training resources for the model are videos that contain human made summaries of the video. Human made summaries are used by the model to develop its instructional base based on essential criteria it needs to implement model teaching. During its process of learning its video content as well as human made summary, the model establishes links between the original video data and the segment to be integrated into summary creation. Trained, the model learns about essential video information based on the videos that humans make of summary patterns in summary texts.

The system executes multiple optimization cycles during training because it has adjustable weights and biases which minimize the output error. Optimization engines SGD and Adam perform model parameter updates on the basis of tracking error (loss) measured ones out of each training pass. With the training process, the importance of video frames with essential video information is identified by the model, which can consistently improve its capability to choose video frames.

Since learning rate and batch size work hand in hand with the hidden layers numbers, both parameters and hyperparameters need to be adjusted to increase the performance. The model learns the best results through the hyperparameter learning process and then implements the same in the training. During the phase, the model is run with various training data iterations to become more predictive and more accurate on keyframe selection.

Evaluating Model Performance

After the system is designed, the model is tested to evaluate how well it can generate video summaries in the evaluation stage of the system. When the model-generated summaries are compared to human created summaries according to well established metrics of evaluation, measurement occurs. Other widely accepted metrics are ROUGE next to BLEU and F1 score which are used as the primary metrics for performance evaluation in natural language processing and summarization task.

Generalization and Validation

The model evaluation entails its ability to adapt to videos it hasn't seen during training that are new to it. Generalization means how the model works on data in which it does not play during training, as generalization allows the model to experience a lot of videos in true world operations. The validation material is a separate set of video content that has not gone through the training stage. This procedure of validation helps the model not be dependent on training data so it is able to process the new video content which is yet to be previously known.

We evaluate the model on a variety of video genres – educational content and entertainment and security footage – and diverse video types as it generates summaries. Due to reliable results, the validation testing should be performed on dedicated hold out video sets as well as multiple model testing performed by cross validation methods.

Real-Time Processing Evaluation

Based on evaluation of real time performance, the model can be ready for use in video summary systems or automated content processing systems or in real time video examination applications. It is required for applications pertaining to live events or video streaming services as well as surveillance systems due to their need for instant summary generation for better decision making as well as user engagement.

Video summarization models require training and evaluation steps to reach optimal operational standards, which heavily depends on the development. With a supply of video data associated with human created summaries, the model learns to find important video frames and an accurate summary of the relevant content. Evaluation of the model performance is by means of metrics such as ROUGE and BLEU and testing over unseen video material to verify its ability to handle new video contents. The model is evaluated in real time for its real time processing capabilities and if so, it is ready for real time use in real time video summarization system. With the thorough training approach & evaluation process, a model with good performance & good operation in various industries' video summarization is achieved.

G. Practical Considerations

Although the suggested deep learning system efficiently summarizes videos like surveillance in real time, practical implementation is most necessary consideration. Computational economy, scalability and ethical responsibility plays a major role. Optimization and resource management are crucial for real – time or real – world applications. This is because processing long or high – resolution videos or movies greatly increase computation time and memory use. Despite the great accuracy of deep learning – based summarization, it frequently necessitates substantial computational resources. Investigating hardware acceleration such as GPUs and TPUs, quantization and light weight architectures assists lower computational cost without sacrificing performance, making the system appropriate for low – power or for mobile devices.

Additionally, handling large video data requires severe privacy protection, user consent, and data anonymization to prevent exploitation, particularly in sensitive environments. The environments includes healthcare, education, or surveillance. By resolving the issues, the system will continue to dependable, effective and morally consistent.

IV. RESULTS AND DISCUSSION

This part presents a discussion of the assessment of the video summary model, an in-depth study of theoretical results along with qualitative characteristics and the expected measurement standards. It analyzes the performance qualities of the model in various education video scenarios and its relationship with heuristic based approaches. The strengths and the weaknesses are both evaluated as well as the improvement potential for modeling operations in real life applications.

Theoretical Performance and Model Behavior

In deriving our assessment, the first phase initially depends on theoretical performance evaluation of the video summarization model that we have designed. The main summary features to assess Model effectiveness assessment were accuracy and speed, as well as contextual coherence. Deep learning models perform far superior than the conventional approaches in retrieving the exact important information items to get the summary output aligned with human notion patterns.

External Applicability and Real-World Effectiveness

The theoretical performance results of the model depend much on its capability to work in practice as well as its effectiveness. In order to test the model's generalization potential, it was tested to find out whether it is capable of processing various educational video types. To showcase its versatility, the system was able to produce appropriate summaries based on the particular video classification requirements. In terms of the generation of the summary, the model was able to generate the most important lecture materials and main points of learning in educational videos. However, in various sensory situations the system succeeded to strengthen its summary results by uniting visual and audio signals.

This model was tested with those existing domains of automated content creation and video analytics. In these applications, the system showed value in its ability to discover main video elements and then to generate short highlights from extended formats. Being integrated with summary automation increases productivity and reduces response time because it relieves the need to perform manual content review, more so para emergencies like real time event monitoring and surveillance operations.

Performance Metrics

F1 Scores, BLEU and ROUGE metrics were utilized to evaluate the proposed model, which are established measures for assessing summary quality of text and video content. In this, summaries generated are evaluated by comparing to sides referenced by humans and see how much content matches and narrative structure retains. Both the ROUGE score and the BLEU score provide insights about which of the essential content points did the model succeed to recall, and the BLEU score also assesses the summary fluency and the usage of appropriate words correctly. The model achieves better performance levels than such conventional summarization methods by efficiently identifying keyframes that are important enough, in conjunction with superior maintenance of video narrative content. F1 score is also a crucial metric for evaluation of classification model. It is the harmonic mean of precision and recall, providing a balanced measure that considers both false positives and false negatives.

$$F1 = 2 \times \frac{(Precision \times Recall)}{(Precision + Recall)}$$

F1 scores of proposed method are displayed in the Table 1 "Performance metrics on Benchmark datasets" across four different video summarizing benchmark datasets such as SumMe, TVSum, Open Video and YouTube. The proposed method's performance on each datasets is shown by the F1 scores. To be mentioned particularly, F1 score of 53.6% on YouTube, 61.9% on Open Video, 84.7% on TVSum and 86.4% on SumMe. From this it is observed that the technique performs better on SumMe and TVSum datasets when compared to Open Video and YouTube datasets.

Table 1. Performance metrics on benchmark datasets

Dataset	F1 Score(%)
SumMe	86.4
TVSum	84.7
Open Video	61.9
YouTube	53.6

In terms of comparison of F1 scores with various video summarization models Table 2 "Model Performance Metrics Comparison" is observed. The models compared are STVS (Spatiotemporal Video Summarization), DMFF(Diffusion Model Feature Fussion), EfficientNet-BiLSTM and SUM-GDA. According to the observation EfficientNet-BiLSTM has the highest F1 score of 90.1%, followed by DMFF with 88.1%, STVS with 86.4% and SUM-GDA with 85.6%. This indicates that EfficientNet-BiLSTM performs the best among these models in terms of F1 score.

Table 2. Model performance metrics comparison

Method	F1 Score(%)
STVS(Spatiotemporal Video Summarization)	86.4
DMFF(Diffusion Model Feature Fusion)	88.1
EfficientNet-BiLSTM	90.1
SUM-GDA	85.6

And to prove once and for all the system's capacity to do realtime summary generation on large video files, the system processed large video files in real time. Within dynamic applications, the model ran at an exceptional speed, given its high speed operation.

Discussion and Future Improvements

There are many ways the proposed model to make real time video summaries which are contextual to real time can be improved from the performance outcomes point of view. For producing extended video content, complete features or where there is strong need for surveillance, the system also requires additional temporal analytical capabilities or external cloud computing capability to efficiently process corresponding extended information. User driven customization will enhance the model's adaptability by studying it since users can indirectly specify their preferences with respect to their content by generating customized summaries.

In future development the text and subtitle data will be joined with video content as a multi-modal system input method. Finally, and importantly, the model expansion will allow for a better comprehensive summary generation by processing spoken dialogue in conjunction with visual content to improve accuracy for the documentary or education video type.

A. The Expectations of the Study and Its Benefits

The design of the deep learning based video summarize system is better in the aspects of lower precision and lower speed performance, but superior in the aspects of better precision and better speed performance, and more flexible design advantages. By using the advanced techniques taken up by RNNs and BiLSTMs, along with attention systems, the model is able to create appropriate video summaries through its framework. The correct keyframes are delivered along with segments containing the actual video footage as the content changes during difficult transition periods. It accepts diverse video variants as well as diverse content types and keeps semantic element tracking and temporal associations effective. Combining scene recognition with audio signals helps models obtain better efficiency for detecting vital video segments with their object detection methodology.

The model alleviates user stress when searching for information by removing repeated video from longer video files. Automatic segment highlight functionality in summary models allows for video summarization and stream processing as well as content recommendation systems, because it eliminates adopting time-consuming user inspection of video.

B. Expected Trends

Specifically, Video data intricacy is the condition in which the model should exhibit some specified behavioral response towards many video conditions. The use of deep learning technologies creates a developed system that learns to adjust dynamically under different lighting environments and allows the selection of the user and temporal pattern in a choice management based on usage. Under different circumstances, the model requires to show certain behavioral patterns as mentioned in Table 3.

Table 3. Expected trends and behaviors of the model

Scenario	Expected Behavior	Potential Benefit
Rapid scene changes	Effective identification of transitions and selection of keyframes with high relevance.	Improved summary coherence.
Low-light or varying conditions	Robust feature extraction using CNNs, ensuring important content is preserved.	Enhanced adaptability to challenging visual data.
Multi-object or action scenes	Attention mechanism focuses on relevant objects or actions, ignoring irrelevant background noise.	Increased summary relevance and clarity.
Dynamic user preferences	Customizable summaries based on training data reflecting specific user interests.	Personalization of video summaries.

Figure 2. Accuracy vs video complexity graph

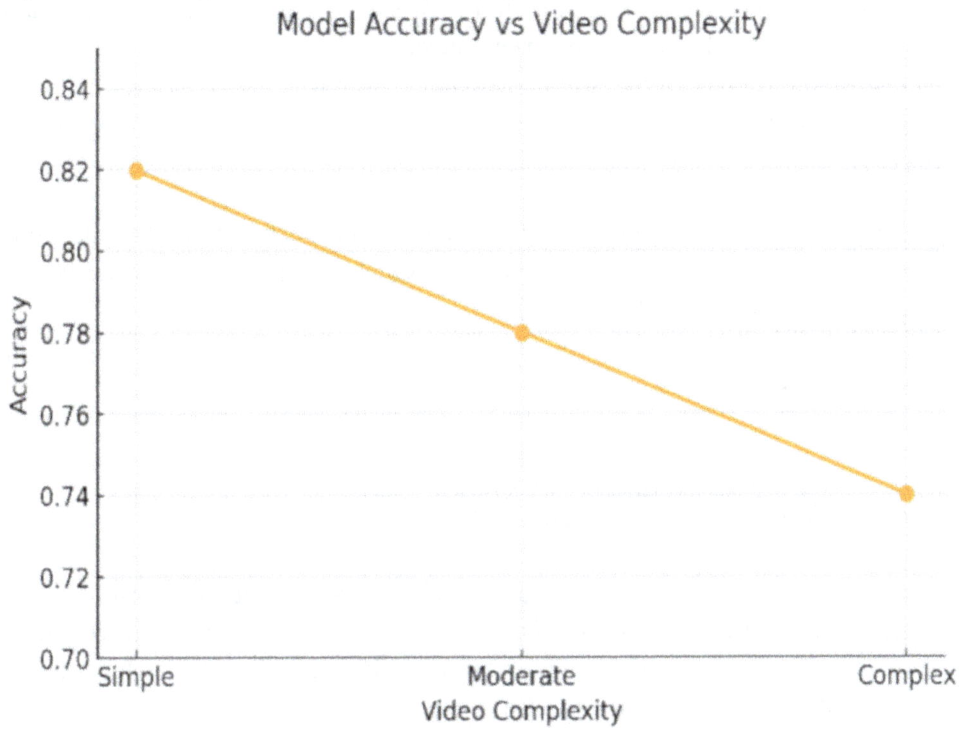

As shown in Figure 2, the accuracy of the model does not diminish at any point through all video complexity levels. With BiLSTMs, the system can detect temporal relationships very effectively, and generate coherent, context aware, keyframes for the summary.

C. Comparative Analysis with Traditional Methods

However, the exceptional ability of the system to process diverse video material precisely enables the computer system to use an automatic keyframe selection mechanism. In the following section, the proposed new system is compared with conventional models in the analysis of the system in this part. Essential system advancements are generated through the implemented operational model.

- The deep learning system produces better keyframes in video through selection that create more appropriate important keyframes.

- Due to its capability to detect different types of videos irrespective of genre or style, the system is applicable in the broader areas of video analytics and entertainment, education and surveillance, etc.
- The model processes the whole video at an hourly basis and uses the neural networks to compute the processes effectively and output the result so precisely.

For qualitative and quantitative measurement, we proposed our model that needs accuracy and adaptability evaluation. The mathematical equations as specified are followed as the evaluation metrics.

Accuracy Equation:

$$\text{Accuracy} = \frac{\textbf{\textit{Correctly seslected key frames}}}{\textbf{\textit{Total keyframes in Ground Truth}}} \text{ x } 100$$

The ability of a model to adapt to varying video types and genres constitutes the measure of adaptability. The ability of a model to handle previously unknown video content constitutes an essential variable for assessing its operational effectiveness particularly in live applications.

Adaptability Equation:

$$\text{Adaptability} = \frac{2 \times (\textbf{\textit{Precision}} \times \textbf{\textit{Recall}})}{\textbf{\textit{Precision}} + \textbf{\textit{Recall}}}$$

Where:

$$\text{Precision} = \frac{\textbf{\textit{Correctly selected keyframes}}}{\textbf{\textit{Total selected keyframes}}}$$

$$\text{Recall} = \frac{\textbf{\textit{Correcty selected keyframes}}}{\textbf{\textit{Total keyframes in Ground Truth}}}$$

Figure 3. Conceptual comparison of traditional vs proposed methods

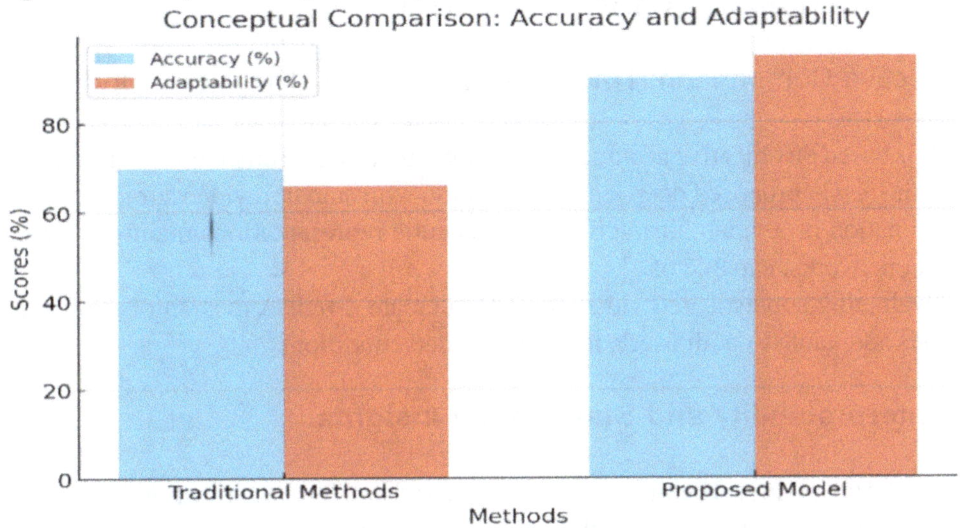

These metrics will be used by the experts in the Figure 3 to perform an unbiased evaluation of traditional summary methods and their proposed model. Precision is the number of relevant keyframes the models choose out of which, recall is the proportion of all the relevant keyframes that were correctly selected. The actual adaptability is realized as the balanced harmonic average of precision and recall for it to regulate its performance ratio. Its adaptability score turns out to perform better on various video contents compared to the model.

Figure 4. Performance comparison graph (ROUGE and BLEU)

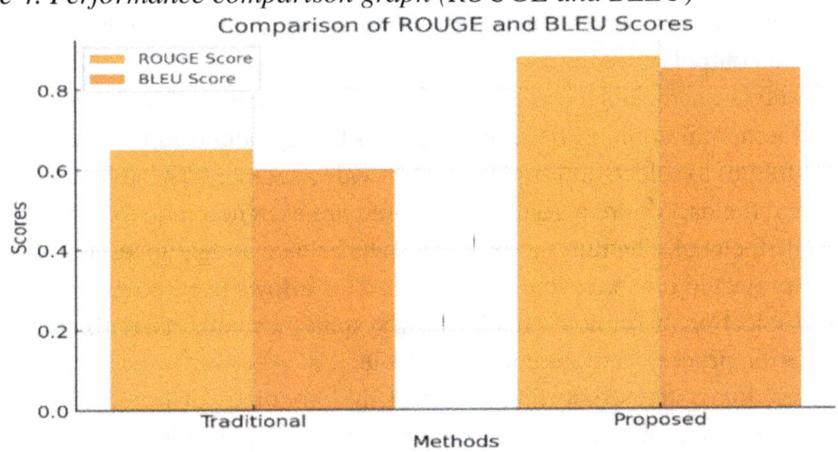

A performance evaluation using ROUGE and BLEU proves that Figure 4 is able to outperform traditional summarization methods.

Objective Comparison: Traditional Methods vs. Proposed Model

It is based on objective accuracy and adaptability measurement methods to compare the newly proposed deep learning solution with standard video summaries. Its combination of a video abstraction and semantic representations mainly leverage neural networks, capable of

evaluating sophisticated video content to create efficient meaning based summaries adaptable to both user's needs and video conditions.

D. Interpretability and Stakeholder Insights

As the technologies behind making system decision functions are transparent and easy to understand for humans, they are likely to be a crucial tool for deployment of AI based video summarization tools. When the system operates on sensitive data such as educational or security material or media content, it is very important for users to understand how the system comes to select frames and segments during the summary generation process transparently.

Attention Mechanisms and Transparency in Decision-Making

Attention mechanisms are applied during all phases of frame and segment assessment as defined by the proposed system. The model tracks what it assumes is relevant in the video content using these mechanisms and gives it weighted value to frames based on their discriminative context and visual aspects. The system thus focuses on which frames, and hence allows users to understand what the system decides on its output.

These attention mechanisms give us an understanding of what parts of the visual and temporal content the model decides to pay attention to when deciding which keyframes to select, and find important video segments. Match video frames which reveal the ball or are a goal being scored are assigned more attention by the system. The focus of a lecture model is on speaker face appearances and diagrams which are projected on some screen displays. This allows users to gain knowledge about how selection of frames is made using system mechanisms, realizing that the summarization process is more understandable.

However, for systems that directly affect the outcomes of users, trust of such systems is necessary and the interpretability makes this possible. With its decision explanation feature, users feel better about the system recommendations and having a higher chance of adoption by stakeholders.

Real-Time Audio-Visual Indicators and Live-Streaming Capabilities

This aspect of the proposed system allows the processing of audio-visual indicators while the system is being used in real time. The model can take advantage of live streaming to interactively summarize content that is fast, such as extended and alive conferences and lectures. In real time, the system can detect important audio indicators such as either variations in tone loudness, or variations in speech patterns, and can detect visual indicators such as either changes in movement of the face, or changes in movement of specific objects in the frame for highlighting important time points.

For a news summarization operation it can automatically monitor important announcements such as breaking news frames or important speeches. The model uses two kinds of cues such that the summary contains entire information beyond purely visual elements with audio inputs to achieve multi-dimensional understanding. We show that the system is useful when short and precise summarization becomes crucial as in sports feature production and live event scientific studies.

Stakeholder Benefits

In various business fields, the flexible and understandable system functionality offers the stakeholders with multiple advantages.

The system consequently helps Media and News organizations to economise their newsroom operations in allocating their informative resources by making it possible for them to create fast summary updates about current (recent) events that can meet editorial standard technical specifications. Besides that, the system allows stakeholders to check and edit summary output items for better quality control purposes and standards of the editors. The interpretability attributes are used by security personnel to inspect flagged content and then confirm important threats, thus increasing the ability of the surveillance response and threat recognition accuracy.

This system allows the content producers who work with entertainment and sports media to produce short highlights from their programs and allow users to choose preferred content for customized viewing.

As educational institutions are already using the system they are helping teachers to condense lectures with presentations and study materials that students can get teach essential content and make adjustments. The video summarization model shown by him matches industry needs by providing transparent decision processes, custom editing tools, and continued oversight over decision making steps.

To create a commercial success, we find that the proposed system will depend on stakeholder's insights along with the interpretability features. By adding human monitoring functions, real time visual and audible alerts, and real time streaming capabilities, the system achieves more reliable performance and the summary creation process is dynamic across multiple fields of use. Table 4 enumerates the predicted stakeholder advantages that they will accumulate from adopting the AML.

Table 4. Interpretability features and expected stakeholder benefits

Feature	Expected Stakeholder Insight	Application
Attention-weighted keyframe selection	Identifies the most critical parts of the video for summarization.	Enhances highlight detection for live-streaming.
Customizable training parameters	Tailors summaries to meet user-specific or genre-specific requirements.	Allows personalized content summarization.
Real-time summary generation	Provides immediate feedback and summaries during video processing.	Improves decision-making for video platform operators.

E. Anticipated Integration of External Factors

Additional outside components added in will make the proposed model development succeed better. By the merging of textual/metadata with speech analyses and scene classification, the system will generate better context based summaries. Purpose design summary functions must be part of the model in order to accommodate the requirements of the learning management platforms while also permitting the automation of the documentary edits.

V. CONCLUSION

To use these techniques of attention based ranking to discern those video segments that are important and still maintain context, these video summary creation techniques need temporal analysis at time and keyframe extraction algorithms. Implementation of the model is shown to work for abstract production because it supports multiple video file types, removes repeated content during segment extraction, and provides support for this type of production. The real time automated processing system offers dependable technical solutions to be employed in video content retrieval systems and in live stream analysis and automated video editing. By showing it has successful keyframe selection and computes at a high speed, the system achieves better results than existing summarization approaches. Our work contributes to deep learning video summarization methods yielding new creation tools based on personal creation and multi-modal processing systems.

VI. FUTURE SCOPE

Metadata text is integrated with audio signals, speech recognition systems and textual data to improve the precision of the video summarization model. For example, combining texts like subtitles or transcripts, audios like voice, background music and visuals like scene changes, object movements could assist create summaries that more accurately convey the video content and emotions. Pitch ad intensity are the major examples that models can use to detect speaker emotions that allows emotion – aware summarization. There is a need for the experts to develop a methodology to guide the model to automatically create summary actions according to personal preference needs as well as specific content attributes. Real time video summarisation features available in cloud based systems improve the system's scalability since one is able to perform streaming requirements and surveillance demands at the same time. Reinforcement learning algorithms are selected to optimize the selection of the keyframes, with which vast amounts of user-controlled feedback are obtained during true running operations, up to a maximum summary effectiveness. During development phase, video transformers should be used to discover distant interdependencies, which are spread across the video sequence. Since multiple security and digital marketing organizations need the automated video summary, this original research is valuable for the development of the automated summarization.

REFERENCES

Ahmed, A. H., Ibraheem, I. N., & Ibrahim, D. A. (2025). From frames to shots: A deep learning perspective on multimodal, graph-based, and transformer video summarization—A review. *Al-Salam Journal for Engineering and Technology*, *4*(2), 108–128. DOI: 10.55145/ajest.2025.04.02.009

Basu, A., Pramanik, R., & Sarkar, R. (2024). WANet: Weight and attention network for video summarization. *Discover Artificial Intelligence*, *4*(1), 5. DOI: 10.1007/s44163-024-00101-y

Feng, S.. (2022). Transformer-based video summarization with spatial-temporal representation. In *Proceedings of the 8th International Conference on Big Data and Information Analytics (BigDIA)* (pp. xx–xx). IEEE.

Hsu, T.-C., Liao, Y.-S., & Huang, C.-R. (2023). Video summarization with spatiotemporal vision transformer. *IEEE Transactions on Image Processing*, *32*, 3013–3026. DOI: 10.1109/TIP.2023.3275069

Ji, Z., Zhao, Y., Pang, Y., Li, X., & Han, J. (2020). Deep attentive video summarization with distribution consistency learning. *IEEE Transactions on Neural Networks and Learning Systems*, *32*(4), 1765–1775. DOI: 10.1109/TNNLS.2020.2991083

Kadam, B. D., & Deshpande, A. M. (2024). Multi-head attention with reinforcement learning for supervised video summarization. *Journal of Electronic Imaging*, *33*(5), 053010. DOI: 10.1117/1.JEI.33.5.053010

Kashid, S., Awasthi, L. K., Berwal, K., & Saini, P. (2024). STVS: Spatio-temporal feature fusion for video summarization. *IEEE MultiMedia*, *31*(3), 88–97. DOI: 10.1109/MMUL.2024.3428933

Lin, F., Yuan, J., Chen, Z., & Abiri, M. (2024). Enhancing multimedia management: Cloud-based movie type recognition with hybrid deep learning architecture. *Journal of Cloud Computing (Heidelberg, Germany)*, *13*(1), 104. DOI: 10.1186/s13677-024-00668-y

Lin, J., Hua, H., Chen, M., Li, Y., Hsiao, J., Ho, C., & Luo, J. (2023). Videoxum: Cross-modal visual and textural summarization of videos. *IEEE Transactions on Multimedia*, *26*, 5548–5560. DOI: 10.1109/TMM.2023.3335875

Mahasseni, B., Lam, M., & Todorovic, S. (2017). Unsupervised video summarization with adversarial lstm networks. In *Proceedings of the IEEE conference on Computer Vision and Pattern Recognition* (pp. 202-211). DOI: 10.1109/CVPR.2017.318

Saini, P., Kumar, K., Kashid, S., Saini, A., & Negi, A. (2023). Video summarization using deep learning techniques: A detailed analysis and investigation. *Artificial Intelligence Review*, *56*(11), 12347–12385. DOI: 10.1007/s10462-023-10444-0

Sreeja, M. U., & Kovoor, B. C. (2023). A multi-stage deep adversarial network for video summarization with knowledge distillation. *Journal of Ambient Intelligence and Humanized Computing*, *14*(8), 9823–9838. DOI: 10.1007/s12652-021-03641-8

Tian, X., Jin, Y., Zhang, Z., Liu, P., & Tang, X. (2025). Video summarization with temporal-channel visual transformer. *Pattern Recognition*, *165*, 111631. DOI: 10.1016/j.patcog.2025.111631

Yu, Q., Yu, H., Sun, Y., Ding, D., & Jian, M. (2024). Unsupervised video summarization based on the diffusion model of feature fusion. *IEEE Transactions on Computational Social Systems*, *11*(5), 6010–6021. DOI: 10.1109/TCSS.2024.3384627

Zhang, Y., Liu, Y., Kang, W., & Zheng, Y. (2023). Mar-net: Motion-assisted reconstruction network for unsupervised video summarization. *IEEE Signal Processing Letters*, *30*, 1282–1286. DOI: 10.1109/LSP.2023.3313091

Zhao, B., Gong, M., & Li, X. (2022). Hierarchical multimodal transformer to summarize videos. *Neurocomputing*, *468*, 360–369. DOI: 10.1016/j.neucom.2021.10.039

Chapter 10
The Next Level Emerging Trends in Gamification

Munir Ahmad
https://orcid.org/0000-0003-4836-6151
Survey of Pakistan, Pakistan

Nodira Shodiyeva
Termez University of Economics and Service, Uzbekistan

Saboxat Kabulova
Mamun University, Uzbekistan

Zamira Atamuratova
Urgench State University, Uzbekistan

Atabayeva Nargis Batirovna
National Pedagogical University of Uzbekistan, Uzbekistan

ABSTRACT

This chapter examines the evolving landscape of gamification, shaped by the convergence of artificial intelligence, immersive environments, blockchain, and social technologies. Once reliant on simple point-and-reward mechanisms, gamification has matured into a dynamic, intelligent, and decentralized ecosystem. AI and machine learning now drive hyper-personalized experiences; augmented and virtual reality enable embodied engagement; and blockchain technologies introduce verifiable rewards, digital ownership, and decentralized governance. These innovations expand gamification's purpose, from individual motivation to community building, equity, and sustainable behavior change. Emerging frontiers such as emotional AI and multimodal interfaces promise even deeper responsiveness by integrating gesture,

DOI: 10.4018/979-8-3373-3690-9.ch010

voice, and biometric data. As gamification systems increasingly permeate education, healthcare, the workplace, and civic life, ethical design becomes imperative, prioritizing inclusion, autonomy, and well-being.

INTRODUCTION

Gamification [the use of game design techniques in non-games] has changed a lot since first appearing in the early 2000s (Ligorio et al., 2025; Liu, 2024; Triantafyllou et al., 2025; Zeybek & Saygı, 2024). In the early days, it basically depended on the primitive reward system of points, badges, and leaderboards to generate user motivation and engagement. These initial applications tended to be transactional and extrinsically motivating, wherein a record of improvement was recorded, but most often failed to generate sustained interest or subsequent engagement. These simple mechanics could not sustain customer expectations that had become more demanding and digital ecosystems that are more complex as users became more sophisticated. Gamification started to evolve in providing more meaningful, flexible, and user-oriented experiences-i.e., the proliferation of psychological knowledge with powerful technologies to generate more effective and immersive systems of engagement. (Kok et al., 2024; Rana & Chicone, 2025; Wang et al., 2024).

Gamification is in its next phase today, and perhaps this can be described as Gamification 2.0 due to the decline of controlling forces that shape the world within the technological and social spectrum (da Silva Junior et al., 2025). Personalized and adaptive gamification systems can become a reality with the help of Artificial Intelligence (AI) and Machine Learning (ML), altering themselves according to user behavior, desires, and achievement. The differences between real and digital worlds are being blurred out by Augmented Reality (AR) and Virtual Reality (VR), which enable users to engage in an immersive, embodied experience with gamified content. Blockchain-based digital assets, such as smart contracts, help improve reward systems by enhancing trust, transparency, and decentralization. It should also be noted that social media, online communities, and multiplayer design principles are transforming gamification through socio and collaborative digital environments. This transformation will help to align with social media and online communities with shared objectives on teamwork (Haoming & Wei, 2024; Lampropoulos et al., 2022; Ribeiro et al., 2024).

The focus of this chapter is to explore the new trends in gamification by providing a detailed view of state-of-the-art technologies and user expectations in the context of gamified systems design and implementations. The second section brings to the fore the application of AI and ML in the development of smart and personalized experiences. Section 3 discusses the way AR and VR develop immersive experiences to increase user interaction in various fields. Section 4 is devoted to the discussion of the blockchain integration in the creation of transparent and secure gamified ecosystems. The main trend in the use of social and collaborative gamification pointed out in Section 5 is that social and collaborative gamification promotes community-based interaction. Lastly, the findings are summarized and future directions are provided in Section 6, which proposes a gamification ecosystem that is more ethical, inclusive, with innovative.

MACHINE LEARNING AND AI IN GAMIFICATION

Gamification is taking a huge leap towards its boundaries and maturity with the use of AI and ML systems that give systems the power to think, learn, adjust, and evolve. Traditional gamification was based on static systems, such as fixed-point systems, fixed-level systems, or fixed-reward systems, whereas AI Gamification appears dynamic and can change with user interaction. These changes enable higher responsiveness to the individual behavior, preferences, and progress and take gamified experiences back to a one-size-fits-all model to a highly personalized and adaptive one. With AI-driven gamification systems, it is possible to analyze user data in real-time, e.g., the speed at which users can complete their tasks, where they struggle, and how frequently they use the system, allowing for adjustments to be made to the system. These may involve swapping the force of challenges, choosing the best encouraging form of feedback, or swapping the schedule and quality of rewards to uphold user interest (Bachiri et al., 2023; Bezzina & Dingli, 2023; Castellano et al., 2024; Suresh Babu & Dhakshina Moorthy, 2024).

Machine Learning Algorithms

The focus of this innovation is the idea of adaptive feedback loops that enable the system to modify itself every moment according to the user's actions (Gheibi et al., 2021). These loops keep a track of what is happening, evaluate the results, and produce an individual response, just as a knowledgeable instructor or coach would in a physical classroom. As an example, when one user is learning faster than another, the system may have more challenging tasks in order to keep things interesting and avoid a sense of boredom; when learning has become difficult, the system could provide easier tasks or encourage by nice feedback the user. Such an equilibrium of challenge and difficulty level assists users in attaining the state of cognitive flow, when the engagement is at its highest and when learning or performance is optimized. This is how AI and ML not only increase the level of gamification, but also add emotional and psychological sensitivity, making it smarter, but also pleasant and beneficial.

Intelligent gamification systems are based on machine learning algorithms, especially those grounded in reinforcement learning and supervised learning (Bennani et al., 2022; Ramadhan et al., 2024). Such algorithms can study and learn about large-scale data sets based on interaction with the user, things like how long a user takes on a certain task, how accurate or successful they are at it, the decisions they make when presented with some choice problem, and when combined with wearable or other sensor-based data, even their moods or other physical reactions. Labeled groups are used to train supervised learning models in order to detect patterns, e.g., when to expect users to deactivate or on what kinds of issues users will be successful. Reinforcement learning is instead a method that allows systems to learn to get better over time by being shown feedback regarding the environment; for example, being a game-playing AI learning which actions yield rewards.

Based on these, it would allow gamified platforms to build robust and dynamic user profiles, including preferences, learning styles, motivational drivers, and behavior patterns. With these profiles, the system will be able to make educated guesses as to what kinds of content, what kinds of tasks, or what kinds of reward mechanisms will be most likely to attract the attention of a specific user at a specific time. To take one example, different users might be either more motivated by progression through the story, or responding to a visual reward more readily, or be more motivated by the promise of social recognition, or competition. Machine learning algorithms of different types support the different ends of personalization, prediction, and adaptation of gamified systems. Table 1 below presents some more important algorithms and directions of their application.

Table 1. Machine learning algorithms and their roles in gamification

Algorithm Type	Function in Gamification	Example Use Case
Supervised Learning	Pattern recognition, performance prediction	Predict dropout points in a learning platform
Reinforcement Learning	Behavior shaping via reward-based optimization	Optimize in-game decision strategies
Collaborative Filtering	Recommendation based on similar users' behavior	Suggest the next learning module in an ed-tech app
Natural Language Processing	Interaction with users via chatbots or feedback analysis	Adaptive dialogue in learning games

Recommendation Engines

This intelligence is frequently implemented with recommendation engines, often leveraged by other applications such as Netflix or Amazon, and shows the next best thing to do or receive based on past action and contextual information. It could translate into a recommendation of the next course of study that would fill in a knowledge gap that a learner has, without losing interest in a gamified learning environment. Within a fitness or mental health application, it may prompt a personalized challenge that correlates to the energy level or mood of a user at a particular point in time. Through constant refinement of such ideas, machine learning transforms the concept of gamification into a most receptive, user-specific experience which adapts to the individual as he or she goes along, and as such maximizes the level of engagement and results alike (Awan et al., 2021; Geng et al., 2022). Figure 1 shows the recommendation engine in gamified systems.

Figure 1. Recommendation engine in gamified systems

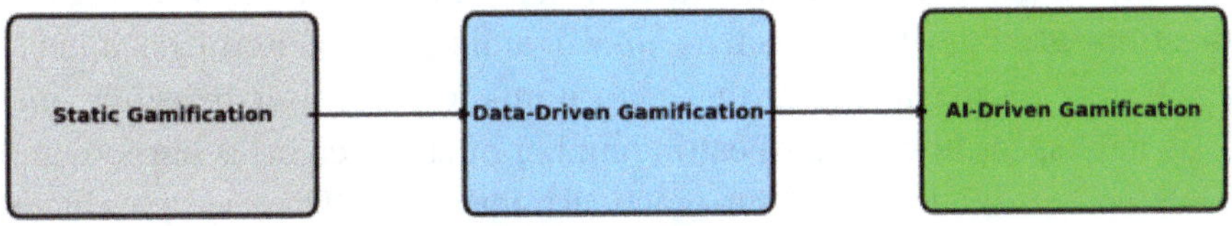

Machine Learning in Education

Machine learning as part of gamification has led to the use of intelligent tutoring systems (ITS) in the education sector that will customize the learning experience to the individual requirements of students. Such systems constantly track the pace of learning of a student, his performance record, how he makes mistakes, and how much he is involved to adjust the delivery and the content of the information. In contrast to conventionally used learning tools, which arrange the same content for every user, ITS learners improvise the learning path depending on the real-time analysis of the data, deciding what to teach, the form in which to present it, and when to revise the earlier material (Bilotti et al., 2023; Hilbert et al., 2021; Shah et al., 2021).

One of the most famous cases is that of Duolingo, the language learning application that applies the idea of machine learning to the domain of teaching a language by testing the knowledge and competency of a learner at different levels through many kinds of linguistic expertise, including vocabulary, grammar, and pronunciation. (Duolingo, 2025; Kazu & Kuvvetli, 2025). It bases this analysis on intelligently modifying the degree and kind of exercises so that more of the user's time is spent on strengthening poor abilities, yet still developing the strengths. It also repetitively goes over the same material shortly before a learner is apt to forget the material, taking advantage of the science of spaced repetition and predictive forgetting curves.

These systems keep learners in the sweet spot between tasks too hard and too easy, with the ideal level of challenge. Experience points, streaks, badges, and the like are provided because they will make a difference in the level of motivation; however, all the information is always informed by data-driven insights. For example, gamification in conjunction with adaptive learning can improve the efficiency of learning on one hand and provide a prominent and enjoyable education process on the other hand.

Machine Learning in Health

Similarly, gamification informed by AI is transforming the way people learn to control and enhance their health and well-being in the field of health and fitness. Applications used in fitness, such as Nike Training Club, Fitbit Coach, and Apple Fitness+, rely on machine learning algorithms to track user behavior, including exercise habits, cardiovascular health, number of steps, calories burned, and sleep schedule, and convert their data into practical information. These systems incorporate AI to configure smart and personal goals, which can change as a user advances, so that fitness programs correspond to the prevailing capacity, routine, and health conditions (Alanazi, 2022; Aldahiri et al., 2021; An et al., 2023; Sabry et al., 2022).

These applications are able to indicate the performance of a user compared to the general population as they can compare individual performance to larger population metrics. With this kind of comparison, the app might advise variations in forms of intensity, changing the type of workout exercise to prevent the plateau, and timing periods of rest to prevent overtraining. This produces a responsive progression system, which changes in real time: it no longer leaves a user exhausted or burned out, or underperforming, but rather at the correct level: neither too easy nor too difficult.

In more detail, these platforms are usually designed so as to be supported by behavioral nudging practices. As an example, we can give the user some celebratory animations upon reaching a milestone, some personalized support upon completing a challenging session, reminders to take it easy when activity level decreases, etc. Such nudging is based on machine learning on historic user data, which in turn serves to predict potential disengagements or when a user needs additional motivation. At its core, AI-powered gamification in health and fitness uses personalization and predictive analytics with the help of motivational psychology to provide a powerful and engaging wellness experience that can individually fit each user. Although the techniques used in AI behind them are similar, the AI techniques used in education and health areas are different in nature, metrics, and goals as compared in Table 2.

Table 2. Comparison of AI-driven gamification in education and health

Aspect	Education (e.g., Duolingo)	Health & Fitness (e.g., Fitbit Coach)
Data Inputs	Quiz scores, error patterns, and engagement time	Steps, heart rate, workout history, sleep cycles
Goals	Knowledge retention, skill progression	Physical improvement, habit formation
Personalization Logic	Learning path adaptation, topic review timing	Exercise intensity, recovery planning
Motivation Strategies	XP, badges, streaks, level-ups	Goal tracking, nudges, milestone celebrations
Feedback Frequency	Per task or session	Real-time and daily

IMMERSIVE GAMIFICATION WITH AR AND VR

AR and VR are transforming the landscape of gamification by enabling users to interact with digital environments in ways that are immersive, spatially aware, and physically engaging. Figure 2 shows the evolution of gamification from the perspective of immersive technologies. AR technology overlays images, sounds or other interactive data elements onto the real-world landscape with the help of smartphones, tablets and AR glasses. VR technology creates an illusion by projecting the users into entirely simulated 3D environments with the help of specialized devices such as headsets and motion sensors. Hence, both AR and VR technologies serve different purposes and offer distinct user experiences (Damaševičius & Sidekersniene, 2023a; Haoming & Wei, 2024). Table 3 below outlines the key differences and use cases of AR and VR in the context of immersive gamification.

Figure 2. Evolution of gamification systems

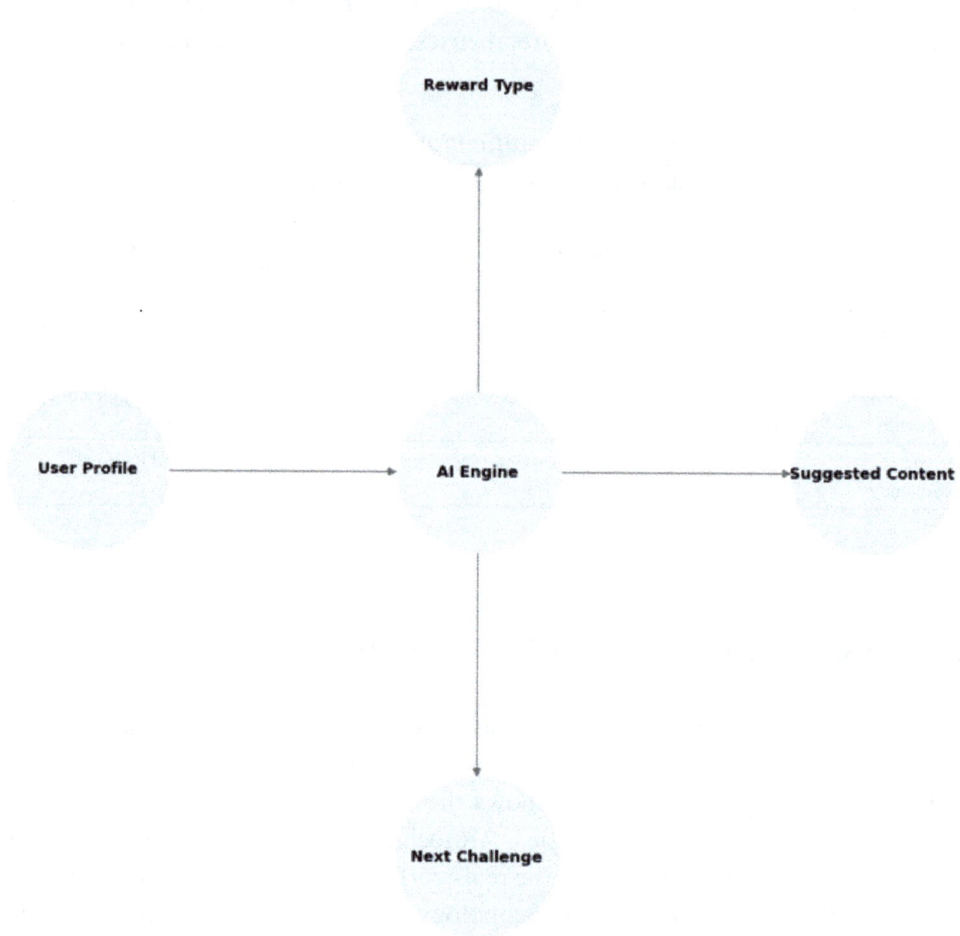

Table 3. Comparison between AR and VR in gamification context

Feature	Augmented Reality	Virtual Reality
Environment	Enhances the real world	Replaces the real world with the virtual
Hardware	Smartphones, tablets, and smart glasses	Head-mounted displays (e.g., Oculus, HTC Vive)
Movement	Limited to real-world space	Full virtual navigation and interaction
Interaction Type	Touch, gaze, hand gestures	Motion tracking, spatial input

continued on following page

Table 3. Continued

Feature	Augmented Reality	Virtual Reality
Common Use Cases	Try-ons, product previews, anatomy overlays	Virtual field trips, rehab games, scenario training
Engagement Style	Contextual, layered information	Full immersion, emotional storytelling

The main focal point of the AR and VR technologies is to make the user experience more natural using the different sensors, ranging from sight, sound, and touch. This type of interaction provides a deep sense of presence in the context of a gamified scenario to amplify emotional involvement and cognitive focus. These technologies also allow users to move around, manipulate virtual objects and receive real-time feedback based on their actions (Choube & Mhamane, 2025; Srdanović et al., 2025; Vorrink et al., 2024). In the context of gamification, AR and VR enable a wide range of embodied learning and participation models to provide users with a multisensory experience. For example, instead of simply clicking through quiz questions or leveling up by collecting points, users might walk through a reconstructed historical site in VR or use AR to interact with a 3D model of a human heart floating in their living room. This interactive experience provides users with a sense of the liveliness of the object, while still accessing these objects virtually. Table 4 summarizes key benefits tied to immersive design features.

Table 4. Behavioral and cognitive benefits of immersive gamification

Design Feature	Cognitive Benefit	Behavioral Outcome
Spatial interaction	Improved spatial reasoning	Greater task engagement
Real-time feedback	Faster learning cycles	Increased motivation
Embodiment & presence	Deep emotional involvement	Higher retention and adherence
Contextual exploration	Enhanced critical thinking	Curiosity-driven exploration

Immersive Gamification in Education

AR and VR have also been transforming the landscape of education - immersion and interaction may place the students in a stimulating learning environment. In contrast to the traditional digital devices, which provide the information on a plane screen, AR and VR provide a 3D spatial experience where learners can move around, manipulate, and interact with the educational content directly. AR takes place using mobile devices or smart glasses displaying a digital information on top of the real world- an example being a spinning model of the solar system on the desk of a classroom and VR engulfs the learners in virtual environments where they can navigate purely synthetic surroundings, like the inside of a cell or a battle place in an ancient war (Damaševičius & Sidekersniene, 2023b; Lampropoulos et al., 2022).

Used with gamification, however, the technologies have the potential to provide a potent value in the educational sector by transforming lessons into adventure lessons or game missions. A scenario in science teaching (where virtual labs could be used) would be an example where students are allowed to carry out experiments in their virtual chemistry laboratories, where they can combine compounds, including learning of safety measures, without having to worry about the dangers or the limitations of resources in a physical lab. History classes are transformed with the help of 3D reenactments to enable the learner to walk through any type of historical period or ancient society that including the ability to interact with the historical characters and solve a range of quests based on real historical events. AR apps can be used by biology and medicine students to study the anatomy of the human body in three dimensions, turn organs and systems, zoom into systems, and see how things inside the body work in first-person.

Such immersive environments turn learning, which is mainly a passive process, into an active, gamified one. Activities can be constructed in the form of a level, goal, or puzzle, where students can earn or unlock a reward by reading (completing) the simulation requirement or alignment with the objectives of a problem area, demonstrating knowledge. This helps boost interest, but other than that, it helps develop the conceptual grasp and memorize the subject matter, especially in complicated or abstract topics, which do not lend themselves to being visualized as easily by traditional teaching methods. The inclusion of AR and VR in educational gamification makes the whole process more interesting, worthwhile, and more closely related to the experience of digital-native learners than those applied in learning.

Immersive Gamification in Healthcare

The use of immersive gamification in the healthcare sector has opened new doors for patient rehabilitation and clinical training processes. The power of immersive technologies to interact in real time with health care objects in a gamified style has increased the effectiveness of these technologies more profoundly. VR headset with motion tracking sensors enables the patient to control virtual objects and spaces with body movements, transforming otherwise tedious or labor-intensive rehabilitation activities into engaging exercises that arouse both physical and cognitive activity (Khan et al., 2024; Queirós et al., 2023; Sridhar et al., 2024; Tao et al., 2021; Yang, 2023).

To give an illustration, in physical rehabilitation, VR-based gamified platforms may assist stroke sufferers in regaining motor abilities by offering activities that demand accuracy, coordination, and balance, like catching the collapsing objects, putting together virtual pieces, or walking an avatar through mazes. The activities are adaptable to the patient's progress and capabilities, and therefore, the plan of therapy is individual, and over time, it will be modified. The feedback given by the visuals and audio components increases motivation, whereas the virtual reality-like experience of the tasks reduces the possibilities of distraction and promotes longer and more uniform engagement, which is also essential to successful recovery. Furthermore, the information obtained in the sessions allows therapists to supervise and track performance, assess changes, and modify exercises, respectively.

In mental health care, VR gamification has lately been applied in exposure therapy, a technique in which patients approach their fears or phobias in a controlled and safe digital setting. As an example, a patient with social anxiety disorder may learn to speak in public, addressing a virtual audience, and patients with PTSD may, over time, re-experience tense situations using interactive and controlled simulation. They are usually placed in a form of levels or quests, and the interaction is driven with a sense of control and progress being given to users. With the gamified framework, the gamification of therapy lessens the emotional load of the treatment process and strengthens coping mechanisms and resiliency via experience-based learning.

Combining the immersive capabilities of VR with the motivation mechanics of game design would allow healthcare providers to give patients treatments that are more effective, more pleasant, and more empowering. The implementation of this groundbreaking solution is particularly promising when producing an improved patient adherence rate, faster recovery, and general optimization of the therapeutic process in the physical and mental areas.

Gamification in the Retail

Cases of AR and VR are being used in the retailing industry to provide a gamified experience to the consumer to satisfy all three functions of entertainment, interactivity, and purchasing in one smooth customer path. These technologies give brands a chance to surpass the passive experience of a catalog or conventional online storefront to develop an environment in which users can roam around the products, touch or absorb virtual objects, and be engaged in interesting goal-driven actions. Available through smartphones or smart glasses, AR apps lay information, animations, challenges, and more about products across the real world, and VR platforms allow people to visit a completely virtualized store or branded space through headsets (Disse & Olsson, 2023; Lopes et al., 2023; Sheetal et al., 2023).

Retailers are relying on these functionalities to create gamified shopping expeditions, loyalty-related missions, and scavenger hunts with the help of AR. As an example, a fashion company could make a VR-boutique where the users explore various rooms to find the secret deals and open special virtual items. In the same manner, an AR application could encourage customers to look up virtual coins in physical retail units or accomplish product-based assignments and acquire discounts and awards. Such mechanisms create a sense of play and exploration, so shopping becomes not quite a shopping experience, as one might expect, but rather an adventure.

The try-before-you-buy AR simulation is one of the strongest examples of this technology in the retail industry since it allows people to imagine in a virtual environment how certain products, such as clothes, accessories, or home decor, will appear or work in real life. The retailers of furniture, like IKEA, provide people with an opportunity to see how a particular sofa may suit in their very own living room with the help of AR, and newly-released cosmetic products enable users to apply a certain model of makeup to their faces, also with the help of AR filters and face recognition. It not only boosts confidence in the purchasing experience but also increases overall satisfaction with such engagements.

AR and VR gamification make retailing more personalized and interactive, which in turn increases customer engagement, shopping duration and brand loyalty. Such a combination of gamification and immersive technologies promotes retail not as a stagnated service but as a living, emotionally interactive experience, restoring the concept of how consumers find, consider, and build associations with the products in the digital era. They provide retailers with useful behavioral data as well, which would allow them to customize promotions and improve the design of their stores. Table 5 presents some AR/VR gamification applications across sectors.

Table 5. AR/VR gamification applications across sectors

Sector	AR/VR Application	Gamified Outcome
Education	Virtual labs, 3D anatomy	Deeper learning, retention
Healthcare	VR rehab, exposure therapy	Higher adherence, personalization
Retail	Try-ons, virtual shopping	Engagement, loyalty, fewer returns

BLOCKCHAIN AND DECENTRALIZED GAMIFICATION

Blockchain technology improves the gamification experience by providing a decentralized, transparent and secure architecture. In contrast to the traditional databases, which are centralized and managed by one person/organization, blockchain is a digital ledger that is distributed across a network of computers (nodes) whereby each transaction is stored in a block and meshed with earlier ones to create an unchangeable chain. Data on the blockchain is non-recursive and hence once data is placed there, it cannot be edited or destroyed, which offers a tamper-free system that can be audited. This immutability makes gamified interactions more solid: the users know that points, rewards, achievements, and transactions are safe and unchangeable (Lopez-Barreiro et al., 2024; Padeli et al., 2024; Wijaya et al., 2024).

The other main aspect of the blockchain is the aspect of transparency. Transaction histories are also visible to all members of the blockchain network, thereby establishing trust among the users since an unnecessary sense of veil often exists with centralized networks. Be it knowing who received which reward, when, and even authenticating the token of digital assets, transparency increases the fair play and accountability when gamifying the environment. In addition to this, the blockchain utilizes cryptographic changes of verification; hence, no authorized centralized body is required to confirm whatever is done; therefore, decentralized authentication holds.

More importantly, blockchain also represents the introduction of smart contracts, a set of self-executing codes with code that automatically enact the predetermined set of actions upon fulfillment of conditions. Smart contracts used in gamification can be used to issue rewards, complete challenges, or enforce game rules automatically with no human or administrative overhead. As an example, a smart contract can unlock a reward token to a gamer who accomplishes a task or implement cool-down times between the game stages. Such automation means that the logic of a gamified system is reliable, fair, and consistent. Table 6 briefly identifies how the features involved with the implementation of blockchain ensure decentralized gamification design.

Table 6. Core features of blockchain for gamification

Blockchain Feature	Function in Gamification	Example
Immutability	Ensures the permanence and integrity of rewards and achievements	Tamper-proof NFT badges for skill completion
Transparency	Builds trust via auditable user actions and reward issuance	Public logs of community contributions
Smart Contracts	Automates rule enforcement and reward delivery	Token auto-release after challenge completion
Decentralization	Removes central authority, empowering users as system stakeholders	Community voting on platform features via DAOs

These fundamental characteristics, namely, immutability, transparency, and automation with the use of smart contracts, unitedly form a trustless but trustworthy realm of gamified relations. They enable the user to be a trusted participant, certain that results cannot be faked and that the system works based on deterministic rules that can be audited. In that sense, blockchain offers the technical basis of a new era of gamification models focusing on user autonomy, ownership, and integrity to open the way to more robust, fair, and participatory digital environments.

Non-Fungible Tokens (NFTs)

Often in legacy gamification, there would be a centralized, non-fungible, non-portable reward which could be represented as points, badges, or virtual trophies, which are usually limited in application, and only have value in the environment in which they are used. The disadvantage in this closed-loop model is that it does not allow users to possess or capitalize on their success in the wider scope beyond the application. The paradigm of having verifiable and decentralized digital assets, which can be owned, managed, and exchanged by their users, is radically altered by blockchain technology. Blockchain enables individuals to put their in-game or in-application achievements in control and transform them into resources, which may be exchanged and potentially sold using mechanisms such as NFTs and cryptographic tokens (Davidová et al., 2022; Queiroz et al., 2024; Razi et al., 2024).

Unique digital items on the blockchain in the form of NFTs can symbolize any manner of achievements in a gamified context, including certificates of mastered skills, collectible tokens reflecting a set milestone, and others. As an example, when a user completes a learning exercise or fitness challenge, they could be awarded an NFT instead of a generic badge that they can forget or lose track of, but can instead be provided with a blockchain-verifiable badge permanently associated with that persona that can be used as a lasting mark of their participation. This NFT would then be able to be displayed in digital portfolios, traded with others, and even redeemed into tangible rewards like discounts, memberships, or special access to content. The fact that NFTs are exclusive and rare also brings with them a feeling of prestige and collectability, which would boost their emotional and symbolic significance.

Besides the NFTs, token economies of gamified systems feature the introduction of fungible tokens, i.e., reward points that have their utility and value in the real world, such as cryptocurrency-based ones. The tokens are earned by either accomplishing the tasks, providing the content, or interacting with the community, and are used to access premium features, avatar up-leveling, special levels, or involvement in the community governance. SEE also Some sites permit users to exchange in decentralized exchanges, transforming their gamified activities into real financial earnings. This combination of economic reward and user undermining changes the dynamics between motivation, shifting the motivational aspect to be intrinsic, as users are able to be stakeholders instead of the passive pool.

Blockchain also transforms the consumer experience involved in the use of the rewards because ownership, portability, and economic value are incorporated into gamified rewards. This makes the user experience more than participation since it gives them significance and investment in the reward. Besides this, it also promotes cross-platform development to achieve a sustainable digital identity and assets portfolio.

Gamified Governance

In addition to remaking reward systems, blockchain is making it possible to create new models of participatory decision-making, gamified governance, where users cease being passive consumers and become active contributors with actual control over a platform and how it develops. The center of this change lies in Decentralized Autonomous Organizations (DAOs), blockchain governance organizations that run via smart contracts and decentralized governance by issuing tokens to act on them. In a DAO, a central authority that makes decisions is replaced by users proposing and voting to make the changes to platform rules, content policies, feature development, or how community funds are spent. The blockchain plays this role as votes are carried out publicly and irreversibly, making them free and impartial, traceable, and resistant to interference (Bernovskis et al., 2023; Ly & Shojaei, 2025).

In gamified systems, DAOs present one potential for incorporating governance into the user experience. Users have the chance to obtain governance tokens by participating in the life of the platform: completing tasks, developing or sharing educational material, or moderating the community process, etc. These tokens not only act as a reward system, but as a tool in the democratic decision-making process in that platform, where users of the tokens have the power to propose and vote on decisions of the platform. It forms a positive feedback mechanism wherein users will have an incentive to produce quality contributions, and in turn, they obtain a stake in the future of the system.

An example of this could be on a blockchain-based learning platform, where the best learners or the most prolific creators can be afforded the right to vote on which new courses are created, the basis and ideals of any certification, and how any token could be issued, etc. Within decentralized games, consumers may cast ballots to establish narrative plots, new game processes, or changes to the in-game market. Such a model enables user interests to be consistent with the sustainability of the platform because they become a part-owner of the ecosystem, but not end-users.

Not only does gamified governance based on the blockchain empower the users, but it also leads to the feeling of ownership, responsibility, and engagement of the community. When the users understand that their voice counts, they will tend to be active, loyal, and interested. This shifts gamified platforms from an upwards, provider-controlled type of system into a side-to-side, co-evolving system where innovation is spawned by the collective intelligence and creativity of the general community.

Interoperability and Portability

Not only can decentralized gamification improve the level of transparency and user ownership, but it also provides another innovation that is sorely lacking in classic systems: the ability to take achievements across platforms and port them seamlessly. In most gamified settings, user-reward, say badges, point level, etc., is generally on only one application, centralized within the platform owner, which can be lost when the user changes service or when the platform goes offline. Blockchain and NFTs change this narrative by allowing users to hold their digital resources, including NFTs or cryptographic tokens, using personal blockchain wallets decoupled from any one platform.

They could be accessed and identified by any other network or system because they are stored on a decentralized and public ledger, and could be accessed by another application or ecosystem that uses the same blockchain technology (e.g., Ethereum, Polygon, Solana). As an example, an NFT of a skill certification achieved in one single learning platform might be shown on a digital portfolio of a user in another learning network, or a token reward inscribed as a game-based health-engaged winning might be exchanged for discounts in a health app or retail store online. This nature of cross-platform transportability means that the accomplishments of the users are persistent, viewable, and applicable in various digital landscapes, which strongly raises their utility over a long period.

Interoperability of decentralized gamification provides a user with control of their digital experience. It helps to realize the ecosystem of a user-centric Web3 world, where people can control their own experiences by carrying their credentials, assets, and identities with them between services. Table 7 compares the traditional models of gamification and gamification in the blockchain format.

Table 7. Traditional vs. blockchain-based gamification

Aspect	Traditional Gamification	Blockchain Gamification
Reward Ownership	Controlled by the platform	User-owned (stored in personal wallets)
Portability	Locked within a single app	Cross-platform and interoperable
Trust Model	Based on the central authority	Based on cryptographic verification
Governance	Top-down decision-making	Community-driven via DAOs
Asset Value	Symbolic, non-transferable	Economically valuable and tradable

COMMUNITY-DRIVEN GAMIFICATION

Transformation from user-centric models to community-driven ecosystems has revolutionized the gamification trends by shifting the focus beyond solo achievements to embrace social connection, collective purposes and collaborative dynamics. This shift has been triggered by the application of social networking technologies, real-time communication platforms, and scalable community management tools. The revolution of gamification trends provides the infrastructure for a sustainable and cooperative user experience. Table 8 provides an overview of the transformation trends.

Table 8. Evolution from individual to community-driven gamification

Gamification Model	Primary Focus	User Interaction	Motivational Driver
Individual-Centric	Personal Progress	Solo Tasks, Leaderboards	Achievement, Competition
Social Recognition-Based	Peer Feedback	Endorsements, Upvotes, Badges	Reputation, Validation
Community-Driven	Shared Goals, Teamwork	Team Quests, Crowdsourced Tasks	Belonging, Collaboration

Table 9 outlines some of the most impactful collaborative gamification mechanics, describing their function and typical applications.

Table 9. Key collaborative mechanics in community gamification

Mechanic	Description	Example Platforms/ Contexts
Team Quests	Users work in groups to achieve shared goals	Classcraft, Discord communities
Peer Recognition Badges	Users nominate/vote for one another's contributions	Stack Overflow, Reddit Awards
Crowdsourced Challenges	Users define and complete community-generated tasks	GitHub, Coursera Forums
Role-Based Teaming	Users take on specific roles with unique responsibilities	Educational RPGs, Corporate LMSs
Community Events	Group milestones or themed challenges to foster collective participation	Discord Servers, Reddit Competitions

Digital technologies help in the transformation of community-based gamification to provide immediate interaction, quick responses and scalable collaboration. To this effect, the in-app messaging applications, social media APIs and gamification-integrated modules can stimulate the development of teams to support real-time interactions and collaborations. These digital technologies include moderation algorithms, reputation systems, as well as bot-aided roles and can help to develop dynamic as well as self-controlled communities. These communities revolutionized the gamified experiences through generating the content, rewarding their peers and taking up leadership roles.

With the use of these new technologies, gamification is turning into a social architecture that is able to support learning, innovation, and cooperation. Community-centered systems are powerful ways to engage people who want to adapt in groups with shared challenges and by the beneficial influence of those who surround us. Figure 3 shows the funnel of community participation in gamification.

Figure 3. Funnel of community participation in gamification

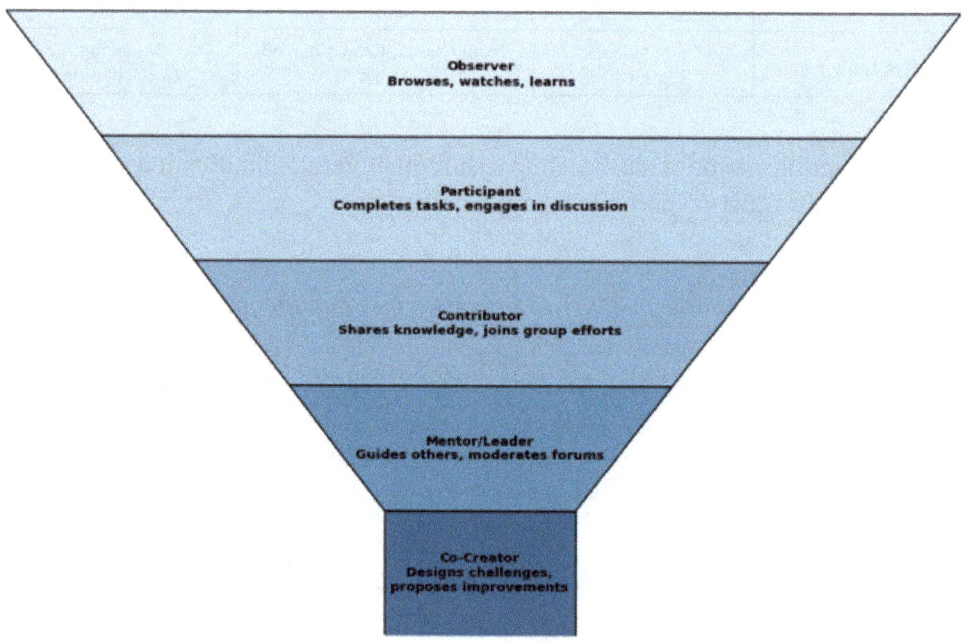

Shared Goals and Social Interaction

The center of this change in the direction of community-based gamification is the set of mechanics that evoke team goals, collaboration, and serious social interaction. The idea of team quests, the missions in which users should cooperate to fulfill a common goal, can be seen as among the most powerful ones. Team quests, unlike conventional challenges that require individual performance and effort, require their own players to work as a team, achieve coordination, and have complementary skills and abilities, and frequently involve communication, planning, and reliance among the users. This system not only fosters collaboration and solving of problems but also adds a stronger feeling of belonging, comradeship, and group responsibility, all of which act as strong agents of continued involvement and repetition of involvement.

People in such settings find a sense of accomplishment together, and the emotional reward gained in the completion of an objective is enhanced by mutual group celebration and celebration. Gamification in a team format is ideally applicable in learning and working environments, where cooperative and collaborative learning is crucial, and peer education boosts knowledge exchange and trust towards others.

At the same time, platforms are further and more closely incorporating social badges and peer award systems by which a user can recognize and award peers. In contrast to traditional achievement systems (where badging occurs automatically or under the direction of administrators), the accolades generated within the community are more valued since they are of immediate appreciation by others. Depending on the nomination or votes of other participants, a user could get a badge that has a label of the person being the most helpful, creative problem solver, or team motivator. The peer-initiated confirmation not only contributes to increased self-esteem but also promotes the overall positive participatory culture where the users are supposed to actively contribute and help one another.

Integration of collaborative mechanics and social validation in gamified systems allows platforms to shift toward rich, interconnected community-building platforms, instead of transactional community participation. These design elements enable gamification that is no longer concerned with a tool of individual behavior shaping, but with a community-building model, where the degree of progress of a user is not assessed by what he or she has successfully done separately, but by what people have done together.

Crowdsourced Challenges

The emergence of crowdsourced challenges is another strong aspect of community-driven gamification, making it a switch from the user being only a passive recipient of rules, content, and experiences, towards the user being an active co-editor of those items. Crowdsourced gamification, unlike a traditional gamified system, where challenges and interactions are pre-designed, encourages the community to set a challenge as well as create and assess content. With the help of such a participatory model, the related user collective intelligence and creativity can be engaged to enhance adaptability, inclusion, responsiveness to user needs, and interests in the gamified environment.

The examples of this practice are the users on these websites (GitHub, Stack Overflow, etc.) who gain reputation points, ranks, and badges according to the usefulness, relevance, and good consequences of their contributions. Development of these ecosystems presents challenges in a natural way by real-life issues that the community proposes and is judged in a direct way, by peers, by upvotes, votes of approval, or accepted answers. This introduces a merit-based reward system in which cooperation and problem-solving are gamified by means of social recognition and status visibility.

Crowdsourced Gamification in Education

Within the learning setting, gamification in crowdsourcing has flourished in open learning communities like the discussion boards on Duolingo or in Coursera courses, where students can help each other with trouble spots, describe their understanding of concepts, and give study strategies. The most productive users may be awarded with digital certifications, taking up the position of a moderator, or receiving a badge of expertise and helpfulness. These websites create a peer-to-peer learning environment of knowledge exchange, not only between an instructor and student but between the different users, and lead to a perceived feeling that knowledge belongs to all.

The crowd-sourced environment has been revolutionized in a way that has changed the focus to a community-driven experience in gamification. A community, such as users of the games, can now influence the way games are played; they can influence the working and reward systems of the games. To this effect, the gamification has now become an organic and self-growing process. The growth of games is diversified as the nature and behavior of the users are also diversified.

Social Platforms

During recent years, social media platforms have been revolutionized by supporting the gamification feature. Now, the user interaction is the most important feature of the social media platform to fuel the gamification behaviors. These platforms have improved the quality and quantity of the content on side side and developed interactive and collaborative communities on the other hand. This has all improved the conversational talk, personalization, and group involvement over the internet applications. Having incorporated game mechanics that heavily focus on peer commentary, group work, and rewards, such platforms are reshaping the way individuals communicate and interact.

An example like Reddit can be given, and it is one of the best-known cases of socially gamified architecture. The karma points are given to the users when their posts or comments can be upvoted by other people, which indicates that their contributions have value. In the long term, such a gamified metric can develop reputation and trust among peers, and, in many cases, affect the visibility and credibility. Gamified activity is also present in the form of themed challenges or general community rivalries where gamers can experience recognition in the form of digital trophies, flair, or temporary privileges by coming together and teaming up. Such features form a loop of contributions, acknowledgment, and inspiration that retain users and make them engaged by and loyal to their communities.

In the same manner, Discord, which is a platform initially made with gamer audiences in mind but in reality used in education, wellness, and working circles, is integrated with gamification with the help of bots and the creation of custom roles. Bots can be used by community organizers, issuing challenges on a daily or weekly basis, adding points to participation, and rewarding milestones of the group with new access privileges, role upgrades, or digital tokens. They tend to replicate in-game mechanics, such as leveling up, team missions, or collaborative quests, and may be adjusted to work with various communities, including coding bootcamps, mental care groups, and others.

In the learning scenarios, even the collaborative gamification is stretched further to the gamification of the entire classroom ecosystem, such as Classcraft. Students receive the assignment (warrior, healer, or mage) and organize into teams and are rewarded with points due to collaborative work, coordination, and meeting expectations regarding behavior. The teachers are given an opportunity to create the quests that match the education objectives, and the whole class is being trained to achieve a common result. This strategy combines both scholarly lecturing and the dynamics of play in team games, providing the students with not only information, but also a sense of human compassion and the ability of communication, as well as the feeling of responsibility towards fellow students. Table 10 compares how major platforms have integrated community-driven gamification elements into their user experiences.

Table 10. Social platform features supporting collaborative gamification

Platform	Collaborative Features	Gamification Mechanics
Reddit	Upvotes, Karma, Community Trophies, Themed Events	Reputation points, Peer validation
Discord	Roles, Bots for team challenges, Server-level rewards	XP systems, Team missions, Role-based access
Classcraft	Group quests, Role assignments (healer, mage, warrior), Collaborative XP	Points, Levels, Shared goals
Stack Overflow	Peer-voted answers, Community moderation privileges	Reputation, Peer badges, Earned privileges
Coursera	Peer-reviewed assignments, Forum-based help	Badges, Top Contributor status

Table 10, as shown above, highlights that many social media platforms are providing engagement tools, team building and participatory cultures in the context of social and educational settings. These settings provide a sense of mission and emotion to foster self-gain for the user of the collaborative gaming environment on these platforms. These kinds of social media platforms, as noted in Table 10 above, provide a clear way forward to the gamification industry. Such platforms offer co-worker-focused collaboration, inclusiveness, and rewarding performance as a team rather than an individual.

To this effect, the main difference between collaborative gamification and the individual game models is that collaborative gamification uses community interaction rather than individual interaction. This underscores that humans are social learners by nature, and when they are put in a collaborative and shared environment, they perform better than in an individual setting. Moreover, community-driven gamification taps into the greater emotional connection and creates a sense of trust through cooperation, peer-to-peer learning, and social reinforcement.

CONCLUSION

Artificial intelligence, machine learning, virtual reality, augmented reality, metaverse, blockchain, social media platforms, and other relevant technologies are interacting with each other to transform the gamification landscape. To this effect, artificial intelligence and machine learning technologies are fueling hyper-personalized feedback loops within a gamified environment. This phenomenon is prompting the development of immersive technologies, such as augmented reality and virtual reality, to make them more intuitive and more suitable for developing games that use a virtual environment. Besides other technologies mentioned above, it should be noted that blockchain is also redefining digital ownership through its features, such as trust means, verifiable rewards, decentralized governance and collaborative models. The trends are expanding the possibilities of gamification on one hand, also redefining the motivations and purposes of using gamification, personal motivation on the other hand, in the context of community building, equity and sustainable behavior.

In recent years, the emergence of emotional AI has been developed to the next level to make gamified systems emotional to react instantly to the mood of a user, their stress, or their motivation. The analysis of recent trends on gamification shows that body gesture, voice, biometric data, and other things that interact with the real world can be combined to achieve more natural and fluid participation in the context of multimodal feedback in games. Recent examples of the use of gamification systems in education, healthcare, the workplace, and retail show that there is an urgent need to design and develop an ethical framework to augment the gamification environment for better results.

Based on the above discussion, it can be concluded that the future of gamification should not only focus on innovative thinking but also on responsible game designs to support the emotional AI context. Technologists, educators, behavioral scientists, ethicists, and policymakers should put their combined efforts into making future AI-based games more human-friendly alongside ethically responsible. The potential uses of gamification are limitless as the lines between digital systems and our daily lives become increasingly blurred.

REFERENCES

Alanazi, A. (2022). Using machine learning for healthcare challenges and opportunities. *Informatics in Medicine Unlocked, 30*, 100924. DOI: 10.1016/j.imu.2022.100924

Aldahiri, A., Alrashed, B., & Hussain, W. (2021). Trends in Using IoT with Machine Learning in Health Prediction Systems. *Forecasting 2021, Vol. 3, Pages 181-206, 3*(1), 181–206. DOI: 10.3390/forecast3010012

An, Q., Rahman, S., Zhou, J., & Kang, J. J. (2023). A Comprehensive Review on Machine Learning in the Healthcare Industry: Classification, Restrictions, Opportunities and Challenges. *Sensors 2023, Vol. 23, Page 4178, 23*(9), 4178. DOI: 10.3390/s23094178

Awan, M. J., Khan, R. A., Nobanee, H., Yasin, A., Anwar, S. M., Naseem, U., & Singh, V. P. (2021). A Recommendation Engine for Predicting Movie Ratings Using a Big Data Approach. *Electronics 2021, Vol. 10, Page 1215, 10*(10), 1215. DOI: 10.3390/electronics10101215

Bachiri, Y. A., Mouncif, H., & Bouikhalene, B. (2023). Artificial Intelligence Empowers Gamification: Optimizing Student Engagement and Learning Outcomes in E-learning and MOOCs. *International Journal of Engineering Pedagogy, 13*(8), 4–19. Advance online publication. DOI: 10.3991/ijep.v13i8.40853

Bennani, S., Maalel, A., & Ben Ghezala, H. (2022). Adaptive gamification in E-learning: A literature review and future challenges. *Computer Applications in Engineering Education, 30*(2), 628–642. DOI: 10.1002/cae.22477

Bernovskis, A., Stibe, A., Sceulovs, D., Zhang, Y., & Li, J. (2023). Gamified DAOs as Blockchain-Based Catalysts for Prosocial and Environmentally Oriented Cities. *Lecture Notes in Computer Science (Including Subseries Lecture Notes in Artificial Intelligence and Lecture Notes in Bioinformatics), 13977 LNCS*, 38–51. DOI: 10.1007/978-3-031-39764-6_3

Bezzina, S., & Dingli, A. (2023). Rethinking Gamification Through Artificial Intelligence. *Lecture Notes in Computer Science (Including Subseries Lecture Notes in Artificial Intelligence and Lecture Notes in Bioinformatics), 14046 LNCS*. DOI: 10.1007/978-3-031-35930-9_17

Bilotti, U., Di Dario, D., Palomba, F., Gravino, C., & Sibilio, M. (2023). Machine Learning for Educational Metaverse: How Far Are We? *Digest of Technical Papers - IEEE International Conference on Consumer Electronics, 2023-January*. DOI: 10.1109/ICCE56470.2023.10043465

Castellano, M. S., Contreras-McKay, I., Neyem, A., Farfán, E., Inzunza, O., Ottone, N. E., del Sol, M., Alario-Hoyos, C., Alvarado, M. S., & Tubbs, R. S. (2024). Empowering human anatomy education through gamification and artificial intelligence: An innovative approach to knowledge appropriation. *Clinical Anatomy (New York, N.Y.), 37*(1), 12–24. Advance online publication. DOI: 10.1002/ca.24074 PMID: 37453079

Choube, D. P. R., & Mhamane, Prof. S. C. (2025). The Role of Technology in Education: Exploring AI, VR, AR, and Gamification. *Educator Insights: Journal of Teaching Theory and Practice, 1*(1), 8–14. https://brightmindpublishing.com/index.php/EI/article/view/2

da Silva, J. N.Junior, & Teotônio, M. (2025). Gamification 2.0: Gamifying an Entire Introductory Organic Chemistry Course Again. *Journal of Chemical Education, 102*(2), 679–687. DOI: 10.1021/acs.jchemed.4c01183

Damaševičius, R., & Sidekersniene, T. (2023). Designing Immersive Gamified Experiences in the Metaverse for Enhanced Student Learning. *2023 International Conference on Intelligent Metaverse Technologies and Applications, IMETA 2023.* DOI: 10.1109/iMETA59369.2023.10294971

Davidová, M., Sharma, S., McMeel, D., & Loisides, F. (2022). Co-De|GT: The Gamification and Tokenisation of More-Than-Human Qualities and Values. *Sustainability 2022, Vol. 14, Page 3787, 14*(7), 3787. DOI: 10.3390/su14073787

Disse, I. K., & Olsson, M. (2023). Uncovering the gamified customer experience in the retail environment. *International Journal of Retail & Distribution Management, 51*(7), 955–971. DOI: 10.1108/IJRDM-07-2022-0268

Duolingo. (2025). *Duolingo - The world's best way to learn a language.* https://www.duolingo.com/

Geng, S., Liu, S., Fu, Z., Ge, Y., & Zhang, Y. (2022). Recommendation as Language Processing (RLP): A Unified Pretrain, Personalized Prompt & Predict Paradigm (P5). *RecSys 2022 - Proceedings of the 16th ACM Conference on Recommender Systems*, 299–315. DOI: 10.1145/3523227.3546767

Gheibi, O., Weyns, D., & Quin, F. (2021). Applying Machine Learning in Self-adaptive Systems. *ACM Transactions on Autonomous and Adaptive Systems, 15*(3), 1–37. Advance online publication. DOI: 10.1145/3469440

Haoming, L., & Wei, W. (2024). A systematic review on vocabulary learning in AR and VR gamification context. *Computers & Education: X Reality, 4*, 100057. DOI: 10.1016/j.cexr.2024.100057

Hilbert, S., Coors, S., Kraus, E., Bischl, B., Lindl, A., Frei, M., Wild, J., Krauss, S., Goretzko, D., & Stachl, C. (2021). Machine learning for the educational sciences. *Review of Education, 9*(3), e3310. DOI: 10.1002/rev3.3310

Kazu, İ. Y., & Kuvvetli, M. (2025). Digital language learning with Duolingo: Assessing its impact on listening, speaking, reading, and writing skills. *Journal of Computers in Education*, •••, 1–27. DOI: 10.1007/s40692-025-00355-0

Khan, H. U., Ali, Y., Khan, F., & Al-antari, M. A. (2024). A comprehensive study on unraveling the advances of immersive technologies (VR/AR/MR/XR) in the healthcare sector during the COVID-19: Challenges and solutions. *Heliyon, 10*(15), e35037. Advance online publication. DOI: 10.1016/j.heliyon.2024.e35037 PMID: 39157361

Kok, C. L., Koh, Y. Y., Ho, C. K., Teo, T. H., & Lee, C. (2024). Enhancing Learning: Gamification and Immersive Experiences with AI. *IEEE Region 10 Annual International Conference, Proceedings/TENCON*, 1853–1856. DOI: 10.1109/TENCON61640.2024.10902870

Lampropoulos, G., Keramopoulos, E., Diamantaras, K., & Evangelidis, G. (2022). Augmented Reality and Gamification in Education: A Systematic Literature Review of Research, Applications, and Empirical Studies. *Applied Sciences 2022, Vol. 12, Page 6809, 12*(13), 6809. DOI: 10.3390/app12136809

Ligorio, L., Venturelli, A., Rosato, P., & Campo, R. (2025). Fostering sustainable development goals through gamification. *Journal of Management & Organization, 31*(2), 945–966. DOI: 10.1017/jmo.2023.54

Liu, Y. (2024). *Gamification in Climate Action*. 359–380. : Lopes, J. M., Gomes, S., Lopes, P., Silva, A., Lourenço, D., Esteves, D., Cardoso, M., & Redondo, V. (2023). Exploring the Role of Gamification in the Online Shopping Experience in Retail Stores: An Exploratory Study. *Social Sciences 2023, Vol. 12, Page 235, 12*(4), 235. https://doi.org/DOI: 10.4018/979-8-3693-7001-8.ch013

Lopez-Barreiro, J., Alvarez-Sabucedo, L., Garcia-Soidan, J. L., & Santos-Gago, J. M. (2024). Towards a Blockchain Hybrid Platform for Gamification of Healthy Habits: Implementation and Usability Validation. *Applied System Innovation 2024, Vol. 7, Page 60, 7*(4), 60. DOI: 10.3390/asi7040060

Ly, R., & Shojaei, A. (2025). Decentralized autonomous organization in built environments: Applications, potential and limitations. *Information Systems and e-Business Management, 23*(2), 1–46. DOI: 10.1007/s10257-025-00699-1

Padeli, L. C., Fahrurroji, Purnama, S., Rizky, A., & Fazri, M. F. (2024). Analysis of Gamification and Blockchain Integration in Intelligent Learning Systems. *2024 3rd International Conference on Creative Communication and Innovative Technology, ICCIT 2024*. DOI: 10.1109/ICCIT62134.2024.10701220

Queirós, R., Swacha, J., Damaševičius, R., Maskeli, R., Unas, ¯, & Blažauskas, T. (2023). Serious Games and Gamification in Healthcare: A Meta-Review. *Information 2023, Vol. 14, Page 105, 14*(2), 105. DOI: 10.3390/info14020105

Queiroz, B. A., Westphall, J., & Martina, J. E. (2024). Badges as a Gamification Tool in Higher Education Through Tokenization. *2024 7th IEEE Biennial Congress of Argentina, ARGENCON 2024*. DOI: 10.1109/ARGENCON62399.2024.10735887

Ramadhan, A., Warnars, H. L. H. S., & Razak, F. H. A. (2024). Combining intelligent tutoring systems and gamification: A systematic literature review. *Education and Information Technologies, 29*(6), 6753–6789. DOI: 10.1007/s10639-023-12092-x

Rana, S., & Chicone, R. (2025). Gamification and Immersive Learning with AI. *Fortifying the Future*, 51–75. DOI: 10.1007/978-3-031-81780-9_3

Razi, Q., Devrani, A., Abhyankar, H., Chalapathi, G. S. S., Hassija, V., & Guizani, M. (2024). Non-Fungible Tokens (NFTs) - Survey of Current Applications, Evolution, and Future Directions. *IEEE Open Journal of the Communications Society, 5*, 2765–2791. DOI: 10.1109/OJCOMS.2023.3343926

Ribeiro, M., Santos, J., Lobo, J., Araújo, S., Magalhães, L. G., & Adão, T. (2024). VR, AR, gamification and AI towards the next generation of systems supporting cultural heritage: addressing challenges of a museum context. *Proceedings - Web3D 2024: 29th International ACM Conference on 3D Web Technology*. DOI: 10.1145/3665318.3677172

Sabry, F., Eltaras, T., Labda, W., Alzoubi, K., & Malluhi, Q. (2022). Machine Learning for Healthcare Wearable Devices: The Big Picture. *Journal of Healthcare Engineering, 2022*(1), 4653923. DOI: 10.1155/2022/4653923 PMID: 35480146

Shah, D., Patel, D., Adesara, J., Hingu, P., & Shah, M. (2021). Exploiting the Capabilities of Blockchain and Machine Learning in Education. *Augmented Human Research 2021 6:1, 6*(1), 1–14. DOI: 10.1007/s41133-020-00039-7

Sheetal, T., Tyagi, R., & Singh, G. (2023). Gamification and customer experience in online retail: A qualitative study focusing on ethical perspective. *Asian Journal of Business Ethics, 12*(1), 49–69. DOI: 10.1007/s13520-022-00162-1

Srdanović, P., Skala, T., & Maričević, M. (2025). InHeritage—A Gamified Mobile Application with AR and VR for Cultural Heritage Preservation in the Metaverse. *Applied Sciences (Basel, Switzerland), 15*(1), 257. DOI: 10.3390/app15010257

Sridhar, S., Saraswathi, S., Bharathi, S. V. S., & Devipriya, A. (2024). Gamification applications based on metaverse for healthcare industry. *Metaverse Technologies in Healthcare*, 233–244. DOI: 10.1016/B978-0-443-13565-1.00011-7

Suresh Babu, S., & Dhakshina Moorthy, A. (2024). Application of artificial intelligence in adaptation of gamification in education: A literature review. In *Computer Applications in Engineering Education* (Vol. 32, Issue 1). DOI: 10.1002/cae.22683

Tao, G., Garrett, B., Taverner, T., Cordingley, E., & Sun, C. (2021). Immersive virtual reality health games: A narrative review of game design. *Journal of Neuroengineering and Rehabilitation, 18*(1), 1–21. DOI: 10.1186/s12984-020-00801-3 PMID: 33573684

Triantafyllou, S. A., Georgiadis, C., & Sapounidis, T. (2025). Gamification in education and training: A literature review. *International Review of Education 2025 71:3, 71*(3), 483–517. DOI: 10.1007/s11159-024-10111-8

Vorrink, N., Wicaksono, H., & Fatahi Valilai, O. (2024). Analyzing VR/AR Technology Capabilities for Enhancing the Effectiveness of Learning Processes with Focus on Gamification. *Lecture Notes in Networks and Systems, 823 LNNS*, 806–817. DOI: 10.1007/978-3-031-47724-9_53

Wang, H., Gao, Z., Zhang, X., Du, J., Xu, Y., & Wang, Z. (2024). Gamifying cultural heritage: Exploring the potential of immersive virtual exhibitions. *Telematics and Informatics Reports, 15*, 100150. DOI: 10.1016/j.teler.2024.100150

Wijaya, S., Husain, A., Laurens, M., & Birgithri, A. (2024). iLearning Education Challenge: Combining the Power of Blockchain with Gamification Concepts. *Journal of Computer Science and Technology Application, 1*(1), 8–15. DOI: 10.33050/corisinta.v1i1.11

Yang, E. (2023). Implications of immersive technologies in healthcare sector and its built environment. *Frontiers in Medical Technology, 5*, 1184925. DOI: 10.3389/fmedt.2023.1184925 PMID: 37799269

Zeybek, N., & Saygı, E. (2024). Gamification in Education: Why, Where, When, and How?—A Systematic Review. *Games and Culture, 19*(2), 237–264. DOI: 10.1177/15554120231158625

Compilation of References

Abbasi, M., Váz, P., Silva, J., & Martins, P. (2024). Enhancing Visual Perception in Immersive VR and AR Environments: AI-Driven Color and Clarity Adjustments Under Dynamic Lighting Conditions. *Technologies*, *12*(11), 11. Advance online publication. DOI: 10.3390/technologies12110216

Agarwal, G., Gupta, S., Agarwal, S., & Rai, A. K. (2023). Emotion classification for musical data using deep learning techniques. *Int J Reconfigurable & Embedded Syst ISSN*, *2089*(4864), 4864.

Ahmed, A. H., Ibraheem, I. N., & Ibrahim, D. A. (2025). From frames to shots: A deep learning perspective on multimodal, graph-based, and transformer video summarization—A review. *Al-Salam Journal for Engineering and Technology*, *4*(2), 108–128. DOI: 10.55145/ajest.2025.04.02.009

Ahmed, M. A., Mahamid, F., & Hilo, G. (2025). Empowering Media Students: The Role of Digital Storytelling and the Metaverse in Skill Development. [JALLS]. *International Journal for Arabic Linguistics & Literature Studies*, *7*(1), 41–48. DOI: 10.31559/JALLS2025.7.1.4

Alanazi, A. (2022). Using machine learning for healthcare challenges and opportunities. *Informatics in Medicine Unlocked*, *30*, 100924. DOI: 10.1016/j.imu.2022.100924

Alavi, S. H., Perez, G. R., & Togelius, J. (2023). GamePlot: Co-creating narrative games with generative AI. *Proceedings of the ACM on Human-Computer Interaction*, *7*(CHI PLAY), 1–27. https://doi.org/DOI: 10.1145/3574198

Alcántara-Rubio, L., Valderrama-Hernández, R., Solís-Espallargas, C., & Ruiz-Morales, J. (2022). The implementation of the SDGs in universities: A systematic review. *Environmental Education Research*, *28*(11), 1585–1615. DOI: 10.1080/13504622.2022.2063798

Aldahiri, A., Alrashed, B., & Hussain, W. (2021). Trends in Using IoT with Machine Learning in Health Prediction Systems. *Forecasting 2021, Vol. 3, Pages 181-206, 3*(1), 181–206. DOI: 10.3390/forecast3010012

Aleksić, V. (2024). Using Artificial Intelligence Concepts to Design Non-Playable Characters in Road Traffic Safety Games. In *10th International Scientific Conference Technics, Informatics and Education-TIE 2024*. Faculty of Technical Sciences Čačak, University of Kragujevac. DOI: 10.46793/TIE24.239A

Alharthi, S. A. (2025). Generative AI in Game Design: Enhancing Creativity or Constraining Innovation? *Journal of Intelligence, 13*(6), 13. DOI: 10.3390/jintelligence13060060

Alonso, E., Jelley, A., Micheli, V., Kanervisto, A., Storkey, A. J., Pearce, T., & Fleuret, F. (2024). Diffusion for world modeling: Visual details matter in atari. *Advances in Neural Information Processing Systems, 37*, 58757–58791.

Alsaedi, A. A. (2024). AI-POWERED PEDAGOGY: REVOLUTIONIZING STUDENTS'LEARNING EXPERIENCES THROUGH INTEGRATION OF AI TECHNOLOGIES.

Alvarado, Y., Guerrero, R., & Serón, F. (2023). Inclusive Learning through Immersive Virtual Reality and Semantic Embodied Conversational Agent: A case study in children with autism. *Journal of Computer Science and Technology, 23*(2), e09. DOI: 10.24215/16666038.23.e09

Amer-Yahia, S. (2022). Towards AI-powered data-driven education. *Proceedings of the VLDB Endowment International Conference on Very Large Data Bases, 15*(12), 3798–3806. DOI: 10.14778/3554821.3554900

Amos, Z. (2022, August). How AI is bringing the Metaverse to life. *Unite.AI.* https://www.unite.ai/how-ai-is-bringing-the-metaverse-to-life/

An, Q., Rahman, S., Zhou, J., & Kang, J. J. (2023). A Comprehensive Review on Machine Learning in the Healthcare Industry: Classification, Restrictions, Opportunities and Challenges. *Sensors 2023, Vol. 23, Page 4178, 23*(9), 4178. DOI: 10.3390/s23094178

Anand Thoutam, V., Srivastava, A., Badal, T., Kumar Mishra, V., Sinha, G. R., Sakalle, A., Bhardwaj, H., & Raj, M. (2022). Yoga pose estimation and feedback generation using deep learning. *Computational Intelligence and Neuroscience, 2022*(1), 4311350. DOI: 10.1155/2022/4311350 PMID: 35371230

Anderson, A., Huttenlocher, D., Kleinberg, J., & Leskovec, J. (2013). Steering user behavior with badges. *Proceedings of the 22nd International Conference on World Wide Web*, 95–106. DOI: 10.1145/2488388.2488398

Anwar, M. R., & Ahyarudin, H. A. (2023). Ai-powered arabic language education in the era of society 5.0. [ITSDI]. *IAIC Transactions on Sustainable Digital Innovation*, *5*(1), 50–57. DOI: 10.34306/itsdi.v5i1.607

Augusto, J. C. (2022). Contexts and Context-awareness Revisited from an Intelligent Environments Perspective. *Applied Artificial Intelligence*, *36*(1), 2008644. DOI: 10.1080/08839514.2021.2008644

Awan, M. J., Khan, R. A., Nobanee, H., Yasin, A., Anwar, S. M., Naseem, U., & Singh, V. P. (2021). A Recommendation Engine for Predicting Movie Ratings Using a Big Data Approach. *Electronics 2021, Vol. 10, Page 1215*, *10*(10), 1215. DOI: 10.3390/electronics10101215

Bachiri, Y. A., Mouncif, H., & Bouikhalene, B. (2023). Artificial Intelligence Empowers Gamification: Optimizing Student Engagement and Learning Outcomes in E-learning and MOOCs. *International Journal of Engineering Pedagogy*, *13*(8), 4–19. Advance online publication. DOI: 10.3991/ijep.v13i8.40853

Bae, Y. H., & Bennett, C. C. (2025). *Multimodal Transformer Models for Turn-taking Prediction: Effects on Conversational Dynamics of Human-Agent Interaction during Cooperative Gameplay.*

Bag, S., Srivastava, G., Bashir, M. M. A., Kumari, S., Giannakis, M., & Chowdhury, A. H. (2021). Journey of customers in this digital era: Understanding the role of artificial intelligence technologies in user engagement and conversion. *Benchmarking*, *29*(7), 2074–2098. DOI: 10.1108/BIJ-07-2021-0415

Bakkes, S. C. J., Spronck, P. H. M., & van Lankveld, G. (2012). Player behavioural modelling for video games. *Entertainment Computing*, *3*(3), 71–79. DOI: 10.1016/j.entcom.2011.12.001

Balasubramaniam, S., Vijesh Joe, C., Sivakumar, T. A., Prasanth, A., Satheesh Kumar, K., Kavitha, V., & Dhanaraj, R. K. (2023). Optimization enabled deep learning-based ddos attack detection in cloud computing. *International Journal of Intelligent Systems*, *2023*(1), 2039217. DOI: 10.1155/2023/2039217

Banik, B. G., & Gullapelly, A. (2025). AI-Powered Gamification and Interactive Learning Tools for Enhancing Student Engagement. In Driving Quality Education Through AI and Data Science (pp. 283–310). IGI Global Scientific Publishing.

Bartle, R. (1996). Hearts, clubs, diamonds, spades: Players who suit MUDs. *Journal of MUD Research, 1*(1).

Basheer, S., Walia, S., Farooq, S., Shah, M. A., & Mir, F. A. (2024). Exploring the Metaverse: The future of tourism through AI and virtual reality. In Basheer, S. (Ed.), *Exploring the Metaverse: The Future of Tourism Through AI and Virtual Reality* (pp. 195–204). IGI Global.

Basu, A., Pramanik, R., & Sarkar, R. (2024). WANet: Weight and attention network for video summarization. *Discover Artificial Intelligence, 4*(1), 5. DOI: 10.1007/s44163-024-00101-y

Behera, G., Meenakshi, S., Rajini, J., Pravin, T., Boopathi, S., & Associates. (2025). Entrepreneurial Insights From Higher Education: Startup Business Ventures. In Real-World Tools and Scenarios for Entrepreneurship Exploration (pp. 101–132). IGI Global.

Belabed, Z., Tounsi, A., Bousahla, A. A., Tounsi, A., & Yaylacı, M. (2024). Accurate free and forced vibration behavior prediction of functionally graded sandwich beams with variable cross-section: A finite element assessment. *Mechanics Based Design of Structures and Machines, 52*(11), 9144–9177. DOI: 10.1080/15397734.2024.2337914

Bennani, S., Maalel, A., & Ben Ghezala, H. (2022). Adaptive gamification in E-learning: A literature review and future challenges. *Computer Applications in Engineering Education, 30*(2), 628–642. DOI: 10.1002/cae.22477

Berkman, M. I., & Akan, E. (2019). Presence and Immersion in Virtual Reality. In Lee, N. (Ed.), *Encyclopedia of Computer Graphics and Games* (pp. 1–10). Springer International Publishing., DOI: 10.1007/978-3-319-08234-9_162-1

Bernovskis, A., Stibe, A., Sceulovs, D., Zhang, Y., & Li, J. (2023). Gamified DAOs as Blockchain-Based Catalysts for Prosocial and Environmentally Oriented Cities. *Lecture Notes in Computer Science (Including Subseries Lecture Notes in Artificial Intelligence and Lecture Notes in Bioinformatics), 13977 LNCS*, 38–51. DOI: 10.1007/978-3-031-39764-6_3

Bethke, E. (2003). *Game Development and Production.* Wordware Pub.

Beukman, M., Cleghorn, C. W., & James, S. (2022, July). Procedural content generation using neuroevolution and novelty search for diverse video game levels. In *Proceedings of the genetic and evolutionary computation conference* (pp. 1028-1037).

Bezzina, S., & Dingli, A. (2023). Rethinking Gamification Through Artificial Intelligence. *Lecture Notes in Computer Science (Including Subseries Lecture Notes in Artificial Intelligence and Lecture Notes in Bioinformatics), 14046 LNCS*. DOI: 10.1007/978-3-031-35930-9_17

Bhattacharya, S., & Singla, B. (2024). Metaverse Banking 2.0: Future Trends and Challenges in Metaverse Banking Strategies. *Exploring the Use of Metaverse in Business and Education*, 166-192.

Bilotti, U., Di Dario, D., Palomba, F., Gravino, C., & Sibilio, M. (2023). Machine Learning for Educational Metaverse: How Far Are We? *Digest of Technical Papers - IEEE International Conference on Consumer Electronics, 2023-January*. DOI: 10.1109/ICCE56470.2023.10043465

Bojić, L., Cinelli, M., Ćulibrk, D., & Delibašić, B. (2024). CERN for AI: A theoretical framework for autonomous simulation-based artificial intelligence testing and alignment. *European Journal of Futures Research*, *12*(1), 1–19. DOI: 10.1186/s40309-024-00238-0

Boopathi, S. (2024). Harnessing the power of distributed cloud and edge computing for advanced healthcare systems. In *Internet of Things enabled Machine Learning for Biomedical Applications* (pp. 248–272). CRC Press. DOI: 10.1201/9781003487647-14

Boyd, E. M., & Fales, A. W. (1983). Reflective Learning. *Journal of Humanistic Psychology*, *23*(2), 99–117. DOI: 10.1177/0022167883232011

Bucher, J. (2017). *Storytelling for Virtual Reality*. Routledge., DOI: 10.4324/9781315210308

Cai, Y., van Joolingen, W., & Veermans, K. (Eds.). (2021). *Virtual and augmented reality, simulation and serious games for education*. Springer. DOI: 10.1007/978-981-16-1361-6

Camerlengo, F., Frittelli, A., & Pagliarello, R. (2022). CRISPR towards a Sustainable Agriculture. *Encyclopedia*, *2*(1), 538–558. DOI: 10.3390/encyclopedia2010036

Camilleri, M. A. (2024). Artificial intelligence governance: Ethical considerations and implications for social responsibility. *Expert Systems: International Journal of Knowledge Engineering and Neural Networks*, *41*(7), e13406. DOI: 10.1111/exsy.13406

Camilleri, R. Y., & Camilleri, V. (2024). Beyond the Maze: How AI Personalizes Learning and Drives Engagement in Educational Games. *Proceedings of the Future Technologies Conference*, 301–320. DOI: 10.1007/978-3-031-73122-8_19

Cant, P. (2018). *SXSW: The State of Immersive Journalism*. The State of Immersive Journalism.

Cao, L., Zhang, H., Peng, C., & Hansberger, J. T. (2023). Real-time multimodal interaction in virtual reality, A case study with a large virtual interface. *Multimedia Tools and Applications*, *82*(16), 25427–25448. DOI: 10.1007/s11042-023-14381-6

Carrera-Rivera, A., Larrinaga, F., & Lasa, G. (2022). Context-awareness for the design of Smart-product service systems: Literature review. *Computers in Industry*, *142*, 103730. DOI: 10.1016/j.compind.2022.103730

Castellano, M. S., Contreras-McKay, I., Neyem, A., Farfán, E., Inzunza, O., Ottone, N. E., del Sol, M., Alario-Hoyos, C., Alvarado, M. S., & Tubbs, R. S. (2024). Empowering human anatomy education through gamification and artificial intelligence: An innovative approach to knowledge appropriation. *Clinical Anatomy (New York, N.Y.)*, *37*(1), 12–24. Advance online publication. DOI: 10.1002/ca.24074 PMID: 37453079

Cavazza, M., & Charles, F. (2021). Dialogue Generation in Character-Based Interactive Storytelling. *Proceedings of the AAAI Conference on Artificial Intelligence and Interactive Digital Entertainment*, *1*(1), 21–26. DOI: 10.1609/aiide.v1i1.18710

Chalkiadakis, A., Seremetaki, A., Kanellou, A., Kallishi, M., Morfopoulou, A., Moraitaki, M., & Mastrokoukou, S. (2024). Impact of artificial intelligence and virtual reality on educational inclusion: A systematic review of technologies supporting students with disabilities. *Education Sciences*, *14*(11), 1223. DOI: 10.3390/educsci14111223

Chamola, V., Bansal, G., Das, T. K., Hassija, V., Reddy, N. S. S., Wang, J., . . . Niyato, D. (2023). Beyond reality: The pivotal role of generative ai in the metaverse. *arXiv preprint arXiv:2308.06272*.

Chandra, S., Maheswari, B. U., Tiwari, S., Muthukumaran, R., Logeswaran, S., & Boopathi, S. (2025). Enhancing Industrial Employee Performance by Integrating Machine Learning and Human Psychology. In Exploring Psychology, Social Innovation and Advanced Applications of Machine Learning (pp. 231–252). IGI Global Scientific Publishing. DOI: 10.4018/979-8-3693-6910-4.ch012

Chen, J., & Cao, L. (2024). AI-enabled rendering technology for the construction and development of Dunhuang Virtual Pavilion. *Front. Comput. Intell. Syst*, *7*(3), 1–5. DOI: 10.54097/yv2hpa48

Chen, X., Gao, W., Chu, Y., & Song, Y. (2024). Enhancing interaction in virtual-real architectural environments: A comparative analysis of generative AI-driven reality approaches. *Building and Environment, 266*, 112113. DOI: 10.1016/j.buildenv.2024.112113

Chhabra, G., Kumar, S., Gupta, S., & Nagpal, P. (2023). *Artificial intelligence to analyze psychophysical and human lifestyle*. Springer Nature Singapore. DOI: 10.1007/978-981-99-3039-5

Chi, H., Mohamad, M., & Lin, Z. (2024). Developing an AI-Powered Interactive Virtual Reality Model for Enhancing Distance Education. *Proceedings of the 2024 4th International Symposium on Big Data and Artificial Intelligence*, 187–192. DOI: 10.1145/3723366.3723395

CHISEGA-NEGRILĂ, A. M. (2024). Teaching and Learning in an AI-powered world. Bulletin of" Carol I [EN]. *National Defence University, 13*(03), 105–116.

Choube, D. P. R., & Mhamane, Prof. S. C. (2025). The Role of Technology in Education: Exploring AI, VR, AR, and Gamification. *Educator Insights: Journal of Teaching Theory and Practice, 1*(1), 8–14. https://brightmindpublishing.com/index.php/EI/article/view/2

Chugh, A., Jain, C., & Kumar, A. (2022). Design of artificial intelligence enabled game engine. *In Proceedings of the 4th International Conference on Information Management & Machine Intelligence (ICIMMI '22)* (Article No. 99, pp. 1–5). ACM.

Cinar, O. E., Rafferty, K., Cutting, D., & Wang, H. (2024). AI-Powered VR for Enhanced Learning Compared to Traditional Methods. *Electronics (Basel), 13*(23), 4787. DOI: 10.3390/electronics13234787

Coplan, A., & Goldie, P. (2011). *EmpathyPhilosophical and Psychological Perspectives*. Oxford University Press., DOI: 10.1093/acprof:oso/9780199539956.001.0001

Crogman, H. T., Cano, V. D., Pacheco, E., Sonawane, R. B., & Boroon, R. (2025). Virtual Reality, Augmented Reality, and Mixed Reality in Experiential Learning: Transforming Educational Paradigms. *Education Sciences, 15*(3), 303. DOI: 10.3390/educsci15030303

Csikszentmihalyi, M. (1990). Flow: The Psychology of Optimal Experience.

da Silva, J. N.Junior, & Teotônio, M. (2025). Gamification 2.0: Gamifying an Entire Introductory Organic Chemistry Course Again. *Journal of Chemical Education, 102*(2), 679–687. DOI: 10.1021/acs.jchemed.4c01183

Damaševičius, R., & Sidekersniene, T. (2023). Designing Immersive Gamified Experiences in the Metaverse for Enhanced Student Learning. *2023 International Conference on Intelligent Metaverse Technologies and Applications, IMETA 2023*. DOI: 10.1109/iMETA59369.2023.10294971

Datta, S. D., Islam, M., Sobuz, M. H. R., Ahmed, S., & Kar, M. (2024). Artificial intelligence and machine learning applications in the project lifecycle of the construction industry: A comprehensive review. *Heliyon, 10*(5), e26888. DOI: 10.1016/j.heliyon.2024.e26888 PMID: 38444479

Davidová, M., Sharma, S., McMeel, D., & Loisides, F. (2022). Co-De|GT: The Gamification and Tokenisation of More-Than-Human Qualities and Values. *Sustainability 2022, Vol. 14, Page 3787, 14*(7), 3787. DOI: 10.3390/su14073787

De Carlo, M. E., & Limone, P. (2024, June). Metaverse Narratives and Artificial Creativity: Fostering Divergent Thinking in the Education of the Future. In *Conference on Artificial Creativity: Looking at the Future of Digital Culture* (pp. 97-109). Cham: Springer Nature Switzerland.

Delgado, G. (2024, July 31). NVIDIA Researchers Harness Real-Time Gen AI to Build Immersive Desert World. NVIDIA Blog. https://blogs.nvidia.com/blog/real-time-3d-generative-ai-research-siggraph-2024/

Devagiri, J. S., Paheding, S., Niyaz, Q., Yang, X., & Smith, S. (2022). Augmented Reality and Artificial Intelligence in industry: Trends, tools, and future challenges. *Expert Systems with Applications, 207*, 118002. DOI: 10.1016/j.eswa.2022.118002

Din, I. U., Awan, K. A., Almogren, A., & Rodrigues, J. J. P. C. (2023). Integration of IoT and blockchain for decentralized management and ownership in the Metaverse. *International Journal of Communication Systems, 36*(18), e5612. Advance online publication. DOI: 10.1002/dac.5612

Dionisio, J. D. N., Burns, W. G.III, & Gilbert, R. (2013). 3D virtual worlds and the Metaverse. *ACM Computing Surveys, 45*(3), 1–38. DOI: 10.1145/2480741.2480751

Disse, I. K., & Olsson, M. (2023). Uncovering the gamified customer experience in the retail environment. *International Journal of Retail & Distribution Management, 51*(7), 955–971. DOI: 10.1108/IJRDM-07-2022-0268

Drachen, A., & Canossa, A. (2009). Analyzing spatial user behavior in computer games using geographic information systems. *Proceedings of the 13th International MindTrek Conference: Everyday Life in the Ubiquitous Era*, 182–189. DOI: 10.1145/1621841.1621875

Drachen, A., Thurau, C., Togelius, J., Yannakakis, G. N., & Bauckhage, C. (2013). Game Data Mining. In *Game Analytics* (pp. 205–253). Springer London., DOI: 10.1007/978-1-4471-4769-5_12

Duolingo. (2025). *Duolingo - The world's best way to learn a language.* https://www.duolingo.com/

Dutta, S., & Ganapathy, S. (2025). *LLM supervised pre-training for multimodal emotion recognition in conversations*. arXiv. https://arxiv.org/abs/2501.11468 DOI: 10.1109/ICASSP49660.2025.10889998

Dyulicheva, Y. Y., & Glazieva, A. O. (2022). Game based learning with artificial intelligence and immersive technologies: An overview.

Eiris, R., & Al-Bayati, A. (2023). *Using Immersive Storytelling to Improve Engagement and Motivation During Fall Prevention Training*. www.cpwr.com•www.elcosh.org

Engage, V. R. (n.d.). Retrieved from https://engagevr.io/

Epstein, Z., Hertzmann, A., Herman, L. M., Mahari, R., Frank, M. R., Groh, M., Schroeder, H., Smith, A., Akten, M., Fjeld, J., Farid, H., Leach, N., Pentland, A., & Russakovsky, O. (2023). Art and the science of generative AI. *Science*, *380*(6650), 1110–1111. DOI: 10.1126/science.adh4451

Fadhel, M. A., Duhaim, A. M., Albahri, A. S., Al-Qaysi, Z. T., Aktham, M. A., Chyad, M. A., Abd-Alaziz, W., Albahri, O. S., Alamoodi, A. H., Alzubaidi, L., Gupta, A., & Gu, Y. (2024). Navigating the Metaverse: Unraveling the impact of artificial intelligence—A comprehensive review and gap analysis. *Artificial Intelligence Review*, *57*(264), 264. Advance online publication. DOI: 10.1007/s10462-024-10881-5

Fang, J., Wang, F., Xue, J., & Chua, T. S. (2024). Behavioral intention prediction in driving scenes: A survey. *IEEE Transactions on Intelligent Transportation Systems*, *25*(8), 8334–8355. DOI: 10.1109/TITS.2024.3374342

Fang, J., Zhang, R., Zhao, Y., Zheng, K., Zhou, X., & Zhou, A. (2020). A-DSP: An Adaptive Join Algorithm for Dynamic Data Stream on Cloud System. *IEEE Transactions on Knowledge and Data Engineering*, •••, 1–1. DOI: 10.1109/TKDE.2019.2947055

Fan, S., Yecies, B., Zhou, Z. I., & Shen, J. (2024). Challenges and opportunities for the web 3.0 metaverse turn in education. *IEEE Transactions on Learning Technologies*, *17*, 1935–1950. DOI: 10.1109/TLT.2024.3385505

Feng, S.. (2022). Transformer-based video summarization with spatial-temporal representation. In *Proceedings of the 8th International Conference on Big Data and Information Analytics (BigDIA)* (pp. xx–xx). IEEE.

Fischer, J. M. & R. M. (1998). *Responsibility and control: A theory of moral responsibility*. Cambridge: Cambridge University Press.

Floridi, L., Cowls, J., Beltrametti, M., Chatila, R., Chazerand, P., Dignum, V., Luetge, C., Madelin, R., Pagallo, U., Rossi, F., Schafer, B., Valcke, P., & Vayena, E. (2018). AI4People—An Ethical Framework for a Good AI Society: Opportunities, Risks, Principles, and Recommendations. *Minds and Machines*, *28*(4), 689–707. DOI: 10.1007/s11023-018-9482-5 PMID: 30930541

Fussell, S. G., & Truong, D. (2022). Using virtual reality for dynamic learning: An extended technology acceptance model. *Virtual Reality (Waltham Cross)*, *26*(1), 249–267. DOI: 10.1007/s10055-021-00554-x PMID: 34276237

Gee, J. P. (2003). What video games have to teach us about learning and literacy. *Computers in Entertainment*, *1*(1), 20–20. DOI: 10.1145/950566.950595

Geng, S., Liu, S., Fu, Z., Ge, Y., & Zhang, Y. (2022). Recommendation as Language Processing (RLP): A Unified Pretrain, Personalized Prompt & Predict Paradigm (P5). *RecSys 2022 - Proceedings of the 16th ACM Conference on Recommender Systems*, 299–315. DOI: 10.1145/3523227.3546767

Gheibi, O., Weyns, D., & Quin, F. (2021). Applying Machine Learning in Self-adaptive Systems. *ACM Transactions on Autonomous and Adaptive Systems*, *15*(3), 1–37. Advance online publication. DOI: 10.1145/3469440

Ghosh, A., Lavanya, V., Hassija, V., Chamola, V., & El Saddik, A. (2024). A survey on decentralized Metaverse using blockchain and Web 3.0 technologies, applications, and more. *IEEE Access : Practical Innovations, Open Solutions*, *12*, 146915–146948. DOI: 10.1109/ACCESS.2024.3469193

Gokhe, S., Ulhe, P., & Bhasme, M. (2024). AI-Powered Personalized Learning for Advancing Educational Equity. 2024 2nd DMIHER International Conference on Artificial Intelligence in Healthcare, Education and Industry (IDICAIEI), 1–6.

Goodwin, N. L., Choong, J. J., Hwang, S., Pitts, K., Bloom, L., Islam, A., Zhang, Y. Y., Szelenyi, E. R., Tong, X., Newman, E. L., Miczek, K., Wright, H. R., McLaughlin, R. J., Norville, Z. C., Eshel, N., Heshmati, M., Nilsson, S. R. O., & Golden, S. A. (2024). Simple Behavioral Analysis (SimBA) as a platform for explainable machine learning in behavioral neuroscience. *Nature Neuroscience*, *27*(7), 1411–1424. DOI: 10.1038/s41593-024-01649-9 PMID: 38778146

Gulyamov, S. S., Mamanazarov, S., & Rodionov, A. A. (2024, June). Creating Self-Updating Digital Platforms Using Artificial Intelligence Technologies for Continuous Education and Professional Development. In *2024 4th International Conference on Technology Enhanced Learning in Higher Education (TELE)* (pp. 337-339). IEEE. DOI: 10.1109/TELE62556.2024.10605683

Haoming, L., & Wei, W. (2024). A systematic review on vocabulary learning in AR and VR gamification context. *Computers & Education: X Reality, 4*, 100057. DOI: 10.1016/j.cexr.2024.100057

Hardin, S. (2001). John Seely Brown: Leveraging the Social Life of Information in the E-Age: Idea Sparkers. *Bulletin of the American Society for Information Science, 27*(3), 15–17. DOI: 10.1002/bult.197

Hendriks Vettehen, P., Wiltink, D., Huiskamp, M., Schaap, G., & Ketelaar, P. (2019). Taking the full view: How viewers respond to 360-degree video news. *Computers in Human Behavior, 91*, 24–32. DOI: 10.1016/j.chb.2018.09.018

He, X., Tang, Y., Ma, S., Ai, Q., Tao, F., & Qiu, R. (2024). Redefinition of digital twin and its situation awareness framework designing toward fourth paradigm for energy internet of things. *IEEE Transactions on Systems, Man, and Cybernetics. Systems, 54*(11), 6873–6888. DOI: 10.1109/TSMC.2024.3407061

Hilbert, S., Coors, S., Kraus, E., Bischl, B., Lindl, A., Frei, M., Wild, J., Krauss, S., Goretzko, D., & Stachl, C. (2021). Machine learning for the educational sciences. *Review of Education, 9*(3), e3310. DOI: 10.1002/rev3.3310

Holmgard, C., Green, M. C., Liapis, A., & Togelius, J. (2019). Automated Playtesting With Procedural Personas Through MCTS With Evolved Heuristics. *IEEE Transactions on Games, 11*(4), 352–362. DOI: 10.1109/TG.2018.2808198

Hsu, T.-C., Liao, Y.-S., & Huang, C.-R. (2023). Video summarization with spatiotemporal vision transformer. *IEEE Transactions on Image Processing, 32*, 3013–3026. DOI: 10.1109/TIP.2023.3275069

Hu, D., Bao, Y., Wei, L., ... (2023) Supervised adversarial contrastive learning for emotion recognition in conversations. In: Proceedings of the 61st Annual Meeting of the Association for Computational Linguistics (Volume 1: Long Papers), ACL 2023. Association for Computational Linguistics, pp 10835–10852. DOI: 10.18653/v1/2023.acl-long.606

Hu, B. A., & Ting, F. (2024, October). EverForest: A More-Than-AI Sustainability Manifesto from an On-Chain Artificial Life. In *Proceedings of the Halfway to the Future Symposium* (pp. 1-6). DOI: 10.1145/3686169.3686209

Hussain, R., Sabir, A., Lee, D. Y., Zaidi, S. F. A., Pedro, A., Abbas, M. S., & Park, C. (2024). Conversational AI-based VR system to improve construction safety training of migrant workers. *Automation in Construction, 160*, 105315. DOI: 10.1016/j.autcon.2024.105315

Hu, Z., Ding, Y., Wu, R., Li, L., Zhang, R., Hu, Y., Qiu, F., Zhang, Z., Wang, K., Zhao, S., Zhang, Y., Jiang, J., Xi, Y., Pu, J., Zhang, W., Wang, S., Chen, K., Zhou, T., Chen, J., & Fan, C. (2023). Deep learning applications in games: A survey from a data perspective. *Applied Intelligence*, *53*(24), 31129–31164. DOI: 10.1007/s10489-023-05094-2

Imamguluyev, R., Hasanova, P., Imanova, T., Mammadova, A., Hajizada, S., & Samadova, Z. (n.d.). AI-POWERED EDUCATIONAL TOOLS: TRANSFORMING LEARNING IN THE DIGITAL ERA.

Inworld, A. I. (2023). *Inworld: AI characters for games and the metaverse.* https://www.inworld.ai/

Isbister, K. (2016). *How Games Move Us: Emotion by Design.* MIT Press. DOI: 10.7551/mitpress/9267.001.0001

Järvinen, A. (2009). Game design as a research field. *In Proceedings of DiGRA 2009: Breaking New Ground: Innovation in Games, Play, Practice and Theory.*

Jhaveri, R. H., Revathi, A., Ramana, K., Raut, R., & Dhanaraj, R. K. (2022). A review on machine learning strategies for real-world engineering applications. *Mobile Information Systems*, *2022*(1), 1833507. DOI: 10.1155/2022/1833507

Jing, X.. (2025). "MELT: Towards Automated Multimodal Emotion Data Annotation by Leveraging LLM Embedded Knowledge." *ArXiv*, https://arxiv.org/abs/2505.24493

Ji, Z., Zhao, Y., Pang, Y., Li, X., & Han, J. (2020). Deep attentive video summarization with distribution consistency learning. *IEEE Transactions on Neural Networks and Learning Systems*, *32*(4), 1765–1775. DOI: 10.1109/TNNLS.2020.2991083

Jobin, A., Ienca, M., & Vayena, E. (2019). The global landscape of AI ethics guidelines. *Nature Machine Intelligence*, *1*(9), 389–399. DOI: 10.1038/s42256-019-0088-2

Joe Romm. (2018, July 9). *Steve Jobs on the awesome viral power of storytelling.* Medium .

Johansson, T., & Eladhari, M. P. (2024, December). Emotional Believability of Non-playable Game Characters-Animations of Anger, Sadness and Happiness. In *International Conference on Interactive Digital Storytelling* (pp. 72-99). Cham: Springer Nature Switzerland.

Joseph, G. V., P, A., Thomas M, A., Jose, D., V Roy, T., & Prasad, M. P. (2024). Impact of Digital Literacy, Use of AI tools and Peer Collaboration on AI Assisted Learning- Perceptions of the University students. *Digital Education Review*, *45*(45), 43–49. DOI: 10.1344/der.2024.45.43-49

Jose, S., Nguyen, K. T. P., Medjaher, K., Zemouri, R., Lévesque, M., & Tahan, A. (2024). Advancing Multimodal Diagnostics: Integrating Industrial Textual Data and Domain Knowledge with Large Language Models. *Expert Systems with Applications*, *255*, 124603. DOI: 10.1016/j.eswa.2024.124603

Kadam, B. D., & Deshpande, A. M. (2024). Multi-head attention with reinforcement learning for supervised video summarization. *Journal of Electronic Imaging*, *33*(5), 053010. DOI: 10.1117/1.JEI.33.5.053010

Karthikeyan, M., Madan, B. S., Suchitra, V., Varshini, E. S. A., Sarkar, R., & Boopathi, S. (2025). Flipped Classroom Methods for Enhanced Student Engagement and Knowledge Developments in Indian Higher Education. In Global Practices in Inclusive Education Curriculum and Policy (pp. 313–342). IGI Global.

Kashid, S., Awasthi, L. K., Berwal, K., & Saini, P. (2024). STVS: Spatio-temporal feature fusion for video summarization. *IEEE MultiMedia*, *31*(3), 88–97. DOI: 10.1109/MMUL.2024.3428933

Kazu, İ. Y., & Kuvvetli, M. (2025). Digital language learning with Duolingo: Assessing its impact on listening, speaking, reading, and writing skills. *Journal of Computers in Education*, •••, 1–27. DOI: 10.1007/s40692-025-00355-0

Kent, S. L. (2001). *The ultimate history of video games: From Pong to Pokémon and beyond*. Three Rivers Press.

Khan, M. A. A., Tashfi, M. M. I., Nur, F. N., & Sultana, S. (2024, December). Effects of Emotional Behavior Tree in Non-Playable Characters in Games. In *2024 6th International Conference on Sustainable Technologies for Industry 5.0 (STI)* (pp. 1-7). IEEE. DOI: 10.1109/STI64222.2024.10951084

Khan, H. U., Ali, Y., Khan, F., & Al-antari, M. A. (2024). A comprehensive study on unraveling the advances of immersive technologies (VR/AR/MR/XR) in the healthcare sector during the COVID-19: Challenges and solutions. *Heliyon*, *10*(15), e35037. Advance online publication. DOI: 10.1016/j.heliyon.2024.e35037 PMID: 39157361

Khare, S. K., Blanes-Vidal, V., Nadimi, E. S., & Acharya, U. R. (2024). Emotion recognition and artificial intelligence: A systematic review (2014–2023) and research recommendations. *Information Fusion, 102*, 102019. DOI: 10.1016/j.inffus.2023.102019

King, D. L., & Delfabbro, P. H. (2019). Video Game Monetization (e.g., 'Loot Boxes'): A Blueprint for Practical Social Responsibility Measures. *International Journal of Mental Health and Addiction, 17*(1), 166–179. DOI: 10.1007/s11469-018-0009-3

Kok, C. L., Koh, Y. Y., Ho, C. K., Teo, T. H., & Lee, C. (2024). Enhancing Learning: Gamification and Immersive Experiences with AI. *IEEE Region 10 Annual International Conference, Proceedings/TENCON*, 1853–1856. DOI: 10.1109/TENCON61640.2024.10902870

Kollias, D., Zafeiriou, S., Kotsia, I., Dhall, A., Ghosh, S., Shao, C., & Hu, G. (2024, September). 7th abaw competition: Multi-task learning and compound expression recognition. In *European Conference on Computer Vision* (pp. 31-45). Cham: Springer Nature Switzerland.

Ko, R.. (2025). "Seven Security Challenges That Must Be Solved in Cross-domain Multi-agent LLM Systems." *ArXiv*, https://arxiv.org/abs/2505.23847

Kostadimas, D., Kasapakis, V., & Kotis, K. (2025). A Systematic Review on the Combination of VR, IoT and AI Technologies, and Their Integration in Applications. *Future Internet, 17*(4), 163. DOI: 10.3390/fi17040163

Kozyreva, A., Lewandowsky, S., & Hertwig, R. (2020). Citizens Versus the Internet: Confronting Digital Challenges With Cognitive Tools. *Psychological Science in the Public Interest, 21*(3), 103–156. DOI: 10.1177/1529100620946707 PMID: 33325331

Kumar, K., Veena, N., Aravind, T., Bhatt, C., Kuppusamy, U., & Jain, P. (2025). Game-changing intelligence: Unveiling the societal impact of artificial intelligence in game software. *Entertainment Computing, 52*, 100862. DOI: 10.1016/j.entcom.2024.100862

Lacle-Melendez, J., Silva-Medina, S., & Bacca-Acosta, J. (2024). Virtual and augmented reality to develop empathy: A systematic literature review. *Multimedia Tools and Applications*. Advance online publication. DOI: 10.1007/s11042-024-19191-y

Laird, J., & VanLent, M. (2001). Human-Level AI's Killer Application: Interactive Computer Games. *AI Magazine, 22*(2). Advance online publication. DOI: 10.1609/aimag.v22i2.1558

Lampropoulos, G., Keramopoulos, E., Diamantaras, K., & Evangelidis, G. (2022). Augmented Reality and Gamification in Education: A Systematic Literature Review of Research, Applications, and Empirical Studies. *Applied Sciences 2022, Vol. 12, Page 6809, 12*(13), 6809. DOI: 10.3390/app12136809

Lantz, B. (2019). *Machine Learning with R: Expert Techniques for Predictive Modeling*. Packt Publishing.

LeCun, Y., Bengio, Y., & Hinton, G. (2015). Deep learning. *Nature, 521*(7553), 436–444. DOI: 10.1038/nature14539 PMID: 26017442

Lerman, D. C., Vorndran, C., Addison, L., & Kuhn, S. A. C. (2004). A RAPID ASSESSMENT OF SKILLS IN YOUNG CHILDREN WITH AUTISM. *Journal of Applied Behavior Analysis, 37*(1), 11–26. DOI: 10.1901/jaba.2004.37-11

Liang, J., Li, R., & Jin, Q. (2020) Semi-supervised multi-modal emotion recognition with cross-modal distribution matching. In: MM '20: The 28th ACM International Conference on Multimedia. ACM, pp 2852–2861. DOI: 10.1145/3394171.3413579

Liang, X., Tao, M., Xia, Y., Wang, J., Li, K., Wang, Y., He, Y., Yang, J., Shi, T., Wang, Y., Zhang, M., & Wang, X. (2025). SAGE: Self-evolving Agents with Reflective and Memory-augmented Abilities. *Neurocomputing, 647*, 130470. DOI: 10.1016/j.neucom.2025.130470

Ligorio, L., Venturelli, A., Rosato, P., & Campo, R. (2025). Fostering sustainable development goals through gamification. *Journal of Management & Organization, 31*(2), 945–966. DOI: 10.1017/jmo.2023.54

Li, J., & Li, Y. (2025). Interactive Narrative and Scenario Building. In *Digital Futures in Human-Computer Interaction* (pp. 139–148). CRC Press. DOI: 10.1201/9781032693606-12

Lin, F., Yuan, J., Chen, Z., & Abiri, M. (2024). Enhancing multimedia management: Cloud-based movie type recognition with hybrid deep learning architecture. *Journal of Cloud Computing (Heidelberg, Germany), 13*(1), 104. DOI: 10.1186/s13677-024-00668-y

Lin, J., Hua, H., Chen, M., Li, Y., Hsiao, J., Ho, C., & Luo, J. (2023). Videoxum: Cross-modal visual and textural summarization of videos. *IEEE Transactions on Multimedia, 26*, 5548–5560. DOI: 10.1109/TMM.2023.3335875

Liu, R. (2024). *Generative AI Agent for Autonomous Match-3 Gameplay through Real-Time Image-Based Decision-Making* [Master's thesis]. Aalto University.

Liu, Y. (2024). *Gamification in Climate Action*. 359–380. : Lopes, J. M., Gomes, S., Lopes, P., Silva, A., Lourenço, D., Esteves, D., Cardoso, M., & Redondo, V. (2023). Exploring the Role of Gamification in the Online Shopping Experience in Retail Stores: An Exploratory Study. *Social Sciences 2023, Vol. 12, Page 235, 12*(4), 235. https://doi.org/DOI: 10.4018/979-8-3693-7001-8.ch013

Liu, H., & Zhong, K. (2025). SSMIM: Semi-supervised Multimodal Interaction Model for real-time conversational emotion recognition. *The Journal of Supercomputing, 81*(8), 897. DOI: 10.1007/s11227-025-07373-w

Liu, Z. J., Tretyakova, N., Fedorov, V., & Kharakhordina, M. (2020). Digital Literacy and Digital Didactics as the Basis for New Learning Models Development. [IJET]. *International Journal of Emerging Technologies in Learning, 15*(14), 4. DOI: 10.3991/ijet.v15i14.14669

Li, Y. (2017). *Deep reinforcement learning: An overview*. ArXiv Preprint.

Lopez-Barreiro, J., Alvarez-Sabucedo, L., Garcia-Soidan, J. L., & Santos-Gago, J. M. (2024). Towards a Blockchain Hybrid Platform for Gamification of Healthy Habits: Implementation and Usability Validation. *Applied System Innovation 2024, Vol. 7, Page 60, 7*(4), 60. DOI: 10.3390/asi7040060

Lucchi, E. (2025). Digital twins, artificial intelligence and immersive technologies for heritage preservation and cultural tourism in smart cities. In *Digital Twin, Blockchain, and Sensor Networks in the Healthy and Mobile City* (pp. 507-520). Elsevier. DOI: 10.1016/B978-0-443-34174-8.00026-0

Ly, R., & Shojaei, A. (2025). Decentralized autonomous organization in built environments: Applications, potential and limitations. *Information Systems and e-Business Management, 23*(2), 1–46. DOI: 10.1007/s10257-025-00699-1

Lyu, Z. (2023). State-of-the-art human–computer interaction in Metaverse. *International Journal of Human-Computer Interaction, 40*(21), 6690–6708. DOI: 10.1080/10447318.2023.2248833

Mahalakshmi, S., Bharath, H., Kautish, S., & Singh, D. (2025). Virtual Storytelling for Sustainable Development: Engaging Audiences with SDG Narratives. In *Metaverse and Sustainability: Business Resilience Towards Sustainable Development Goals* (pp. 361–375). Springer Nature Switzerland. DOI: 10.1007/978-3-031-89545-6_19

Mahasseni, B., Lam, M., & Todorovic, S. (2017). Unsupervised video summarization with adversarial lstm networks. In *Proceedings of the IEEE conference on Computer Vision and Pattern Recognition* (pp. 202-211). DOI: 10.1109/CVPR.2017.318

Mansouri, B., Roozkhosh, A., & Farbeh, H. (2021). A Survey on Implementations of Adaptive AI in Serious Games for Enhancing Player Engagement. *2021 International Serious Games Symposium (ISGS)*, 48–53. DOI: 10.1109/ISGS54702.2021.9684760

Mao, X. (2021). Procedural level generation with generative adversarial networks: Techniques and challenges. *Entertainment Computing*, *37*, 100412.

Marczewski, A. (2015). *Even Ninja Monkeys like to play* (Vol. 1). Blurb Inc.

Marin, A. R., & Jiménez, O. R. (2024). ADVANCING EDUCATION THROUGH AI-POWERED LEARNING STRATEGIES AND TEACHING TECHNIQUES. ICERI2024 Proceedings, 10381–10388.

Martin, K. (2019). Designing Ethical Algorithms. *MIS Quarterly Executive*, •••, 129–142. DOI: 10.17705/2msqe.00012

Maslych, M., Pumarada, C., Ghasemaghaei, A., & LaViola, J. J., Jr. (2024). Takeaways from applying llm capabilities to multiple conversational avatars in a vr pilot study. *arXiv preprint arXiv:2501.00168*

Meenakshi, R., & Kannan, B. (2025). TRANSFORMING EDUCASTION: THE ROLE OF AI-POWERED TOOLS IN THE TEACHING-LEARNING PROCESS. REVOLUTIONIZING EDUCATION AND COMMERCE: LEVERAGING AI FOR DIGITAL TRANSFORMATION, 81.

Mehra, R. K. (2024). Evolutionary Advantages of Virtual Reality in Education. In *Transforming Education with Virtual Reality* (pp. 73–86). Wiley., DOI: 10.1002/9781394200498.ch5

Mehra, R. K., & Kapoor, N. (2025). The Role of Assistive Technology in Supporting Special Education Needs. In *Blending Human Intelligence With Technology in the Classroom* (pp. 209–222). IGI Global., DOI: 10.4018/979-8-3373-0771-8.ch009

Mittelstadt, B. D., Allo, P., Taddeo, M., Wachter, S., & Floridi, L. (2016). The ethics of algorithms: Mapping the debate. *Big Data & Society*, *3*(2), 2053951716679679. Advance online publication. DOI: 10.1177/2053951716679679

Mnih, V., Kavukcuoglu, K., Silver, D., Rusu, A. A., Veness, J., Bellemare, M. G., Graves, A., Riedmiller, M., Fidjeland, A. K., Ostrovski, G., Petersen, S., Beattie, C., Sadik, A., Antonoglou, I., King, H., Kumaran, D., Wierstra, D., Legg, S., & Hassabis, D. (2015). Human-level control through deep reinforcement learning. *Nature*, *518*(7540), 529–533. DOI: 10.1038/nature14236 PMID: 25719670

Moon, J., Jeong, M., Oh, S., Laine, T. H., & Seo, J. (2022). Data Collection Framework for Context-Aware Virtual Reality Application Development in Unity: Case of Avatar Embodiment. *Sensors (Basel)*, *22*(12), 12. Advance online publication. DOI: 10.3390/s22124623 PMID: 35746405

Munir, A., Aved, A., & Blasch, E. (2022). Situational Awareness: Techniques, Challenges, and Prospects. *AI*, *3*(1), 1. Advance online publication. DOI: 10.3390/ai3010005

Natarajan, T., Pragha, P., Dhalmahapatra, K., & Veera Raghavan, D. R. (2024). Exploring tourist's metaverse experience using destination spatial presence quality & perceived augmentation: Metaverse exploration, physical expedition (MEPE). *Current Issues in Tourism*, ●●●, 1–23.

Nechesov, A., Dorokhov, I., & Ruponen, J. (2025). Virtual cities: From digital twins to autonomous ai societies. *IEEE Access : Practical Innovations, Open Solutions*, *13*, 13866–13903. DOI: 10.1109/ACCESS.2025.3531222

Nettey, S. (2024). *Vision Vantage: A Decision Support System for Football Player Scouts*. Ashesi University.

Neumann, M., & Vu, N. T. (2019) Improving speech emotion recognition with unsupervised representation learning on unlabeled speech. In: IEEE International Conference on Acoustics, Speech and Signal Processing, ICASSP. IEEE, pp 7390–7394. DOI: 10.1109/ICASSP.2019.8682541

Newzoo. (2024). *Global games market report.*

Nicolaidou, I., Tozzi, F., & Antoniades, A. (2022). A gamified app on emotion recognition and anger management for pre-school children. *International Journal of Child-Computer Interaction*, *31*, 100449. Advance online publication. DOI: 10.1016/j.ijcci.2021.100449

Nilsson, N., Nordahl, R., & Serafin, S. (2016). Immersion Revisited: A Review of Existing Definitions of Immersion and Their Relation to Different Theories of Presence. *Human Technology*, *12*(2), 108–134. DOI: 10.17011/ht/urn.201611174652

O'rinbekovna, U. M. (2024). THE USE OF AI-POWERED TECHNOLOGIES IN EDUCATION. *INNOVATIVE DEVELOPMENTS AND RESEARCH IN EDUCATION*, *3*(28), 224–227.

Ojha, A., Narain, S., Raj, A., Agrawal, T., Wadhwa, B., & Joshi, M. (2024). Dynamic virtual reality horror sports enhanced by artificial intelligence and player modeling. *Multimedia Tools and Applications*, *83*(32), 77415–77432. DOI: 10.1007/s11042-024-18414-6

Olsen, A. F., & Torresen, J. (2016). Smartphone accelerometer data used for detecting human emotions. *2016 3rd International Conference on Systems and Informatics (ICSAI)*, 410–415. DOI: 10.1109/ICSAI.2016.7810990

Omirgaliyev, R., Kenzhe, D., & Mirambekov, S. (2024, April). Simulating life: The application of generative agents in virtual environments. In *2024 IEEE AITU: Digital Generation* (pp. 181-187). IEEE.

Padeli, L. C., Fahrurroji, Purnama, S., Rizky, A., & Fazri, M. F. (2024). Analysis of Gamification and Blockchain Integration in Intelligent Learning Systems. *2024 3rd International Conference on Creative Communication and Innovative Technology, ICCIT 2024*. DOI: 10.1109/ICCIT62134.2024.10701220

Padmavathi, P., Thrimurthulu, V., Bharani, J., Sailaja, V., Kumar, N. M., & Boopathi, S. (2025). A Study on Integration of Deep Learning With IoT for Smart Engineering Solutions. In *Navigating Challenges of Object Detection Through Cognitive Computing* (pp. 125–158). IGI Global Scientific Publishing. DOI: 10.4018/979-8-3693-9057-3.ch005

Pakniyat, N., Abdullah, J., Agarwal, G., Krejcar, O., & Namazi, H. (2025). Harnessing Fractal Theory for Biomedical Signal Analysis: A Comprehensive Review. [fractals]. *Fractals*, *33*(05), 1–11. DOI: 10.1142/S0218348X25300016

Panchanadikar, R., Gonzalez, L., & Sarkar, A. (2023). Generative AI and indie game developers: Innovation, risks, and ethical concerns. *CHI Conference on Human Factors in Computing Systems Extended Abstracts*.

Paneva, V., Winterhalter, V., Malladi, N. S. S. V., Strauss, M., Schneegass, S., & Alt, F. (2025). Usable Privacy in Virtual Worlds: Design Implications for Data Collection Awareness and Control Interfaces in Virtual Reality (No. arXiv:2503.10915). arXiv. https://doi.org//arXiv.2503.10915DOI: 10.48550

Papadopoulou, A., Mystakidis, S., & Tsinakos, A. (2024). Immersive storytelling in social virtual reality for human-centered learning about sensitive historical events. *Information (Basel)*, *15*(5), 244. DOI: 10.3390/info15050244

Pareek, P., & Thakkar, A. (2021). A survey on video-based Human Action Recognition: Recent updates, datasets, challenges, and applications. *Artificial Intelligence Review*, *54*(3), 2259–2322. DOI: 10.1007/s10462-020-09904-8

Pathirana, A., Rajakaruna, D. K., Kasthurirathna, D., Atukorale, A., Aththidiye, R., & Yatipansalawa, M. (2024). A reinforcement learning-based approach for promoting mental health using multimodal emotion recognition. *Journal of Future Artificial Intelligence and Technologies*, *1*(2), 124–142. DOI: 10.62411/faith.2024-22

Pellowski, A. (1977). *The world of storytelling*. Bowker.

Pereira, R. (2024). Intelligence artificial and Metaverse: An integrative review. *Arquétipos*, *1*(1), 45–62.

Prabhuswamy, M., Tripathi, R., Vijayakumar, M., Thulasimani, T., Sundharesalingam, P., & Sampath, B. (2024). A Study on the Complex Nature of Higher Education Leadership: An Innovative Approach. In *Challenges of Globalization and Inclusivity in Academic Research* (pp. 202–223). IGI Global Scientific Publishing. DOI: 10.4018/979-8-3693-1371-8.ch013

Prokopenko, O., & Sapinski, A. (2024). Using virtual reality in education: Ethical and social dimensions. *E-Learning Innovations Journal*, *2*(1), 41–62. DOI: 10.57125/ELIJ.2024.03.25.03

Proma, A. M.. (2025). "Personalized Large Language Models Can Increase the Belief Accuracy of Social Networks." *ArXiv*, https://arxiv.org/abs/2506.06153

Promethean, A. I. (2023). *Promethean AI – Artificial intelligence for virtual worlds*. https://www.prometheanai.com/

Przybylski, A. K., Rigby, C. S., & Ryan, R. M. (2010). A Motivational Model of Video Game Engagement. *Review of General Psychology*, *14*(2), 154–166. DOI: 10.1037/a0019440

Qiu, S. (2023). Generative AI Processes for 2D Platformer Game Character Design and Animation. *Lecture Notes in Education Psychology and Public Media*, *29*(1), 146–160. DOI: 10.54254/2753-7048/29/20231440

Queirós, R., Swacha, J., Damaševičius, R., Maskeli, R., Unas, ¯, & Blažauskas, T. (2023). Serious Games and Gamification in Healthcare: A Meta-Review. *Information 2023, Vol. 14, Page 105*, *14*(2), 105. DOI: 10.3390/info14020105

Queiroz, B. A., Westphall, J., & Martina, J. E. (2024). Badges as a Gamification Tool in Higher Education Through Tokenization. *2024 7th IEEE Biennial Congress of Argentina, ARGENCON 2024*. DOI: 10.1109/ARGENCON62399.2024.10735887

Rabin, S. (Ed.). (2013). *Game AI pro: collected wisdom of game AI professionals*. CRC Press. DOI: 10.1201/b16725

Rachha, A., & Seyam, M. (2024, October). LLM-Enhanced Learning Environments for CS: Exploring Data Structures and Algorithms with Gurukul. In *2024 IEEE Frontiers in Education Conference (FIE)* (pp. 1-9)

Rahimi, S. (2025). Going beyond the brick: Assessing and supporting creativity using AI-powered digital games. *Creativity Research Journal*, *37*(2), 275–283. DOI: 10.1080/10400419.2023.2241779

Rai, A. K., Agarwal, S., Gupta, S., & Agarwal, G. (2023, November 08). An effective fuzzy based segmentation and twin attention based convolutional gated recurrent network for skin cancer detection. *Multimedia Tools and Applications*, *83*(17), 52113–52140. DOI: 10.1007/s11042-023-17538-5

Raji, I. D., & Buolamwini, J. (2019). Actionable Auditing. *Proceedings of the 2019 AAAI/ACM Conference on AI, Ethics, and Society*, 429–435. DOI: 10.1145/3306618.3314244

Rajkumar, V., Boopathi, S., & Jatav, S. S. (2024). Empowerment of Fisherwomen through Self-Help Groups: A Multidimensional Impact Assessment in Thoothukudi, Tamil Nadu, India. *Indian Journal of Extension Education*, *60*(4), 47–52. DOI: 10.48165/IJEE.2024.60409

Ramadan, Z., & Ramadan, J. (2025). AI avatars and co-creation in the Metaverse. *Consumer Behavior in Tourism and Hospitality*, *20*(1), 131–147. DOI: 10.1108/CBTH-07-2024-0246

Ramadhan, A., Warnars, H. L. H. S., & Razak, F. H. A. (2024). Combining intelligent tutoring systems and gamification: A systematic literature review. *Education and Information Technologies*, *29*(6), 6753–6789. DOI: 10.1007/s10639-023-12092-x

Rana, S., & Chicone, R. (2025). Gamification and Immersive Learning with AI. *Fortifying the Future*, 51–75. DOI: 10.1007/978-3-031-81780-9_3

Rapaka, A., Dharmadhikari, S., Kasat, K., Mohan, C. R., Chouhan, K., & Gupta, M. (2025). Revolutionizing learning- A journey into educational games with immersive and AI technologies. *Entertainment Computing*, *52*, 100809. DOI: 10.1016/j.entcom.2024.100809

Razi, Q., Devrani, A., Abhyankar, H., Chalapathi, G. S. S., Hassija, V., & Guizani, M. (2024). Non-Fungible Tokens (NFTs) - Survey of Current Applications, Evolution, and Future Directions. *IEEE Open Journal of the Communications Society*, *5*, 2765–2791. DOI: 10.1109/OJCOMS.2023.3343926

Reddy, C. V., Reddy, N. U., Sharma, S., Kumar, J. P., Lakhanpal, S., & Albawi, A. (2024, May). Advanced Deep Learning Architectures for Real-Time Human Emotion Recognition and Behavioral Prediction. In *2024 International Conference on Communication, Computer Sciences and Engineering (IC3SE)* (pp. 1306-1311). IEEE. DOI: 10.1109/IC3SE62002.2024.10592940

Reiners, D., Davahli, M. R., Karwowski, W., & Cruz-Neira, C. (2021). The Combination of Artificial Intelligence and Extended Reality: A Systematic Review. *Frontiers in Virtual Reality*, *2*, 721933. Advance online publication. DOI: 10.3389/frvir.2021.721933

Ribeiro, M., Santos, J., Lobo, J., Araújo, S., Magalhães, L. G., & Adão, T. (2024). VR, AR, gamification and AI towards the next generation of systems supporting cultural heritage: addressing challenges of a museum context. *Proceedings - Web3D 2024: 29th International ACM Conference on 3D Web Technology*. DOI: 10.1145/3665318.3677172

Riedl, M. O., & Harrison, B. (2016). Using Stories to Teach Human Values to Artificial Agents. *AAAI Workshop: AI, Ethics, and Society*, 105–112.

Rong, Z. (2024). Application of Natural Language Processing in Virtual Experience AI Interaction Design. *Journal of Intelligent Learning Systems and Applications*, *16*(4), 4. Advance online publication. DOI: 10.4236/jilsa.2024.164020

Roohi, S., Guckelsberger, C., Relas, A., Heiskanen, H., Takatalo, J., & Hämäläinen, P. (2021). Predicting Game Difficulty and Engagement Using AI Players. Proc. ACM Hum.-Comput. Interact., 5(CHI PLAY), 231:1-231:17. DOI: 10.1145/3474658

Rudschies, C., & Schneider, I. (2024). Ethical, legal, and social implications (ELSI) of virtual agents and virtual reality in healthcare. *Social Science & Medicine*, *340*, 116483. DOI: 10.1016/j.socscimed.2023.116483 PMID: 38064822

Rutrecht, H., Wittmann, M., Khoshnoud, S., & Igarzábal, F. A. (2021). Time Speeds Up During Flow States: A Study in Virtual Reality with the Video Game Thumper. DOI: 10.1163/22134468-bja10033

Ryan, R. M., & Rigby, C. S. (2019). Motivational foundations of game-based learning. In *Handbook of game-based learning* (pp. 153–176).

Ryan, R. M., & Deci, E. L. (2000). Self-determination theory and the facilitation of intrinsic motivation, social development, and well-being. *The American Psychologist*, *55*(1), 68–78. DOI: 10.1037/0003-066X.55.1.68 PMID: 11392867

Ryan, R. M., Rigby, C. S., & Przybylski, A. (2006). The Motivational Pull of Video Games: A Self-Determination Theory Approach. *Motivation and Emotion*, *30*(4), 344–360. DOI: 10.1007/s11031-006-9051-8

Sabry, F., Eltaras, T., Labda, W., Alzoubi, K., & Malluhi, Q. (2022). Machine Learning for Healthcare Wearable Devices: The Big Picture. *Journal of Healthcare Engineering*, *2022*(1), 4653923. DOI: 10.1155/2022/4653923 PMID: 35480146

Saini, P., Kumar, K., Kashid, S., Saini, A., & Negi, A. (2023). Video summarization using deep learning techniques: A detailed analysis and investigation. *Artificial Intelligence Review, 56*(11), 12347–12385. DOI: 10.1007/s10462-023-10444-0

Sankaran, S., Arun, M., & Kottaimalai, R. (2025). Virtualization of Smart Society 5.0 Using Artificial Intelligence and Virtual Reality. *Networked Sensing Systems*, 297-321.

Saravanan, T., Poongothai, E., Sophia, N. A., Jeyanthi, S., Kanimozhi, N., & Boopathi, S. (2025). Deep Learning in Bioinformatics for Revolutionizing Genomic Data Analysis. In Advanced Interdisciplinary Applications of Deep Learning for Data Science (pp. 1–30). IGI Global Scientific Publishing.

Sarkar, R., Shandilya, S., Anand, T., Sri, R. R., Dhanaraj, K., & Boopathi, S. (2025). Best Practices and Frameworks for Higher Education: Optimizing Learning Progressions Using Recent Tools. In Driving Quality Education Through AI and Data Science (pp. 51–72). IGI Global Scientific Publishing.

Selinger, E., & Hartzog, W. (2017). Obscurity and privacy. In *Spaces for the Future* (pp. 119–129). Routledge. DOI: 10.4324/9780203735657-12

Shah, D., Patel, D., Adesara, J., Hingu, P., & Shah, M. (2021). Exploiting the Capabilities of Blockchain and Machine Learning in Education. *Augmented Human Research 2021 6:1, 6*(1), 1–14. DOI: 10.1007/s41133-020-00039-7

Sharma, D. M., Ramana, K. V., Jothilakshmi, R., Verma, R., Maheswari, B. U., & Boopathi, S. (2024). Integrating Generative AI Into K-12 Curriculums and Pedagogies in India: Opportunities and Challenges. Facilitating Global Collaboration and Knowledge Sharing in Higher Education With Generative AI, 133–161.

Sheetal, T., Tyagi, R., & Singh, G. (2023). Gamification and customer experience in online retail: A qualitative study focusing on ethical perspective. *Asian Journal of Business Ethics, 12*(1), 49–69. DOI: 10.1007/s13520-022-00162-1

Sherman, W., & C. A. (2013). *Understanding Virtual Reality: Interface, Application, and Design.* Amsterdam: Elsevier.

Shi, F., Ning, H., Zhang, X., Li, R., Tian, Q., Zhang, S., Zheng, Y., Guo, Y., & Daneshmand, M. (2023). A new technology perspective of the Metaverse: Its essence, framework and challenges. *Digital Communications and Networks*. Advance online publication. DOI: 10.1016/j.dcan.2023.02.017

Shirazi, B. N., Safavi, A. A., Aftabi, E., & Salimi, G. (2024). The Integration of Virtual Reality and Artificial Intelligence in Educational Paradigms. 2024 11th International and the 17th National Conference on E-Learning and E-Teaching (ICeLeT), 1–6. DOI: 10.1109/ICeLeT62507.2024.10493089

Short, T., & Adams, T. (Eds.). (2017). *Procedural generation in game design*. CRC Press. DOI: 10.1201/9781315156378

Sifa, R., Drachen, A., & Bauckhage, C. (2018). Profiling in games: Understanding behavior from telemetry. *Social Interactions in Virtual Worlds: An Interdisciplinary Perspective*, 337–374.

Singh, G., & Goel, A. K. (2020, March). Face detection and recognition system using digital image processing. In *2020 2nd International Conference on Innovative Mechanisms for Industry Applications (ICIMIA)* (pp. 348-352). IEEE. DOI: 10.1109/ICIMIA48430.2020.9074838

Slater, M. (2009). Place illusion and plausibility can lead to realistic behaviour in immersive virtual environments. *Philosophical Transactions of the Royal Society of London. Series B, Biological Sciences, 364*(1535), 3549–3557. DOI: 10.1098/rstb.2009.0138 PMID: 19884149

Soliman, M. M., Ahmed, E., Darwish, A., & Hassanien, A. E. (2024). Artificial intelligence powered Metaverse: Analysis, challenges and future perspectives. *Artificial Intelligence Review, 57*(36), 36. Advance online publication. DOI: 10.1007/s10462-023-10641-x

Song, Y., Wu, K., & Ding, J. (2024). Developing an immersive game-based learning platform with generative artificial intelligence and virtual reality technologies – "LearningverseVR". Computers & Education: X Reality, 4, 100069. DOI: 10.1016/j.cexr.2024.100069

Srdanović, P., Skala, T., & Maričević, M. (2025). InHeritage—A Gamified Mobile Application with AR and VR for Cultural Heritage Preservation in the Metaverse. *Applied Sciences (Basel, Switzerland), 15*(1), 257. DOI: 10.3390/app15010257

Sreeja, M. U., & Kovoor, B. C. (2023). A multi-stage deep adversarial network for video summarization with knowledge distillation. *Journal of Ambient Intelligence and Humanized Computing, 14*(8), 9823–9838. DOI: 10.1007/s12652-021-03641-8

Sridhar, S., Saraswathi, S., Bharathi, S. V. S., & Devipriya, A. (2024). Gamification applications based on metaverse for healthcare industry. *Metaverse Technologies in Healthcare*, 233–244. DOI: 10.1016/B978-0-443-13565-1.00011-7

Stephenson, N. (2022, January 13). *Snow Crash*. Penguin Books Australia. (Original work published 1992)

Sugiyama, M. S. (n.d.). *Literary Prehistory: The Origins and Psychology of Storytelling*. https://www.researchgate.net/publication/316861108

Summerville, A., & Mateas, M. (2016). Super Mario as a String: Platformer Level Generation Via LSTMs. *Summerville*. /arXiv.1603.00930DOI: 10.26503/dl.v2016i1.752

Summerville, A., Snodgrass, S., & Mateas, M. (2018). Procedural content generation via machine learning (PCGML). *IEEE Transactions on Games*, *10*(3), 257–270. DOI: 10.1109/TG.2018.2846639

Sun, Y., Li, Z., Fang, K., Lee, C. H., & Asadipour, A. (2023, October). Language as reality: a co-creative storytelling game experience in 1001 nights using generative AI. In *Proceedings of the AAAI Conference on Artificial Intelligence and Interactive Digital Entertainment* (Vol. 19, No. 1, pp. 425-434). DOI: 10.1609/aiide.v19i1.27539

Suresh Babu, S., & Dhakshina Moorthy, A. (2024). Application of artificial intelligence in adaptation of gamification in education: A literature review. In *Computer Applications in Engineering Education* (Vol. 32, Issue 1). DOI: 10.1002/cae.22683

Sutton, R. S., & Barto, A. G. (2018). *Reinforcement Learning: An Introduction* (2nd ed.). MIT Press.

Tabassum, A., Elmahjub, E., Padela, A. I., Zwitter, A., & Qadir, J. (2025). Generative AI and the Metaverse: A scoping review of ethical and legal challenges. *IEEE Open Journal of the Computer Society*, *6*, 348–359. DOI: 10.1109/OJCS.2025.3536082

Tao, G., Garrett, B., Taverner, T., Cordingley, E., & Sun, C. (2021). Immersive virtual reality health games: A narrative review of game design. *Journal of Neuroengineering and Rehabilitation*, *18*(1), 1–21. DOI: 10.1186/s12984-020-00801-3 PMID: 33573684

Thakur, S. S., Bandyopadhyay, S., & Datta, D. (2023). Artificial intelligence and the Metaverse: Present and future aspects. In Hassanien, A. E., Darwish, A., & Torky, M. (Eds.), *The future of Metaverse in the virtual era and physical world* (Vol. 123). Springer., DOI: 10.1007/978-3-031-29132-6_10

Thawonmas, R., Yoshida, K., Lou, J.-K., & Chen, K.-T. (2011). Analysis of revisitations in online games. *Entertainment Computing*, *2*(4), 215–221. DOI: 10.1016/j.entcom.2011.01.003

Tian, X., Jin, Y., Zhang, Z., Liu, P., & Tang, X. (2025). Video summarization with temporal-channel visual transformer. *Pattern Recognition, 165*, 111631. DOI: 10.1016/j.patcog.2025.111631

Tissot, C., & Evans, R. (2003). Visual Teaching Strategies for Children with Autism. *Early Child Development and Care, 173*(4), 425–433. DOI: 10.1080/0300443032000079104

Todd, G., Padula, A. G., Stephenson, M., Piette, É., Soemers, D. J., & Togelius, J. (2024). Gavel: Generating games via evolution and language models. *Advances in Neural Information Processing Systems, 37*, 110723–110745.

Togelius, J., & Yannakakis, G. N. (2026). General general game AI. *2016 IEEE Conference on Computational Intelligence and Games*, 1–8.

Tran, T., Ho, M.-T., Pham, T.-H., Nguyen, M.-H., Nguyen, K.-L. P., Vuong, T.-T., Nguyen, T.-H. T., Nguyen, T.-D., Nguyen, T.-L., Khuc, Q., La, V.-P., & Vuong, Q.-H. (2020). How Digital Natives Learn and Thrive in the Digital Age: Evidence from an Emerging Economy. *Sustainability (Basel), 12*(9), 3819. DOI: 10.3390/su12093819

Triantafyllou, S. A., Georgiadis, C., & Sapounidis, T. (2025). Gamification in education and training: A literature review. *International Review of Education 2025 71:3, 71*(3), 483–517. DOI: 10.1007/s11159-024-10111-8

Triberti, S., Sapone, C., & Riva, G. (2025). Being there but where? Sense of presence theory for virtual reality applications. *Humanities & Social Sciences Communications, 12*(1), 79. Advance online publication. DOI: 10.1057/s41599-025-04380-3

Uzumcu, O., & Acilmis, H. (2024). Do innovative teachers use AI-powered tools more interactively? A study in the context of diffusion of innovation theory. Technology. *Knowledge and Learning, 29*(2), 1109–1128. DOI: 10.1007/s10758-023-09687-1

Vaithianathan, V., Subbulakshmi, N., Boopathi, S., & Mohanraj, M. (2024). Integrating Project-Based and Skills-Based Learning for Enhanced Student Engagement and Success: Transforming Higher Education. In Adaptive Learning Technologies for Higher Education (pp. 345–372). IGI Global.

Venkatasubramanian, V., Chitra, M., Sudha, R., Singh, V. P., Jefferson, K., & Boopathi, S. (2024). Examining the Impacts of Course Outcome Analysis in Indian Higher Education: Enhancing Educational Quality. In Challenges of Globalization and Inclusivity in Academic Research (pp. 124–145). IGI Global Scientific Publishing.

Verma, K., Chaudhary, A., Bhati, H., & Bisht, G. (2025). Advanced AI & ML applications in satellite image processing and industry. In *Proceedings of the 3rd International Conference on Disruptive Technologies (ICDT 2025)* (pp. 66–69). IEEE. DOI: 10.1109/ICDT63985.2025.10986339

Verma, R. K. (2025). Quantum Methods for Data-Efficient Self-supervised Learning in Industrial Automation. In Ghosh, A., Dutta, S., Das, A. K., Shukla, V. K., & Moreira, F. (Eds.), *Quantum Machine Learning in Industrial Automation. Information Systems Engineering and Management* (Vol. 65). Springer., DOI: 10.1007/978-3-031-99786-0_11

Verma, R. K. (2025). The Role of Artificial Intelligence in Optimizing Cybersecurity for Industrial Control Systems. In Pandey, H., & Goel, P. (Eds.), *AI-Enhanced Cybersecurity for Industrial Automation* (pp. 493–508). IGI Global Scientific Publishing., DOI: 10.4018/979-8-3373-3241-3.ch023

Verma, R. K., & Kishor, K. (2024). Image Processing Applications in Agriculture With the Help of AI. In Khan, M., Khan, R., Praveen, P., Verma, A., & Panda, M. (Eds.), *Infrastructure Possibilities and Human-Centered Approaches With Industry 5.0* (pp. 162–181). IGI Global Scientific Publishing., DOI: 10.4018/979-8-3693-0782-3.ch010

Verma, R. K., Kishor, K., & Jha, S. K. (2024). Big Data Analytics in Bioinformatics and Healthcare. In Khan, R., Kumar, I., & Praveen, P. (Eds.), *Applications of Parallel Data Processing for Biomedical Imaging* (pp. 25–43). IGI Global Scientific Publishing., DOI: 10.4018/979-8-3693-2426-4.ch002

Victory, X. R. (n.d.). Retrieved from https://www.victoryxr.com/

Vinyals, O., Babuschkin, I., Czarnecki, W. M., Mathieu, M., Dudzik, A., Chung, J., & Silver, D. (2019). Grandmaster level in StarCraft II using multi-agent reinforcement learning. *Nature*, *575*(7782), 350–354. DOI: 10.1038/s41586-019-1724-z PMID: 31666705

Vorrink, N., Wicaksono, H., & Fatahi Valilai, O. (2024). Analyzing VR/AR Technology Capabilities for Enhancing the Effectiveness of Learning Processes with Focus on Gamification. *Lecture Notes in Networks and Systems, 823 LNNS*, 806–817. DOI: 10.1007/978-3-031-47724-9_53

Wang, G. X., Deng, J., & Ali, S. (2025). Evaluating the Impact of AI-Powered Audiovisual Personalization on Learner Emotion, Focus, and Learning Outcomes. *arXiv preprint arXiv:2505.03033*

Wang, A., Thompson, M., Uz-Bilgin, C., & Klopfer, E. (2021). Authenticity, Interactivity, and Collaboration in Virtual Reality Games: Best Practices and Lessons Learned. *Frontiers in Virtual Reality*, *2*, 734083. Advance online publication. DOI: 10.3389/frvir.2021.734083

Wang, B., Zhang, X., Pei, J., & Chen, Y. (2022). *Towards understanding chain-of-thought prompting: An empirical study of what matters*. arXiv. https://arxiv.org/abs/2212.10001

Wang, H., Gao, Z., Zhang, X., Du, J., Xu, Y., & Wang, Z. (2024). Gamifying cultural heritage: Exploring the potential of immersive virtual exhibitions. *Telematics and Informatics Reports*, *15*, 100150. DOI: 10.1016/j.teler.2024.100150

Wang, Y., Wang, L., & Siau, K. L. (2024). Human-centered interaction in virtual worlds: A new era of generative artificial intelligence and Metaverse. *International Journal of Human-Computer Interaction*, *41*(2), 1459–1501. DOI: 10.1080/10447318.2024.2316376

Washington, P., Voss, C., Haber, N., Tanaka, S., Daniels, J., Feinstein, C., Winograd, T., & Wall, D. (2016). A Wearable Social Interaction Aid for Children with Autism. *Proceedings of the 2016 CHI Conference Extended Abstracts on Human Factors in Computing Systems*, 2348–2354. DOI: 10.1145/2851581.2892282

Werning, S. (2024). Generative AI and the technological imaginary of game design. In *Creative tools and the softwarization of cultural production* (pp. 67–90). Springer Nature Switzerland. DOI: 10.1007/978-3-031-45693-0_4

West, S. M., Whittaker, M., & Crawford, K. (2019). Discriminating systems. *AI Now*, 1–33.

White, R. (2017). Walter Benjamin: "The Storyteller" and the Possibility of Wisdom. *Journal of Aesthetic Education*, *51*(1), 1–14. DOI: 10.5406/jaesteduc.51.1.0001

Wijaya, S., Husain, A., Laurens, M., & Birgithri, A. (2024). iLearning Education Challenge: Combining the Power of Blockchain with Gamification Concepts. *Journal of Computer Science and Technology Application*, *1*(1), 8–15. DOI: 10.33050/corisinta.v1i1.11

Wilujeng, P. R., Sugihartati, R., Saud, M., & Wijayanti, N. (2025, July). Non-Playable Characters (NPC) in Video Games. In *Proceedings of the International Conference on Cultural Studies (ICCUS) 2024* (Vol. 930, p. 165). Springer Nature. DOI: 10.2991/978-2-38476-418-1_13

Xu, C., Sun, Y., Tao, Y., Zhao, B., Hu, R., & Jiu, L. (2024). Exploring the confluence of bioinspired technologies and the metaverse: Business and societal implications in the anthropocene era. *Journal of Cleaner Production*, *450*, 141873. DOI: 10.1016/j.jclepro.2024.141873

Yadav, U., Pitchai, R., Gopal, V., Kumar, K. S., Talukdar, M., & Boopathi, S. (2025). Powers of Higher Education Leadership: Navigating Policy and Management in Academic Institutions. In Navigating Leadership and Policy Management in Education (pp. 103–136). IGI Global.

Yang, M., Li, J., Fang, Z., Chen, S., Yu, Y., Fu, Q., . . . Ye, D. (2024). Playable game generation. arXiv preprint arXiv:2412.00887.

Yang, E. (2023). Implications of immersive technologies in healthcare sector and its built environment. *Frontiers in Medical Technology*, *5*, 1184925. DOI: 10.3389/fmedt.2023.1184925 PMID: 37799269

Yang, L., Allen, G., Zhang, Z., & Zhao, Y. (2024). Achieving on-site trustworthy AI implementation in the construction industry: A framework across the AI lifecycle. *Buildings (Basel, Switzerland)*, *15*(1), 21. DOI: 10.3390/buildings15010021

Yang, S., & Zhang, W. (2022). Presence and Flow in the Context of Virtual Reality Storytelling: What Influences Enjoyment in Virtual Environments? *Cyberpsychology, Behavior, and Social Networking*, *25*(2), 101–109. DOI: 10.1089/cyber.2021.0037

Yannakakis, G. N. (2012). Game AI revisited. *Proceedings of the 9th Conference on Computing Frontiers*, 285–292. DOI: 10.1145/2212908.2212954

Yannakakis, G. N., & Togelius, J. (2018). *Artificial intelligence and games* (Vol. 2). Springer. DOI: 10.1007/978-3-319-63519-4

Yao, C., Zhan, Q., Cao, Z., Li, D., Lin, Y., Shao, Y., & Dong, Z. (2025). Generative AI for Simulating Real World Dynamics Applications and Challenges. *Authorea Preprints*. DOI: 10.36227/techrxiv.176049719.90048379/v1

Yee, N. (2006). Motivations for Play in Online Games. *Cyberpsychology & Behavior*, *9*(6), 772–775. DOI: 10.1089/cpb.2006.9.772 PMID: 17201605

Yin, Q.-Y., Yang, J., Huang, K.-Q., Zhao, M.-J., Ni, W.-C., Liang, B., Huang, Y., Wu, S., & Wang, L. (2023). AI in Human-computer Gaming: Techniques, Challenges and Opportunities. *Machine Intelligence Research*, *20*(3), 299–317. DOI: 10.1007/s11633-022-1384-6

Yuan, H., Liu, M., Lu, K., Yang, C., & Hao, N. (2023). The effect of example abstraction on creativity from the perspectives of example modality and generality. *Thinking Skills and Creativity*, *47*, 101234. DOI: 10.1016/j.tsc.2023.101234

Yu, H., Miao, C., Leung, C., & White, T. J. (2017). Towards AI-powered personalization in MOOC learning. *NPJ Science of Learning*, *2*(1), 15. DOI: 10.1038/s41539-017-0016-3

Yu, J., Dickinger, A., So, K. K. F., & Egger, R. (2024). Artificial intelligence-generated virtual influencer: Examining the effects of emotional display on user engagement. *Journal of Retailing and Consumer Services*, *76*, 103560. DOI: 10.1016/j.jretconser.2023.103560

Yu, Q., Yu, H., Sun, Y., Ding, D., & Jian, M. (2024). Unsupervised video summarization based on the diffusion model of feature fusion. *IEEE Transactions on Computational Social Systems*, *11*(5), 6010–6021. DOI: 10.1109/TCSS.2024.3384627

Zacharia, K. (2018). *3D Escape Room Based on Personality Traits*. Aristotle University of Thessaloniki.

Zeng, B., Huang, Q., El Saddik, A., Li, H., Jiang, S., & Fan, X. (2018). Advances in Multimedia Information Processing–PCM 2017. *18th Pacific-Rim Conference on Multimedia*.

Zeybek, N., & Saygı, E. (2024). Gamification in Education: Why, Where, When, and How?—A Systematic Review. *Games and Culture*, *19*(2), 237–264. DOI: 10.1177/15554120231158625

Zhang, R., Liu, G., Zhang, Q., Lu, X., Dian, R., Yang, Y., & Xu, L. (2025). Detail-aware network for infrared image enhancement. *IEEE Transactions on Geoscience and Remote Sensing*, *63*, 1–14. DOI: 10.1109/TGRS.2024.3504240

Zhang, Y., Liu, Y., Kang, W., & Zheng, Y. (2023). Mar-net: Motion-assisted reconstruction network for unsupervised video summarization. *IEEE Signal Processing Letters*, *30*, 1282–1286. DOI: 10.1109/LSP.2023.3313091

Zhao, S., Gao, Y., Jiang, X., ... (2014) Exploring principles-of-art features for image emotion recognition. In: Proceedings of the ACM International Conference on Multimedia, MM. ACM, pp 47–56. DOI: 10.1145/2647868.2654930

Zhao, B., Gong, M., & Li, X. (2022). Hierarchical multimodal transformer to summarize videos. *Neurocomputing*, *468*, 360–369. DOI: 10.1016/j.neucom.2021.10.039

Zhu, T., Li, L., Yang, J., Zhao, S., Liu, H., & Qian, J. (2023). Multimodal sentiment analysis with image-text interaction network. *IEEE Transactions on Multimedia*, *25*, 3375–3385. DOI: 10.1109/TMM.2022.3160060

About the Contributors

Jeffrey Saltz research focuses on the socio-technical issues relating to AI and Data science, such as how to effectively leverage AI and Data Science within an organizational context and how teams should work together to "do" data science and AI projects. HIs 20+ years of industry information systems experience has often focused on building new teams that leverage emerging technologies to deliver innovative business solutions. In his last corporate role, he worked at JPMorgan Chase. At JPMC, he reported to the firm's Chief Information officer while helping to drive innovation throughout the firm. He also held several other key technology management positions at the company, including CTO (Consumer and Community Banking Risk Management), Chief Information Architect (Chase Financial Services), global head of eBusiness technology and vice president of computational technology. He previously served as chief technology officer and principal investor at Goldman Sachs/Goldman Sachs Ventures, where he invested and helped incubate technology start-ups. He started his career as a programmer, project leader and consulting engineer with Digital Equipment Corp (now part of HP).

Jasmina Tacheva is an Assistant Professor in the School of Information Studies. She studied Philosophy, Economics and German at Canisius College and earned her Ph.D. from the University at Buffalo's (UB) School of Management, where she was part of the NAVIGATE Project, an NSF-sponsored initiative for supporting women in STEM.

Shamik Tiwari, Dean and Professor at the School of Computer Science & Engineering, IILM University, Gurugram, brings over two decades of comprehensive expertise encompassing research, teaching, and administration. His leading-edge research has earned him recognition as one of the world's top 2% of research scientists, acknowledged by Stanford University in 2023 & 2024. Dr. Tiwari's proficiency extends across diverse domains, including Data Analytics, Statistical

Modeling, Predictive Modeling, Machine Learning, Deep Learning, NLP, Image Processing, Computer Vision, and Data Visualization.

Anurag Jain, is a Professor of Computer Science and Engineering with over 22 years of teaching and research experience. He holds a Ph.D. in Computer Science and Engineering and specializes in machine learning, deep learning, natural language processing, and algorithm design. He has published extensively in indexed journals and conferences, completed government-funded research projects, and served in key academic leadership roles. His research interests include intelligent systems, explainable AI, and applied data-driven solutions.

***

Munir Ahmad is a seasoned professional in the realm of Spatial Data Infrastructure (SDI), Geo-Information Productions, Information Systems, and Information Governance, boasting over 25 years of dedicated experience in the field. With a PhD in Computer Science, Dr. Ahmad's expertise spans Spatial Data Production, Management, Processing, Analysis, Visualization, and Quality Control. Throughout his career, Dr. Ahmad has been deeply involved in the development and deployment of SDI systems specially in the context of Pakistan, leveraging his proficiency in Spatial Database Design, Web, Mobile & Desktop GIS, and Geo Web Services Architecture. His contributions to Volunteered Geographic Information (VGI) and Open Source Geoportal & Metadata Portal have significantly enriched the geospatial community. As a trainer and researcher, Dr. Ahmad has authored over 50 publications, advancing the industry's knowledge base and fostering innovation in Geo-Tech, Data Governance, and Information Infrastructure, and Emerging Technologies. His commitment to Research and Development (R&D) is evident in his role as a dedicated educator and mentor in the field.

Zamira Atamuratova is working at the Department of Pedagogy and Psychology, Urgench State University, Urgench, Uzbekistan.

Reno Yuri Camilleri is an Artificial Intelligence engineer and Researcher at the University of Malta, where he is pursuing a Doctorate in Artificial Intelligence. He also works as a Research Support Officer within the university.

Vanessa Camilleri is an academic at the Department of Artificial Intelligence, Faculty of ICT, University of Malta. Her expertise is in the area of Human Computer Interactions, with a specialisation in Virtual Worlds and Serious Games. Her areas of interest include Virtual Reality applications for developing emotional intelligence values. Her previous experience in the area of education and pedagogy, as well as educational technologies and use of games for learning have contributed to her overall academic profile. Her main publications are in the areas of online learning and the use of innovative and emerging technologies for learning. She also has worked on a number of EU funded projects in the areas of game-based learning. More recently she has started working on developing virtual reality experiences for teaching and learning purposes related to various aspects of emotional intelligence.

Aarti Chugh is a seasoned academic with over 22 years of extensive teaching and research experience in the field of computer science and engineering. Her research interests are deeply rooted in Big Data, Database Management Systems (DBMS), and Artificial Intelligence. She has contributed to various national and international conferences and journals and is actively involved in academic leadership and program coordination.

S. Ida Evangeline, presently working as an Assistant Professor in the Department of Electrical and Electronics Engineering at the Government College of Engineering, Tirunelveli, Tamilnadu, India. She obtained her Bachelor's in Electrical and Electronics Engineering from Manonmaniam Sundaranar University in 2003, and Master's in Power Systems Engineering from Anna University, Chennai, Tamilnadu, India in 2005. She completed her PhD degree in 2023 at Anna University, Chennai, Tamilnadu, India. She has published six research papers in international journals. Her current research interests include optimal power flow, renewable energy, soft computing, machine learning, and deep learning.

Richa Kapoor Mehra is working as an Associate Professor of Philosophy and Area chair of Social Sciences and Humanities (SSH) at O.P. Jindal Global University, India; she has earned her PhD in Philosophy from Jawaharlal Nehru University, Delhi. While pursuing a PhD, she received a Junior Research Fellowship from the prestigious Indian Council of Philosophical Research (ICPR). She has completed a Master's and a Bachelor's in philosophy from Miranda House, University of Delhi. She was awarded the Miranda House and Delhi University Rankers prizes for scoring the highest marks in the bachelor's program. She has also worked at Miranda House, the University of Delhi, Amity University, Noida, B.M.L Munjal University, and IIIT Kalyani. Recently, she designed a course on critical thinking and analysis for undergraduate business students at O.P. Jindal Business School. Dr. Mehra has launched the Department of Philosophy at Amity University, Noida, designing various philosophy courses for undergraduate students. She is one of the members of the new National Advisory Board for the Centre for Positive Philosophy and Interdisciplinary Studies (CPPIS) and Society for Positive Philosophy and Interdisciplinary Studies (SPPIS), Haryana, and also the Editorial Advisory Board for Lokāyata: Journal of Positive Philosophy (ISSN 2249-8389). She is one of the Editorial board members of the prestigious "The Journals." She has been a reviewer and reviewed several research book chapters and articles for various national and international journals and books. She was awarded the Excellent Academician Award at an international conference organized by the University of Sri Jayewardenepura, Sri Lanka. She has presented and published several research papers at national and international conferences. Her specialization involves the philosophy of mind and the philosophy of language. Her research interests include spiritual and emotional intelligence, human well-being, virtual reality, artificial intelligence, and ethical concerns.

Ridwan Ishola Mogaji is a passionate philosopher and environmental advocate with a degree in Philosophy from Lagos State University, where he is currently pursuing his Master's while also serving as a graduate assistant. Ridwan is deeply committed to promoting sustainability and tackling climate change, focusing on how philosophy can drive positive environmental change. He strives to develop practical solutions that address the pressing global environmental shifts, always looking for ways to make a meaningful impact both academically and in the world around him.

Matthew Montebello is a full professor and Head of the Department of Artificial Intelligence at the Faculty of ICT, University of Malta. He joined the University in 1999 after completing a PhD in Computer Science, following earlier work in secondary education after graduating with a B.Ed. (Hons) in 1990. He later obtained a Masters and Doctorate from Cardiff University in 1996 and 1998, and went on to complete an M.A. and Ed.D. in Higher Education, specialising in the application of artificial intelligence to e-learning. In 2017 he was awarded visiting academic status at the University of Illinois in Urbana-Champaign, where he collaborated on research projects, and in 2018 was appointed Adjunct Professor, contributing to the development of a next-generation virtual learning environment. At the University of Malta he serves on several committees, including the Web Editorial Board and Digital Education Committee. Since 2022 he has supported the University in addressing the impact of Generative AI on higher education, co-authoring guidelines and delivering workshops on its use in teaching and learning.

Pooja Nagpal Ph.D. (CSE/CPU, Kota), MTech (CSE/NIT Kurukshetra University), B. Tech (CSE/Kurukshetra University), MBA (IT & Systems/IMT Ghaziabad) Dr. Pooja Nagpal has more than 18 years of academic and industry experience. Her research areas are DevOps, Agile methodologies, AI and machine learning, and data science. Currently she is an associate professor in the Computer Science Department at IILM University in Gurugram, Haryana, India. Her expertise lies in translating complex technical concepts into easily understandable content, fostering an engaging learning environment for diverse audiences. She has published over 40 research papers in reputable and indexed journals, authored numerous patents and books, and delivered presentations at international conferences. She has been the recipient of numerous awards, including the Women Scientist Award from a government organization. She has also served as a keynote speaker in numerous organizations.

Jothi Chitra R. is working as Professor in the Department of Electronics and Communication Engineering at Velammal Institute of Technology, Chennai. She received her Bachelor Degree in Electronics and Communication Engineering from Bharathidasan University and Master's Degree in Microwave and Television Engineering from Kerala University and Doctorate in Microstrip Patch Antenna from Anna University, Chennai. Her research interest includes Microstrip patch antenna, RF and Microwave Engineering, Communication systems, Wireless Networks and Image Processing. She has contributed around 32 Scopus indexed research papers in various reputed journals and Conferences. She is an Editor of Nova Science Book Chapter and published 2 books. She has been granted one patent and published three patents. She is a recognized Research supervisor of Anna university and presently guiding 4 research scholars. She received fund form TNSCST. She received Outstanding Woman in Engineering award from International Agency. . She is an active member of IEEE and life member of ISTE.

Om Rohilla is a B.Tech (CSE) student in the Computer Science Department at IILM University, Gurugram. He was a member of the runner-up team of SIH, Chhattisgarh. His areas of expertise are AI and generative AI.

Varshini S. R., UG Final Year, Electronics and Communication Engineering, Velammal Institute of Technology, Tiruvallur, TamilNadu

M. Sivarathinabala working as Professor in Electronics and Communication Engineering at Velammal Institute of Technology, Tamilnadu, India. She has been teaching in the Electronics and Communication field since 2007. She received her PhD from College of Engineering, Guindy, Anna University Chennai. Her research interest includes Computer vision, Image and video processing. She has published 25 international journals, 30 national and international conference papers and 3 patents. She received best researcher award and SEEE Awards from International Agencies. She is a member of IEEE Image Processing society. She is acting as reviewer for various Elsevier, Springer and IEEE journals. She acted as resource person for various institutions.

Raj Kishor Verma is a seasoned academician and researcher with over 12 years of teaching experience in the field of Computer Science and Engineering (CSE). He is currently pursuing a Ph.D. in CSE from Galgotias University, focusing on developing innovative solutions to address contemporary challenges in technology. Raj Kishor Verma holds an M.Tech. in Mobile Computing from the Central University of Jharkhand, where he gained expertise in Automatic Text Summarization by the using Python, mobile systems, and pervasive computing. He completed his B.Tech. in Computer Science and Engineering from RVS College of Engineering & Technology, Jamshedpur, building a strong academic foundation. Throughout his career, Raj Kishor Verma has demonstrated excellence in teaching and research. He has published four research papers in Scopus-indexed journals, contributing significantly to fields such as mobile computing, artificial intelligence, wireless networks, and emerging technologies. He is actively working on additional research projects to advance knowledge in his domain. Currently, he serves as an Assistant Professor at ABES Institute of Technology (ABESIT),

Ester Novi Kurnia Zebua is a student of the Master of Biology Education programme at the State University of Malang (UM) with the support of the Republic of Indonesia Education Fund Management Agency (LPDP) scholarship in 2023. Previously, she completed her undergraduate education at the Biology Education Study Programme, FKIP University of Nias Raya (UNIRAYA). Her professional experience includes her role as a subject teacher at SMK Negeri 1 Alasa Talumuzoi, as well as being the founder of Creative Youth of Nias Community (CYNC), a community that focuses on the development of Nias youth. Ester actively writes as a form of contribution in the field of educational research and innovation, especially those related to literacy, ethnobotany, and the development of local wisdom-based learning media.

Nofamataro Zebua is an academic and researcher in the field of biology education. He earned his bachelor's degree from Universitas Nias Raya in the Faculty of Teacher Training and Education, and his master's degree from Universitas Negeri Malang in the Faculty of Mathematics and Natural Sciences. He has received a scholarship from the Education Fund Management Institution (LPDP) of the Republic of Indonesia. He is active in writing scientific articles for reputable national (Indonesian) and international journals. His research interests and scope include biology education, science education, learning assessment, AI for education, thinking skills, literacy, STEM, and SSI.

Yan Piter Basman Ziraluo started higher education in 2005 and continued his studies in Biology Education at IKIP Gunung Sitoli, which he completed in

2010. During college, he actively worked as an honorary teacher in several private schools on Nias. After graduating, she served as Principal of Senora Private Junior High School and Regional Auxiliary Teacher at SMA Negeri 1 Fanayama, which strengthened her dedication to education. In 2011, she continued her Master of Education Management studies at HKBP Nommensen University with the support of the foundation where she teaches. Despite experiencing health problems, in 2013 he was accepted as a lecturer at STKIP Nias Selatan (now Nias Raya University), where he has served until now. She completed her master's degree in 2015 at Padang State University through a scholarship from the South Nias Education Foundation. At Universitas Nias Raya, she is active as a lecturer, student supervisor, and involved in various academic quality development activities, both at the study program level and internal quality assurance institutions. In 2022, he successfully passed the doctoral program selection at the State University of Malang through the LPDP scholarship, marking his long-term commitment to improving the quality of higher education in Indonesia.

Index

www.ingramcontent.com/pod-product-compliance
Lightning Source LLC
LaVergne TN
LVHW081532300926
849161LV00006B/1394